Truly Yours
G.A.Custer

By

General

George

Armstrong

Custer

A Citadel Press Book
Published by Carol Publishing Group

EDITED BY

MILO MILTON QUAIFE

Carol Publishing Group Edition - 1993

A Citadel Press Book
Published by Carol Publishing Group
Citadel Press is a registered trademark of Carol Communications, Inc.

Editorial Offices: 600 Madison Avenue, New York, NY 10022
Sales & Distribution Offices: 120 Enterprise Avenue, Secaucus, NJ 07094
In Canada: Canadian Manda Group, P.O. Box 920, Station U, Toronto,
Ontario, M8Z 5P9, Canada

Queries regarding rights and permissions should be addressed to:
Carol Publishing Group, 600 Madison Avenue, New York, NY 10022

Manufactured in the United States of America
ISBN 0-8065-1439-6

Carol Publishing Group books are available at special discounts
for bulk purchases, for sales promotions, fund raising, or
educational purposes. Special editions can also be created to
specifications. For details contact: Special Sales Department,
Carol Publishing Group, 120 Enterprise Ave., Secaucus, NJ 07094

Contents

PUBLISHER'S NOTE

———

Citadel Pioneer Books are devoted to telling the story of the American frontier, and the life of the men and women who were the pioneers in shaping the American West. These are the intimate memoirs, journals, autobiographies and other writings that provide the basic source material for an understanding of the rise of the American Nation. For, basically, the story of the expanding frontier is the story of the United States.

𝕳istorical 𝕴ntroduction

GENERAL George A. Custer was perhaps the most brilliant cavalry leader America has produced. His solid claim to military fame rests upon his achievements in the Civil War, yet paradoxically he is chiefly remembered by reason of his death in the minor action of the Little Big Horn in June, 1876.

Over it, as over much else in Custer's career and character, warm controversy still wages. Custer, in short, was an exceedingly complex character whose military brilliance and admirable qualities were marred by certain outstanding defects of character and temperament. In life he won devoted friends and admirers, and no less outspoken and bitter enemies. Nor did his tragic death suffice to still the tumult. Today despite the lapse of two generations of time and the upheavals produced by two world wars, Custer's career continues to supply fuel for heated controversy. Even as this introduction is being composed a bulletin issued by the South Dakota Historical Society bluntly observes that he is "either a hero or a heel, and the propo-

Historical Introduction

nents of both postulates can produce evidence
entirely satisfactory to themselves in proof."[1]

It necessarily follows that my own interpretation will in its turn afford food for further controversy. Although historians wist-
fully aspire to be known as scientists, human
actions are shaped by uncounted influences
and in appraising them the historian encounters no such thing as simple facts. Caesar
crossed the Rubicon 2000 years ago, and in
my boyhood I crossed hundreds of times
another brook which ran through my father's
farm. Why does the world remember Caesar's exploit and remain contentedly ignorant
of mine? Evidently because of background
circumstances which necessarily become the
subject of the narrator's interpretation; and
historians, like theologians, are able to base
widely differing expositions upon identical
"simple" facts.

In interpreting Custer we encounter at the
outset the mystery of how so fiery an eaglet
could spring from such an unlikely nest. The
Pennsylvania Dutch, to whose stock he belonged, are notably phlegmatic and peace-
loving, and their environment seems wholly
unsuited to the propagation of a Prince Ru-
pert or a Hannibal. Yet, surprisingly, in the
case of Custer it did.

[1] *The Wi-Iy-Ohi*, V, No. 11 (February, 1952).

Historical Introduction

Bearers of the family name are widely distributed throughout America and we have no assurance that all of them are descendants of one common ancestor. In 1684 Paul Custer migrated from the German Rhineland to Pennsylvania as one of a company of Mennonites who constituted the second band of immigrants to settle in William Penn's new colony. Conceivably he may have been the General's first American ancestor, but the known family line of the latter begins with Emanuel Custer who died in 1854, aged "about 100 years." Despite a statement frequently repeated, he was not a Hessian officer in Burgoyne's army. In 1778 he married Mary Fadley, and a few years later was residing at Cresaptown, in western Maryland.

Emanuel Custer was the General's great-grandfather, and one may speculate that from him the latter inherited his amazing physical vigor. Emanuel's second son, and the General's grandfather, Jacob Custer, was born at Cresaptown February 26, 1782. He became a blacksmith, as did his son, the General's father. In May, 1802 he married Catherine Vallentine and in sturdy Pennsylvania Dutch fashion fathered a family of eight children, at Cresaptown.

The third member of this progeny was Emanuel Henry Custer, the General's father,

who was born December 10, 1806. In 1824,
he removed to New Rumley in Harrison
County, Ohio. It was not a long migration,
hardly more than 100 miles, and older members of the Custer clan had long since preceded him there. Jacob Custer, his uncle, in
fact, had laid out the village as early as 1812.

Neither Cresaptown or New Rumley ever
developed beyond mere hamlets, and gazet-
teers and atlases accord them but scanty
notice. At New Rumley and Monroe, Michigan, the General grew up. Monroe, although
Michigan's second oldest settlement, numbered less than 4000 population as late as
1860. Save for it, Custer's ancestral background and his early life were both completely rural. Harrison County, Ohio was
peopled by two widely disparate groups of
settlers: the Pennsylvania Dutch, to which
the Custers belonged, and the Virginians, of
Scotch-Irish and Cavalier stock. Young Custer, therefore, may have been exposed to a
certain degree of cosmopolitanism in his native county, although it is unlikely that his
family associated with the Virginians to any
appreciable extent. As for Yankees, they
were so rare in the county as to be an unknown species.[2]

[2]Charles A. Hanna, *Historical Collections of Harrison
County* . . . , Chap. 3.

Historical Introduction

On August 7, 1828 Emanuel Henry Custer married Matilda Viers, who mothered three children and died untimely on July 13, 1835. The lot of a widower with small children on the frontier was difficult, and that of a widow even more so. Living in New Rumley was Maria Kirkpatrick, a recent widow and the mother of two children. On February 23, 1836 Custer and Maria married, and to the two groups of children thus brought together they presently began to add a third, born of the new union. Yet so harmonious were the domestic relations that only by a conscious effort could the General in after years recall the identity of the three groups of children.

Of Maria Kirkpatrick's first brood we need note only Lydia, who was to become the General's second mother. He was born December 5, 1839, the third of seven children born to Maria and Emanuel Custer. In practical effect he was the oldest, since the first two died in infancy. Following George Armstrong came in due order Nevin J., Thomas W., Boston, and Margaret.

Conspicuous among General Custer's better qualities was his devotion to his family. Thomas Custer entered the Union Army as a private soldier, attained a commission, and won two medals for twice within a few days capturing Confederate battle flags. Like the General he was a man of great physical energy and overflowing love of life. Throughout their lives the two brothers were exceedingly close, and in death they were not divided.

Along with them, Margaret's husband, Lieutenant James Calhoun, Boston, and Armstrong Reed, the General's nephew, were slain in the battle of the Little Big Horn. Terrible indeed must have been the shock to Emanuel and "Mother" Custer upon receiving the news of this wholesale destruction of their family. Of them all, only Nevin remained aloof from the General's military orbit. Lacking in physical vigor, he lived the life of a farmer until his death in 1915.

In 1845 Lydia Kirkpatrick, Custer's elder half-sister, married David Reed and the young couple settled in Monroe, Michigan. Explanation of how they met or why they migrated to Monroe is lacking, but a possible clue is afforded by the fact that George W., son of John and Vallentine Custer and an uncle of the General, had married Sidney Ann Reed and in the early forties was a resident of Monroe. Sidney Ann's parents were natives of Fermanagh County, Ireland, and presumably David Reed was of Scotch-Irish stock.

However correct these surmises may be,

Historical Introduction

Lydia took her young half-brother with her to Monroe, where he remained during several of his formative years, and where he obtained much of his schooling. Monroe became his spiritual home, although it is impossible to determine just how many, or which, years he resided there. At sixteen he became a rural schoolmaster at Hopedale, near New Rumley, and at seventeen applied to the local Congressman for an appointment to West Point. It was granted a year later, and in July, 1857 Custer entered the Academy as a member of the class of 1861.

With the attainment of subsequent fame went the usual weaving of myths about the hitherto uncelebrated youth. Whittaker, Custer's first and most worshipful biographer, would have us believe that from his earliest childhood Custer displayed a precocious liking for military activities. Such tales may safely be classed with the ones invented by Parson Weems about young George Washington or the ones woven about the infant Hercules strangling serpents while still in his cradle.

In fact, it still remains a mystery why Custer aspired to admission to West Point, for nothing in his pacifist-minded ancestry offers an explanation. At Monroe, however, he had come into physical proximity with

the Yankee breed of Americans, who domi-
nated the community both politically and
socially. Mid-century Monroe harbored numerous men of state-wide or even national
influence, and it harbored also a number of
army families. "Remember the Raisin" had
been the battle-cry of the Nation in the War
of 1812, and military memories and tradi-
tions were vital in the community.

A knowledge of these things may have
turned young Custer's thoughts to a military
career, although he lived in a world apart
from the Yankee and army families. Within
recent years elderly men and women have
related to me their memories of the Custers.
"Of course we did not associate with them,"
commented Major Joseph R. Smith, descendant of a line of army officers. In greater detail, a life-long friend of Mrs. Custer recalled:

"General Custer was born in Ohio. One of
his older half-sisters married David Reed and
came on to Monroe. Young Custer went to
her home and from there attended school in
Monroe. His father was a blacksmith. . . .
We did not associate with the Custers. They
were quite ordinary people, no intellectual
interests, very little schooling. Young Custer got a little job working for the Bacons.
He used to hang around the back yard and
wait for Libby (Mrs. Elizabeth Custer). He

was not received in her home. He was of good character but the family just couldn't see him. After he became famous for his military service, however, the judge (Bacon) finally assented to their marriage.[3]

From July, 1857 to July, 1861 Custer toiled as a cadet to master the profession of arms. Perhaps the word "toiled" is inappropriate for it is safe to say that in all the long history of the Military Academy it was never afflicted with a less promising or more cantankerous pupil. A recent biographer who has examined the Academy records characterizes him as "a slovenly soldier and a deplorable student . . . a tardy and a clumsy recruit who persistently was punished for slackness in drill, dirty equipment, or disorderly uniform.[4]

One hundred demerits acquired in any six-months period called for automatic expulsion. In his first half-year Custer earned 129, and was only spared to future fame by some unknown benefactor who reduced them to 69. In the first and second halves of his second year he again came perilously close to expulsion by acquiring 98 and 94 demerits respectively. He constantly remained at or

[3]Interview with the present writer, July 11, 1938. Printed in *Burton Hist. Collection Leaflet*, May, 1939.

[4]Frederic F. Van De Water, *Glory Hunter.—A Life of General Custer* (Indianapolis, 1939), Chap. 2.

close to the bottom of his class throughout the four years and graduated number 34 in a class of 34.

As if determined to climax this sorry record, Custer ended his academic career with a characteristic defiance of discipline. While he was serving as officer of the guard, two of the cadets engaged in a fist fight. Others quickly gathered around, and some were in the act of interfering to separate the gladiators when Custer rushed to the scene shouting to them to "stand back and have a fair fight." In his own subsequent recital of the affair, Custer states: "My duty as officer of the guard was plain and simple. I should have arrested the two combatants and sent them to the guard tents for violating the peace and the regulations of the Academy. But the instincts of the boy prevailed over the obligation of the officer of the guard."

They continued to do so to the end of his life, for to the end he remained an incorrigible, impulsive boy. This quality, admirable enough from a certain point of view, became something else when exercised by an officer responsible for the lives of his men and the safety of his country. The incident illustrates Custer's most conspicuous failing as a soldier and officer. The self-control which four years of West Point failed to instill in him, he never acquired. To the end of life he remained an impulsive adolescent who never hesitated to snap his fingers at discipline and "plain and simple duty," although as an officer in command of others he became a furious disciplinarian.

Custer himself relates that for this final West Point offense he was court-martialed and thereby prevented from going with the rest of his class to Washington where the armies of blue and gray were gathering for the first blood-bath of the Civil War. For whatever reason, he remained at the Point until Mid-July. Meanwhile the nation was fast falling apart and in urgent need of the service of her trained soldiers. At length on July 18 Custer set out for Washington. On his arrival he reported at the War Department for orders and for some inscrutable reason was ushered before General Scott. Although that aged warrior was immersed in preparations for the impending battle of Bull Run, which was fought the next day, he took time to question the young shavetail about his preferences and to assign him the task of proceeding to the front as a courier, bearing dispatches to General McDowell.

So it came about that, fresh from his arrest at West Point, Custer participated in the

first battle of the war. Until its close at
Appomattox four years later he was engaged
in every important battle of the Army of the
Potomac, besides sharing in or leading uncounted cavalry raids and engagements. At
the close, to Custer came the flag of surrender tendered by Lee's Army of Northern
Virginia, and to Mrs. Custer General Sheridan presented the table on which the articles
of surrender were signed, accompanied by
the statement that he knew of no one who
had been more instrumental than her "gallant husband" in bringing the surrender to
pass.

We have neither space nor desire to trace
in detail Custer's Civil War career. It is one
with the history of the war, which may be
read in many books. Our present task is limited to commenting upon certain aspects of
Custer's amazing ascent from obscurity to
fame which serve to shed light upon his personality and character.

Outstanding is the famed "Custer luck,"
which examination discloses to have been in
large degree the natural consequence of his
own enterprise. The ebullient energy which
had found earlier outlet in harum-scarum
escapades and rough practical jokes was now
directed to the more entrancing game of war.
Even his assignment to the cavalry arm of

the service was not wholly due to luck, for at West Point, along with his many demerits he had won a reputation as a superb horseman, and it was his own enterprise and combative temperament that advanced him to the leadership of his profession.

Probably no soldier ever experienced greater zest for combat, into which he was ever ready to rush without pausing to count the odds. The story is told of Anthony Wayne that when asked by Washington whether he was willing to undertake the capture of Stony Point he answered that he would storm hell itself if his General wished it. Custer, we may feel sure, was ready to storm hell without awaiting his General's command.

He fought joyously and fiercely at every opportunity, and when opportunities were lacking he frequently went in search of them. In the Peninsular Campaign of 1862, while still an obscure lieutenant he was ordered to conduct a lone-man reconnaisance of a ford across the Chickahominy River. Having waded the river in safety, he went on to discover an isolated outpost. Returning, he was taken before General McClellan, and the commander of the army listened while the drenched and mud-stained youth eagerly related his discovery. The brief interview ended with an invitation from the Commander for Custer to join his personal staff. Although the opportune meeting with McClellan may have been blind luck, the capital which Custer made of it was the result of his own enterprise and personality. "In those days," McClellan subsequently wrote in his *Own Story*, "Custer was simply a reckless, gallant boy, undeterred by fatigue, unconscious of fear; but his head was always clear in danger and he always brought me clear and intelligible reports of what he saw under the heaviest fire. I became much attached to him."

So, too, did General Pleasanton, the first notable commander of Union cavalry, under whom Custer, still a lieutenant, was serving a year later. At Aldie on June 17, 1863 he showed the mettle which had attracted the attention of General McClellan by leading a desperate charge against Stuart's famed Confederate troopers and driving them in headlong retreat.

A year earlier, Custer had captured the first prisoner made by the Army of the Potomac; now he had led victoriously the first charge made by the reorganized Union cavalry. Five days later Pleasanton was made a major general and in the attendant shakeup of the command Custer, who had hopefully aspired to a captaincy, was commis-

Historical Introduction

sioned a brigadier and given command of the Michigan Cavalry Brigade.

At twenty-three the slovenly cadet of West Point days had become the youngest general in the Union army, passing at a single bound from lowly lieutenant to brigadier general. There were many colonels, majors, and captains older in years and in service whom he thus passed by. Something more than mere blind luck must have dictated the promotion, and this something was evidently the fiery spirit of combativeness which was presently to command the admiration of General Sheridan and the popular esteem of the nation.

The youthful general was not backward about enjoying the perquisites of his rank. Always a showman with a pronounced theatrical bent, he proceeded to devise for himself a uniform such as had never been seen in the United States Army and to discard forever the slovenly attire which had hitherto been his trademark. In his new apparel, set off by his shoulder-length golden curls, he looked "as if he had just stepped out of Van Dyke's pictures, the image of the seventeenth century."[5]

More important, he imposed upon his mid-

[5]Frederick Whittaker, *Complete Life of Gen. George A. Custer* (New York, 1876), 169.

western volunteer soldiers a strict regime of
regular army discipline. Before long they
responded to his leadership, under which the
Michigan Cavalry Brigade acquired a reputation no less notable than that of its foot-
slogging counterpart, the famed Wisconsin-
Indiana-Michigan Iron Brigade.

Custer's most notable service and his most
fruitful friendship were yet to come. In 1864
General Grant made General Sheridan commander of all the cavalry of the Army of the
Potomac. A born fighter of marked intellectual ability, Sheridan quickly learned to appreciate the fighting qualities of the flamboy-
ant leader of the Michigan Cavalry Brigade.
Under Sheridan's competent oversight Custer led repeated raids and charges and at the
end, when Lee was desperately seeking to
escape the toils of Grant's encircling army
Custer was launching the last charge of the
war, to be stopped by a soldier bearing a
white towel in token of Lee's desire to surrender.

Appomattox was the climax of Custer's career. With the war safely ended the Government turned its attention to the intervention
of France in Mexico and an army was dis-
patched to the Rio Grande to reinforce our
diplomatic demands. General Sheridan was
given command of the military demonstra-

tion and Custer, too, was ordered to the Southwest, where he passed several months in command of troops at Alexandria and Austin. When the prospect of armed intervention in Mexico subsided the troops were dispersed and in the process early in 1866 Custer was mustered out of the volunteer service.

Therewith he reverted to his rank of captain in the regular army and his salary was reduced to one-fourth of its former amount. In common with hundreds of other Union officers he was suddenly made aware of the impermanency of volunteer commissions and brevets. For a short time he toyed with the idea of becoming a mercenary soldier in Mexico at an extravagant salary and even General Grant loaned the influence of his prestige to the project. Opportunely, however, a better future was opened to him. Intensified troubles with the Indians of the western Plains induced Congress to increase the size of the standing army, with consequent promotion of the officers then in service and the commissioning of scores of new ones. In this connection the organization of the Seventh U.S. Cavalry was authorized, and the powerful influence of General Sheridan procured the appointment of his old-time favorite as its lieutenant colonel. Since neither General

Smith, its colonel, or his successor joined the regiment, save for a few weeks' time, Custer became its actual leader until his death ten years later.

Both for Custer and the nation an era had ended and a new one was dawning. From the founding of Jamestown and Plymouth colonies the white man had pushed the native inhabitants of America ever westward before his relentless advance. Early in the nineteenth century the conception of the Great Plains as a desert unfit for civilized habitation gained currency, and the surviving remnants of numerous eastern tribes were granted new homes in this area, which was conceived as a permanent Indian reserve. The passage of two generations served to dispel this conception, however, and before 1860 white settlers were crossing the Missouri and the lower Mississippi to occupy the Great Plains, already occupied by numerous nomadic tribes for whom the vast herds of buffaloes provided an all-embracing source of life.

Relations with the Indian tribes had always been a vexed problem wherever the frontier existed. Until President Grant's Administration, when a radical change in governmental policy was made, the fiction that the tribes were sovereign or semi-sovereign entities had been observed, and scores of treaties had been made with them. In fact, however, tribal government was exceedingly rudimentary. The chiefs had no power to compel their followers to observe the provisions of a treaty, nor was the Government able to restrain its own land-hungry citizens from wholesale violations of the agreements it entered into with the tribes.

Friction, followed by warfare and forcible conquest of the Indians, was thus inevitable. However much one may deplore such wrongs as were committed against them, the broad fact is clear that in taking forcible possession of the continent the white race was following a practice as old as human history. But for it there would be today no United States, since every square league of our national domain was forcibly wrested, at one time or another, from the original possessors.

Now, in the later sixties, the Government was pushing the Pacific Railroad across the Plains, settlers were steadily following in its wake, and the wholesale slaughter of the buffaloes on which the Plains tribes were dependent for their continued existence, was beginning. Unless the savages were willing peaceably to abandon their immemorial way of life and follow "the white man's road" they must resist the invasion. They did, to the best of their ability, and it became the duty of the army, led by such generals as Sherman, Sheridan, and Custer, along with scores of others, to subdue them.

Unfortunately for all concerned, both the Government and public sentiment were swayed by divided counsels. In the resultant confusion the absurdity was witnessed of the Indian Bureau feeding, clothing, and even arming the Indians at the very time the Army was engaged in fighting them.[6] The bitterness which developed between spokesmen of the contending policies has long since been forgotten, but readers of General Custer's narrative will once more come in contact with that leader's forcible expression of it. Some knowledge of the background here but inadequately sketched, is essential to any understanding of his attitude.

Such was the state of confusion under which General Custer's Plains service was performed. Readers of Mrs. Carrington's *Absaraka*[7] are familiar with the deplorable

[6]"Something should be done to stop this anomaly" wrote Sheridan to Sherman in a report of Dec. 2, 1868. "I am ordered to fight these Indians and General Hazen is permitted to feed them." Although all the Arapahoes, he continued, had taken part in the recent battle of the Washita, "still they are now having flour, sugar, and coffee issued to them, and even to war parties going out to depredate and kill." U. S. Serial 1360, Ex. Doc. 18, p. 43.

[7]The Lakeside Classics volume for 1950.

lack of military support accorded General Carrington at Fort Phil Kearny, and the even more deplorable fire in the rear to which he was subjected by the spokesmen of the Indian Department. Sheridan and Custer were subjected to the same back fire, while engaged in protecting the frontier settlers and punishing their red tormentors.

Although Custer came to the Plains as a veteran soldier, he had yet to learn the methods of Indian warfare. Despite early mistakes his progress was rapid; he presently acquired the reputation of being the country's best Indian fighter and the regiment whose character he moulded became renowned throughout the Army. His undoubted brilliance was marred, however, by certain defects of character which caused him infinite trouble to the end of his life. Space to discuss them adequately is lacking, but some passing notice of them will be of assistance in understanding his career.

Underlying all of them was his perennial boyishness, which frequently betrayed him into sorry exhibitions of misjudgment. Although his final escapade at West Point, when eagerness to prolong a fist-fight led him to ignore his "plain and simple duty" as an officer, entailed no serious consequences, its implications were portentous. The lesson of

subjection to duty and to discipline which
during four years as a cadet he failed to learn
was never mastered. General McClellan
characterized him as a "mere boy" in 1862,
and a boy he remained to the end of his
life.

To this characteristic may be attributed
his sudden outbursts of wild enthusiasm upon
the receipt of some piece of good news, when,
as Mrs. Custer relates, his common response
was to break up the furniture by way of giving outlet to his exuberant joy. To it, also,
may be attributed his senseless abandonment
of his command, as at Culpepper in 1863, in
the eagerness to participate in an assault
upon a train; as also his recklessness, repeatedly displayed on the Plains, in ignoring his
responsibility as commander in face of the
enemy to engage in some hunt for wild game.
His own account of his conduct when he engaged in his first buffalo hunt affords a perfect illustration of the adolescence which he
never outgrew.[8] So pronounced was this pro-
pensity that Sheridan placed him under orders not to go outside the lines to hunt while
leading the Black Hills expedition of 1874.

Impulsiveness combined with uxoriousness
explains certain of his gravely foolish actions
during the Hancock campaign of 1867. While

[8]For this incident, see *Post*, Chap. 3.

actively campaigning against a foe which as
yet he had signally failed to match, he sent
for his wife to join him in the field, thereby
exposing her to a fate whose hideousness
staggers the imagination. Belatedly realizing
this, he sent a squadron of cavalry post haste
to rescue the wagon train with which he had
directed her to come. Fortunately she had not
left the protection of the fort, had she joined
him in safety, however, her presence would
only have served to hamper the command in
its further operations.[9]

This performance serves to illustrate a
curious inconsistency in Custer's character.
Commonly indifferent to hardship and physical exertion, he catered to his personal pleasure in ways that raised further questions
concerning his good judgment. Almost as
soon as he acquired his brigadier's stars he
annexed a negro contraband woman to serve
as his personal cook. She followed him to the
end of the war and for years afterward, until
she finally succumbed to the charms of a
dusky wooer and returned to domestic life.

[9]Custer says, because his letter had miscarried, Van
De Water states (*Glory Hunter*, 167) that General Smith
intervened to deny her permission to leave. Uxoriousness also largely accounts for the terrific march in the
summer of 1867, followed by leaving his command to
pay a visit to his wife, which precipitated his arrest
and attendant trial and conviction.

Historical Introduction

General Stanley complained that on the arduous Yellowstone expedition of 1873 he took along another "old negro woman," and with her a cast iron stove and other impedimenta whose daily packing delayed the scheduled early marches: and on the difficult pursuit of the hostiles to the Texas Panhandle in the winter of 1869 he took with him a white female cook.

Such exhibitions argue a degree of self-centeredness which help to account for certain exhibitions of shocking callousness toward the men under his command. Unmindful of the fact that but few of them possessed his own remarkable stamina, and that none were mounted, like himself, on thoroughbreds, he subjected them to terrific marches of which he boasts in his narrative. On the one of 1867 which led to his arrest he drove them on a 55-hour march of 150 miles. Watchful Indians swooped down upon a handful who had lagged behind—"without authority" he tells us, but quite possibly from sheer inability to keep up—and killed two of them. Although he properly excoriates General Sully's inhuman abandonment of a captured soldier, he made no effort on this occasion to punish the marauders or to recover the bodies of his men: his only reason, "time [was] important," although why it was remains still a mystery.

Historical Introduction

More notable, and the most serious blot upon Custer's entire career on the Plains, was the indifference he displayed at the battle of the Washita to the fate of Major Elliot's detachment.

Although Custer's own narrative presents a plausible defense of this action, careful scrutiny of the attendant circumstances discloses its inadequacy; and his headlong retreat before an enemy only intent upon fleeing in the opposite direction seems to indicate that for perhaps the only time in his career he had lost his nerve. That he greatly exaggerated the opposition made by the warriors from the lower villages is testified by Lieutenant Godfrey and by the obvious facts disclosed in large part in his own narrative.

The sharpest possible criticism of this abandonment of Major Elliot's party began at once, to continue ever afterward. Although Keim, who followed the campaign as a reporter and whose book, *Sheridan's Troopers on the Border* appeared within a few months, attempts a defense of the action on technical military grounds, he concedes that it "would appear as a gross abandonment" of Elliot.

Even General Sheridan, whose faith in Custer seemed to have no limit, notes in his *Personal Memoirs* that Custer was severely criticized for making "no effort" to discover Elliot's fate. Captain Benteen excoriated him in a letter which was published anonymously in a St. Louis newspaper and when Custer announced to his officers that he would dogwhip the author if he could learn his identity, Benteen acknowledged his responsibility and suggested that the whipping begin. Custer's own narrative discloses that the "most thorough search" he caused to be made for Elliot's men was limited to the immediate vicinity of the captured village; and the fact that their mangled corpses, conspicuous in their snowy background, were lying only two miles away exposes the "thoroughness" of the search that was made.

Still stranger were Custer's fears for the safety of his wagon train. The one reason for making the winter campaign was the fact that the ponies of the Indians, weakened by lack of forage, made the warriors incapable of evading the white cavalry. Even had they been insane enough to leave their women and children unprotected while they went off in the opposite direction to attack the wagon train, Custer's better mounted troops could readily have followed them. Quite apart from this consideration the train was impregnable to any attack they could have made upon it. Custer himself in describing the at-

Historical Introduction

tack upon Lieutenant Robbins' train (*Post*,
Chap. 6) when 48 troopers without even halting beat off for several hours an attack by
600 or more warriors, tells us that if necessary the wagons could have been halted to
use as breastworks, which would have made
the defenders "almost invincible," although
they were outnumbered more than ten to
one. Evidently the defenders of Custer's
train were secure against Indians attacking
on weakened ponies operating in foot-deep
snow and with the knowledge that Custer's
entire force was close at hand.[10]

[10]Quite apart from the foregoing considerations there
was no reason to anticipate any attack on the train.
In his official report to Sheridan written on the night of
November 28 (U.S. Serial 1360, Ex. Doc. 18, pp. 27–28),
in reciting the reasons for his retreat Custer says nothing of any fear for his train; instead, he recites only the
exhaustion of his supplies and the weariness of his men
and horses. It was a three-day march to the train
(actually he reached it in a night march of 4 hours and
a morning march from daylight until 10 o'clock), the
country was so cut up that it was difficult even for
the cavalry to traverse it, and he knew the wagons
could not follow him; hence he began his return march
to discover, upon rejoining them, that since leaving
them behind they had advanced but sixteen miles. All
this implies that the train was some thirty miles from
the battlefield. How then could the warriors, who had
come to the scene of the conflict from the opposite
direction, know anything of its existence or whereabouts;
or, knowing, how could they, without supplies, have

Historical Introduction

With the war in the Southwest triumphant-
ly ended, the Seventh Regiment marched to
Fort Hays near where (on Big Creek) it remained until autumn. During this period
Custer was occupied in entertaining many
guests and conducting them on hunting expeditions. In October he removed to Fort
Leavenworth where he devoted the winter
season to writing his Civil War memoirs.
The summer of 1870 was passed at Fort Hays
in much the same fashion as the preceding

covered such a distance even if freed from the menace
of pursuit by Custer's army?

That his horses and men were weary and in want of
supplies is evident, but for these conditions Custer was
himself responsible, since in Black Kettle's village he
had captured ample supplies of food, blankets, and buffalo robes, all of which he had voluntarily burned. If
ammunition was short (of which he gives no hint) he
could have saved the important supply which was ex-
pended in shooting the 875 captured ponies. So, too,
although he emphasizes the handicap imposed by the
necessity of guarding the captured squaws and children
and the handful of wounded men, he had only to turn
the former loose, and his narrative shows that the latter
(14 in all) did not materially impede his progress.

In his final battle of the Little Big Horn the commands of Reno and Benteen, beleaguered on their hill-
top by swarms of warriors, mistakenly believed that
Custer had abandoned them to their fate and cursed
him for his supposed desertion. Was this lack of confidence a legacy from his indifference to the fate of
Elliot's command at the Washita eight years earlier?

one. Following another winter at Fort Leavenworth the Regiment was withdrawn from
the Plains and in March, 1871 Custer began
a two-year sojourn as commandant of a two-
company post at Elizabethtown, Kentucky,
not far from the childhood home of Abraham
Lincoln. His duties were insignificant and
with ample leisure time on his hands he began and finished the series of articles which
were published in the *Galaxy*, entitled *My
Life on the Plains*,[11] beginning in January,
1872 and ending in October, 1874.

Judged by present-day standards the editorial skill exhibited by the *Galaxy* was curi-
ously vestigial. Publication of the Custer
series was begun with no single word of introduction or explanation. For a long time
installments appeared monthly, then inter-
missions followed without explanation to the
reader. In all, twenty installments were published in the thirty-four-month period from
January, 1872 to October, 1874. Almost the
only editorial comment during the entire period was devoted to a brief summary appended to the July, 1874 installment, giving
General Hazen's rejoinder to Custer's stric-
tures upon his conduct, published in the issue
of the preceding February.[12]

[11]The later installments omitted the adjective from
the title.   [12]Chapter 14 of the present volume.

Historical Introduction

Having thus belatedly embarked upon a literary career, Custer became a persistent addict to the pen. With *My Life on the Plains* completed, he undertook the design of writing for *Galaxy* publication the story of his life in the Army of the Potomac. This no doubt would have attained heroic dimensions had not death prematurely stayed his diligent pen. He wrote at times under conditions of hardship unexampled perhaps in the annals of literature—at night in his tent by a feeble light while all his companions were sleeping. At least one contribution to the *Galaxy* was thus composed after a fifty-mile march through the badlands of the Yellowstone, from notes which he had taken along on the march. He succeeded in carrying his Civil War narration only to the Peninsular Campaign of 1862, and Whittaker records that his final contribution to the *Galaxy* was written during his last march to the Little Big Horn and was received by the publisher some days after the arrival of the news of his death.

Literary fashions two generations ago differed in numerous respects from that of the present time. Custer's contributions should be judged in the light of their contemporary background and generous allowance should be made for the nature of his literary preparation. His formal education was that of the frontier schools of his time, and his mature life until 1871 had been devoted to making history rather than writing it. Unlike most present-day men of action, he employed no ghost writer, and if at times his sentences make heavy going the charitable reader will reflect that he is deserving credit for producing them at all in the conditions under which many of them were written. Whatever his literary faults may have been, we are indebted to him for a remarkably vivid firsthand picture of Great Plains life and warfare when dominion over them was in the moment of passing from the red race to the white.

The type employed in printing Custer's articles in the *Galaxy* was utilized to reprint them as a book, first issued by Sheldon and Company at New York in 1874, the only editing provided for the volume consisting in supplying a title page and several illustrations. The same type was utilized—by this time much worn—to print a second issue of the book in 1881. Professor Rister lists another edition "expanded and reedited by W. I. Holloway *et al*," published at St. Louis in 1891 with the title *Wild Life on the Plains and the Horrors of Indian Warfare*. I have not seen this volume. Since the copyright of Sheldon and Company had not expired, its publishers must have secured the permission of the copyright owner to issue it.

Although the Indian is still with us, in numbers perhaps as large as ever, he long since ceased to figure as a military factor and now excites public interest chiefly as a character on the silver screen. There, like the synthetic cowboy of moviedom, he still continues to entertain the multitudes who are thrilled by the mixture of a little bad history and a plethora of imaginative melodrama.

The task of editing *My Life on the Plains* entailed the making of a number of decisions which should be explained to the reader. The narrative as originally printed in the magazine is unduly long, and some of its contents possess but slight present-day interest. There is also a good deal of second-hand narration of such events as the Fetterman massacre and Colonel Forsyth's battle on the Arikaree which it seemed best to excise. Considerable additional matter devoted to Custer's exposition of the controversy between the Army and the Indian Department over the policy pursued toward the Indians has also been excluded. The present volume, therefore, although taken direct from the pages of the *Galaxy*, does not contain all of the material Custer contributed to it. Nor is our present volume a verbatim reprint. Chapter heads (of which the original contained none) have been supplied by the Editor, punctuation has been altered (in particular, hundreds of the commas in which our ancestors revelled have been deleted) and such other changes as seemed clearly desirable have been made. The result, it is believed, is not only a more compact volume, but one which presents Custer's essential story in better form than any earlier printing has done.

"Were you ever in a charge, you who read this now, by the winter fireside, long after the bones of the slain have turned to dust, when peace covers the land? If not, you have never known the fiercest pleasure of life. The chase is nothing to it, the most headlong hunt is tame in comparison. In the chase, the game flees and you shoot: here the game shoots back, and every leap of the charging steed is a peril escaped or dashed aside. The sense of power and audacity that possesses the cavalier, the unity with his steed, both are perfect. The horse is as wild as the man: with glaring eye-balls and red nostrils he rushes frantically forward at the very top of his speed, with huge bounds, as different from the rhythmic precision of the gallop as the sweep of the hurricane is from the rustle of the breeze. Horse and rider are drunk with excitement, feeling and seeing nothing but the cloud of dust, the scattered flying figures, conscious of only one mad desire, to reach them, to smite, smite, smite!" Frederick Whittaker, *Complete Life of Gen. George A. Custer . . . 157–8.*

MY LIFE on the PLAINS

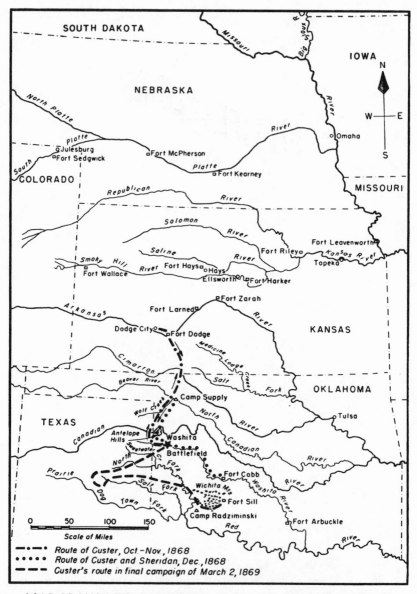

MAP DRAWN TO ILLUSTRATE "MY LIFE ON THE PLAINS"
Note that General Custer's route in March, 1869
is represented only approximately

My Life on the Plains

—

Chapter 1

THE GREAT PLAINS

AS a fitting introduction to some of the
personal incidents and sketches which
I shall hereafter present to the readers
of the *Galaxy*, a brief description of the country in which these events transpired may not
be deemed inappropriate.

It is but a few years ago that every school-
boy, supposed to possess the rudiments of a
knowledge of the geography of the United
States, could give the boundaries and a general description of the Great American Desert. As to the boundary the knowledge seemed
to be quite explicit: on the north bounded by
the Upper Missouri, on the east by the Lower
Missouri and Mississippi, on the south by
Texas, and on the west by the Rocky Mountains. The boundaries on the northwest and
south remained undisturbed, while on the
east civilization, propelled and directed by
Yankee enterprise, adopted the motto: Westward the star of empire takes its way. Count-

less throngs of emigrants crossed the Mississippi and Missouri rivers, selecting homes in the rich and fertile territories lying beyond. Each year this tide of emigration, strengthened and increased by the flow from foreign shores, advanced toward the setting sun, slowly but surely narrowing the preconceived limits of the Great American Desert, and correspondingly enlarging the limits of civilization. At last the geographical myth was dispelled. It was gradually discerned that the Great American Desert did not exist, that it had no abiding place, but that within its supposed limits and instead of what had been regarded as a sterile and unfruitful tract of land incapable of sustaining either man or beast there existed the fairest and richest portion of the national domain, blessed with a climate pure, bracing, and healthful, while its undeveloped soil rivalled if it did not surpass the most productive portions of the eastern, middle, or southern states.[1]

[1] Zebulon M. Pike, whose narrative of his southwestern exploring expedition of 1806–07 was reprinted as the Lakeside Classics volume for 1925, described the Plains country as a desert and proposed that it be set aside as a permanent home for Indians, whom the westward push of white settlement was depriving of their homes. Secretary of War Calhoun recommended this program to Congress, which adopted it. The removal of numerous tribes from east of the Mississippi to the

The Great Plains

Discarding the name Great American Desert, this immense tract of country, with its eastern boundary moved back by civilization to a distance of nearly three hundred miles west of the Missouri River, is now known as the Plains, and by this more appropriate title it shall be called when reference to it is necessary. The Indian tribes which have caused the Government most anxiety and whose depredations have been most serious against our frontier settlements and prominent lines of travel across the Plains, infest that portion of the Plains bounded on the north by the valley of the Platte River and its tributaries, on the east by a line running north and south between the 97th and 98th meridians, on the south by the valley of the Arkansas River, and west by the Rocky Mountains—although by treaty stipulations almost every tribe with which the Government has recently been at war is particularly debarred from entering or occupying any portion of this tract of country.

Of the many persons whom I have met on the Plains as transient visitors from the

area followed, and in many cases their descendants still reside there. The conception of the Great American Desert lying westward of the Missouri and the lower Mississippi, which General Custer in the present chapter labors to dispel, obsessed the minds of Americans until toward the close of the nineteenth century.

States or from Europe, there are few who
have not expressed surprise that their original ideas concerning the appearance and
characteristics of the country were so far
from correct, or that the Plains in imagination, as described in books, tourists' letters,
or reports of isolated scientific parties, differed so widely from the Plains as they actually exist and appear to the eye. Travellers,
writers of fiction, and journalists have spoken
and written a great deal concerning this immense territory, so unlike in all its qualities
and characteristics to the settled and cultivated portion of the United States; but to a
person familiar with the country the conclusion is forced, upon reading these published
descriptions, either that the writers never
visited but a limited portion of the country
they aim to describe, or, as is most commonly
the case at the present day, that the journey
was made in a stage-coach or Pullman car,
half of the distance travelled in the night
time, and but occasional glimpses taken during the day. A journey by rail across the
Plains is at best but ill adapted to a thorough
or satisfactory examination of the general
character of the country, for the reason that
in selecting the route for railroads the valley
of some stream is, if practicable, usually chosen to contain the road-bed. The valley be-

ing considerably lower than the adjacent country, the view of the tourist is correspondingly limited. Moreover, the vastness and varied character of this immense tract could not fairly be determined or judged of by a flying trip across one portion of it. One would scarcely expect an accurate opinion to be formed of the swamps of Florida from a railroad journey from New York to Niagara.

After indulging in criticisms on the written descriptions of the Plains, I might reasonably be expected to enter into what I conceive a correct description, but I forbear. Beyond a general outline embracing some of the peculiarities of this slightly known portion of our country, the limits and character of these sketches of western life will not permit me to go.

* * *

In proceeding from the Missouri River to the base of the Rocky Mountains the ascent, although gradual, is quite rapid. For example, at Fort Riley, Kansas, the bed of the Kansas River is upward of 1,000 feet above the level of the sea, while Fort Hays, at a distance of nearly 150 miles farther west, is about 1,500 feet above the level of the sea. Starting from almost any point near the central portion of the Plains, and moving in any direction, one seems to encounter a series of undulations at a more or less remote distance from each other, but constantly in view. Comparing the surface of the country to that of the ocean, a comparison often indulged in by those who have seen both, it does not require a very great stretch of the imagination, when viewing this boundless ocean of beautiful living verdure, to picture these successive undulations as gigantic waves, not wildly chasing each other to or from the shore, but standing silent and immovable, and by their silent immobility adding to the impressive grandeur of the scene. These undulations, varying in height from fifty to five hundred feet, are sometimes formed of a light sandy soil, but often of different varieties of rock, producing at a distance the most picturesque effect.

The constant recurrence of these waves, if they may be so termed, is quite puzzling to the inexperienced plainsman. He imagines, and very naturally too, judging from appearances, that when he ascends to the crest he can overlook all the surrounding country. After a weary walk or ride of perhaps several miles, which appeared at starting not more than one or two, he finds himself at the desired point, but discovers that directly beyond in the direction he desires to go rises a second wave, but slightly higher than the first, and from the crest of which he must certainly be able to scan the country as far as the eye can reach. Thither he pursues his course, and after a ride of from five to ten miles, although the distance did not seem half so great before starting, he finds himself on the crest, or, as it is invariably termed, the "divide," but again only to discover that another and apparently a higher divide rises in his front, and at about the same distance. Hundreds, yes, thousands of miles may be journeyed over, and this same effect witnessed every few hours.

As you proceed toward the west from the Missouri, the size of the trees diminishes, as well as the number of kinds. As you penetrate the borders of the Indian country, leaving civilization behind you, the sight of forests is no longer enjoyed, the only trees to be seen being scattered along the banks of the streams, these becoming smaller and more rare, finally disappearing altogether and giving place to a few scattering willows and osiers. The greater portion of the Plains may be said to be without timber of any kind.

* * *

While dwarfed specimens of almost all varieties of trees are found fringing the banks

of some of the streams, the prevailing species
are cottonwood and poplar trees (*Populus
monilifera* and *Populus angulosa*). Intermingled with these are found clumps of osiers
(*Salix longifolia*). In almost any other portion of the country the cottonwood would be
the least desirable of trees; but to the Indian,
and, in many instances which have fallen
under my observation, to our troops, the
cottonwood has performed a service for which
no other tree has been found its equal, and
that is as forage for horses and mules during
the winter season, when the snow prevents
even dried grass from being obtainable. During the winter campaign of 1868–'69 against
the hostile tribes south of the Arkansas it not
infrequently happened that my command,
while in pursuit of Indians, exhausted its
supply of forage, and the horses and mules
were subsisted upon the young bark of the
cottonwood tree. In routing the Indians
from their winter villages, we invariably discovered them located upon that point of the
stream promising the greatest supply of cottonwood bark, while the stream in the vicinity of the village was completely shorn of its
supply of timber, and the village itself was
strewn with the white branches of the cottonwood entirely stripped of their bark. It was
somewhat amusing to observe an Indian pony

feeding on cottonwood bark. The limb being usually cut into pieces about four feet in length and thrown upon the ground, the pony, accustomed to this kind of "long forage," would place one fore foot on the limb in the same manner as a dog secures a bone, and gnaw the bark from it. Although not affording anything like the amount of nutriment which either hay or grain does, yet our horses invariably preferred the bark to either, probably on account of its freshness.

The herbage to be found on the principal portion of the Plains is usually sparse and stunted in its growth. Along the banks of the streams and in the bottom lands there grows generally in rich abundance a species of grass often found in the states east of the Mississippi; but on the uplands is produced what is there known as the buffalo grass, indigenous and peculiar in its character, differing in form and substance from all other grasses. The blade under favorable circumstances reaches a growth usually of from three to five inches, but instead of being straight, or approximately so, it assumes a curled or waving shape, the grass itself becoming densely matted and giving to the foot, when walking upon it, a sensation similar to that produced by stepping upon moss or the most costly of velvet carpets.

Nearly all graminivorous animals inhabiting the Plains except the elk and some species of the deer prefer the buffalo grass to that of the lowland; and it is probable that even these exceptions would not prove good if it were not for the timber on the bottom land, which affords good cover to both the elk and the deer. Both are often found in large herds grazing upon the uplands, although the grass is far more luxuriant and plentiful on the lowlands. Our domestic animals invariably choose the buffalo grass, and experience demonstrates beyond question that it is the most nutritious of all varieties of wild grass.

The favorite range of the buffalo is contained in a belt of country running north and south, about two hundred miles wide, and extending from the Platte River on the north to the valley of the Upper Canadian on the south. In migrating, if not grazing or alarmed, the buffalo invariably moves in single file, the column generally being headed by a patriarch of the herd, who is not only familiar with the topography of the country, but whose prowess in the field entitles him to become the leader of his herd. He maintains this leadership only so long as his strength and courage enable him to remain the successful champion in the innumerable contests which he is called upon to maintain. The buffalo trails are always objects of interest and inquiry to the sight-seer on the Plains. These trails made by the herds in their migrating movements are so regular in their construction and course as to well excite curiosity. They vary but little from eight to ten inches in width, and are usually from two to four inches in depth; their course is almost as unvarying as that of the needle, running north and south. Of the thousands of buffalo trails which I have seen, I recollect none of which the general direction was not north and south. This may seem somewhat surprising at first thought, but it admits of a simple and satisfactory explanation.

The general direction of all streams, large and small, on the Plains, is from the west to the east, seeking as they do an entrance to the Mississippi. The habits of the buffalo incline him to graze and migrate from one stream to another, moving northward and crossing each in succession as he follows the young grass in the spring, and moving southward seeking the milder climate and open grazing in the fall and winter. Throughout the buffalo country are to be seen what are termed buffalo wallows. The number of these is so great as to excite surprise; a moderate estimate would give from one to three to each acre of ground throughout this vast tract of

country. These wallows are about eight feet
in diameter and from six to eighteen inches
in depth, and are made by the buffalo bulls
in the spring when challenging a rival to combat for the favor of the opposite sex. The
ground is broken by pawing—if an animal
with a hoof can be said to paw—and if the
challenge is accepted, as it usually is, the
combat takes place; after which the one who
comes off victorious remains in possession of
the battle-field, and, occupying the wallow
of fresh upturned earth, finds it produces a
cooling sensation to his hot and gory sides.

Sometimes the victory which gives possession of the battle-field and drives a hated
antagonist away is purchased at a dear price.
The carcass of the victor is often found in the
wallow, where his brief triumph has soon terminated from the effects of his wounds. In
the early spring, during the shedding season,
the buffalo resorts to his wallow to aid in
removing the old coat. These wallows have
proved of no little benefit to man, as well as
to animals other than the buffalo. After a
heavy rain they become filled with water, the
soil being of such a compact character as to
retain it. It has not infrequently been the
case when making long marches that the
streams would be found dry, while water in
abundance could be obtained from the wal-

lows. True, it was not of the best quality, particularly if it had been standing long and the buffalo had patronized the wallows as summer resorts; but on the Plains a thirsty man or beast, far from any streams of water, does not parley long with these considerations.

Wherever water is found on the Plains, particularly if it is standing, innumerable gadflies and mosquitoes generally abound. To such an extent do these pests to the animal kingdom exist, that to our thinly-coated animals, such as the horse and mule, grazing is almost an impossibility, while the buffalo with his huge shaggy coat can browse undisturbed. The most sanguinary and determined of these troublesome insects are the buffalo flies; they move in myriads, and so violent and painful are their assaults upon horses that a herd of the latter has been known to stampede as the result of an attack from a swarm of these flies.

But here again is furnished what some reasoners would affirm is evidence of the eternal fitness of things. In most localities where these flies are found in troublesome numbers, there are also found flocks of starlings, a species of blackbird; these, more, I presume, to obtain a livelihood than to become the defender of the helpless, perch

themselves upon the backs of the animals,
when woe betide the hapless gadfly who ventures near, only to become a choice morsel
for the starling. In this way I have seen our
herds of cavalry horses grazing undisturbed,
each horse of the many hundreds having
perched upon his back from one to dozens of
starlings, standing guard over him while he
grazed.

One of the first subjects which addresses
itself to the mind of the stranger on the
Plains, particularly if he be of a philosophical
or scientific turn of mind, is the mirage, which
is here observed in all its perfection. Many
a weary mile of the traveller has been whiled
away in endeavors to account for the fitful
and beautifully changing visions presented
by the mirage. Sometimes the distortions
are wonderful, and so natural as to deceive
the most experienced eye. Upon one occasion I met a young officer who had spent
several years on the Plains and in the Indian
country. He was, on the occasion alluded to,
in command of a detachment of cavalry in
pursuit of a party of Indians who had been
committing depredations on our frontier.
While riding at the head of his command he
suddenly discovered, as he thought, a party
of Indians not more than a mile distant. The
latter seemed to be galloping toward him.

The attention of his men was called to them, and they pronounced them Indians on horseback. The trot was sounded, and the column moved forward to the attack. The distance between the attacking party and the supposed foe was rapidly diminishing, the Indians appearing plainer to view each moment. The charge was about to be sounded, when it was discovered that the supposed party of Indians consisted of the decayed carcasses of half a dozen slain buffaloes, which number had been magnified by the mirage, while the peculiar motion imparted by the latter had given the appearance of Indians on horseback.

I have seen a train of government wagons with white canvas covers moving through a mirage which, by elevating the wagons to treble their height and magnifying the size of the covers, presented the appearance of a line of large sailing vessels under full sail, while the usual appearance of the mirage gave a correct likeness of an immense lake or sea. Sometimes the mirage has been the cause of frightful suffering and death by its deceptive appearance.

Trains of emigrants making their way to California and Oregon have, while seeking water to quench their thirst and that of their animals, been induced to depart from their

17

course in the endeavor to reach the inviting lake of water which the mirage displayed before their longing eyes. It is usually represented at a distance of from five to ten miles. Sometimes, if the nature of the ground is favorable, it is dispelled by advancing toward it; at others it is like an *ignis fatuus*, hovering in sight, but keeping beyond reach. Here and there throughout this region are pointed out the graves of those who are said to have been led astray by the mirage until their bodies were famished and they succumbed to thirst.

The routes usually chosen for travel across the Plains may be said to furnish, upon an average, water every fifteen miles. In some instances, however, and during the hot season of the year, it is necessary in places to go into what is termed a dry camp, that is, to encamp where there is no water. In such emergencies, with a previous knowledge of the route, it is practicable to transport from the last camp a sufficient quantity to satisfy the demands of the people composing the train, but the dumb brutes must trust to the little moisture obtained from the night grazing to quench their thirst.

The animals inhabiting the Plains resemble in some respects the fashionable society of some of our larger cities. During the extreme heat of the summer they forsake their accustomed haunts and seek a more delightful retreat. For, although the Plains are drained by streams of all sizes, from the navigable river to the humblest of brooks, yet at certain seasons the supply of water in many of them is of the most uncertain character. The pasturage, from the excessive heat, the lack of sufficient moisture, and the withering hot winds which sweep across from the south, becomes dried, withered, and burnt, and is rendered incapable of sustaining life. Then it is that the animals usually found on the Plains disappear for a short time, and await the return of a milder season.

Having briefly grouped the prominent features of the central Plains, and as some of the incidents connected with my service among the Indian tribes occurred far to the south of the localities already referred to, a hurried reference to the country north of Texas, and in which the Wichita Mountains are located, a favorite resort of some of the tribes, is here made. To describe it as one would view it in journeying upon horseback over this beautiful and romantic country, to picture with the pen those boundless solitudes—so silent that their silence alone increases their grandeur—to gather inspiration from nature and to attempt to paint the scene as my eye beheld it, is a task before which a much readier pen than mine might well hesitate.

It was a beautiful and ever-changing panorama which at one moment excited the beholder's highest admiration, at the next impressed him with speechless veneration. Approaching the Wichita Mountains from the north, and after the eye has perhaps been wearied by the tameness and monotony of the unbroken Plains, one is gladdened by the relief which the sight of these picturesque and peculiarly beautiful mountains affords.

* * *

Unlike most mountains, the Wichita cannot properly be termed a range or chain, but more correctly a collection or group, as many of the highest and most beautiful are detached, and stand on a level plain, solitary and alone. They are mainly composed of granite, the huge blocks of which exhibit numerous shades of beautiful colors, crimson, purple, yellow, and green predominating. They are conical in shape, and seem to have but little resemblance to the soil upon which they are founded. They rise abruptly from a level surface—so level and unobstructed that it would be an easy matter to drive a carriage to any point of the circumference at the base; and yet so steep and broken are the sides that it is only here and there that it is possible to ascend them. From the foot of almost every mountain pours a stream of limpid water, of almost icy coldness.

* * *

It is to be regretted that the character of the Indian as described in Cooper's interesting novels is not the true one. But as, in emerging from childhood into the years of a maturer age we are often compelled to cast aside many of our earlier illusions and replace them by beliefs less inviting but more real, so we, as a people, with opportunities enlarged and facilities for obtaining knowledge increased, have been forced by a multiplicity of causes to study and endeavor to comprehend thoroughly the character of the red man. So intimately has he become associated with the Government as ward of the nation, and so prominent a place among the questions of national policy does the much mooted Indian question occupy, that it behooves us no longer to study this problem from works of fiction, but to deal with it as it exists in reality.

Stripped of the beautiful romance with which we have been so long willing to envelop him, transferred from the inviting pages of the novelist to the localities where we are compelled to meet with him, in his native village, on the war path, and when raiding upon our frontier settlements and lines of travel, the Indian forfeits his claim to the appellation of the *noble* red man. We see him as he is, and, so far as all knowledge goes, as he ever has been, a *savage* in every sense of the word; not worse, perhaps, than his white brother would be, similarly born and bred, but one whose cruel and ferocious nature far exceeds that of any wild beast of the desert.

That this is true no one who has been brought into intimate contact with the wild tribes will deny. Perhaps there are some who as members of peace commissions or as wandering agents of some benevolent society may have visited these tribes or attended with them at councils held for some pacific purpose, and who, by passing through the villages of the Indian while *at peace,* may imagine their opportunities for judging of the Indian nature all that could be desired. But the Indian, while he can seldom be accused of indulging in a great variety of wardrobe, can be said to have a character capable of adapting itself to almost every occasion. He has one character, perhaps his most serviceable one, which he preserves carefully, and only airs it when making his appeal to the

Government or its agents for arms, ammunition, and license to employ them. This character is invariably paraded, and often with telling effect, when the motive is a peaceful one. Prominent chiefs invited to visit Washington invariably don this character, and in their talks with the Great Father and other less prominent personages they successfully contrive to exhibit but this one phase. Seeing them under these or similar circumstances only, it is not surprising that by many the Indian is looked upon as a simple-minded son of nature, desiring nothing beyond the privilege of roaming and hunting over the vast unsettled wilds of the West, inheriting and asserting but few native rights, and never trespassing upon the rights of others.

This view is equally erroneous with that which regards the Indian as a creature possessing the human form but divested of all other attributes of humanity, and whose traits of character, habits, modes of life, disposition, and savage customs disqualify him from the exercise of all rights and privileges, even those pertaining to life itself. Taking him as we find him, at peace or at war, at home or abroad, waiving all prejudices, and laying aside all partiality, we will discover in the Indian a subject for thoughtful study

23

and investigation. In him we will find the representative of a race whose origin is, and promises to be, a subject forever wrapped in mystery; a race incapable of being judged by the rules or laws applicable to any other known race of men; one between which and civilization there seems to have existed from time immemorial a determined and unceasing warfare—a hostility so deep-seated and inbred with the Indian character that in the exceptional instances where the modes and habits of civilization have been reluctantly adopted, it has been at the sacrifice of power and influence as a tribe, and the more serious loss of health, vigor, and courage as individuals.

Chapter 2

GENERAL HANCOCK'S CAMPAIGN

THERE are two classes of people who are always eager to get up an Indian war—the army and our frontiersmen." I quote from an editorial on the Indian question, which not long since appeared in the columns of one of the leading New York daily newspapers. That this statement was honestly made I do not doubt, but that instead of being true it could not have been farther from the truth I will attempt to show. I assert, and all candid persons familiar with the subject will sustain the assertion, that of all classes of our population the army and the people living on the frontier entertain the greatest dread of an Indian war, and are willing to make the greatest sacrifices to avoid its horrors. This is a proposition the assertion of which almost carries its proof with it.

Under the most auspicious circumstances, and in time of peace with the Indians, the life of an army officer on the Plains or along our frontier is at best one involving no little personal discomfort, and demanding the sacrifice of many of the luxuries and benefits which he could obtain were he located within the limits of civilization. To many officers, service in the West amounts almost to social exile. Some can have their families with or near them. There is a limited opportunity for social intercourse; travel from the States, to and across the Plains, either for business or pleasure, is uninterrupted, and mail facilities with friends and relations in the States are maintained.

An Indian war changes all this. The troops must prepare to take the field. Provided with but few comforts, necessarily limited in this respect by the amount of transportation, which on the Plains is narrowed down to the smallest practicable, the soldier bids adieu— often a final one—to the dear ones at home, and with his comrades in arms sets out, no matter how inclement the season, to seek what? fame and glory? How many military men have reaped laurels from their Indian campaigns? Does he strive to win the approving smile of his countrymen? That is indeed, in this particular instance, a difficult task. For let him act as he may in conducting or assisting in a campaign against the Indians, if he survives the campaign he can feel assured of this fact, that one-half of his fellow-citizens at home will revile him for his zeal and pronounce his success, if he achieves

General Hancock's Campaign

any, a massacre of poor, defenseless, harmless
Indians; while the other half, if his efforts to
chastise the common enemy are not crowned
with satisfactory results, will cry "Down with
him. Down with the regular army, and give
us brave volunteers who can serve the Government in other ways besides eating rations
and drawing pay."

An unsuccessful campaign, under which
head nineteen out of twenty may reasonably
be classed, satisfies no portion of the public
and greatly dissatisfies that portion of the
western population whose knowledge of the
murders and depredations committed by
the Indians is, unlike that of the people of
the States farther east, of too recent origin to
be swept away by false notions of clemency.
During the continuance of the campaign
both officers and soldiers are generally cut off
from all communication with the friends left
behind. Couriers, sent as bearers of a few
despatches and letters, are sometimes under
cover of the night enabled to make their way
back to the forts; but even these fail sometimes. I now recollect the circumstance of
two trusty scouts being sent with despatches
and a small mail to make their way from the
southern portion of Kansas to Fort Dodge on
the Arkansas. When we saw them again we
beheld their lifeless, mangled remains, their

27

bodies pierced with numerous arrows, and mutilated almost beyond recognition—our letters scattered here and there by the savages, who had torn open the little canvas mail-bag in search of plunder. The Indians had surrounded these faithful fellows when within about ten miles of the end of their perilous journey. The numerous empty cartridge shells which lay around and near the bodies of the two men proved how persistently and bravely they had struggled for their lives.

The opening of an Indian campaign is also the signal for the withdrawal of all privileges and enjoyments, such as leaves of absence, visits from eastern friends, hunting and pleasure parties of all kinds. The reception from the East of all luxuries and delicacies for the table and of all current literature, such as the numerous railroads being constructed in the West, particularly the two Pacifics, render easy of procurement, ceases; and not only the private soldier but the officer is limited in his mess fare to an indifferent portion of the ordinary ration. Is it probable or reasonable that these objects and results, the principal ones generally, so far as the army as individuals is concerned, would be considered sufficient to render either officers or soldiers "eager to get up an Indian war"? I have yet to make the acquaintance of that officer of the army who, in time of undisturbed peace, desired a war with the Indians. On the contrary, the army is the Indian's best friend so long as the latter desires to maintain friendship. Is it pleasant at all times, and always interesting, to have a village of peaceable Indians locate their lodges near our frontier posts or camps. The daily visits of the Indians, from the most venerable chief to the strapped papoose, their rude interchange of civilities, their barterings, races, dances, legends, strange customs, and fantastic ceremonies, all combine to render them far more agreeable as friendly neighbors than as crafty, bloodthirsty enemies.

As to the frontiersman, he has everything to lose, even to life, and nothing to gain by an Indian war. "His object is to procure a fat contract or a market for his produce," adds the journal from which the opening lines of this chapter are quoted. This seems plausible and likely enough. But does that journal, and do the people who believe on this question as it does, know that there are two reasons—more are not required—why its statement is a very great error? First, our frontier farmers, busily employed as they are in opening up their farms, never have any produce to dispose of, but consider them-

selves fortunate if they have sufficient for
their personal wants. They are never brought
in contact with the Indian except when the
latter makes a raid or incursion of at least
hundreds of miles, and attacks the settlements. It is another case of Mohammed and
the mountain. The frontiersman never goes
beyond the settlements. The Indian forsakes
his accustomed hunting-grounds when am-
bitious of obtaining scalps or plunder, and
visits the settlements.

The only ground upon which the frontiersman can be accused of inspiring or inciting a
war with the Indian is, that when applied to
by the latter to surrender his life, family, and
property, scalp thrown in, he stoutly refuses,
and sometimes employs force to maintain
this refusal.

I have shown that this abused class of the
pioneers of civilization have no hand in the
fat contracts. Who are the fortunate parties?
With but rare exceptions our most expensive
expeditions against the Indians on the Plains
have been supplied by contracts made with
parties far inside the limits of civilization,
who probably never saw a hostile Indian, and
who never even visited the Indian country.
The supplies are purchased far from the frontiers, in the rich and thickly settled portions
of the States, then shipped by rail and boat

to the most available military post, from which point they are generally drawn by huge trains of army wagons, or carried on pack animals.

Of the many important expeditions organized to operate in the Indian country, none, perhaps, of late years has excited more general and unfriendly comment, considering the slight loss of life inflicted upon the Indians, than the expedition organized and led in person by Major-General Hancock in the spring of 1867. The clique generally known as the Indian ring were particularly malevolent and bitter in their denunciations of General Hancock for precipitating, as they expressed it, an Indian war. This expedition was quite formidable in appearance, being made up of eight troops of cavalry, seven companies of infantry, and one battery of light artillery, numbering altogether about 1,400 men. As General Hancock at the time and since has been so often accused of causelessly bringing on an Indian war, a word in explanation may not be amiss.[2]

[2] General Winfield Scott Hancock, a West Point graduate in the class of 1840, was a veteran and distinguished soldier. Criticism of his Indian campaign of 1867, in which General Custer participated, still continues. Basically it was not occasioned by any lack of ability on Hancock's part; instead, it reflected the underlying cleavage of views between advocates of a policy of

﬩y Life on the Plains

Being in command of the cavalry connected
with the expedition, I had ample and frequent opportunities for learning the true purposes and objects of the march into the heart
of the Indian country. I know no better
mode of explaining these than by quoting
the following extract from letters written by
General Hancock to the agents of the various
tribes with which we expected to be brought
in contact: "I have the honor to state for
your information that I am at present preparing an expedition to the Plains, which will
soon be ready to move. My object in doing
so at this time is to convince the Indians
within the limits of this department that we
are able to punish any of them who may
molest travellers across the Plains, or who
may commit other hostilities against the
whites. We desire to avoid if possible any
troubles with the Indians, and to treat them
with justice, and according to the requirements of our treaties with them; and I wish
especially in my dealings with them to act

peaceful persuasion of the Indians as opposed to one of
forcible control. Practically all military men were committed to the latter, and Hancock is still charged with
needlessly precipitating a new Indian war. See, for
example, Frederic F. Van De Water, *Glory Hunter. A
Life of General Custer* (New York, 1934) 158–67; Joseph
B. Thoburn, *Standard History of Oklahoma* (Chicago,
1916), I, 393–96.

through the agents of the Indian Department as far as it is possible so to do. . . . If you as their agent can arrange these matters satisfactorily with them, we will be pleased to defer the whole subject to you. In case of your inability to do so, I would be pleased to have you accompany me when I visit the country of your tribes, to show that the officers of the Government are acting in harmony. I will be pleased to talk with any of the chiefs whom we may meet."

Surely there was no hostile intent here expressed. In another communication to the agents of different tribes, General Hancock, in referring to certain murders which had been recently committed, and which had been traced to the tribes in question, said: "These cases will now be left entirely in the hands of the Indian Department, and I do not expect to make war against any of the Indians of your agency unless they commence war against us."

It may be asked, what had the Indians done to make this incursion necessary? They had been guilty of numerous thefts and murders during the preceding summer and fall, for none of which had they been called to account. They had attacked the stations of the overland mail route, killed the employees, burned the stations, and captured the stock.

Citizens had been murdered in their homes on the frontier of Kansas; murders had been committed on the Arkansas route. The principal perpetrators of these acts were the Cheyennes and Sioux. The agent of the former, if not a party to the murder on the Arkansas, knew who the guilty persons were, yet took no steps to bring the murderers to punishment. Such a course would have interfered with his trade and profits. It was not to punish for these sins of the past that the expedition was set on foot, but rather by its imposing appearance and its early presence in the Indian country to check or intimidate the Indians from a repetition of their late conduct. This was deemed particularly necessary from the fact that the various tribes from which we had greatest cause to anticipate trouble had during the winter, through their leading chiefs and warriors, threatened that as soon as the grass was up in the spring a combined outbreak would take place along our entire frontier, and especially against the main routes of travel. To assemble the tribes for the desired council, word was sent early in March to the agents of those tribes whom it was desirable to meet. The agents sent runners to the villages inviting them to meet us at some point near the Arkansas River.

General Hancock's Campaign

General Hancock, with the artillery and six companies of infantry, reached Fort Riley, Kansas, from Fort Leavenworth by rail the last week in March; here he was joined by four companies of the Seventh Cavalry and an additional company of the Thirty-seventh Infantry. It was at this point that I joined the expedition. And as a very fair sample of the laurels which military men may win in an Indian campaign by a zealous discharge of what they deem their duty, I will here state, in parenthesis, that after engaging in the expedition, some of the events of which I am about to relate, and undergoing fatigue, privations, and dangers equal to those of a campaign during the Rebellion, I found myself at the termination of the campaign again at Fort Riley in arrest. This is not mentioned in a fault-finding spirit. I have no fault to find. It is said that blessings sometimes come in disguise. Such proved to be true in this instance, although I must say the disguise for some little time was most perfect.

From Fort Riley we marched to Fort Harker, a distance of ninety miles, where our force was strengthened by the addition of two more troops of cavalry. Halting only long enough to replenish our supplies, we next directed our march toward Fort Larned, near the Arkansas, about seventy miles to

35

the southeast.[2] A march from the 3d to the 7th of April brought us to Fort Larned. The agent for the Comanches and Kiowas accompanied us. At Fort Larned we found the agent of the Cheyennes, Arapahoes, and

[2] Brief historical sketches of many of these frontier forts are given in Frank W. Blackmar's *Kansas. A Cyclopaedia of State History* (Chicago, 1912) and in Thoburn's *Standard History of Oklahoma.* Contemporary descriptions of several of them are given in Henry M. Stanley's, *My Early Travels and Adventures* . . . (New York, 1895).

Fort Leavenworth, near the city of Leavenworth, Kansas, was established in 1827 and for half a century was an important center of frontier military operations. In 1881 the service school for the instruction of officers in the infantry and cavalry arms was established here.

Fort Riley, on the Kansas River just east of the mouth of the Republican and 100 miles west of Fort Leavenworth, was established in 1852. It still remains an important center of service school instruction and military administration.

Fort Harker was established in 1864 on the Smoky Hill River, four miles southeast of present-day Ellsworth, Kansas. At first it was named Fort Ellsworth, the change to Fort Harker being made in 1866. In 1867 the fort was reestablished on a new site, about a mile distant from the old one. For years it was a shipping center for goods bound for New Mexican points. It was abandoned as a military establishment in April, 1872.

Fort Larned, on the Arkansas River at present-day Larned, Kansas, was established in 1859. General Hancock made it his base of military operations for his Cheyenne campaign of 1867. The military establishment was abandoned in 1878.

36

Apaches; from the latter we learned that he had, as requested, sent runners to the chiefs of his agency inviting them to the council, and that they had agreed to assemble near Fort Larned on the 10th of the month, requesting that the expedition would remain there until that date. To this request General Hancock acceded.

On the 9th of April, while encamped awaiting the council, which was to be held the following day, a terrible snow-storm occurred, lasting all day until late in the evening. It was our good fortune to be in camp rather than on the march; had it been otherwise, we could not well have escaped without loss of life from the severe cold and blinding snow. The cavalry horses suffered seriously, and were only preserved by doubling their ration of oats, while to prevent their being frozen during the intensely cold night which followed, the guards were instructed to keep passing along the picket lines with a whip, and to keep the horses moving constantly. The snow was eight inches in depth. The council, which was to take place the next day, had to be postponed until the return of good weather. Now began the display of a kind of diplomacy for which the Indian is peculiar. The Cheyennes and a band of the Sioux were encamped on Pawnee Fork, about

thirty miles above Fort Larned. They neither desired to move nearer to us nor have
us approach nearer to them. On the morning
of the 11th they sent us word that they had
started to visit us, but discovering a large
herd of buffalo near their camp, they had
stopped to procure a supply of meat. This
message was not received with much confidence, nor was a buffaloes hunt deemed of sufficient importance to justify the Indians in
breaking their engagement. General Hancock decided, however, to delay another day,
when, if the Indians still failed to come in,
he would move his command to the vicinity
of their village and hold the conference there.

Orders were issued on the evening of the
12th for the march to be resumed on the
following day. Later in the evening two chiefs
of the Dog Soldiers, a band composed of the
most warlike and troublesome Indians on the
Plains, chiefly made up of Cheyennes, visited
our camp. They were accompanied by a
dozen warriors, and expressed a desire to
hold a conference with General Hancock, to
which he assented. A large council fire was
built in front of the General's tent, and all
the officers of his command assembled there.
A tent had been erected for the accommodation of the chiefs a short distance from the
General's. Before they could feel equal to

the occasion, and in order to obtain time to collect their thoughts, they desired that supper might be prepared for them, which was done. When finally ready they advanced from their tent to the council fire in single file, accompanied by their agent and an interpreter. Arrived at the fire, another brief delay ensued. No matter how pressing or momentous the occasion, an Indian invariably declines to engage in a council until he has filled his pipe and gone through with the important ceremony of a smoke. This attended to, the chiefs announced that they were ready to "talk." They were then introduced to the principal officers of the group, and seemed much struck with the flashy uniforms of the few artillery officers who were present in all the glory of red horsehair plumes, aigulets, etc. The chiefs seemed puzzled to determine whether these insignia designated chieftains or medicine men.

General Hancock began the conference by a speech in which he explained to the Indians his purpose in coming to see them, and what he expected of them in the future. He particularly informed them that he was not there to make war, but to promote peace. Then expressing his regret that more of the chiefs had not visited him, he announced his intention of proceeding on the morrow with his command to the vicinity of their village and there holding a council with all of the chiefs. Tall Bull, a fine, warlike-looking chieftain, replied to General Hancock, but his speech contained nothing important, being made up of allusions to the growing scarcity of the buffaloes, his love for the white man, and the usual hint that a donation in the way of refreshments would be highly acceptable; he added that he would have nothing new to say at the village.[4]

Several years prior to the events referred to, our people had captured from the Indians two children. I believe they were survivors of the Chivington massacre at Sand Creek, Colorado. These children had been kindly cared for, and were being taught to lead a civilized mode of life. Their relatives, how-

[4] Henry M. Stanley, who accompanied the expedition as a reporter for the St. Louis *Democrat,* recorded the speeches of General Hancock and Tall Bull, apparently in full. Reprinted in his *My Early Travels and Adventures,* I, 29–35.

In the spring of 1869 Major E. A. Carr led a command of several hundred soldiers in search of the hostiles who were ravaging the Kansas frontier settlements. After an arduous march of some 300 miles he surprised Tall Bull's village in northeastern Colorado and in the ensuing action Tall Bull and most of his warriors were killed. For an account of this affair see Carl C. Rister's *Border Command. General Phil Sheridan in the West* (Norman, Okla., 1944), 149–53.

ever, made demands for them, and we by treaty stipulation agreed to deliver them up. One of them, a little girl, had been cared for kindly in a family living near Denver, Colorado; the other, a boy, had been carried East to the States, and it was with great difficulty that the Government was able to learn his whereabouts and obtain possession of him. He was finally discovered, however, and sent to General Hancock, to be by him delivered up to his tribe. He accompanied the expedition, and was quite a curiosity for the time being. He was dressed comfortably, in accordance with civilized custom; and, having been taken from his people at so early an age, was apparently satisfied with the life he led.

The Indians who came to our camp expressed a great desire to see him, and when he was brought into their presence they exhibited no emotion such as white men under similar circumstances might be expected to show. They evidently were not pleased to see him clothed in the white man's dress. The little fellow, then some eight or ten years of age, seemed little disposed to go back to his people. I saw him the following year in the village of his tribe; he then had lost all trace of civilization, had forgotten his knowledge of the English language, and was as shy and suspicious of the white man as any of his dusky comrades. From older persons of the tribe we learned that their first act after obtaining possession of him was to deprive him of his "store clothes," and in their stead substitute the blanket and leggings.[5]

Rightly concluding that the Indians did not intend to come to our camp as they had at first agreed to, it was decided to move nearer to their village. On the morning following the conference held with the two chiefs of the Dog Soldiers, our entire force therefore marched from Fort Larned up Pawnee Fork in the direction of the main village, encamping the first night about twenty-one miles from the fort. Several parties of Indians were seen in our advance during the

[5] The Chivington or Sand Creek massacre of November 29, 1864 was one of the more ghastly incidents in the history of white-Indian warfare. Several hundred Indians, chiefly Cheyennes, were surprised in their camp on Sand Creek near Fort Lyon, Colorado by about 1000 white soldiers commanded by Colonel J. M. Chivington, and some 150 to 500, according to varying estimates, were killed. The soldiers had been ordered by Chivington to take no prisoners, and children, women, and men were slaughtered indiscriminately. Over the whole affair controversy still rages, and it has been characterized as the most controversial subject in Colorado history. A detailed and reasonably judicial account of it is given in Baker and Hafen's (eds.) *History of Colorado*, Vol. 1, Chap. 7. The massacre further embittered the Plains Indians and precipitated a fresh series of hostilities.

day, evidently watching our movements; while a heavy smoke, seen to rise in the direction of the Indian village, indicated that something more than usual was going on. This smoke we afterwards learned arose from the burning grass. The Indians, thinking to prevent us from encamping in their vicinity, had set fire to and burned all the grass for miles in the direction from which they expected us. Before we arrived at our camping-ground we were met by several chiefs and warriors belonging to the Cheyennes and Sioux. Among the chiefs were Pawnee Killer of the Sioux and White Horse of the Cheyennes.

It was arranged that these chiefs should accept our hospitality and remain with us during the night, and in the morning all the chiefs of the two tribes then in the village were to come to General Hancock's headquarters and hold a council. On the morning of the 14th Pawnee Killer left our camp at an early hour, for the purpose, as he said, of going to the village to bring in the other chiefs to the council. Nine o'clock had been agreed upon as the hour at which the council should assemble. The hour came, but the chiefs did not. Now an Indian council is not only often an important but always an interesting occasion. And, somewhat like a famous recipe for making a certain dish, the first thing necessary in holding an Indian council is to get the Indian. Half-past nine o'clock came, and still we were lacking this one important part of the council. At this juncture Bull Bear, an influential chief among the Cheyennes, came in and reported that the chiefs were on their way to our camp, but would not be able to reach it for some time. This was a mere artifice to secure delay. General Hancock informed Bull Bear that as the chiefs could not arrive for some time, he would move his forces up the stream nearer to the village, and the council could be held at our camp that night. To this proposition Bull Bear gave his assent.

At 11 A.M. we resumed the march, and had proceeded but a few miles when we witnessed one of the finest and most imposing military displays, prepared according to the Indian art of war, which it has ever been my lot to behold. It was nothing more nor less than an Indian line of battle drawn directly across our line of march; as if to say: thus far and no farther. Most of the Indians were mounted; all were bedecked in their brightest colors, their heads crowned with the brilliant warbonnet, their lances bearing the crimson pennant, bows strung, and quivers full of barbed arrows. In addition to these weapons, which with the hunting-knife and tomahawk are considered as forming the armament of the warrior, each one was supplied with either a breech-loading rifle or revolver, sometimes with both—the latter obtained through the wise foresight and strong love of fair play which prevails in the Indian Department, which, seeing that its wards are determined to fight, is equally determined that there shall be no advantage taken, but that the two sides shall be armed alike; proving, too, in this manner the wonderful liberality of our Government, which not only is able to furnish its soldiers with the latest improved style of breech-loaders to defend it and themselves, but is equally able and willing to give the same pattern of arms to their common foe. The only difference is, that the soldier, if he loses his weapon, is charged double price for it; while to avoid making any such charge against the Indian, his weapons are given him without conditions attached.

In the line of battle before us there were several hundred Indians, while farther to the rear and at different distances were other organized bodies acting apparently as reserves. Still farther were small detachments who seemed to perform the duty of couriers, and were held in readiness to convey messages to the village. The ground beyond was favorable for an extended view, allowing the eye to sweep the plain for several miles. As far as the eye could reach small groups or individuals could be seen in the direction of the village; these were evidently parties of observation, whose sole object was to learn the result of our meeting with the main body and hasten with the news to the village.

For a few moments appearances seemed to foreshadow anything but a peaceful issue. The infantry was in the advance, followed closely by the artillery, while my command, the cavalry, was marching on the flank. General Hancock, who was riding with his staff at the head of the column, coming suddenly in view of the wild fantastic battle array, which extended far to our right and left and not more than half a mile in our front, hastily sent orders to the infantry, artillery, and cavalry to form line of battle, evidently determined that if war was intended we should be prepared. The cavalry, being the last to form on the right, came into line on a gallop, and, without waiting to align the ranks carefully, the command was given to draw saber. As the bright blades flashed from their scabbards into the morning sunlight, and the infantry brought their muskets to a carry, a most beautiful and wonderfully interesting sight was spread out before and around us, presenting a contrast which, to a military eye, could but be striking.

General Hancock's Campaign

Here in battle array, facing each other, were the representatives of civilized and barbarous warfare. The one, with but few modifications, stood clothed in the same rude style of dress, bearing the same patterned shield and weapon that his ancestors had borne centuries before; the other confronted him in the dress and supplied with the implements of war which the most advanced stage of civilization had pronounced the most perfect. Was the comparative superiority of these two classes to be subjected to the mere test of war here? Such seemed the prevailing impression on both sides. All was eager anxiety and expectation. Neither side seemed to comprehend the object or intentions of the other; each was waiting for the other to deliver the first blow. A more beautiful battleground could not have been chosen. Not a bush or even the slightest irregularity of ground intervened between the two lines which now stood frowning and facing each other. Chiefs could be seen riding along the line as if directing and exhorting their braves to deeds of heroism.

After a few moments of painful suspense General Hancock, accompanied by General A. J. Smith[6] and other officers, rode forward,

[6] General Andrew J. Smith was a West Point graduate in the class of 1834 and a veteran frontier and Civil

47

and through an interpreter invited the chiefs to meet us midway for the purpose of an interview. In response to this invitation Roman Nose, bearing a white flag, accompanied by Bull Bear, White Horse, Gray Beard, and Medicine Wolf on the part of the Cheyennes, and Pawnee Killer, Bad Wound, Tall Bear that Walks under the Ground, Left Hand, Little Bear, and Little Bull on the part of the Sioux, rode forward to the middle of the open space between the two lines. Here we shook hands with all of the chiefs, most of them exhibiting unmistakable signs of gratification at this apparently peaceful termination of our encounter. General

War soldier. Upon the organization of the Seventh U.S. Cavalry in 1866 he was appointed Colonel of the regiment. Save for a few weeks, however, he never exercised the actual command, which fell to Custer, as lieutenant colonel, until the death of the latter in 1876. Henry M. Stanley described General Smith as a tough old soldier who made light of the "dandified young bucks" who wore shoulder straps and were afraid of a little snow. "During the wildest snowstorm that has visited this post for many a year, and which we experienced yesterday [described by Custer earlier in the present chapter] he was out on foot, stamping through the snow, performing duties with as much celerity as the youngest subaltern." *My Early Travels and Adventures,* I, 24–25. President Grant appointed Smith postmaster of St. Louis, and in the spring of 1869 he resigned his army commission.

General Hancock's Campaign

Hancock very naturally inquired the object of the hostile attitude displayed before us, saying to the chiefs that if war was their object we were ready then and there to participate. Their immediate answer was that they did not desire war, but were peacefully disposed. They were then told that we would continue our march toward the village and encamp near it, but would establish such regulations that none of the soldiers would be permitted to approach or disturb them. An arrangement was then effected by which the chiefs were to assemble at General Hancock's headquarters as soon as our camp was pitched. The interview then terminated, and the Indians moved off in the direction of their village, we following leisurely in rear.

A march of a few miles brought us in sight of the village, which was situated in a beautiful grove on the banks of the stream up which we had been marching. The village consisted of upwards of three hundred lodges, a small fraction over half belonging to the Cheyennes, the remainder to the Sioux. Like all Indian encampments, the ground chosen was a most romantic spot, and at the same time fulfilled in every respect the requirements of a good camping-ground; wood, water, and grass were abundant. The village was placed on a wide, level plateau, while on the north and west, at a short distance off, rose high bluffs, which admirably served as a shelter against the cold winds which at that season of the year prevail from these directions. Our tents were pitched within half a mile of the village. Guards were placed between to prevent intrusion upon our part. A few of the Indian ponies found grazing near our camp were caught and returned to them, to show that our intentions were at least neighborly. We had scarcely pitched our tents when Roman Nose, Bull Bear, Gray Beard, and Medicine Wolf, all prominent chiefs of the Cheyennes, came into camp with the information that upon our approach their women and children had all fled from the village, alarmed by the presence of so many soldiers, and imagining a second Chivington massacre to be intended.

General Hancock insisted that they should all return, promising protection and good treatment to all; that if the camp was abandoned he would hold it responsible. The chiefs then stated their belief in their ability to recall the fugitives, could they be furnished with horses to overtake them. This was accordingly done, and two of them set out mounted on two of our horses. An agreement was also entered into at the same time that one of our interpreters, Ed. Guerrier, a half-

General Hancock's Campaign

breed Cheyenne who was in the employ of the Government, should remain in the village and report every two hours as to whether any Indians were leaving the village. This was about seven o'clock in the evening. At half past nine the half-breed returned to headquarters with the intelligence that all the chiefs and warriors were saddling up to leave, under circumstances showing that they had no intention of returning, such as packing up such articles as could be carried with them, and cutting and destroying their lodges this last being done to obtain small pieces for temporary shelter.

I had retired to my tent, which was located some few hundred yards from that of General Hancock, when a messenger from the latter awakened me with the information that General Hancock desired my presence at his tent. Imagining a movement on the part of the Indians, I made no delay in responding to the summons. General Hancock briefly stated the situation of affairs, and directed me to mount my command as quickly and as silently as possible, surround the Indian village, and prevent the departure of its inhabitants. Easily said, but not so easily done. Under ordinary circumstances, silence not being necessary, I could have returned to my camp, and by a few blasts from the trumpet placed every soldier in his saddle almost as quickly as it has taken time to write this sentence. No bugle calls must be sounded; we were to adopt some of the stealth of the Indian—how successfully remains to be seen.

By this time every soldier, officers as well as men, was in his tent sound asleep. How to awaken them and impart to each the necessary order? First going to the tent of the adjutant and arousing him, I procured an experienced assistant in my labors. Next the captains of companies were awakened and orders imparted to them. They in turn transmitted the order to the first sergeant, who similarly aroused the men. It has often surprised me to observe the alacrity with which disciplined soldiers, experienced in campaigning, will hasten to prepare themselves for the march in an emergency like this. No questions are asked, no time is wasted. A soldier's toilet on an Indian campaign is a simple affair, and requires little time for arranging. His clothes are gathered up hurriedly, no matter how, so long as he retains possession of them. The first object is to get his horse saddled and bridled, and until this is done his own toilet is a matter of secondary importance, and one button or hook must do the duty of half a dozen. When his horse is ready for the mount the rider will be seen completing his own equipment; stray buttons will receive attention, arms be overhauled, spurs restrapped; then, if there still remain a few spare moments, the homely black pipe is filled and lighted, and the soldier's preparation is completed.

The night was all that could be desired for the success of our enterprise. The air was mild and pleasant; the moon, although nearly full, kept almost constantly behind the clouds, as if to screen us in our hazardous undertaking. I say hazardous, because there were none of us who imagined for one moment that if the Indians discovered us in our attempt to surround them and their village, we would escape without a fight—a fight, too, in which the Indians, sheltered behind the trunks of the stately forest trees under which their lodges were pitched, would possess all the advantage. General Hancock, anticipating that the Indians would discover our approach, and that a fight would ensue, ordered the artillery and infantry under arms to await the result of our moonlight venture.

My command was soon in the saddle, and silently making its way toward the village. Instructions had been given forbidding all conversation except in a whisper. Sabers were so disposed of as to prevent clanging. Taking a camp-fire which we could see in the village as our guiding point, we made a detour so as to place the village between ourselves and the infantry. Occasionally the moon would peep out from behind the clouds and enable us to catch a hasty glance at the village. Here and there under the thick foliage we could see the white, conical-shaped lodges. Were their inmates slumbering, unaware of our close proximity, or were their dusky defenders concealed, as well they might have been, along the banks of the Pawnee, quietly awaiting our approach, and prepared to greet us with their well-known war-whoop? These were questions that were probably suggested to the mind of each individual of my command. If we were discovered approaching in the stealthy, suspicious manner which characterized our movements, the hour being midnight, it would require a more confiding nature than that of the Indian to assign a friendly or peaceful motive to our conduct. The same flashes of moonlight which gave us hurried glimpses of the village enabled us to see our own column of horsemen stretching its silent length far into the dim darkness, and winding its course, like some huge anaconda about to envelop its victim. The method by which it was determined to establish a cordon of armed troopers about the fated village was to direct the march in

a circle with the village in the center, the
commanding officer of each rear troop halting his command at the proper point and
deploying his men similarly to a line of skirmishers—the entire circle, when thus formed,
facing toward the village, and distant from it
perhaps a few hundred yards. No sooner was
our line completely formed than the moon,
as if deeming darkness no longer essential to
our success, appeared from behind her screen
and lighted up the entire scene. And a beautiful scene it was. The great circle of troops,
each individual of which sat on his steed
silent as a statue, the beautiful and in some
places dense foliage of the cotton trees shel-
tering and shading the bleached, skin-clad
lodges of the red man, while in the midst of
all murmured undisturbedly in its channel
the little stream on whose banks the village
was located, all combined to produce an artistic effect as beautiful as it was interesting.
But we were not there to study artistic effects.
The next step was to determine whether we
had captured an inhabited village, involving
almost necessarily a fierce conflict with its
savage occupants, or whether the red man
had again proved too wily and crafty for his
more civilized brothers.

Directing the entire line of troopers to remain mounted with carbines held at the "ad-

vance," I dismounted, and taking with me Guerrier, the half-breed, Dr. Coates, one of our medical staff, and Lieutenant Moylan, the adjutant, proceeded on our hands and knees toward the village. The prevailing opinion was that the Indians were still asleep. I desired to approach near enough to the lodges to enable the half-breed to hail the village in the Indian tongue, and if possible establish friendly relations at once. It became a question of prudence with us, which we discussed in whispers as we proceeded on our "tramp, tramp, tramp, the boys are creeping," how far from our horses and how near to the village we dared to go. If so few of us were discovered entering the village in this questionable manner it was more than probable that, like the returners of stolen property, we should be suitably rewarded and no questions asked. The opinions of Guerrier, the half-breed, were eagerly sought for and generally deferred to. His wife, a full-blooded Cheyenne, was a resident of the village. This with him was an additional reason for wishing a peaceful termination to our efforts. When we had passed over two-thirds of the distance between our horses and the village, it was deemed best to make our presence known. Thus far not a sound had been heard to disturb the stillness of the night. Guerrier called out at the top of his voice in the Cheyenne tongue. The only response came from the throats of a score or more of Indian dogs which set up a fierce barking. At the same time one or two of our party asserted that they saw figures moving beneath the trees. Guerrier repeated his summons, but with no better result than before.

A hurried consultation ensued. The presence of so many dogs in the village was regarded by the half-breed as almost positive assurance that the Indians were still there. Yet it was difficult to account for their silence. Guerrier in a loud tone repeated who he was, and that our mission was a friendly one. Still no answer. He then gave it as his opinion that the Indians were on the alert, and were probably waiting in the shadow of the trees for us to approach nearer, when they would pounce upon us. This comforting opinion induced another conference. We must ascertain the truth of the matter; our party could do this as well as a larger number, and to go back and send another party in our stead could not be thought of.

Forward was the verdict. Each one grasped his revolver, resolved to do his best, whether it was in running or fighting. I think most of us would have preferred to take our own chances at running. We had approached near enough to see that some of the lodges were detached some distance from the main encampment. Selecting the nearest of these, we directed our advance on it. While all of us were full of the spirit of adventure, and were further encouraged with the idea that we were in the discharge of our duty, there was scarcely one of us who would not have felt more comfortable if we could have got back to our horses without loss of pride. Yet nothing, under the circumstances, but a positive order would have induced any one to withdraw. The doctor, who was a great wag, even in moments of greatest danger, could not restrain his propensities in this direction. When everything before us was being weighed and discussed in the most serious manner, he remarked: "General, this recalls to my mind those beautiful lines:

Backward, turn backward, O Time, in thy flight, Make me a child again just for one night—

this night of all others."

We shall meet the doctor again before daylight, but under different circumstances.

Chapter 3

CAUTIOUSLY approaching, on all fours, to within a few yards of the nearest lodge, occasionally halting and listening to discover evidence as to whether the village was deserted or not, we finally decided that the Indians had fled before the arrival of the cavalry, and that none but empty lodges were before us. This conclusion somewhat emboldened as well as accelerated our progress. Arriving at the first lodge, one of our party raised the curtain or mat which served as a door, and the doctor and myself entered. The interior of the lodge was dimly lighted by the decaying embers of a small fire built in the center. All around us were to be seen the usual adornments and articles which constitute the household effects of an Indian family. Buffalo robes were spread like carpets over the floor; head-mats, used to recline upon, were arranged as if for the comfort of their owners; parfleches, a sort of Indian bandbox, with their contents apparently undisturbed, were to be found carefully stowed away under the edges or borders of the lodge. These, with the door-mats, paint-bags, rawhide ropes, and other articles of Indian equipment, were left as if the owners had only absented themselves for a brief period.

To complete the picture of an Indian lodge, over the fire hung a camp-kettle, in which, by means of the dim light of the fire, we could see what had been intended for the supper of the late occupants of the lodge. The doctor, ever on the alert to discover additional items of knowledge, whether pertaining to history or science, snuffed the savory odors which arose from the dark recesses of the mysterious kettle. Casting about the lodge for some instrument to aid him in his pursuit of knowledge, he found a horn spoon, with which he began his investigation of the contents, finally succeeding in getting possession of a fragment which might have been the half of a duck or rabbit, judging merely from its size. "Ah!" said the doctor, in his most complacent manner, "here is the opportunity I have long been waiting for. I have often desired to test and taste of the Indian mode of cooking. What do you suppose this is?" holding up the dripping morsel. Unable to obtain the desired information, the Doctor, whose naturally good appetite had been sensibly sharpened by his recent exercise *a la quadrupede*, set to with a will and ate heartily of the mysterious contents of the kettle.

A Futile Pursuit

"What can this be?" again inquired the doctor. He was only satisfied on one point, that it was delicious—a dish fit for a king.

Just then Guerrier, the half-breed, entered the lodge. He could solve the mystery, having spent years among the Indians. To him the doctor appealed for information. Fishing out a huge piece, and attacking it with the voracity of a hungry wolf, he was not long in determining what the doctor had supped so heartily upon. His first words settled the mystery: "Why, this is dog." I will not attempt to repeat the few but emphatic words uttered by the heartily disgusted member of the medical fraternity as he rushed from the lodge.

Other members of our small party had entered other lodges, only to find them, like the first, deserted. But little of the furniture belonging to the lodges had been taken, showing how urgent and hasty had been the flight of the owners. To aid in the examination of the village, reinforcements were added to our party, and an exploration of each lodge was determined upon. At the same time a messenger was despatched to General Hancock, informing him of the flight of the Indians. Some of the lodges were closed by having brush or timber piled up against the entrance, as if to preserve the contents. Others had

61

huge pieces cut from their sides, these pieces evidently being carried away to furnish temporary shelter to the fugitives. In most of the lodges the fires were still burning.

I had entered several without discovering anything important. Finally, in company with the doctor I arrived at one the interior of which was quite dark, the fire having almost died out. Procuring a lighted fagot, I prepared to explore it as I had done the others; but no sooner had I entered the lodge than my fagot failed me, leaving me in total darkness. Handing it out to the doctor to be relighted, I began feeling my way about the interior of the lodge. I had almost made the circuit when my hand came in contact with a human foot; at the same time a voice unmistakably Indian, and which evidently came from the owner of the foot, convinced me that I was not alone. My first impression was that in their hasty flight the Indians had gone off leaving this one asleep. My next, very naturally, related to myself. I would have gladly placed myself on the outside of the lodge, and there matured plans for interviewing its occupant; but unfortunately, to reach the entrance of the lodge I must either pass over or around the owner of the beforementioned foot and voice. Could I have been convinced that among its other possessions there was neither tomahawk nor scalping-knife, pistol nor war-club, or any similar article of the noble red man's toilet, I would have risked an attempt to escape through the low narrow opening of the lodge; but who ever saw an Indian without one or all of these interesting trinkets? Had I made the attempt, I should have expected to encounter either the keen edge of the scalping-knife or the blow of the tomahawk, and to have engaged in a questionable struggle for life. This would not do. I crouched in silence for a few moments, hoping the doctor would return with the lighted fagot.

I need not say that each succeeding moment spent in the darkness of that lodge seemed like an age. I could hear a slight movement on the part of my unknown neighbor, which did not add to my comfort. Why does not the doctor return? At last I discovered the approach of a light on the outside. When it neared the entrance I called to the doctor and informed him that an Indian was in the lodge, and that he had better have his weapons ready for a conflict. I had, upon discovering the foot, drawn my hunting-knife from its scabbard, and now stood waiting the *dénouement*. With his lighted fagot in one hand and cocked revolver in the other, the doctor cautiously entered the lodge.

And there, directly between us, wrapped in a buffalo robe, lay the cause of my anxiety— a little Indian girl, probably ten years old; not a full-blood, but a half-breed. She was terribly frightened at finding herself in our hands, with none of her people near. Why was she left behind in this manner? Guerrier, our half-breed interpreter, was called in. His inquiries were soon answered. The little girl, who at first was an object of our curiosity, became at once an object of pity. The Indians, an unusual thing for them to do toward their own blood, had wilfully deserted her; but this, alas! was the least of their injuries to her. After being shamefully abandoned by the entire village, a few of the young men of the tribe returned to the deserted lodge, and upon the person of this little girl committed outrages, the details of which are too sickening for these pages.

She was carried to the fort and placed under the care of kind hands and warm hearts, where everything was done for her comfort that was possible. Other parties in exploring the deserted village found an old, decrepit Indian of the Sioux tribe, who also had been deserted, owing to his infirmities and inability to travel with the tribe. He also was kindly cared for by the authorities of the fort. Nothing was gleaned from our search of the village which might indicate the direction of the flight. General Hancock, on learning the situation of affairs, despatched some companies of infantry to the deserted village with orders to replace the cavalry and protect the village and its contents from disturbance until its final disposition could be determined upon. Starting my command back to our camp near General Hancock's headquarters, I galloped on in advance to report the particulars to the General. It was then decided that with eight troops of cavalry I should start in pursuit of the Indians at early dawn on the following morning (April 15). There was no sleep for my command the remainder of the night, the time being fully occupied in preparation for the march, neither the extent nor direction of which was known.

Mess kits were overhauled and fresh supplies of coffee, sugar, flour, and the other articles which go to supply the soldier's larder were laid in. Blankets were carefully rolled so as to occupy as little space as possible; every useless pound of luggage was discarded, for in making a rapid pursuit after Indians much of the success depends upon the lightness of the order of march. Saratoga trunks and their accompaniments are at a discount. Never was the old saying that in Rome one must do as Romans do more aptly illustrated than on an Indian campaign. The Indian, knowing that his safety either on offensive or defensive movements depends in a great measure upon the speed and endurance of his horse, takes advantage of every circumstance which will favor either the one or the other. To this end he divests himself of all superfluous dress and ornament when preparing for rapid movements. The white man, if he hopes for success, must adopt the same rule of action and encumber his horse as little as possible. Something besides well-filled mess chests and carefully rolled blankets is necessary in preparing for an Indian campaign. Arms must be reëxamined, cartridge-boxes refilled, so that each man should carry about one hundred rounds of ammunition on his person, while each troop commander must see that in the company wagon there are placed a few boxes of reserve ammunition. Then, when the equipment of the soldier has been attended to, his horse, without whose assistance he is helpless, must be looked after; loose shoes are tightened by the driving of an additional nail, and to accomplish this one may see the company blacksmith, a soldier, with the few simple tools of his kit on the ground beside him, hurriedly fastening the last shoe by the uncertain light of a candle held in the hands of the rider of the horse, their mutual labor being varied at times by queries as to "How long shall we be gone?" "I wonder if we will catch Mr. Lo?" "If we do, we'll make it lively for him."

So energetic had everybody been that before daylight everything was in readiness for the start. In addition to the regularly organized companies of soldiers which made up the pursuing column, I had with me a detachment of white scouts or Plainsmen, and one of friendly Indians, the latter belonging to the tribe of Delawares, once so famous in Indian wars.[7] Of the Indians one only could speak English; he acted as interpreter for the party. Among the white scouts were numbered some of the most noted of their class. The most prominent man among them was Wild Bill, whose highly varied career was

[7] The Delaware Indians, so called by the English who found them occupying the Delaware River Valley, were at one time the most important division of the Algonquin family. William Penn made a treaty with them in 1682, when their council house was at Germantown, now a suburb of Philadelphia. By successive removals, crowded by the whites, they reached Oklahoma, Kansas, and Texas, having sojourned at different periods in Ohio, Indiana, Missouri, and elsewhere. They were notable warriors, and prior to the treaty of Greenville of 1795 were among the most determined opponents of the whites. The Tammany Society of New York City takes its name from Tamenend, an earlier notable Delaware chieftain.

made the subject of an illustrated sketch in one of the popular monthly periodicals a few years ago.[8] Wild Bill was a strange character, just the one which a novelist might gloat over. He was a Plainsman in every sense of the word, yet unlike any other of his class. In person he was about six feet one in height, straight as the straightest of the warriors whose implacable foe he was; broad shoulders, well-formed chest and limbs, and a face strikingly handsome; a sharp, clear, blue eye, which stared you straight in the face when in conversation; a finely-shaped nose, inclined to be aquiline; a well-turned mouth, with lips only partially concealed by a handsome moustache. His hair and complexion were those of the perfect blond. The former was worn in uncut ringlets falling carelessly over his powerfully formed shoulders. Add to this figure a costume blending the immac-

[8] This was James B. Hickok, commonly known as "Wild Bill," whose career as frontier scout, marshal, and tamer of bad men generally has become semi-legendary. Despite his turbulent career, he won the friendship and admiration of many prominent contemporaries. His killings were many, but his biographer affirms that he never killed a man except in self-defense or in the line of official duty. Mrs. Custer, like her husband, admired him profoundly. See her *Following the Guidon* (New York, 1890), chap. 12. Wild Bill was assassinated, August 2, 1876 at Deadwood, South Dakota.

ulate neatness of the dandy with the extravagant taste and style of the frontiersman, and you have Wild Bill, then as now the most famous scout on the Plains. Whether on foot or on horseback, he was one of the most perfect types of physical manhood I ever saw.

Of his courage there could be no question; it had been brought to the test on too many occasions to admit of a doubt. His skill in the use of the rifle and pistol was unerring; while his deportment was exactly the opposite of what might be expected from a man of his surroundings. It was entirely free from all bluster or bravado. He seldom spoke of himself unless requested to do so. His conversation, strange to say, never bordered either on the vulgar or blasphemous. His influence among the frontiersmen was unbounded, his word was law; and many are the personal quarrels and disturbances which he has checked among his comrades by his simple announcement that "this has gone far enough," if need be followed by the ominous warning that when persisted in or renewed the quarreller "must settle it with me."

Wild Bill is anything but a quarrelsome man; yet no one but himself can enumerate the many conflicts in which he has been engaged, and which have almost invariably re-

sulted in the death of his adversary. I have
a personal knowledge of at least half a dozen
men whom he has at various times killed,
one of these being at the time a member of
my command. Others have been severely
wounded, yet he always escapes unhurt. On
the Plains every man openly carries his belt
with its invariable appendages, knife and
revolver, often two of the latter. Wild Bill
always carried two handsome ivory-handled
revolvers of the large size; he was never seen
without them. Where this is the common
custom, brawls or personal difficulties are
seldom if ever settled by blows. The quarrel
is not from a word to a blow, but from a word
to the revolver, and he who can draw and
fire first is the best man. No civil law reaches
him; none is applied for. In fact there is no
law recognized beyond the frontier but that
of "might makes right." Should death result
from the quarrel, as it usually does, no coro-
ner's jury is impanelled to learn the cause of
death, and the survivor is not arrested. But
instead of these old-fashioned proceedings, a
meeting of citizens takes place, the survivor
is *requested* to be present when the circumstances of the homicide are inquired into,
and the unfailing verdict of "justifiable,"
"self-defense," etc., is pronounced, and the
law stands vindicated.

A Futile Pursuit

That justice is often deprived of a victim there is not a doubt. Yet in all of the many affairs of this kind in which Wild Bill has performed a part, and which have come to my knowledge, there is not a single instance in which the verdict of twelve fair-minded men would not be pronounced in his favor. That the even tenor of his way continues to be disturbed by little events of this description may be inferred from an item which has been floating lately through the columns of the press, and which states that "the funeral of Jim Bludso, who was killed the other day by Wild Bill, took place to-day." It then adds: "The funeral expenses were borne by Wild Bill." What could be more thoughtful than this? Not only to send a fellow mortal out of the world, but to pay the expenses of the transit. Guerrier, the half-breed, also accompanied the expedition as guide and interpreter.

Everything being in readiness to move, the column began its march, and reached the vicinity of the village before day had fully dawned. Here a brief halt was necessary, until the light was sufficient to enable our scouts to discover the trail of the Indians. When they finally set out to discover this, their method was highly interesting, and resembled not a little the course of a thorough sportsman, who, with a well-trained pointer or setter, thoroughly "ranges" and "beats" the ground in search of his coveted game. The Indians had set out on their flight soon after dark the preceding night; a heavy frost covered the ground and rendered it difficult to detect the trail from the many pony tracks which are always found in the vicinity of a village. We began to grow impatient at the delay, when one of the Indians gave the "halloo" as the signal that the trail was discovered, and again the column marched forward.

Our order of march was for the Indian and white scouts to keep a few hundred paces in advance of the troops, so that momentary delays upon the part of those watching and following the trail should not extend to the troops. The Indians on leaving the village had anticipated pursuit and had adopted measures to mislead us. In order to prevent their trail from being easily recognizable, they had departed in as many detachments or parties almost as there were families or lodges in the village, each party taking a different direction from the others, having personally agreed, of course, upon the general direction and place of reuniting. Once being satisfied that we were on the right trail, no difficulty was found in following it as rapidly as our horses could walk. The Indians had nearly twelve hours the start of us, but being encumbered by their families, we hoped to overhaul them before many days. Our first obstacle was encountered when we struck Walnut Creek, a small stream running east and west some thirty miles north of the Arkansas at that point. The banks were so high and abrupt that it was impossible to reach the water's edge, let alone clamber up the opposite bank. A few of the Indians had been able to accomplish this feat, as was shown by the tracks on the opposite side; but the main band had moved up stream in search of a favorable crossing, and we were compelled to do likewise.

Here we found that the Indians had called a halt, built fires, and cooked their breakfast. So rapidly had we gained upon them that the fires were burning freshly, and the departure of the Indians had been so abrupt that they left several ponies with their packs tied to trees. One of the packs belonged to a famous chief, Roman Nose, who was one of those who met us at the grand gathering just before we reached their village a few days before.[9] One of our Delawares who made the

[9] Roman Nose was a Cheyenne chief whose proper name was Sauts, or Bat. He was the Indian leader in the celebrated battle of Beecher Island on the Arikaree,

capture was very proud of the success, and was soon seen ornamenting his head-dress with the bright crimson feathers taken from the wardrobe of Roman Nose. Encouraged by our progress, we continued the pursuit as rapidly as a due regard for our horses would permit. Thus far, neither myself nor any of the soldiers had caught sight of any Indians; but our Delaware scouts, who were constantly in the advance and on our flanks, taking advantage of the bluffs to reconnoiter, frequently reported that they saw small parties of Indians observing our movements from a distance. From positive evidences, familiar to those accustomed to the Plains, we were convinced that we were rapidly gaining upon the Indians. The earth upturned by the feet of their ponies and by the ends of the trailing lodge-poles was almost as damp and fresh as that disturbed by the horses of the command.

Soon we discovered additional signs of encouragement. The route now became strewn with various lodge-poles and other obstacles peculiar to an Indian's outfit, showing that

Sept. 17–25, 1868, when 52 white scouts commanded by Col. George A. Forsyth were assailed for several days by several hundred Cheyennes. It was Roman Nose's last battle; he was shot on the first day of the fight and died that night in the Indian camp.

they were "lightening up" so as to facilitate
their escape. So certain did we feel of our
ability to out-trail them, that the only question now was one which has often determined
the success of military operations. Would
darkness intervene to disappoint us? We
must imitate the example of the Indians and
disembarrass ourselves of everything tending to retard our speed. The troops would
march much faster, if permitted to do so,
than the rate at which our wagons had forced
themselves along. It was determined to
leave the wagons under escort of one squadron, to follow our trail as rapidly as they
could, while the other three squadrons
pushed on in pursuit. Should darkness settle
down before overtaking the Indians the advantage was altogether against us, as we
would be compelled to await daylight to enable us to follow the trail, while the Indians
were free to continue their flight, sheltered
and aided by the darkness.

By three o'clock P. M. we felt that we were
almost certain to accomplish our purpose.
No obstacle seemed to stand in our way; the
trail was broad and plain, and apparently as
fresh as our own. A half hour, or an hour at
furthest, seemed only necessary to enable us
to dash in upon our wily enemy. Alas for
human calculations! The Indians, by means

of the small reconnoitering parties observed
by our scouts, had kept themselves constantly informed regarding our movements and
progress. They had first risked their safety
upon the superior speed and endurance of
their ponies—a safe reliance when favored by
the grass season, but in winter this advantage was on our side. Failing in their first resource, they had a second and better method
of eluding us. So long as they kept united
and moved in one body their trail was as
plainly to be seen and as easily followed as
if made by a heavily-laden wagon train. We
were not called upon to employ time and
great watchfulness on the part of our scouts
to follow it. But when it was finally clear to
be seen that, in the race as it was then being
run, the white man was sure to win, the proverbial cunning of the red man came to his
rescue and thwarted the plans of his pursuers. Again dividing his tribe, as when first
setting out from the village, into numerous
small parties, we were discouraged by seeing
the broad well-beaten trail suddenly separate
into hundreds of indistinct routes, leading
fan-shape in as many different directions.
What was to be done?

The general direction of the main trail,
before dissolving into so many small ones,
had been nearly north, showing that if un-

disturbed in their flight the Indians would strike the Smoky Hill overland route, cross it, then pursue their way northward to the headwaters of the Solomon or Republican River, or farther still, to the Platte River. Selecting a central trail, we continued our pursuit, now being compelled often to halt and verify our course. The trail gradually grew smaller and smaller, until by five o'clock it had become so faint as to be followed with the greatest difficulty. We had been marching exactly twelve hours without halting, except to water our horses. Reluctantly we were forced to go into camp and await the assistance of daylight. The Delaware scouts continued the pursuit six miles farther, but returned without accomplishing anything. The Indians, after dividing up into small parties, kept up communication with each other by means of columns of signal smoke. These signal smokes were to be seen to the west, north, and east of us, but none nearer than ten miles. They only proved to us that we were probably on the trail of the main body, as the fires were in front and on both sides of us.

We had marched over thirty-five miles without a halt. The Delawares having determined the direction of the trail for six miles, we would be able next morning to continue

that far at least unaided by daylight. Our
wagons overtook us a few hours after we
reached camp. Reveille was sounded at two
o'clock the next morning, and four o'clock
found us again in the saddle and following
the guidance of our friendly Delawares. The
direction of our march took us up the valley
and almost dry bed of a small stream. The
Delawares thought we might find where the
Indians had encamped during the night by
following the upward course of the stream,
but in this we were disappointed. The trail
became more and more indistinct, until it
was lost in the barren waste over which we
were then moving. To add to our annoy-
ance, the watercourse had become entirely
dry, and our guides were uncertain as to
whether water could be procured in one day's
march in any direction except that from
which we had come. We were, therefore,
forced to countermarch after reaching a
point thirteen miles from our starting-place
in the morning, and retrace our steps until
the uncertain stream in whose valley we
then were would give us water enough for
our wants.

Here I will refer to an incident entirely
personal which came very near costing me my
life. When leaving our camp that morning I
felt satisfied that the Indians, having trav-

elled at least a portion of the night, were
then many miles in advance of us, and there
was neither danger nor probability of encountering any of them near the column.
We were then in a magnificent game country, buffaloes, antelope, and smaller game being in abundance on all sides of us. Although
an ardent sportsman, I had never hunted the
buffalo up to this time, consequently was exceedingly desirous of tasting of its excitement. I had several fine English greyhounds,
whose speed I was anxious to test with that
of the antelope, said to be—which I believe
—the fleetest of animals. I was mounted on
a fine large thoroughbred horse. Taking with
me but one man, the chief bugler, and calling
my dogs around me, I galloped ahead of the
column as soon as it was daylight, for the
purpose of having a chase after some antelope which could be seen grazing nearly two
miles distant.

That such a course was rashly imprudent
I am ready to admit. A stirring gallop of a
few minutes brought me near enough to the
antelope, of which there were a dozen or
more, to enable the dogs to catch sight of
them. Then the chase began, the antelope
running in a direction which took us away
from the command. By availing myself of
the turns in the course, I was able to keep

well in view of the exciting chase until it was
evident that the antelope were in no danger
of being caught by the dogs, which latter had
become blown from want of proper exercise.
I succeeded in calling them off, and was
about to set out on my return to the column.
The horse of the chief bugler, being a com-
mon-bred animal, failed early in the race
and his rider wisely concluded to regain the
command, so that I was alone. How far I
had travelled from the troops I was trying to
determine, when I discovered a large, dark-
looking animal grazing nearly a mile distant.
As yet I had never seen a wild buffalo, but I
at once recognized this as not only a buffalo,
but a very large one.

Here was my opportunity. A ravine near
by would enable me to approach unseen until almost within pistol range of my game.
Calling my dogs to follow me, I slowly pursued the course of the ravine, giving my
horse opportunity to gather himself for the
second run. When I emerged from the ravine I was still several hundred yards from
the buffalo, which almost instantly discovered me and set off as fast as his legs could
carry him. Had my horse been fresh the
race would have been a short one, but the preceding long run had not been without effect.
How long or how fast we flew in pursuit, the

intense excitement of the chase prevented me from knowing. I only knew that even the greyhounds were left behind, until finally my good steed placed himself and me close alongside the game. It may be because this was the first I had seen, but surely of the hundreds of thousands of buffaloes which I have since seen, none have corresponded with him in size and lofty grandeur. My horse was above the average size, yet the buffalo towered even above him. I had carried my revolver in my hand from the moment the race began. Repeatedly could I have placed the muzzle against the shaggy body of the huge beast, by whose side I fairly yelled with wild excitement and delight, yet each time would I withdraw the weapon, as if to prolong the enjoyment of the race.

It was a race for life or death, yet how different the award from what could be imagined. Still we sped over the springy turf, the high breeding and mettle of my horse being plainly visible over that of the huge beast that struggled by his side. Mile after mile was traversed in this way, until the rate and distance began to tell perceptibly on the bison, whose protruding tongue and labored breathing plainly betrayed his distress. Determined to end the chase and bring down my game, I again placed the muzzle of the revolver close to the body of the buffalo, when, as if divining my intention, and feeling his inability to escape by flight, he suddenly determined to fight and at once wheeled, as only a buffalo can, to gore my horse. So sudden was this movement, and so sudden was the corresponding veering of my horse to avoid the attack, that to retain my control over him I hastily brought up my pistol hand to the assistance of the other. Unfortunately as I did so my finger, in the excitement of the occasion, pressed the trigger, discharged the pistol, and sent the fatal ball into the very brain of the noble animal I rode. Running at full speed he fell dead in the course of his leap. Quick as thought I disengaged myself from the stirrups and found myself whirling through the air over and beyond the head of my horse. My only thought, as I was describing this trajectory, and my first thought on reaching *terra firma*, was: "What will the buffalo do with me?" Although at first inclined to rush upon me, my strange procedure seemed to astonish him. Either that or pity for the utter helplessness of my condition inclined him to alter his course and leave me alone to my own bitter reflections.

In a moment the danger into which I had unluckily brought myself stood out in bold relief before me. Under ordinary circumstances the death of my horse would have been serious enough. I was strongly attached to him; had ridden him in battle during a portion of the late war; yet now his death, except in its consequences, was scarcely thought of. Here I was, alone in the heart of the Indian country, with warlike Indians known to be in the vicinity. I was not familiar with the country. How far I had travelled, or in what direction from the column, I was at a loss to know. In the excitement of the chase I had lost all reckoning. Indians were liable to pounce upon me at any moment. My command would not note my absence probably for hours. Two of my dogs overtook me, and with mute glances first at the dead steed, then at me, seemed to inquire the cause of this strange condition of affairs. Their instinct appeared to tell them that we were in misfortune.

While I was deliberating what to do, the dogs became uneasy, whined piteously, and seemed eager to leave the spot. In this desire I sympathized with them, but whither should I go? I observed that their eyes were generally turned in one particular direction; this I accepted as my cue, and with one parting look at my horse, and grasping a revolver in each hand, I set out on my uncertain journey. As long as the body of my horse was visible above the horizon I kept referring to it as my guiding point, and in this way contrived to preserve my direction. This resource soon failed me, and I then had recourse to weeds, buffalo skulls, or any two objects I could find on my line of march. Constantly my eyes kept scanning the horizon, each moment expecting, and with reason too, to find myself discovered by Indians.

I had travelled in this manner what seemed to me about three or four miles, when far ahead in the distance I saw a column of dust rising. A hasty examination soon convinced me that the dust was produced by one of three causes: white men, Indians, or buffaloes. Two to one in my favor at any rate. Selecting a ravine where I could crawl away undiscovered should the approaching body prove to be Indians, I called my dogs to my side and concealed myself as well as I could to await developments. The object of my anxious solicitude was still several miles distant. Whatever it was, it was approaching in my direction, as was plainly discernible from the increasing columns of dust. Fortunately I had my field-glass slung across my shoulder, and if Indians I could discover them before they could possibly discover me. Soon I was able to see the heads of mounted men running in irregular order. This discovery shut out the probability of their being buffaloes, and simplified the question to white men or Indians. Never during the war did I scan an enemy's battery or approaching column with half the anxious care with which I watched the party then approaching me. For a long time nothing satisfactory could be determined, until my eye caught sight of an object which, high above the heads of the approaching riders, told me in unmistakable terms that friends were approaching. It was the cavalry guidon, and never was the sight of stars and stripes more welcome. My comrades were greatly surprised to find me seated on the ground alone and without my horse. A few words explained all. A detachment of my men, following my direction, found my horse and returned with the saddle and other equipments. Another horse, and Richard was himself again, plus a little valuable experience and minus a valuable horse.

In retracing our steps later in the day, in search of water sufficient for camping purposes, we marched over nine miles of our morning route and at two P. M. of April 16 we went into camp. From this point I wrote a despatch to General Hancock and sent it back by two of my scouts, who set out on their journey as soon as it was dark. It was determined to push on and reach the Smoky Hill route as soon as possible, and give the numerous stage stations along that route notice of the presence of warlike Indians. This was before the Pacific Railroad or its branches had crossed the Plains. Resting our animals from two until seven P. M., we were again in the saddle and setting out for a night march, our only guide being the north star. We hoped to strike the stage route near a point called Downer's Station.[10] After riding all night we reached and crossed about daylight the Smoky Hill River, along whose valley the stage route runs. The stations were then from ten to fifteen miles apart; if Indians had crossed this line at any point the station men would be informed of it. To get information as to this, as well as to determine where we were, an officer with one company was at once despatched on this mission. This party had scarcely taken its departure and our pickets been posted before the entire command of tired, sleepy cavalrymen, scouts, and Delawares had thrown them-

[10] Downer's Station was established about the year 1863 on the Smoky Hill River 50 miles west of Fort Hays and 180 miles from Fort Riley. The buildings were burned in 1867 and on May 28, 1868 the fort was abandoned.

86

A Futile Pursuit

selves on the ground and were wrapped in
the deepest slumber. We had slept perhaps
an hour or more, yet it seemed but a few
moments, when an alarm shot from the lookout and the startling cry of "Indians!"
brought the entire command under arms.

Chapter 4

ALTHOUGH in search of Indians and supposed to be always prepared to encounter them, yet the warning shot of the sentry, followed as it was by his cry of "Indians!" could not but produce the greatest excitement in camp. Where all had been quiet before—men sleeping and resting after their long night march, animals grazing unsuspectingly in the midst of the wagons and tents which thickly dotted the Plain here and there—all was now bustle if not confusion. Herders and teamsters ran to their animals to conduct them inside the limits of camp. The troopers of one platoon of each company hastened to secure the cavalry horses and provide against a stampede, while those of the remaining platoons were rapidly marshalled under arms by their troop officers and advanced in the direction from which the lookout reported the enemy to be approaching. All this required but a few moments of time. Recovering from the first shock of surprise, we endeavored, one and all, to discover the number and purpose of the foes who had in so unceremonious a manner disturbed our much-needed slumbers.

Indian Raids and Murders

Daylight had just dawned, but the sun was not yet high enough to render a satisfactory view of the country possible. This difficulty was aggravated, too, by a dull heavy mist which hung like a curtain near the horizon. Yet in spite of all these obstructions we could clearly perceive at a distance of perhaps a mile the dim outlines of numerous figures—horsemen evidently—approaching our camp, not as if simply on the march, but in battle array. First came a deployed line of horsemen, followed in rear, as we could plainly see, by a reserve, also mounted and moving in compact order.

It required no practised eye to comprehend that be they who or what they might, the parties advancing in this precise and determined manner upon us were doing so with hostile purpose, and evidently intended to charge into our camp unless defeated in their purpose. No time was to be lost. Dispositions to meet the coming attack were rapidly made. To better observe the movements and determine the strength of the approaching parties, an officer ascended the knoll occupied by the lookout.

We had often heard of the high perfection of some of the Indian tribes in military evolutions and discipline, but here we saw evidences which went far to convince us that the red man was not far behind his more civilized brother in the art of war. Certainly no troops of my command could have advanced a skirmish line or moved a reserve more accurately than was done in our presence that morning.

As yet we had no means of determining to what tribe the attacking party belonged. We were satisfied they must be either Sioux or Cheyennes, or both; in either case we should encounter troublesome foes. But for the heavy mist we could have comprehended everything. Soon we began receiving reports from the officer who had ascended the lookout. First, there were not more than eighty horsemen to be seen. This number we could easily dispose of. Next, the attacking parties seemed to have changed their plan; a halt was ordered, and two or three horsemen seemed to be advancing to the front as if to parley, or reconnoiter our position. Then the skirmishers were suddenly withdrawn and united with the reserve, when the entire party wheeled about and began to move off. This was mystifying in the extreme, but a couple of young cavalry officers leaped into their saddles and taking a few mounted troopers with them dashed after our late enemies, determined to learn more about them than they seemed willing we should.

A brisk gallop soon cleared away the mystery and furnished another proof of the de-

ceptive effects produced by the atmosphere
on the Plains. Those who have read the preceding article will remember that at the termination of the night march which brought
us to our present camp an officer was despatched with one troop of cavalry to find the
nearest stage station on the overland route,
near which we knew we must then be. Our
camp lay on the Smoky Hill River. The
stage route, better known as the Smoky Hill
route, was known to be but a few miles north
of us. To determine our exact locality, as
we had been marching by compass over a
wild country and in the night-time, and to
learn something regarding the Indians, this
officer was sent out. He was selected for this
service because of his professed experience on
and knowledge of the Plains. He had set out
from our camp an hour or more before daylight, but losing his bearings had marched
his command in a semicircle until daylight
found him on the side of our camp opposite
that from which he had departed. The conical Sibley tent used in my command, resembling the Indian lodge from which it was
taken, seen through the peculiar and uncertain morning atmosphere of that region, had
presented to his eyes and to those of his men
the appearance of an Indian village. The
animals grazing about our camp might well

have been taken for the ponies of the Indians. Besides, it was well known that large
encampments of Indians were in the part of
the country over which we were marching.
The bewilderment of this detachment, then,
was not surprising considering the attending
circumstances. Had the officer in command
been young and inexperienced his mishap
might have been credited to these causes;
but here was an officer who had grown gray
in the service, familiar with the Plains and
with Indians, yet so completely misled by
appearances as to mistake his camp, which
he had left but an hour before, for an Indian
village.

Few officers laboring under the same impression would have acted so creditably. He
and his men imagined they had discovered
the camp of the Indians whom we had been
pursuing, and although believing their enemies outnumbered them ten to one, yet their
zeal and earnestness prompted them, instead
of sending to their main camp for reinforcements, thereby losing valuable time and
probable opportunities to effect a surprise,
to make a dash at once into the village. And
it was only the increasing light of day that
enabled them to discover their mistake and
saved us from a charge from our own troopers. This little incident will show how neces-

sary experienced professional guides are in connection with all military movements on the Plains. It was a long time before the officer who had been so unlucky as to lose his way heard the last of it from his brother officers.

The remainder of his mission was completed more successfully. Aided by daylight, and moving nearly due north, he soon struck the well-travelled overland route, and from the frightened employees at the nearest station he obtained intelligence which confirmed our worst fears as to the extent of the Indian outbreak. Stage stations at various points along the route had been attacked and burned, and the inmates driven off or murdered. All travel across the Plains was suspended, and an Indian war with all its barbarities had been forced upon the people of the frontier.

As soon as the officer ascertaining these facts had returned to camp and made his report, the entire command was again put in motion and started in the direction of the stage route, with the intention of clearing it of straggling bands of Indians, reopening the main line of travel across the Plains, and establishing if possible upon the proper tribes the responsibility for the numerous outrages recently committed. The stage sta-

tions were erected at points along the route
distant from each other from ten to fifteen
miles, and were used solely for the shelter and accommodation of the relays of
drivers and horses employed on the stage
route. We found, in passing over the route
on our eastward march that only about
every fourth station was occupied, the occupants of the other three having congregated there for mutual defense against the
Indians, the latter having burned the deserted stations.

From the employees of the company at
various points we learned that for the few
preceding days the Indians had been crossing the line, going toward the north in large
bodies. In some places we saw the ruins of
the burned stations, but it was not until we
reached Lookout Station, a point about fifteen miles west of Fort Hays, that we came
upon the first real evidences of an Indian
outbreak. Riding some distance in advance
of the command, I reached the station only
to find it and the adjacent buildings in ashes,
the ruins still smoking. Near by I discovered
the bodies of the three station-keepers, so
mangled and burned as to be scarcely recognizable as human beings. The Indians had
evidently tortured them before putting an
end to their sufferings. They were scalped

and horribly disfigured. Their bodies were badly burned, but whether before or after death could not be determined. No arrow or other article of Indian manufacture could be found to positively determine what particular tribe was the guilty one. The men at other stations had recognized some of the Indians passing as belonging to the Sioux and Cheyennes, the same we had passed from the village on Pawnee Fork.

Continuing our march, we reached Fort Hays, from which point I despatched a report to General Hancock, on the Arkansas, furnishing him all the information I had gained concerning the outrages and movements of the Indians.[11] As it has been a

[11] Fort Hays was established in October, 1865 on Big Creek, about 16 miles southwest of present-day Hays, Kansas and was at first named Fort Fletcher. Henry M. Stanley, in a letter of March 9, 1867, described the fort site as a level space entirely surrounded by a deep ravine at whose bottom a stream of fine water trickled, with the soldiers' quarters built in the form of a square at the edge of the ravine. He added that General Hancock was dissatisfied with the site and a new location had been determined upon. Custer was then there, with his horses enfeebled and dying daily from lack of forage, and since Hancock depended upon him for success in pursuing the Indians he was much disappointed with the situation.

Unforeseen by every one, apparently, was another reason for dissatisfaction with the site. Early in June a

My Life on the Plains

question of considerable dispute between the respective advocates of the Indian peace and war policy, as to which party committed the first overt act of war, the Indians or General Hancock's command, I quote from a letter on the subject written by Major-General Hancock to General Grant, in reply to a letter of inquiry from the latter when commanding the armies of the United States. General Hancock says:

"When I learned from General Custer, who investigated these matters on the spot, that directly after they had abandoned the villages they attacked and burned a mail station on the Smoky Hill, killed the white men at it, disembowelled and burned them, fired into another station, endeavored to gain admittance to a third, fired on my expressmen both on the Smoky Hill and on

sudden flood turned the "trickling" stream into a raging torrent which overwhelmed the garrison, drowning six soldiers and seriously imperiling the lives of every one in the place. Custer had already departed on his campaign, described in the following chapter, leaving Mrs. Custer at the fort in his absence. In a section of the *Galaxy* installment not reprinted here he gave a vivid description of the flood and her experience in it. The fort was subsequently removed to Hays, where a military reserve of 7500 acres was established and where the fort was maintained until 1889. Subsequent to its abandonment the site was utilized for a state college and an agricultural experiment station, both still in operation.

96

their way to Larned, I concluded that this must be war, and therefore deemed it my duty to take the first opportunity which presented to resent these hostilities and outrages, and did so by destroying their villages."

The first paragraph of General Hancock's special field order directing the destruction of the Indian village read as follows:

"II. As a punishment for the bad faith practised by the Cheyennes and Sioux who occupied the Indian village at this place, and as a chastisement for murders and depredations committed since the arrival of the command at this point, by the people of these tribes, the village recently occupied by them, which is now in our hands, will be utterly destroyed."

From these extracts the question raised can be readily settled. This act of retribution on the part of General Hancock was the signal for an extensive pen and ink war, directed against him and his forces. This was to be expected. The pecuniary loss and deprivation of opportunities to speculate in Indian commodities, as practised by most Indian agents, were too great to be submitted to without a murmur. The Cheyennes, Arapahoes, and Apaches had been united under one agency; the Kiowas and

Comanches under another. As General
Hancock's expedition had reference to all of
these tribes, he had extended invitations to
each of the two agents to accompany him
into the Indian country, and be present at all
interviews with the representatives of these
respective tribes, for the purpose, as the invitation states, of showing the Indians "that
the officers of the Government are acting in
harmony."

These agents were both present at General
Hancock's headquarters. Both admitted to
General Hancock in conversation that Indians had been guilty of all the outrages
charged against them, but each asserted the
innocence of the particular tribes under his
charge and endeavored to lay their crimes
at the door of their neighbors. The agent of
the Kiowas and Comanches declared to the
department commander that "the tribes of
his agency had been grossly wronged by
having been charged with various offenses
which had undoubtedly been committed by
the Cheyennes, Arapahoes, and Apaches,
and that these tribes deserved severe and
summary chastisement for their numerous
misdeeds, very many of which had been laid
at the doors of his innocent tribes."

Not to be outdone in the profuse use of
fair words, however, the agent of the three

tribes thus assailed informed General Hancock that his three tribes "were peacefully inclined, and rarely committed offenses against the laws, but that most unfortunately they were charged in many instances with crimes which had been perpetrated by other tribes, and that in this respect they had suffered heavily from the Kiowas, who were the most turbulent Indians of the Plains, and deserved punishment more than any others."

Here was positive evidence from the agents themselves that the Indians against whom we were operating were guilty, and deserving of severe punishment. The only conflicting portion of the testimony was as to which tribe was most guilty. Subsequent events proved, however, that all of the five tribes named, as well as the Sioux, had combined for a general war throughout the Plains and along our frontier. Such a war had been threatened to our post commanders along the Arkansas on many occasions during the winter. The movement of the Sioux and Cheyennes toward the north indicated that the principal theater of military operations during the summer would be between the Smoky Hill and Platte Rivers. General Hancock accordingly assembled the principal chiefs of the Kiowas and Arapahoes in

council at Fort Dodge,[12] hoping to induce
them to remain at peace and observe their
treaty obligations.

The most prominent chiefs in council were
Satanta, Lone Wolf, and Kicking Bird of the
Kiowas, and Little Raven and Yellow Bear
of the Arapahoes. During the council extravagant promises of future good conduct
were made by these chiefs.[13] So effective

[12] Fort Dodge, on the north bank of the Arkansas
near present-day Dodge City, was established in 1864
by General Grenville M. Dodge, builder of the Union
Pacific Railroad. During the succeeding decade and a
half it was one of the most important frontier posts. It
was abandoned for military purposes in 1882. When the
railroad reached nearby Dodge City in 1872 it quickly
developed into a roaring cattle town, the resort of the
buffalo hunters and of adventurers and outlaws generally. A movie made in recent years commemorates
more or less accurately this period in the City's history.
For a more scholarly recital see Louis Pelzer, *The Cattle-
man's Frontier* . . . (Glendale, California, 1936), 57–69.

[13] Little Raven, Yellow Bear, and one or two more
Arapahoe chiefs met General Hancock in council at
Fort Dodge on April 28 and promised to remain at
peace with the whites. The major council, however,
was held with Satanta, second chief of the Kiowas, at
Fort Larned on May 1. Henry M. Stanley, who was
present as a reporter, described the council and recorded
the speeches of Hancock and Satanta in extensive detail. At the conclusion of the council General Hancock
presented Satanta a major-general's coat and yellow
sash. See Stanley, *My Early Travels and Adventures*, I,
62–83.

SATANTA, SECOND CHIEF OF THE KIOWAS.

and convincing was the oratorical effort of
Satanta, that at the termination of his address the department commander and staff
presented him with the uniform coat, sash,
and hat of a major-general. In return for
this compliment Satanta, within a few weeks
after, attacked the post at which the council
was held, arrayed in his new uniform. This
said chief had but recently headed an expedition to the frontier of Texas, where, among
other murders committed by him and his
band, was that known as the Box massacre.

The Box family consisted of the father,
mother, and five children, the eldest a girl
about eighteen, the youngest a babe. The
entire family had been visiting at a neighbor's house, and were returning home in the
evening, little dreaming of the terrible fate
impending, when Satanta and his warriors
dashed upon them, surrounded the wagon in
which they were driving, and at the first fire
killed the father and one of the children. The
horses were hastily taken from the wagon,
while the mother was informed by signs that
she and her four surviving children must accompany their captors. Mounting their
prisoners upon led horses, of which they had
a great number stolen from the settlers, the
Indians prepared to set out on their return
to the village, then located hundreds of miles

north. Before departing from the scene of
the massacre, the savages scalped the father
and child, who had fallen as their first victims. Far better would it have been had the
remaining members of the family met their
death in the first attack. From the mother,
whom I met when released from her captivity, after living as a prisoner in the hands of
the Indians for more than a year, I gathered
the details of the sufferings of herself and
children.

Fearing pursuit by the Texans and desiring to place as long a distance as possible between themselves and their pursuers, they
prepared for a night march. Mrs. Box and
each of the three elder children were placed
on separate horses and securely bound. This
was to prevent escape in the darkness. The
mother was at first permitted to carry the
youngest child, a babe of a few months, in
her arms, but the latter, becoming fretful
during the tiresome night ride, began to cry.
The Indians, fearing the sound of its voice
might be heard by pursuers, snatched it from
its mother's arms and dashed its brains out
against a tree, then threw the lifeless remains
to the ground and continued their flight. No
halt was made for twenty-four hours, after
which the march was conducted more deliberately. Each night the mother and three chil-

dren were permitted to occupy one shelter,
closely guarded by their watchful enemies.

After travelling for several days this war
party arrived at the point where they rejoined their lodges. They were still a long
distance from the main village, which was
near the Arkansas. Each night the scalp of
the father was hung up in the lodge occupied
by the mother and children. A long and
weary march over a wild and desolate country brought them to the main village. Here
the captives found that their most serious
troubles were to commence. In accordance
with Indian custom upon the return of a successful war party, a grand assembly of the
tribe took place. The prisoners, captured
horses, and scalps were brought forth, and
the usual ceremonies, terminating in a scalp
dance, followed. Then the division of the
spoils was made. The captives were appor-
tioned among the various bands composing
the tribe, so that when the division was completed the mother fell to the possession of
one chief, the eldest daughter to that of another, the second, a little girl of probably ten
years, to another, and the youngest, a child
of three years, to a fourth. No two members
of the family were permitted to remain in the
same band, but were each carried to separate
villages, distant from each other several days'

march. This was done partly to prevent escape.

No pen can describe the painful tortures of mind and body endured by this unfortunate family. They remained as captives in the hands of the Indians for more than a year, during which time the eldest daughter, a beautiful girl just ripening into womanhood, was exposed to a fate infinitely more dreadful than death itself. She first fell to one of the principal chiefs, who, after robbing her of that which was more precious than life and forcing her to become the victim of his brutal lust, bartered her in return for two horses to another chief; he again, after wearying of her, traded her to a chief of a neighboring band; and in that way this unfortunate girl was passed from one to another of her savage captors, undergoing a life so horribly brutal that, when meeting her upon her release from captivity, one could only wonder how a young girl, nurtured in civilization and possessed of the natural refinement and delicacy of thought which she exhibited, could have survived such degrading treatment.

The mother and second daughter fared somewhat better. The youngest, however, separated from mother and sisters and thrown among people totally devoid of all kind feeling, spent the time in shedding bitter tears.

This so enraged the Indians that, as a punishment as well as preventive, the child was seized and the soles of its naked feet exposed to the flames of the lodge fire until every portion of the cuticle was burned therefrom. When I saw this little girl a year afterward her feet were from this cause still in a painful and unhealed condition. These poor captives were reclaimed from their bondage through the efforts of officers of the army, and by the payment of a ransom amounting to many hundreds of dollars.

The facts relating to their cruel treatment were obtained by me directly from the mother and eldest daughter immediately after their release, which occurred a few months prior to the council held with Satanta and other chiefs. To prove something of the character of the Cheyennes, one of the principal tribes with which we were at war, I will give the following extract from an official communication addressed by me to General Hancock prior to the surrender of the little Indian boy of whom mention was made in a former article. My recommendation was not deemed practicable, as it had been promised by us in treaty stipulation to return the boy unconditionally.

"Having learned that a boy belonging to the Cheyenne tribe of Indians is in the pos-

session of the military authorities, and that
it is the intention of the Major-General commanding the department to deliver him up
to the above-named tribe, I would respectfully state that a little white girl aged from
four to seven years is held captive by the
Cheyenne Indians, and is now in the possession of Cut Nose, a chief of said tribe.

"The child referred to has been in the
hands of the Indians a year or more. She
was captured somewhere in the vicinity of
Cache la Poudre, Colorado. The parents'
name is Fletcher. The father escaped with a
severe wound, the mother and two younger
children being taken prisoners. The Indians
killed one of the children outright, and the
mother, after subjecting her to tortures too
horrible to name.

"The child now held by the Indians was
kept captive. An elder daughter made her
escape and now resides in Iowa. The father
resides in Salt Lake City. I have received
several letters from the father and eldest
daughter and from friends of both, requesting me to obtain the release of the little girl,
if possible. I would therefore request that it
be made a condition of the return of the
Indian boy now in our possession, that the
Cheyennes give up the white child referred
to above."

This proposition failing in its object, and the war destroying all means of communication with the Indians and scattering the latter over the Plains, all trace of the little white girl was lost, and to this day nothing is known of her fate. At the breaking out of the Indian difficulty Cut Nose with his band was located along the Smoky Hill route in the vicinity of Monument Station. He frequently visited the stage stations for purposes of trade, and was invariably accompanied by his little captive. I never saw her, but those who did represented her as strikingly beautiful; her complexion being fair, her eyes blue, and her hair of a bright golden hue, she presented a marked contrast to the Indian children who accompanied her. Cut Nose, from the delicate light color of her hair, gave her an Indian name signifying Little Silver Hair. He appeared to treat her with great affection, and always kept her clothed in the handsomest of Indian garments. All offers from individuals to ransom her proved unavailing. Although she had been with the Indians but a year, she spoke the Cheyenne language fluently, and seemed to have no knowledge of her mother tongue.

The treatment of the Box and Fletcher families is not given as isolated instances, but is referred to principally to show the character of the enemy with whom we were at war. Volume after volume might be filled in recounting the unprovoked and merciless atrocities committed upon the people of the frontier by their implacable foe, the red man. It will become necessary, however, in making a truthful record of the principal events which transpired under my personal observation, to make mention of Indian outrages surpassing if possible in savage cruelty any yet referred to.

As soon as General Hancock had terminated his council with the Kiowas and Arapahoes, he marched with the remaining portion of the expedition across from the Arkansas to Fort Hays, where my command was then encamped, arriving there on the third of May. Here, owing to the neglect or delay of the officers of the Quartermaster's Department in forwarding the necessary stores, the cavalry was prevented from undertaking any extensive movement, but had to content itself for the time being in scouting the adjacent country. The time, however, was well employed in the preparation of men and animals for the work which was to be assigned them.

Unfortunately, desertions from the ranks became so frequent and extensive as to cause no little anxiety. To produce these, several causes combined. Prominent among them

was the insufficiency and inferior quality of
the rations furnished the men. At times the
latter were made the victims of fraud, and it
was only by the zealous care and watchfulness of the officers immediately over them
that their wants were properly attended to.

Dishonest contractors at the receiving depots farther east had been permitted to perpetrate gross frauds upon the Government,
the result of which was to produce want and
suffering among the men. For example, unbroken packages of provisions shipped from
the main depot of supplies, and which it was
impracticable to replace without loss of time,
were when opened discovered to contain
huge stones for which the Government had
paid so much per pound according to contract price. Boxes of bread were shipped and
issued to the soldiers of my command, the
contents of which had been baked in 1861,
yet this was in 1867. It is unnecessary to
state that but little of this bread was eaten,
yet there was none at hand of better quality
to replace it. Bad provisions were a fruitful
cause of bad health. Inactivity led to restlessness and dissatisfaction. Scurvy made
its appearance, and cholera attacked neighboring stations. For all these evils desertion
became the most popular antidote. To such
an extent was this the case, that in one year

one regiment lost by desertion alone more than half of its effective force.

General Hancock remained with us only a few days before setting out with the battery for his headquarters at Fort Leavenworth. Supplies were pushed out and every preparation made for resuming offensive movements against the Indians. To find employment for the few weeks which must ensue before breaking up camp was sometimes a difficult task. To break the monotony and give horses and men exercise, buffalo hunts were organized, in which officers and men joined heartily. I know of no better drill for perfecting men in the use of firearms on horseback, and thoroughly accustoming them to the saddle, than buffalo-hunting over a moderately rough country. No amount of riding under the best of drill-masters will give that confidence and security in the saddle which will result from a few spirited charges into a buffalo herd.

The command, consisting of cavalry alone, was at last in readiness to move. Wagons had been loaded with reserve supplies and we were only waiting the growth of the spring grass to set out on the long march which had previously been arranged. On the first of June, with about three hundred and fifty men and a train of twenty wagons,

My Life on the Plains

I left Fort Hays and directed our line of
march toward Fort McPherson, on the
Platte River, distant by the proposed route
two hundred and twenty-five miles.[14] The
friendly Delawares accompanied us as scouts
and trailers, but our guide was a young white
man known on the Plains as Will Comstock.
No Indian knew the country more thoroughly than did Comstock. He was perfectly
familiar with every divide, water-course, and
strip of timber for hundreds of miles in either
direction. He knew the dress and peculiarities of every Indian tribe, and spoke the
languages of many of them. Perfect in horsemanship, fearless in manner, a splendid
hunter, and a gentleman by instinct, as modest and unassuming as he was brave, he was
an interesting as well as valuable companion
on a march such as was then before us.
Many were the adventures and incidents of

[14] Fort McPherson, at first called Fort Cottonwood,
was established in October, 1863 on the south side of the
Platte in Lincoln County, Nebraska, several miles east
of present-day Platte City. Colonel and Mrs. Carring-
ton, returning in the winter of 1867 from their harrow-
ing sojourn at Fort Phil Kearny, remained here while
Colonel Carrington underwent a court of inquiry, and
were here at the time of Custer's visit. Here, too, Ned
Buntline (Edward Z. Judson) first encountered Buffalo
Bill Cody and started him on his career of showmanship.
See Mrs. Carrington's *Absaraka, Home of the Crows*, the
Lakeside Classics volume for 1950, pp. 46–74 and 273–75.

frontier life with which he was accustomed to
entertain us when around the camp-fire or on
the march. Little did he then imagine that
his own life would soon be given as a sacrifice
to his daring, and that he, with all his experience among the savages, would fall a victim
of Indian treachery.[15]

[15] In one of the *Galaxy* installments which is not included in the present volume Custer characterized Comstock as "the favorite and best known scout on the Central Plains." General Sheridan in his *Personal Memoirs*
(II, 292–94) tells the story of his death. In company
with Abner S. Grover, another scout, he went to Turkey
Leg's Cheyenne village to seek information concerning
the recent raids on the Kansas settlers. Although both
scouts were long-time friends of the band, they now
found the village hostile and were ordered to leave.
Seven young warriors escorted them, under a pretense of
protection, and when several miles had been traversed,
opened fire on them by surprise. Comstock was killed
and Grover wounded in the shoulder. Using his dead
companion's body as a shield, he held the seven Indians
off until nightfall, when he crawled away and escaped to
Fort Wallace. Custer's account of the killing differs in
numerous details from Sheridan's story. He states that
Comstock carried a beautiful white-handled revolver,
which the Indians coveted and which while in Turkey
Leg's village they sought to purchase from him. The
seven warriors who followed the two scouts, on leaving
the village, were chiefly animated in the killing by the
desire to obtain Comstock's revolver. Custer himself
carried a very similar weapon, and Comstock had said
that after the Indians were found and whipped he would
give his own to Custer.

Chapter 5

IT had been decided that my command should thoroughly scout the country from Fort Hays near the Smoky Hill River, to Fort McPherson, on the Platte; thence describe a semicircle to the southward, touching the head waters of the Republican, and again reach the Platte at or near Fort Sedgwick, at which post we would replenish our supplies; then move directly south to Fort Wallace, on the Smoky Hill, and from there march down the overland route to our starting-point at Fort Hays. This would involve a ride of upwards of one thousand miles.

As is usually the case, the first day's march was not to be a long one. The troops, under charge of the officer second in command, Colonel Wickliffe Cooper, left camp and marched up the valley of Big Creek a distance of eighteen miles, and there encamped. Two companies of cavalry and a small force of infantry were to constitute the garrison to remain behind. When the troops composing my command left, it became necessary to rearrange the camp and provide new dispositions for defense. My wife, who always accompanied me when in camp or on the march except when I was engaged in active pursuit of Indians, had rejoined me soon after my arrival at Fort Hays. She was accompanied by a young lady friend from the East, a schoolmate, who had been tempted by the novelties of wild western life to make her a visit in camp. As there were other ladies in camp, wives of officers who were to remain with the garrison, my wife and friend decided to remain and await our return, rather than go back to the protection and luxuries of civilization. To arrange for their comfort and superintend the locating of their tents, I remained behind my command, intending to wait until after midnight, and then, guided by the moonlight, ride on and overtake my command before it should commence its second day's march. I retained with me two soldiers, one scout, and four of the Delawares.

* * *

Soon after midnight, everything being in readiness and my little party having been refreshed by a cup of good army coffee, it only remained to say adieu to those who were to remain behind and we were ready for our moonlight gallop.

But little was said as we made our way rapidly over the plain in the direction taken by the command. Occasionally, as we dashed across a ravine, we would suddenly come upon a herd of antelope or a few scattering buffaloes, startling them from their repose and causing them to wonder what was the occasion and who the strange parties disturbing the peaceful quiet of the night in this unusual manner. On we sped, our good steeds snuffing the early morning air and pressing forward as eagerly as if they knew their companions were awaiting them in the advance.

Daylight had given us no evidence of its coming, when, after a ride of nearly twenty miles we found ourselves descending into a valley in which we knew the command must be encamped. The moon had disappeared below the horizon, and we were left to make our way aided by such light as the stars twinkling in a clear sky afforded us. Our horses gave us unmistakable evidence that camp was near. To convince us beyond all doubt, the clear ringing notes of the bugle sounding the reveille greeted our ears, and directed by the sound we soon found ourselves in camp.

A cavalry camp immediately after reveille always presents an animated and most in-

teresting scene. As soon as the rolls are
called and the reports of absentees made to
headquarters, the men of the companies,
with the exception of the cooks, are employed in the care of the horses. The latter
are fed, and while eating are thoroughly
groomed by the men, under the superinten-
dence of their officers. Nearly an hour is devoted to this important duty. In the meanwhile the company cooks, ten to each company, and the officers' servants are busily
engaged preparing breakfast, so that within
a few minutes after the horses have received
proper attention breakfast is ready, and being very simple it requires but little time to
dispose of it. Immediately after breakfast
the first bugle call indicative of the march is
the "General," and is the signal for tents to
be taken down and everything packed in
readiness for moving. A few minutes later
this is followed by the bugler at headquarters
sounding "Boots and saddles," when horses
are saddled up and the wagon train put in
readiness for pulling out. Five minutes later
"To horse" is sounded, and the men of each
company lead their horses into line, each
trooper standing at the head of his horse. At
the words "Prepare to mount," from the
commanding officer, each trooper places his
left foot in the stirrup; and at the command

"Mount," every man rises on his stirrup and places himself in his saddle, the whole command presenting the appearance to the eye of a huge machine propelled by one power. Woe betide the unfortunate trooper who through carelessness or inattention fails to place himself in his saddle simultaneously with his companions. If he is not for this offense against military rule deprived of the services of his horse during the succeeding half day's march, he escapes luckily.

As soon as the command is mounted the "Advance" is sounded, and the troops, usually in column of fours, move out. The company leading the advance one day march in rear the following day. This successive changing gives each company an opportunity to march by regular turn in advance. Our average daily march, when not in immediate pursuit of the enemy, was about twenty-five miles. Upon reaching camp in the evening the horses were cared for as in the morning, opportunities being given them to graze before dark. Pickets were posted and every precaution adopted to guard against surprise.

Our second day's march brought us to the Saline River, where we encamped for the night. From our camp ground we could see on a knoll some two miles distant a platform or scaffold erected, which resembled some-

what one of our war signal stations. Curious
to discover its purpose, I determined to
visit it.

Taking with me Comstock and a few soldiers, I soon reached the point, and discovered that the object of my curiosity and surprise was an Indian grave. The body, instead of being consigned to mother earth,
was placed on top of the platform. The latter was constructed of saplings, and was
about twenty feet in height. From Comstock I learned that with some of the tribes
this is the usual mode of disposing of the
body after death. The prevailing belief of
the Indian is that when done with this world
the spirit of the deceased is transferred to
the happy hunting-ground, where he is permitted to engage in the same pleasures and
pursuits which he preferred while on earth.
To this end it is deemed essential that after
death the departed must be supplied with
the same equipment and ornaments considered necessary while in the flesh. In accordance with this belief a complete Indian outfit, depending in extent upon the rank and
importance of the deceased, is prepared, and
consigned with the body to the final resting-
place.

The body found on this occasion must
have been that of a son of some important

chief; it was not full grown, but accompanied with all the arms and adornments usually owned by a warrior. There was the bow and quiver full of steel-pointed arrows, the toma-hawk and scalping-knife, and a red clay pipe with a small bag full of tobacco. In order that the departed spirit should not be wholly dependent upon friends after his arrival at the happy hunting-ground, he had been sup-plied with provisions, consisting of small par-cels containing coffee, sugar, and bread. Weapons of modern structure had also been furnished him, a revolver and rifle with powder and ball ammunition for each, and a saddle, bridle, and lariat for his pony. Added to these was a supply of wearing apparel, embracing every article known in an Indian's toilet, not excepting the various colored paints to be used in decorating himself for war. A handsome buckskin scalping-pocket, profusely ornamented with beads, com-pleted the outfit. But for fear that white women's scalps might not be readily obtain-able, and desiring no doubt to be received at once as a warrior who in his own country at least was not without renown, a white wom-an's scalp was also considered as a necessary accompaniment, a letter of introduction to the dusky warriors and chieftains who had gone before. As the Indian of the Plains is himself only when on horseback, provision must be made for mounting him properly in the Indian heaven. To accomplish this, the favorite war pony is led beneath the platform on which the body of the warrior is placed at rest and there strangled to death.

No signs indicating the recent presence of Indians were discovered by our scouts until we neared the Republican River, where the trail of a small war party was discovered running down one of the tributaries of the Republican. After following it far enough to determine the futility of pursuit, the attempt was relinquished. Upon crossing the Republican we suddenly came in full view of about a hundred mounted warriors, who, without waiting for a parley of any kind, set off as fast as their horses could carry them. One squadron was sent in pursuit, but was unable to overhaul the Indians. From the tracks we learned that the Indians were mounted on horses stolen from the stage company. These horses were of a superior quality, and purchased by the company at a price about double that paid by the Government. This was the only occasion on which we saw Indians before reaching the Platte River.

One of our camps was pitched on the banks of a small stream which had been named

Beaver Creek. Comstock informed us that here an opportunity could be had of killing a few beavers, as they were very numerous all along this stream, which had derived its name from that fact. We had gone into camp about 3 P. M. The numerous stumps and fallen trees, as well as the beaver dams, attested the accuracy of Comstock's statement. By his advice we waited until sundown before taking our stations on the bank, not far above the site of our camp, as at that time the beavers would be out and on shore.

Placing ourselves under Comstock's guidance, a small party proceeded to the ground selected, where we were distributed singly at stations along the stream and quietly awaited the appearance of the beavers. Whether the noise from the camp below or the passing of hunting parties of soldiers in the afternoon had frightened them, I know not. I remained at my station with my rifle in hand ready to fire at the first beaver which should offer itself as a sacrifice, until the sun had disappeared and darkness had begun to spread its heavy mantle over everything around me. No living thing had thus far disturbed my reveries. My station was on the immediate bank of the stream, on a path which had evidently been made by wild ani-

mals of some kind. The bank rose above me
to a distance of nearly twenty feet.

I was just on the point of leaving my station and giving up all hope of getting a shot
when I heard the rustling of the long dry
grass a few yards lower down the stream.
Cocking my rifle, I stood ready to deliver its
contents into the approaching animal, which
I presumed would be seen to be a beaver as
soon as it should emerge from the tall grass.
It did not make its appearance in the path in
which I stood until within a few feet of me,
when to my great surprise I beheld instead of
a beaver an immense wildcat. It was difficult
to say which of us was most surprised. Without delaying long to think, I took a hasty
aim and fired. The next moment I heard a
splash which relieved my mind as to which
of us should retain the right of way on shore,
the path being too narrow to admit of our
passing each other. I had either wounded or
killed the wildcat, and its body in the darkness had been carried down with the current,
as the dogs which were soon attracted from
the camp by my shot were unable to find the
trail on either bank.

Nothing occurred to break the monotony
of our march until we reached Fort McPherson, on the Platte River. The country over
which we had marched had been quite varied

in its character, and as we neared the Platte it became very broken and abrupt. It was only by availing ourselves of Comstock's superior knowledge of the country that we found an easy exit from the deep cañons and rough defiles which were encountered.

At Fort McPherson we refilled our wagons with supplies of rations and forage. At the same time, in accordance with my instructions, I reported by telegraph my arrival to General Sherman, who was then farther west on the line of the Union Pacific road. He did not materially change my instructions, further than to direct me to remain near Fort McPherson until his arrival, which would be in the course of a few days.

Moving my command about twelve miles from the fort, I arranged for a council with Pawnee Killer and a few other Sioux chiefs, who had arrived at the Platte about the same time my command had. My object was, if possible, to induce Pawnee Killer and his band, with such other Indians as might choose to join them, to bring their lodges into the vicinity of the fort, and remain at peace with the whites. Pawnee Killer and his chiefs met me in council and the subject was discussed, but with no positive conclusions. While protesting strongly in favor of preserving peaceful relations with us, the subsequent conduct of the chiefs only confirmed the suspicion that they had arranged the council not to perfect a friendly agreement with us, but to spy out and discover, if possible, our future plans and movements. In this they were disappointed. Their numerous inquiries as to where we intended proceeding when we resumed the march were unavailing. Desiring to leave nothing undone to encourage a friendly attitude on their part, I gave the chiefs on parting with them liberal presents of coffee, sugar, and other articles gratifying to the taste of an Indian. They departed after giving utterance to the strongest expressions of their desire to live at peace with their white brothers, and promised to collect their families and bring them in under protection of the fort, and thus avoid becoming entangled in the ravages of an Indian war which now promised to become general throughout the Plains. Pawnee Killer and his chiefs never attempted to keep their promises.

General Sherman arrived at my camp next day. He had no confidence in the faith of Pawnee Killer and his band, and desired that a party be sent in pursuit at once, and bring the chiefs back and retain a few of the prominent ones as hostages for the fulfilment of their agreement. This was decided to be impracticable. It was then judged best for me to move my command in a southwesterly direction to the forks of the Republican, a section of country usually infested by Indians, and there endeavor to find the village of Pawnee Killer, and compel him, if necessary, to move nearer to the fort, so that we might distinguish between those who were friendly and those who were not. Besides, it was known that the Cheyennes and Sioux, whom we had pursued from the Arkansas across the Smoky Hill River, had not crossed north of the Platte, and they were rightly supposed to be located somewhere near the forks of the Republican. I could reach this point in three days' marching after leaving the Platte River, on whose banks we were then encamped.

Owing to the rough and broken character of the bluffs which bound the valley of the Platte on the south side, it was determined to march up the men about fifteen miles from the fort and strike south through an opening in the bluffs known as Jack Morrow's cañon.[16] General Sherman rode with

[16] Jack Morrow conducted a ranch at this time on the south side of the South Platte, two miles from Fort McPherson. When the Union Pacific Railroad passed by on the north side of the river Morrow ferried his ranch house across and resumed business in the new

us as far as this point, where, after com-
mending the Cheyennes and Sioux to us in
his expressive manner, he bade us good-by,
and crossed the river to the railroad station
on the north side. Thus far we had had no
real Indian warfare. We were soon to experience it, attended by all its frightful barbarities.

location. Morrow's Cañon was several miles up river
on the south side. Although Mrs. Carrington characterized Morrow as "the prince of ranchmen and the king of
good fellows," according to others he was known as a
killer and as a stupendous drinker. See *Absaraka, Home
of the Crows*, 62–63.

Chapter 6

THE INDIANS ATTACK THE CAVALRY

BEFORE leaving the Platte I employed two additional interpreters who were familiar with the Sioux language. Both were white men, but, following the example of many frontiersmen they had taken unto themselves Indian wives, and each had become the head of a considerable family of half-breeds.

Starting nearly due south from the Platte, and marching up the cañon, which forms a natural gateway through the otherwise almost impassable barrier of bluffs and deep ravines bordering the valley of the Platte River, we again set out in search of Indians. The latter are sought after so frequently and found so seldom, except when not wanted, that scouting parties, as a general thing, are not overburdened with confidence on beginning an expedition. Most of us, however, felt that we were destined to see Indians—an impression probably due to the fact that we had determined to accomplish our purpose, if hard riding and watchfulness could attain this result.

Our first day's march brought us to a small stream, a tributary of the Republican River, on whose banks we encamped for the night. Daylight the following morning found us in the saddle and ascending from the valley to the table-lands; we were still in the broken country. On reaching the plateau overlooking the valley we found ourselves enveloped in a dense fog, so dense that the sky was not visible, nor was an extended view of the country possible. Had the surface of the plain been, as usual, level and unbroken, we could have pursued our march guided by the unerring compass. But deep and impassable cañons divided the country in all directions and rendered our further progress impracticable. The sun, however, soon rose high enough to drive away the mist, and permitted us to proceed on what might be truly termed our winding way.

The afternoon of the fourth day we reached the forks of the Republican, and there went into camp. We were then located about seventy-five miles southeast of Fort Sedgwick, and about the same distance northeast of Fort Wallace.[17] Intending to

[17] Fort Sedgwick, near Julesburg, Colorado was established as Camp Rankin in September, 1864. Soon afterward it was renamed in honor of General Sedgwick, who was killed in the battle of Spottsylvania Court House in the Civil War. Following the Chivington massacre of November 20, 1864, Fort Sedgwick was twice attacked by the Cheyennes, in January and February, 1865.

scout the surrounding country thoroughly in
search of Indians, we selected our camp with
reference to a sojourn of several days, com-
bining among its essentials wood, water,
good grazing, and last, but not least, facilities for defense.

When I parted from General Sherman the
understanding was, that after beating up the
country thoroughly about the forks of the
Republican River, I should march my command to Fort Sedgwick, and there I would
either see General Sherman again or receive
further instructions from him. Circumstances seemed to favor a modification of
this plan, at least as to marching the entire
command to Fort Sedgwick. It was therefore decided to send a trusty officer with a
sufficient escort to Fort Sedgwick with my
despatch, and to receive the despatches
which might be intended for me. My pro-

Julesburg contained about a dozen houses and stores
when Colonel Carrington passed by in the summer of
1866. Upon the arrival of the Union Pacific some months
later, it became a boom town of 3000, with wall tents
renting for $100 per day. For the visit of the Carring-
ton's see *Absaraka, Home of the Crows*, 49–50.

Fort Wallace was established in 1865 on the south
fork of Smoky Hill River, near present-day Wallace,
Kansas. A reservation of 14 square miles was laid out
and buildings to accommodate 500 soldiers were erected.
The Union Pacific was completed to this point in July,
1868. The fort was maintained until 1882.

posed change of program contemplated a
continuous march, which might be prolonged
twenty days or more. To this end additional
supplies were necessary. The guides all
agreed in the statement that we were then
about equidistant from Fort Wallace on the
south and Fort Sedgwick on the north, at
either of which the required supplies could be
obtained; but that while the country between our camp and the former was generally level and unbroken—favorable to the
movement of our wagon train—that between
us and Fort Sedgwick was almost impassable
for heavily-laden wagons. The train then
was to go to Fort Wallace under sufficient escort, be loaded with fresh supplies, and rejoin us in camp. At the same time the officer
selected for that mission could proceed to
Fort Sedgwick, obtain his despatch, and return.

Major Joel H. Elliot, a young officer of
great courage and enterprise, was selected as
bearer of despatches to Fort Sedgwick.[18] As

[18] Elliot had served in an Indiana cavalry regiment
throughout the Civil War, rising to the rank of captain.
Subsequently for a brief time he was Superintendent of
Schools of Toledo. When the Seventh U.S. Cavalry was
organized he was given the rank of Major in that regiment. Van De Water describes him as "a pleasant and
earnest youth, with a high, fair forehead beneath wavy
hair, and a studious face, framed by sideburns," who

131

the errand was one involving considerable danger, requiring for the round trip a ride of almost two hundred miles through a country which was not only almost unknown but infested by large numbers of hostile Indians, the Major was authorized to arrange the details in accordance with his own judgment.

Knowing that small detachments can move more rapidly than large ones, and that he was to depend upon celerity of movement rather than strength of numbers to evade the numerous war parties prowling in that vicinity, the Major limited the size of his escort to ten picked men and one of the guides, all mounted on fleet horses. To elude the watchful eyes of any parties that might be noting our movements, it was deemed advisable to set out from camp as soon as it was dark, and by making a rapid night ride get beyond the circle of danger. In this way the little party took its departure on the night of the 23d of June.

On the same day our train of wagons set out for Fort Wallace to obtain supplies. Colonel West with one full squadron of cavalry was ordered to escort the train to Beaver Creek, about midway, and there halt

had aspired only to the rank of lieutenant and was embarrassed when he was commissioned a major. *Glory Hunter*, 151–52.

with one of his companies, while the train, under escort of one company commanded by Lieutenant Robbins, should proceed to the fort and return—Colonel West to employ the interval in scouting up and down Beaver Creek. The train was under the special management of Colonel Cooke who on this occasion was acting in the capacity of a staff officer.[19]

While at Fort McPherson, and when under the impression that my command upon arriving at Fort Wallace, after terminating the scouting expedition we were then engaged upon, would remain in camp for several weeks, I wrote to my wife at Fort Hays,

[19] Robert M. West served from 1856 to 1861 as a private in the Mounted Rifle Regiment. During the Civil War he attained the rank of colonel and brevet brigadier general in the volunteer service. He was made a captain in the Seventh U.S. Cavalry in July, 1866. He resigned in March, 1869, and died six months later.

William W. Cooke was a native of Canada who enlisted as a private in a New York cavalry regiment in the Civil War, rising to the rank of lieutenant colonel. He was given the commission of lieutenant in the Seventh U.S. Cavalry upon the organization of that regiment in 1866. He was one of Custer's favorites and followed him to death at the Little Big Horn.

Samuel M. Robbins served in the Civil War as a captain in the First Colorado Cavalry. He joined the Seventh U.S. Cavalry as a lieutenant in July, 1866, and became a captain in November, 1868. He resigned from the service in 1872.

advising her to meet me at Fort Wallace,
provided that travel between the two posts
was considered safe. I expected her to reach
Fort Wallace before the arrival of the train
and escort from my camp, and under this
impression I sent a letter to her by Colonel
Cooke asking her to come to our camp on the
Republican under escort of the Colonel, who
was an intimate friend of the family. I am
thus minute in giving these details in order
that the events of the succeeding few days
may appear in their proper light.

After the departure of the two detachments, which left us in almost opposite directions, our camp settled down to the dull and
unexciting monotony of waiting patiently for
the time when we should welcome our comrades back again, and listen to such items of
news as they might bring to us.

Little did we imagine that the monotony
of idleness was so soon and so abruptly tô be
broken. That night our pickets were posted
as usual; the horses and mules, after being
allowed to graze in the evening, were brought
in and securely tethered close to our tents,
and the stable guards of the different troops
had been assigned to their stations for the
night. At half-past eight the bugler at headquarters sounded the signal for taps, and before the last note had died away every light,

in obedience to this command, disappeared, and nothing remained to the eye, except here and there a faint glimpse of a white tent, to indicate the presence of our camp.

It was just that uncertain period between darkness and daylight on the following morning, and I was lying in my tent deep in the enjoyment of that perfect repose which only camp life offers when the sharp, clear crack of a carbine near by brought me to my feet. I knew in an instant that the shot came from the picket posted not far from the rear of my camp. At the same moment my brother, Colonel Custer, who on that occasion was officer of the day, and whose duties required him to be particularly on the alert, rushed past my tent, halting only long enough to show his face through the opening and shout, "They are here!"

Now I did not inquire who were referred to, or how many were included in the word "they," nor did my informant seem to think it necessary to explain. "They" referred to Indians, I knew full well. Had I doubted, the brisk fusillade which opened the next moment, and the wild war-whoop, were convincing evidences that in truth "they were here!"

Ordinarily, I must confess to having sufficient regard for the customs and courtesies of life to endeavor to appear in society suitably and appropriately dressed. But when the alarm of "Indians" was given, and in such a startling manner as to show they were almost in our midst, the question was not "What shall I wear?" but "What shall I do?" It has become so common—in fact, almost a law—to describe the costumes worn upon memorable occasions, that I may be pardoned if I indulge in a description which I will endeavor to make as brief as the costume itself. A modern Jenkins, if desiring to tell the truth, would probably express himself as follows: "General Custer on this occasion appeared in a beautiful crimson robe (red flannel *robe de nuit*), very becoming to his complexion. His hair was worn *au naturel*, and permitted to fall carelessly over his shoulders. In his hand he carried gracefully a handsome Spencer rifle. It is unnecessary to add that he became the observed of all observers."

My orderly, as was his custom, on my retiring had securely tied all the fastenings to my tent, and it was usually the work of several minutes to undo this unnecessary labor. I had no time to throw away in this manner. Leaping from my bed, I grasped my trusty Spencer, which was always at my side whether waking or sleeping, and with a single dash burst open the tent and, hatless as well as shoeless, ran to the point where the attack seemed to be concentrated.

It was sufficiently light to see our enemies and be seen. The first shot had brought every man of my command from his tent, armed and equipped for battle. The Indians, numbering hundreds, were all around the camp, evidently intending to surround us, while a party of about fifty of their best mounted warriors had, by taking advantage of a ravine, contrived to approach quite close before being discovered. It was the intention of this party to dash through our camp, stampede all our horses, which were to be caught up by the parties surrounding us, and then finish us at their leisure. The picket, however, discovered the approach of this party and by firing gave timely warning, thus frustrating the plan of the Indians, who almost invariably base their hopes of success upon effecting a surprise.

My men opened on them such a brisk fire from their carbines that they were glad to withdraw beyond range. The picket who gave the alarm was shot down at his post by the Indians, the entire party galloping over his body and being prevented from scalping him only by the fire from his comrades, who dashed out and recovered him. He was found to be badly though not mortally wounded by a rifle ball through the body.

The Indians, seeing that their attempt to surprise us and to stampede our horses had failed, then withdrew to a point but little over a mile from us, where they congregated and seemed to hold a conference with each other. We did not fear any further attack at this time. They were satisfied with this attempt, and would await another opportunity.

It was desirable, however, that we should learn if possible to what tribe our enemies belonged. I directed one of our interpreters to advance midway between our camp and the Indians, and make the signal for holding a parley, and in this way ascertain who were the principal chiefs.

The ordinary manner of opening communication with parties known or supposed to be hostile, is to ride toward them in a zigzag manner or to ride in a circle. The interpreter gave the proper signal, and was soon answered by a small party advancing from the main body of the Indians to within hailing distance. It was then agreed that I, with six of the officers, should come to the bank of the river, which was about equidistant from my camp and from the point where the Indians had congregated, and there be met by an equal number of the leading chiefs. To guard against treachery, I placed most of my command under arms and arranged with the officer left in command that a blast from the bugle should bring assistance to me if required.

Six of the officers and myself, taking with us a bugler and an interpreter, proceeded on horseback to the designated point. Dismounting, we left our horses in charge of the bugler, who was instructed to watch every movement of the Indians and upon the first appearance of violence or treachery to sound the "advance." Each of us took our revolvers from their leather cases and stuck them loosely in our belts.

Descending to the river bank, we awaited the arrival of the seven chiefs. On one side of the river the bank was level and covered with a beautiful green sward, while on the opposite side it was broken and thickly covered by willows and tall grass. The river itself was at this season of the year, and at this distance from its mouth, scarcely deserving of the name. The seven chiefs soon made their appearance on its opposite bank, and, after removing their leggings, waded across to where we stood. Imagine our surprise at recognizing as the head chief Pawnee Killer, our friend of the conference of the Platte, who on that occasion had overwhelmed us

with the earnestness of his professions of
peace, and who, after partaking of our hospitality under the guise of friendship, and
leaving our camp laden with provisions and
presents, returned to attack and murder us
within a fortnight. This, too, without the
slightest provocation, for surely we had not
trespassed against any right of theirs since
the exchange of friendly greetings near Fort
McPherson.

Pawnee Killer and his chiefs met us as if
they were quite willing to forgive us for interfering with the success of their intended
surprise of our camp in the morning. I
avoided all reference to what had occurred,
desiring if possible to learn the locality of
their village and their future movements.
All attempts, however, to elicit information
on these points were skilfully parried. The
chiefs in turn were anxious to know our
plans, but we declined to gratify them. Upon
crossing to our side of the river Pawnee
Killer and his companions at once extended
their hands, and saluted us with the familiar
"How." Suspicious of their intentions, I
kept one hand on my revolver during the
continuance of our interview.

When we had about concluded our conference a young brave, completely armed, as
were all the chiefs, emerged from the willows

and tall grass on the opposite bank and waded across to where we were, greeting us as the others had done. Nothing was thought of this act until a few moments after another brave did the same, and so on until four had crossed over and joined our group. I then called Pawnee Killer's attention to the conditions under which we met, and told him he was violating his part of the contract. He endeavored to turn it off by saying that his young men felt well disposed toward us, and came over only to shake hands and say "How." He was told, however, that no more of his men must come. The conversation was then resumed and continued until another party of the warriors was seen preparing to cross from the other side. The conduct of these Indians in the morning, added to our opinions in general as regards treachery, convinced us that it would be in the highest degree imprudent to trust ourselves in their power. They already outnumbered us, eleven to seven, which were as heavy odds as we felt disposed to give. We all felt convinced that the coming over of these warriors, one by one, was but the execution of a preconceived plan whereof we were to become the victims as soon as their advantage in numbers should justify them in attacking us.

Again reminding Pawnee Killer ` of the stipulations of our agreement, and that while we had observed ours faithfully, he had disregarded his, I told him that not another warrior of his should cross the river to our side. And calling his attention to the bugler, who stood at a safe distance from us, I told him that I would then instruct the bugler to watch the Indians who were upon the opposite bank, and, upon any of them making a movement as if to cross, to sound the signal which would bring my entire command to my side in a few moments. This satisfied Pawnee Killer that any further attempt to play us false would only end in his own discomfiture. He at once signalled to the Indians on the other side to remain where they were.

Nothing definite could be gleaned from the replies of Pawnee Killer. I was satisfied that he and his tribe were contemplating mischief. Their previous declarations of peaceful intent went for naught. Their attack on our camp in the morning proved what they would do if able to accomplish their purpose. I was extremely anxious, however, to detain the chiefs near my camp, or induce them to locate their village near us, and keep up the semblance at least of friendship. I was particularly prompted to this desire by the fact that the two detachments which had left my command the previous day would necessarily continue absent several days, and I feared that they might become the victims of an attack from this band if steps were not taken to prevent it. Our anxiety was greatest regarding Major Elliot and his little party of eleven. Our only hope was that the Indians had not become aware of their departure. It was fortunate that the Major had chosen night as the most favorable time for setting out. As to the detachment that had gone with the train to Fort Wallace we felt less anxious, it being sufficiently powerful in numbers to defend itself, unless attacked after the detachment became divided at Beaver Creek.

Finding all efforts to induce Pawnee Killer to remain with us unavailing, I told him that we would march to his village with him. This did not seem satisfactory. Before terminating our interview, the chiefs requested me to make them presents of some sugar, coffee, and ammunition. Remembering the use they had made of the latter article in the morning, it will not appear strange if I declined to gratify them. Seeing that nothing was to be gained by prolonging the interview, we separated, the officers returning to our camp, and the Indians recrossing the river, mounting their ponies, and galloping off to the main body, which was then nearly two miles distant.

My command was in readiness to leap into their saddles and I determined to attempt to follow the Indians and, if possible, get near their village. They were prepared for this move on our part and the moment we advanced toward them set off at the top of their speed. We followed as rapidly as our heavier horses could travel, but the speed of the Indian pony on this occasion, as on many others, was too great for that of our horses. A pursuit of a few hours proved our inability to overtake them and we returned to camp.

Soon after arriving at camp a small party of Indians was reported in sight in a different direction. Captain Louis Hamilton, a lineal descendant of Alexander Hamilton, was immediately ordered to take his troop and learn something of their intentions.[20] The Indians

[20] Louis McLane Hamilton was a grandson of Alexander Hamilton, Washington's Secretary of the Treasury. His maternal grandfather, for whom he was named, was Louis McLane, U.S. Senator, Ambassador to Great Britain, and Secretary of the Treasury and Secretary of State in President Jackson's Cabinet. He enlisted in the army for the Civil War before he was eighteen years of age, and before he was nineteen was commanding a company in battle. At the time of his death in the battle of the Washita he was the youngest officer of his rank in the regular army.

resorted to their usual tactics. There were not more than half a dozen to be seen—not enough to appear formidable. These were there as a decoy. Captain Hamilton marched his troop toward the hill on which the Indians had made their appearance, but on arriving at its crest found that they had retired to the next ridge beyond. This manœuver was repeated several times, until the cavalry found itself several miles from camp. The Indians then appeared to separate into two parties, each going in different directions. Captain Hamilton divided his troop into two detachments, sending one detachment, under command of my brother, after one of the parties, while he with twenty-five men continued to follow the other.

When the two detachments had become so far separated as to be of no assistance to each other, the Indians developed their scheme. Suddenly dashing from a ravine, as if springing from the earth, forty-three Indian warriors burst out upon the cavalry, letting fly their arrows and filling the air with their wild war-whoops. Fortunately Captain Hamilton was an officer of great presence of mind as well as undaunted courage. The Indians began circling about the troops, throwing themselves upon the sides of their ponies and aiming their carbines and arrows over the necks of their well-trained war-steeds. Captain Hamilton formed his men in order to defend themselves against the assaults of their active enemies. The Indians displayed unusual boldness, sometimes dashing close up to the cavalry and sending in a perfect shower of bullets and arrows. Fortunately their aim, riding as they did at full speed, was necessarily inaccurate.

All this time we who had remained in camp were in ignorance of what was transpiring. Dr. Coates, whose acquaintance has been made before, had accompanied Captain Hamilton's command, but when the latter was divided the doctor joined the detachment of my brother. In some unexplained manner the doctor became separated from both parties, and remained so until the sound of the firing attracted him toward Captain Hamilton's party. When within half a mile of the latter, he saw what was transpiring; saw our men in the center and the Indians charging and firing from the outside. His first impulse was to push on and endeavor to break through the line of savages, casting his lot with his struggling comrades. This impulse was suddenly nipped in the bud. The Indians, with their quick, watchful eyes, had discovered his presence, and half a dozen of their best mounted warriors at once galloped toward him.

The Indians Attack

Happily the doctor was in the direction of camp from Captain Hamilton's party, and comprehending the peril of his situation at a glance, turned his horse's head toward camp, and applying the spur freely set out on a ride for life. The Indians saw this move, but were not disposed to be deprived of their victim in this way. They were better mounted than the doctor, his only advantage being in the start and the greater object to be attained. When the race began he was fully four miles from camp, the day was hot and sultry, the country rough and broken, and his horse somewhat jaded from the effects of the ride of the morning. These must have seemed immense obstacles in the eyes of a man who was riding for dear life. A false step, a broken girth, or almost any trifle might decide his fate.

How often, if ever, the doctor looked back, I know not; his eyes more probably were strained to catch a glimpse of camp or of assistance accidentally coming to his relief. Neither the one nor the other appeared. His pursuers, knowing that their success must be gained soon, if at all, pressed their fleet ponies forward until they seemed to skim over the surface of the green plain, and their shouts of exultation falling clearer and louder upon his ear told the doctor that they were surely gaining upon him. Fortunately our domestic horses, until accustomed to their presence, are as terrified by Indians as by a huge wild beast, and will fly from them if not restrained. The yells of the approaching Indians served, no doubt, to quicken the energies of the doctor's horse and impelled him to greater efforts to escape.

So close had the Indians succeeded in approaching that they were almost within arrow range and would soon have sent one flying through the doctor's body, when to the great joy of the pursued and the corresponding grief of his pursuers camp suddenly appeared in full view scarcely a mile distant. The ponies of the Indians had been ridden too hard to justify their riders in venturing near enough to provoke pursuit upon fresh animals. Sending a parting volley of bullets after the flying doctor, they turned about and disappeared. The doctor did not slacken his pace on this account, however; he knew that Captain Hamilton's party was in peril, and that assistance should reach him as soon as possible. Without tightening rein or sparing spur he came dashing into camp, and the first we knew of his presence he had thrown himself from his almost breathless horse and was lying on the ground, unable, from sheer exhaustion and excitement, to utter a word.

The Indians Attack

The officers and men gathered about him in astonishment, eager and anxious to hear his story, for all knew that something far from any ordinary event had transpired to place the doctor in such a condition of mind and body. As soon as he had recovered sufficiently to speak, he told us that he had left Captain Hamilton surrounded by a superior force of Indians, and that he himself had been pursued almost to the borders of camp.

This was enough. The next moment the bugle rang out the signal "To horse," and in less time than would be required to describe it, horses were saddled and arms ready. Then "there was mounting in hot haste." A moment later the command set off at a brisk trot to attempt the rescue of their beleaguered comrades.

Persons unfamiliar with the cavalry service may mentally inquire why, in such an emergency as this, the intended reinforcements were not pushed forward at a rapid gallop? But in answer to this it need only be said that we had a ride of at least five miles before us in order to arrive at the point where Captain Hamilton and his command had last been seen, and it was absolutely necessary to so husband the powers of our horses as to save them for the real work of conflict.

149

We had advanced in this manner probably
two miles, when we discerned in the distance
the approach of Captain Hamilton's party.
They were returning leisurely to camp, after
having succeeded in driving off their assail-
ants and inflicting upon them a loss of two
warriors killed and several wounded. The
Indians could only boast of having wounded
a horse belonging to Captain Hamilton's
party.

This encounter with the Indians occurred
in the direction taken by Major Elliot's detachment on leaving camp, and the Indians,
after this repulse by Captain Hamilton,
withdrew in that direction. This added to
our anxiety concerning the safety of Major
Elliot and his men. There was no doubt now
that all Indians infesting the broad belt of
country between the Arkansas and Platte
rivers were on the war path, and would seek
revenge from any party so unfortunate as to
fall in their way. The loss of the two warriors slain in the fight, and their wounded
comrades, would be additional incentives to
acts of hostility. If there had been any possible means of communicating with Major
Elliot, and either strengthening or warning
him, it would have been done. He left us by
no travelled or defined route, and it was by
no means probable that he would pass over

the same trail in coming from Fort Sedgwick as in going to that point; otherwise reinforcements could have been sent out over his trail to meet him.

On the 27th our fears for the safety of the Major and his escort were dispelled by their safe return to camp, having accomplished a ride of nearly two hundred miles through an enemy's country. They had concealed themselves in ravines during the daytime and travelled at night, trusting to the faithful compass and their guide to bring them safely back.

Now that the Major and his party had returned to us, our anxiety became centered in the fate of the larger party which had proceeded with the train to Fort Wallace for supplies. The fact that Major Elliot had made his trip unmolested by Indians proved that the latter were most likely assembled south of us, that is between us and Fort Wallace. Wherever they were, their numbers were known to be large. It would be impossible for a considerable force, let alone a wagon train, to pass from our camp to Fort Wallace and not be seen by the Indian scouting parties. They had probably observed the departure of the train and escort at the time, and, divining the object which occasioned the sending of the wagons, would permit them to go to the fort unmolested, but would waylay them on their return, in the hope of obtaining the supplies they contained. Under this supposition the Indians had probably watched the train and escort during every mile of their progress; if so, they would not fail to discover that the larger portion of the escort halted at Beaver Creek, while the wagons proceeded to the fort guarded by only forty-eight men; in which case the Indians would combine their forces and attack the train at some point between Fort Wallace and Beaver Creek.

Looking at these probable events, I not only felt impelled to act promptly to secure the safety of the train and its escort, but a deeper and stronger motive stirred me to leave nothing undone to circumvent the Indians. My wife, who, in answer to my letter, I believed was then at Fort Wallace, would place herself under the protection of the escort of the train and attempt to rejoin me in camp. The mere thought of the danger to which she might be exposed spurred me to decisive action. One full squadron, well mounted and armed, under command of Lieutenant-Colonel Meyers, an officer of great experience in Indian affairs, left our camp at dark on the evening of the day that Captain Hamilton had had this engagement

with the Indians, and set out in the direction
of Fort Wallace.[21] His orders were to press
forward as rapidly as practicable, following
the trail made by the train. Written orders
were sent in his care to Colonel West, who
was in command of that portion of the escort
which had halted at Beaver Creek, to join
Colonel Meyers's command with his own, and
then to continue the march toward Fort
Wallace until he should meet the returning
train and escort. The Indians, however,
were not to be deprived of this opportunity
to secure scalps and plunder.

From our camp to Beaver Creek was
nearly fifty miles. Colonel Meyers marched
his command without halting until he joined
Colonel West at Beaver Creek. Here the
two commands united and under the direction of Colonel West, the senior officer of the
party, proceeded toward Fort Wallace, following the trail left by the wagon train and

[21] Edward Meyers was a native of Germany who enlisted as a private in the First U.S. Dragoon Regiment
in 1857, serving until 1862, by which time he had been
made a first sergeant. He served as a lieutenant throughout the remainder of the war in the same regiment (now
the First U.S. Cavalry) and at its close was brevetted a
lieutenant colonel for gallant and meritorious service
during the war. He was commissioned captain in the
Seventh U.S. Cavalry in July 1866. He died July 11,
1871.

escort. If the escort and Colonel West's forces could be united, they might confidently hope to repel any attack made upon them by Indians. Colonel West was an old Indian fighter and too thoroughly accustomed to Indian tactics to permit his command to be surprised or defeated in any manner other than by a fair contest.

Let us leave them for a time and join the wagon train and its escort—the latter numbering, all told, as before stated, forty-eight men under the immediate command of Lieutenant Robbins. Colonel Cooke, whose special duty connected him with the train and its supplies, could also be relied upon for material assistance with the troops in case of actual conflict with the enemy. Comstock, the favorite scout, a host in himself, was sent to guide the party to and from Fort Wallace. In addition to these were the teamsters, who could not be expected to do more than control their teams should the train be attacked.

The march from camp to Beaver Creek was made without incident. Here the combined forces of Colonel West and Lieutenant Robbins encamped together during the night. Next morning at early dawn Lieutenant Robbins's party, having the train in charge, continued the march toward Fort Wallace, while Colonel West sent out scouting parties up and down the stream to search for Indians.

As yet none of their party were aware of the hostile attitude assumed by the Indians within the past few hours, and Colonel West's instructions contemplated a friendly meeting between his forces and the Indians should the latter be discovered. The march of the train and escort was made to Fort Wallace without interruption. The only incident worthy of remark was an observation of Comstock's, which proved how thoroughly he was familiar with the Indian and his customs.

The escort was moving over a beautifully level plateau. Not a mound or hillock disturbed the evenness of the surface for miles in either direction. To an unpractised eye there seemed no recess or obstruction in or behind which an enemy might be concealed, but everything appeared open to the view for miles and miles, look in what direction one might. Yet such was not the case. Ravines of greater or less extent, though not perceptible at a glance, might have been discovered if searched for, extending almost to the trail over which the party was moving. These ravines, if followed, would be found to grow deeper and deeper, until, after running their course for an indefinite extent, they would terminate in the valley of some running stream.

These were the natural hiding-places of Indian war parties, waiting their opportunities to dash upon unsuspecting victims. These ravines serve the same purpose to the Indians of the timberless plains that the ambush did to those Indians of the eastern states accustomed to fighting in the forests and everglades. Comstock's keen eyes took in all at a glance, and he remarked to Colonel Cooke and Lieutenant Robbins, as the three rode together at the head of the column, that "If the Injuns strike us at all, it will be just about the time we are comin' along back over this very spot. Now mind what I tell ye all." We shall see how correct Comstock's prophecy was.

Arriving at the fort, no time was lost in loading up the wagons with fresh supplies, obtaining the mail intended for the command, and preparing to set out on the return to camp the following day. No late news regarding Indian movements was obtained. Fortunately, my letter from Fort McPherson to Mrs. Custer, asking her to come to Fort Wallace, miscarried, and she did not undertake a journey which in all probability would have imperilled her life, if not terminated it in a most tragic manner.

The Indians Attack

On the following morning Colonel Cooke
and Lieutenant Robbins began their return
march. They had advanced one half the distance which separated them from Colonel
West's camp without the slightest occurrence
to disturb the monotony of their march, and
had reached the point where, on passing before, Comstock had indulged in his prognos-
tication regarding Indians; yet nothing had
been seen to excite suspicion or alarm.

Comstock, always on the alert and with
eyes as quick as those of an Indian, had been
scanning the horizon in all directions. Suddenly he perceived, or thought he perceived,
strange figures resembling human heads peering over the crest of a hill far away to the
right. Hastily levelling his field-glass, he pronounced the strange figures, which were
scarcely perceptible, to be neither more nor
less than Indians. The officers brought into
requisition their glasses, and were soon convinced of the correctness of Comstock's report. It was some time before the Indians
perceived that they were discovered. Concealment then being no longer possible, they
boldly rode to the crest and exposed themselves to full view. At first but twenty or
thirty made their appearance; gradually their
number became augmented, until about a
hundred warriors could be seen.

It may readily be imagined that the appearance of so considerable a body of Indians produced no little excitement and speculation in the minds of the people with the train. The speculation was as to the intentions of the Indians, whether hostile or friendly. Upon this subject all doubts were soon dispelled. The Indians continued to receive accessions to their numbers, the reinforcements coming from beyond the crest of the hill on which their presence was first discovered. Finally, seeming confident in their superior numbers, the warriors, all of whom were mounted, advanced leisurely down the slope leading in the direction of the train and its escort.

By the aid of field-glasses Comstock and the two officers were able to determine fully the character of the party now approaching them. The last doubt was thus removed. It was clearly to be seen that the Indians were arrayed in full war costume, their heads adorned by the brilliantly colored war bonnets, their faces, arms, and bodies painted in various colors, rendering their naturally repulsive appearance even more hideous. As they approached nearer they assumed a certain order in the manner of their advance. Some were to be seen carrying the long glistening lance with its pennant of bright colors;

while upon the left arm hung the round shield, almost bullet-proof, and ornamented with paint and feathers according to the taste of the wearer. Nearly all were armed with carbines and one or two revolvers, while many in addition to these weapons carried the bow and arrow.

When the entire band had defiled down the inclined slope, Comstock and the officers were able to estimate roughly the full strength of the party. They were astonished to perceive that between six and seven hundred warriors were bearing down upon them and in a few minutes would undoubtedly commence the attack. Against such odds, and upon ground so favorable for the Indian mode of warfare it seemed unreasonable to hope for a favorable result. Yet the entire escort, officers and men, entered upon their defense with the determination to sell their lives as dearly as possible.

As the coming engagement, so far as the cavalry was concerned, was to be purely a defensive one, Lieutenant Robbins at once set about preparing to receive his unwelcome visitors. Colonel Cooke formed the train in two parallel columns, leaving ample space between for the horses of the cavalry. Lieutenant Robbins then dismounted his men and prepared to fight on foot. The led horses, under charge of the fourth trooper, were placed between the two columns of wagons, and were thus in a measure protected from the assaults which the officers had every reason to believe would be made for their capture. The dismounted cavalrymen were then formed in a regular circle enclosing the train and horses. Colonel Cooke took command of one flank, Lieutenant Robbins of the other, while Comstock, who as well as the two officers remained mounted, galloped from point to point wherever his presence was most valuable. These dispositions being perfected, the march was resumed in this order, and the attack of the savages calmly awaited.

The Indians, who were interested spectators of these preparations for their reception, continued to approach, but seemed willing to delay their attack until the plain became a little more favorable for their operations. Finally, the desired moment seemed to have arrived. The Indians had approached to within easy range, yet not a shot had been fired, the cavalrymen having been instructed by their officers to reserve their fire for close quarters. Suddenly, with a wild ringing warwhoop, the entire band of warriors bore down upon the train and its little party of defenders.

On came the savages, filling the air with their terrible yells. Their first object, evidently, was to stampede the horses and draft animals of the train; then, in the excitement and consternation which would follow, to massacre the escort and drivers. The wagon-master in immediate charge of the train had been ordered to keep his two columns of wagons constantly moving forward and well closed up. This last injunction was hardly necessary, as the frightened teamsters, glancing at the approaching warriors and hearing their savage shouts, were sufficiently anxious to keep well closed upon their leaders.

The first onslaught of the Indians was made on the flank which was superintended by Colonel Cooke. They rode boldly forward as if to dash over the mere handful of cavalrymen, who stood in skirmishing order in a circle about the train. Not a soldier faltered as the enemy came thundering upon them, but waiting until the Indians· were within short rifle range of the train, the cavalrymen dropped upon their knees, and taking deliberate aim, poured a volley from their Spencer carbines into the ranks of the savages, which seemed to put a sudden check upon the ardor of their movements and forced them to wheel off to the right. Several of the warriors were seen to reel in their saddles, while the ponies of others were brought down or wounded by the effectual fire of the cavalrymen.

My Life on the Plains

Those of the savages who were shot from
their saddles were scarcely permitted to fall
to the ground before a score or more of their
comrades dashed to their rescue and bore
their bodies beyond the possible reach of our
men. This is in accordance with the Indian
custom in battle. They will risk the lives of
a dozen of their best warriors to prevent the
body of any one of their number from falling
into the white man's possession. The reason
for this is the belief, which generally prevails
among all the tribes, that if a warrior loses
his scalp he forfeits his hope of ever reaching
the happy hunting-ground.

As the Indians were being driven back by
the well-directed volley of the cavalrymen,
the latter, overjoyed at their first success,
became reassured and sent up a cheer of
exultation, while Comstock, who had not
been idle in the fight, called out to the re-
treating Indians in their native tongue, taunting them with their unsuccessful assault.

The Indians withdrew to a point beyond
the range of our carbines, and there seemed
to engage in a parley. Comstock, who had
closely watched every movement, remarked
that "There's no sich good luck for us as to
think them Injuns mean to give it up so. Six
hundred red devils ain't agoin' to let fifty
men stop them from gettin' at the coffee and

162

THE ATTACK UPON THE TRAIN.

sugar that is in these wagons. And they ain't agoin' to be satisfied until they get some of our scalps to pay for the bucks we popped out of their saddles a bit ago."

It was probable that the Indians were satisfied that they could not dash through the train and stampede the animals. Their recent attempt had convinced them that some other method of attack must be resorted to. Nothing but their greater superiority in numbers had induced them to risk so much in a charge.

The officers passed along the line of skirmishers—for this in reality was all their line consisted of—and cautioned the men against wasting their ammunition. It was yet early in the afternoon, and should the conflict be prolonged until night, there was great danger of exhausting the supply of ammunition. The Indians seemed to have thought of this, and the change in their method of attack encouraged such a result.

But little time was spent at the parley. Again the entire band of warriors, except those already disabled, prepared to renew the attack and advanced as before—this time, however, with greater caution, evidently desiring to avoid a reception similar to the first. When sufficiently near to the troops the Indians developed their new plan of attack. It

was not to advance *en masse*, as before, but
to fight as individuals, each warrior selecting
his own time and method of attack. This is
the habitual manner of fighting among all
Indians of the Plains, and is termed "circling."
First the chiefs led off, followed at regular
intervals by the warriors, until the entire six
or seven hundred were to be seen riding in
single file as rapidly as their fleet-footed ponies could carry them. Preserving this order
and keeping up their savage chorus of yells,
war-whoops, and taunting epithets, this long
line of mounted barbarians was guided in
such manner as to envelop the train and
escort, and make the latter appear like a
small circle within a larger one.

The Indians gradually contracted their circle, although maintaining the full speed of
their ponies, until sufficiently close to open
fire upon the soldiers. At first the shots were
scattering and wide of their mark; but, emboldened by the silence of their few but determined opponents, they rode nearer and
fought with greater impetuosity. Forced now
to defend themselves to the uttermost, the
cavalrymen opened fire from their carbines
with most gratifying results. The Indians,
however, moving at such a rapid gait and in
single file, presented a most uncertain target.
To add to this uncertainty the savages availed

themselves of their superior—almost marvellous—powers of horsemanship. Throwing themselves upon the sides of their well-trained ponies, they left no part of their persons exposed to the aim of the troopers except the head and one foot, and in this posture they were able to aim the weapons either over or under the necks of their ponies, thus using the bodies of the latter as an effective shield against the bullets of their adversaries.

At no time were the Indians able to force the train and its escort to come to a halt. The march was continued at an uninterrupted gait. This successful defense against the Indians was in a great measure due to the presence of the wagons, which, arranged in the order described, formed a complete barrier to the charges and assaults of the savages; and as a last resort the wagons could have been halted and used as a breastwork, behind which the cavalry, dismounted, would have been almost invincible against their more numerous enemies. There is nothing an Indian dislikes more in warfare than to attack a foe, however weak, behind breastworks of any kind. Any contrivance which is an obstacle to his pony is a most serious obstacle to the warrior.

The attack of the Indians, aggravated by their losses in warriors and ponies, as many

166

of the latter had been shot down, was continued without cessation for three hours. The supply of ammunition of the cavalry was running low. The "fourth troopers," who had remained in charge of the led horses between the two columns of wagons, were now replaced from the skirmishers, and the former were added to the list of active combatants. If the Indians should maintain the fight much longer, there was serious ground for apprehension regarding the limited supply of ammunition.

If only night or reinforcements would come! was the prayerful hope of those who contended so gallantly against such heavy odds. Night was still too far off to promise much encouragement; while as to reinforcements, their coming would be purely accidental—at least so argued those most interested in their arrival. Yet reinforcements were at that moment striving to reach them. Comrades were in the saddle and spurring forward to their relief. The Indians, although apparently turning all their attention to the little band inside, had omitted no precaution to guard against interference from outside parties. In this instance, perhaps, they were more·than ordinarily watchful, and had posted some of their keen-eyed warriors on the high line of bluffs which ran almost parallel to the trail over which the combatants moved. From these bluffs not only a good view of the fight could be obtained, but the country for miles in either direction was spread out beneath them; and enabled the scouts to discern the approach of any hostile party which might be advancing. Fortunate for the savages that this precaution had not been neglected, or the contest in which they were engaged might have become one of more equal numbers. To the careless eye nothing could have been seen to excite suspicion. But the warriors on the lookout were not long in discovering something which occasioned them no little anxiety. Dismounting from their ponies and concealing the latter in a ravine, they prepared to investigate more fully the cause of their alarm.

That which they saw was as yet but a faint dark line on the surface of the plain, almost against the horizon. So faint was it that no one but an Indian or practised frontiersman would have observed it. It was fully ten miles from them and directly in their line of march. The ordinary observer would have pronounced it a break or irregularity in the ground, or perhaps the shadow of a cloud, and its apparent permanency of location would have dispelled any fear as to its dangerous character. But was it stationary?

Apparently, yes. The Indians discovered otherwise. By close watching, the long faint line could be seen moving along, as if creeping stealthily upon an unconscious foe. Slowly it assumed a more definite shape, until what appeared to be a mere stationary dark line drawn upon the green surface of the plain developed itself to the searching eyes of the red man into a column of cavalry moving at a rapid gait toward the very point they were then occupying.

Convinced of this fact, one of the scouts leaped upon his pony and flew with almost the speed of the wind to impart this knowledge to the chiefs in command on the plain below. True, the approaching cavalry, being still several miles distant, could not arrive for nearly two hours; but the question to be considered by the Indians was, whether it would be prudent for them to continue their attack on the train—their ponies already becoming exhausted by the three hours' hard riding given them—until the arrival of the fresh detachment of the enemy, whose horses might be in condition favorable to a rapid pursuit, and thereby enable them to overtake those of the Indians whose ponies were exhausted. Unwilling to incur this new risk, and seeing no prospect of overcoming their present adversaries by a sudden or combined dash, the chiefs decided to withdraw from the attack and make their escape while the advantage was yet in their favor. The surprise of the cavalrymen may be imagined at seeing the Indians, after pouring a shower of bullets and arrows into the train, withdraw to the bluffs, and immediately after continue their retreat until lost to view.

This victory for the troopers, although so unexpected, was none the less welcome. The Indians contrived to carry away with them their killed and wounded. Five of their bravest warriors were known to have been sent to the happy hunting-ground, while the list of their wounded was much larger. After the Indians had withdrawn and left the cavalrymen masters of the field, our wounded, of whom there were comparatively few, received every possible care and attention. Those of the detachment who had escaped unharmed were busily engaged in exchanging congratulations and relating incidents of the fight.

In this manner nearly an hour had been whiled away when far in the distance, in their immediate front, fresh cause for anxiety was discovered. At first the general opinion was that it was the Indians again, determined to contest their progress. Field-glasses were again called into requisition, and revealed not Indians, but the familiar blue blouses of the cavalry. Never was the sight more welcome. The next moment Colonel Cooke, with Comstock and a few troopers, applied spurs to their horses and were soon dashing forward to meet their comrades.

The approaching party was none other than Colonel West's detachment, hastening to the relief of the train and its gallant little escort. A few words explained all, and told the heroes of the recent fight how it happened that reinforcements were sent to their assistance; and then was explained why the Indians had so suddenly concluded to abandon their attack and seek safety in quietly withdrawing from the field.

Chapter 7

WHITE DESERTERS AND RED MASSACRE

ON the morning of the 28th the train with its escort returned to the main camp on the Republican. All were proud of the conduct of those detachments of the command which had been brought into actual conflict with the Indians. The heroes of the late fights were congratulated heartily upon their good luck, while their comrades who had unavoidably remained in camp consoled themselves with the hope that the next opportunity might be theirs.

The despatches brought by Major Elliot from General Sherman directed me to continue my march, as had been suggested, up the North Republican, then strike northward and reach the Platte again at some point west of Fort Sedgwick, near Riverside Station. This program was carried out. Leaving our camp on the Republican, we marched up the north fork of that river about sixty miles, then turned nearly due north, and marched for the valley of the Platte.

The only incident connected with this march was the painful journey under a burning July sun of sixty-five miles, without a drop of water for our horses or draft animals. This march was necessarily effected in one day, and produced untold suffering among the poor dumb brutes. Many of the dogs accompanying the command died from thirst and exhaustion. When the sun went down we were still many miles from the Platte. The moon, which was nearly full at the time, lighted us on our weary way for some time; but even this was only an aggravation, as it enabled us from the high bluffs bordering the Platte Valley to see the river flowing beneath us, yet many miles beyond our reach.

Taking Lieutenant Moylan,[22] Dr. Coates, and one attendant with me and leaving the

[22] Myles Moylan entered the regular army as a private soldier in 1857. Dismissed, with the rank of second lieutenant, in October, 1863 he enlisted as a private in the Fourth Massachusetts Cavalry under the name of Charles E. Thomas and attained the rank of captain and brevet major before the close of the war. He again enlisted as a private in the Seventh U.S. Cavalry in January, 1866, attaining the rank of lieutenant in July, 1866 and captain in 1872. He subsequently became major of the Tenth Cavalry. In November, 1894 he was awarded a medal of honor for gallantry in the Bear Paw Mountain action against the Nez Percé's, September 30, 1877, in which he was severely wounded. Van De Water, who is decidedly critical of Custer, states (*Glory Hunter*, 155) that the bachelor officers' mess refused to admit Moy-

command under temporary charge of Major Elliot, I pushed on, intending after arriving at the river to select as good camping ground as the darkness and circumstances would permit. We then imagined ourselves within four or five miles of the river, so near did it appear to us. Mile after mile was traversed by our tired horses, yet we apparently arrived no nearer our journey's end. At last, at about eleven o'clock, and after having ridden at a brisk rate for nearly fifteen miles, we reached the river bank. Our first act was to improve the opportunity to quench our thirst and that of our horses.

Considering the lateness of the hour and the distance we had ridden since leaving the command, it was idle to expect the latter to reach the river before daylight. Nothing was left to us but to bivouac for the night. This we did by selecting a beautiful piece of sward on the river bank for our couch, and taking our saddle blankets for covering and our saddles for pillows. Each of us attached his horse by the halter-strap to the hilt of his

lan, a former private soldier, and Custer, on learning of this, invited him to become a boarder in his own home and made him his adjutant. In view of Moylan's record, as cited above, it seems possible that some other reason may have been responsible for his exclusion from the mess.

saber, then forced the saber firmly into the
ground. Both horses and riders were weary
as well as hungry. At first the horses grazed
upon the fresh green pasture which grew
luxuriantly on the river bank, but fatigue,
more powerful than hunger, soon claimed
the mastery and in a few minutes our little
group, horses and men, were wrapped in the
sweetest of slumber. Had we known that
the Indians were then engaged in murdering
men within a few minutes' ride of where we
slept, and that when we awakened in the
morning it would be to still find ourselves
away from the command, our sleep would
not have been so undisturbed.

Daylight was beginning to make its appearance in the east when our little party of
slumbering troopers began to arouse themselves. Those unfortunate persons who have
always been accustomed to the easy comforts of civilization, and who have never
known what real fatigue or hunger is, cannot
realize or appreciate the blissful luxury of a
sleep which follows a day's ride in the saddle
of half a hundred miles or more.

Being the first to awake, I rose to a sitting
posture and took a hasty survey of our situation. Within a few feet of us flowed the
Platte River. Our group, horses and men,
presented an interesting subject for a paint-

er. To my surprise I discovered that a heavy shower of rain had fallen during the night, but so deep had been our slumber that even the rain had failed to disturb us. Each one of the party had spread his saddle blanket on the ground to serve as his couch, while for covering we had called into requisition the india-rubber poncho or rubber blanket which invariably forms an important part of the Plainsman's outfit. The rain, without awakening any of the party, had aroused them sufficiently to cause each one to pull his rubber blanket over his face and thus protected he continued his repose. The appearance presented by this somber-looking group of sleepers strongly reminded me of scenes during the war when, after a battle, the bodies of the slain had been collected for burial.

But this was no time to indulge in idle reveries. Arousing my comrades, we set about discovering the circumstances of our situation. First, the duties of a hasty toilet were attended to. Nothing, however, could be more simple. As we had slept in our clothes, top boots and all, we had so much less to attend to. The river flowing at our feet afforded a lavatory which, if not complete in its appointments, was sufficiently grand in its extent to satisfy every want.

Deserters and Massacres

It was now becoming sufficiently light to enable us to see indistinctly for almost a mile in either direction, yet our eyes failed to reveal to us any evidence of the presence of the command. Here was fresh cause for anxiety, not only as to our own situation, but as to the whereabouts of the troops. Saddling up our horses, each person acting as his own groom, we awaited the clearing away of the morning mist to seek the main body. We had not long to wait. The light was soon sufficient to enable us to scan the country with our field-glasses in all directions. Much to our joy we discovered the bivouac of the troops about three miles down the river. A brisk gallop soon placed us where we desired to be and a few words explained how, in the darkness, the column had failed to follow us, but instead had headed for the river at a point below us, a portion not reaching the bank until near morning.

Breakfast disposed of, the next question was to ascertain our exact location and distance from the nearest telegraph station. Fortunately Riverside Station was near our camp, and from there we ascertained that we were then about fifty miles west of Fort Sedgwick. The party obtaining this information also learned that the Indians had attacked the nearest stage station west of camp the preceding evening and killed three men. This station was only a few minutes' ride from the point on the river bank where myself and comrades had passed the night in such fancied security.

Believing that General Sherman must have sent later instructions for me to Fort Sedgwick than those last received from him, I sent a telegram to the officer in command at the fort, making inquiry to that effect. To my surprise I received a despatch saying that the day after the departure of Major Elliot and his detachment from Fort Sedgwick with despatches, of which mention has been previously made, a second detachment of equal strength, viz., ten troopers of the Second United States Cavalry, under command of Lieutenant Kidder and guided by a famous Sioux chief Red Bead, had left Fort Sedgwick with important despatches for me from General Sherman, and that Lieutenant Kidder had been directed to proceed to my camp near the forks of the Republican, and failing to find me there he was to follow rapidly on my trail until he should overtake my command. I immediately telegraphed to Fort Sedgwick that nothing had been seen or heard of Lieutenant Kidder's detachment, and requested a copy of the despatches borne by him to be sent me by telegraph. This was done; the instructions of General Sherman were for me to march my command, as was at first contemplated, across the country from the Platte to the Smoky Hill River, striking the latter at Fort Wallace. Owing to the low state of my supplies, I determined to set out for Fort Wallace at daylight next morning.

Great anxiety prevailed throughout the command concerning Lieutenant Kidder and his party. True, he had precisely the same number of men that composed Major Elliot's detachment when the latter went upon a like mission, but the circumstances which would govern in the one case had changed when applied to the other. Major Elliot, an officer of experience and good judgment, had fixed the strength of his escort and performed the journey before it was positively known that the Indians in that section had entered upon the war path. Had the attack on the commands of Hamilton, Robbins, and Cooke been made prior to Elliot's departure, the latter would have taken not less than fifty troopers as escort.

After an informal interchange of opinions between the officers of my command regarding the whereabouts of Lieutenant Kidder and party, we endeavored to satisfy ourselves with the following explanation. Using

179

the capital letter Y for illustration, let us
locate Fort Sedgwick, from which post Lieutenant Kidder was sent with despatches, at
the right upper point of the letter. The camp
of my command at the forks of the Republican would be at the junction of the three
branches of the letter. Fort Wallace rela-
tively would be at the lower termination, and
the point on the Platte at which my command was located the morning referred to
would be at the upper termination of the
left branch of the letter. Robbins and Cooke,
in going with the train to Wallace for supplies, had passed and returned over the lower
branch. After their return and that of Major Elliot and his party my entire command
resumed the march for the Platte. We
moved for two or three miles out on the
heavy wagon trail of Robbins and Cooke,
then suddenly changed our direction to the
right. It was supposed that Kidder and his
party arrived at our deserted camp at the
forks of the Republican about nightfall, but
finding us gone had determined to avail
themselves of the moonlit night and overtake us before we should break camp next
morning. Riding rapidly in the dim light of
evening, they had failed to observe the point
at which we had diverged from the plainer
trail of Robbins and Cooke, and instead of

following our trail had continued on the former in the direction of Fort Wallace. Such seemed to be a plausible if not the only solution capable of being given.

Anxiety for the fate of Kidder and his party was one of the reasons impelling me to set out promptly on my return. From our camp at the forks of the Republican to Fort Wallace was about eighty miles—but eighty miles of the most dangerous country infested by Indians. Remembering the terrible contest in which the command of Robbins and Cooke had been engaged on this very route within a few days, and knowing that the Indians would in all probability maintain a strict watch over the trail to surprise any small party which might venture over it, I felt in the highest degree solicitous for the safety of Lieutenant Kidder and party. Even if he succeeded in reaching Fort Wallace unmolested there was reason to apprehend that, impressed with the importance of delivering his despatches promptly, he would set out on his return at once and endeavor to find my command.

Let us leave him and his detachment for a brief interval, and return to events which were more immediately connected with my command, and which bear a somewhat tragic as well as personal interest.

In a previous chapter reference has been made to the state of dissatisfaction which had made its appearance among the enlisted men. This state of feeling had been principally superinduced by inferior and insufficient rations, a fault for which no one connected with the troops in the field was responsible, but which was chargeable to persons far removed from the theater of our movements, persons connected with the supply departments of the army. Added to this internal source of disquiet, we were then on the main line of overland travel to some of our most valuable and lately discovered mining regions. The opportunity to obtain marvellous wages as miners and the prospect of amassing sudden wealth proved a temptation sufficiently strong to make many of the men forget their sworn obligations to their government and their duties as soldiers. Forgetting for the moment that the command to which they belonged was actually engaged in war and was in a country infested with armed bodies of the enemy, and that the legal penalty of desertion under such circumstances was death, many of the men formed a combination to desert their colors and escape to the mines.

The first intimation received by any person in authority of the existence of this plot was on the morning fixed for our departure from the Platte. Orders had been issued the previous evening for the command to march at daylight. Upwards of forty men were reported as having deserted during the night. There was no time to send parties in pursuit, or the capture and return of a portion of them might have been effected.

The command marched southward at daylight. At noon, having marched fifteen miles, we halted to rest and graze the horses for one hour. The men believed that the halt was made for the remainder of the day, and here a plan was perfected among the disaffected by which upwards of one third of the effective strength of the command was to seize their horses and arms during the night and escape to the mountains. Had the conspirators succeeded in putting this plan into execution it would have been difficult to say how serious the consequences might be, or whether enough true men would remain to render the march to Fort Wallace practicable. Fortunately it was decided to continue the march some fifteen miles farther before night. The necessary orders were given and everything was being repacked for the march when attention was called to thirteen soldiers who were then to be seen rapidly leaving camp in the direction from which we had marched. Seven of these were mounted and were moving off at a rapid gallop; the remaining six were dismounted, not having been so fortunate as their fellows in procuring horses. The entire party were still within sound of the bugle, but no orders by bugle note or otherwise served to check or diminish their flight. The boldness of this attempt at desertion took every one by surprise. Such an occurrence as enlisted men deserting in broad daylight and under the immediate eyes of their officers had never been heard of. With the exception of the horses of the guard and a few belonging to the officers, all others were still grazing and unsaddled. The officer of the guard was directed to mount his command promptly, and if possible overtake the deserters. At the same time those of the officers whose horses were in readiness were also directed to join in the pursuit and leave no effort untried to prevent the escape of a single malcontent. In giving each party sent in pursuit instructions, there was no limit fixed to the measures which they were authorized to adopt in executing their orders. This, unfortunately, was an emergency which involved the safety of the entire command, and required treatment of the most summary character.[23]

[23] Upon this situation some of the sharpest criticism of General Custer centers. His narrative naturally presents his own view of his conduct. To the bad food and

Deserters and Massacres

It was found impossible to overtake that portion of the party which was mounted, as it was afterwards learned that they had selected seven of the fleetest horses in the command. Those on foot, when discovering themselves pursued, increased their speed, but a chase of a couple of miles brought the pursuers within hailing distance.

Major Elliot, the senior officer participating in the pursuit, called out to the deserters to halt and surrender. This command was several times repeated, but without effect. Finally, seeing the hopelessness of further flight, the deserters came to bay, and to Major Elliot's renewed demand to throw down their arms and surrender, the ring-

other causes of discontent felt by the soldiers may properly be added the superhuman, if not inhuman, march to which they had just been subjected. The statement that "no limit" was fixed to the measures the officers in pursuit of the deserters might adopt is an understatement. Custer himself wrote to his wife on June 8, 1867: "I directed Major Elliot and Lts. Custer, Cook, and Jackson, with a few of the guard, to pursue the deserters who were still visible, though more than a mile distant, and to bring the dead bodies of as many as could be taken back to camp." Marguerite Merington, *The Custer Story* (New York, 1950), 205–06. The court martial which tried him two months later found him guilty on seven charges, one of them that he had ordered his subordinate officers to pursue the deserters and bring none back alive.

leader drew up his carbine to fire upon his pursuers. This was the signal for the latter to open fire, which they did successfully, bringing down three of the deserters, although, two of them were worse frightened than hurt.[24]

Rejoining the command with their six captive deserters, the pursuing party reported their inability to overtake those who had deserted on horseback. The march was resumed and continued until near nightfall, by which time we had placed thirty miles between us and our last camp on the Platte. While on the march during the day a trusty sergeant, one who had served as a soldier long and faithfully, imparted the first information which could be relied upon as to the plot which had been formed by the malcontents to desert in a body. The following night had been selected as the time for making the attempt. The best horses and arms in the command were to be seized and taken away. I believed that the summary action adopted during the day would intimidate any who might still be contemplating desertion, and was confident that another day's march would place us so far in a hostile and danger-

[24] One of the six men on foot was killed and two were wounded. The three remaining threw themselves down and by feigning death escaped being shot.

ous country that the risk of encountering war parties of Indians would of itself serve to deter any but large numbers from attempting to make their way back to the settlements. To bridge the following night in safety was the next problem. While there was undoubtedly a large proportion of the men who could be fully relied upon to remain true to their obligations and to render any support to their officers which might be demanded, yet the great difficulty at this time, owing to the sudden development of the plot, was to determine who could be trusted.

This difficulty was solved by placing every officer in the command on guard during the entire night. The men were assembled as usual for roll-call at tattoo, and then notified that every man must be in his tent at the signal "taps," which would be sounded half an hour later; that their company officers, fully armed, would walk the company streets during the entire night, and any man appearing outside the limits of his tent between the hours of taps and reveille would do so at the risk of being fired upon after being once hailed.

The night passed without disturbance, and daylight found us in the saddle and pursuing our line of march toward Fort Wallace. It is proper to here record the fact that from that date onward desertion from that command during the continuance of the expedition was never attempted. It may become necessary in order to perfect the record, borrowing a term from the War Department, to refer in a subsequent chapter to certain personal and official events which resulted partially from the foregoing occurrences.

Let us now turn our attention to Lieutenant Kidder and his detachment. The third night after leaving the Platte my command encamped in the vicinity of our former camp near the forks of the Republican. So far nothing had been learned which would enable us to form any conclusion regarding the route taken by Kidder. Comstock, the guide, was frequently appealed to for an opinion which, from his great experience on the Plains, might give us some encouragement regarding Kidder's safety. But he was too cautious and careful a man, both in word and deed, to excite hopes which his reasoning could not justify. When thus appealed to he would usually give an ominous shake of the head and avoid a direct answer.

On the evening just referred to, the officers and Comstock were grouped near headquarters discussing the subject which was then uppermost in the mind of every one in camp.

Comstock had been quietly listening to the various theories and surmises advanced by different members of the group, but was finally pressed to state his ideas as to Kidder's chances of escaping harm.

"Well, gentle*men*," emphasizing the last syllable as was his manner, "before a man kin form any ijee as to how this thing is likely to end, thar are several things he ort to be acquainted with. For instance, now, no man need tell me any p'ints about Injuns. Ef I know anything, it's Injuns. I know jest how they'll do anything and when they'll take to do it; but that don't settle the question, and I'll tell you why. Ef I knowed this young lootenint—I mean Lootenint Kidder—ef I knowed what for sort of a man he is, I could tell you mighty near to a sartainty all you want to know; for you see Injun huntin' and Injun fightin' is a trade all by itself, and like any other bizness a man has to know what he's about, or ef he don't he can't make a livin' at it. I have lots uv confi*dence* in the fightin' sense of Red Bead the Sioux chief, who is guidin' the lootenint and his men, and ef that Injun kin have his own way thar is a fair show for his guidin' 'em through all right; but as I sed before, there lays the difficulty. Is this lootenint the kind of a man who is willin' to take advice, even ef it does

cum from an Injun? My experience with
you army folks has allus bin that the youngsters among ye think they know the most,
and this is particularly true ef they hev just
cum from West P'int. Ef some of them
young fellars knowed half as much as they
b'lieve they do, you couldn't tell them
nothin'. As to rale book-larnin', why I 'spose
they've got it all; but the fact uv the matter
is, they couldn't tell the difference twixt the
trail of a war party and one made by a
huntin' party to save their necks. Half uv
'em when they first cum here can't tell a
squaw from a buck, just because both ride
straddle; but they soon larn. But that's
neither here nor thar. I'm told that the
lootenint we're talkin' about is a new-comer
and that this is his first scout. Ef that be
the case it puts a mighty onsartain look on
the whole thing, and twixt you and me, gentle*men*, he'll be mighty lucky ef he gits
through all right. To-morrow we'll strike
the Wallace trail and I kin mighty soon tell
ef he has gone that way."

But little encouragement was to be derived from these expressions. The morrow
would undoubtedly enable us, as Comstock
had predicted, to determine whether or not
the lieutenant and his party had missed our
trail and taken that leading to Fort Wallace.

Deserters and Massacres

At daylight our column could have been seen stretching out in the direction of the Wallace trail. A march of a few miles brought us to the point of intersection. Comstock and the Delawares had galloped in advance, and were about concluding a thorough examination of the various tracks to be seen in the trail, when the head of the column overtook them. "Well, what do you find, Comstock?" was my first inquiry. "They've gone toward Fort Wallace, sure," was the reply; and in support of this opinion he added, "The trail shows that twelve American horses, shod all round, have passed at a walk, goin' in the direction of the fort; and when they went by this p'int they were all right, because their horses were movin' along easy and there are no pony tracks behind 'em, as wouldn't be the case ef the Injuns had got an eye on 'em." He then remarked, as if in parenthesis, "It would be astonishin' ef that lootenint and his lay-out gits into the fort without a scrimmage. He may; but ef he does, it will be a scratch ef ever there was one, and I'll lose my confidence in Injuns."

The opinion expressed by Comstock as to the chances of Lieutenant Kidder and party making their way to the fort across eighty miles of danger unmolested was the concur-

rent opinion of all the officers. And now that
we had discovered their trail, our interest and
anxiety became immeasurably increased as
to their fate. The latter could not remain in
doubt much longer, as two days' marching
would take us to the fort. Alas! we were to
solve the mystery without waiting so long.

Pursuing our way along the plain, heavy
trail made by Robbins and Cooke, and directing Comstock and the Delawares to
watch closely that we did not lose that of
Kidder and his party, we patiently but hopefully awaited further developments. How
many miles we had thus passed over without
incident worthy of mention, I do not now
recall. The sun was high in the heavens,
showing that our day's march was about half
completed, when those of us who were riding
at the head of the column discovered a
strange-looking object lying directly in our
path, and more than a mile distant. It was
too large for a human being, yet in color and
appearance, at that distance, resembled no
animal frequenting the Plains with which
any of us were familiar. Eager to determine
its character, a dozen or more of our party,
including Comstock and some of the Delawares, galloped in front.

Before riding the full distance the question
was determined. The object seen was the

body of a white horse. A closer examination showed that it had been shot within the past few days, while the brand, U. S., proved that it was a government animal. Major Elliot then remembered that while at Fort Sedgwick he had seen one company of cavalry mounted upon white horses. These and other circumstances went far to convince us that this was one of the horses belonging to Lieutenant Kidder's party. In fact there was no room to doubt that this was the case.

Almost the unanimous opinion of the command was that there had been a contest with Indians, and this only the first evidence we should have proving it. When the column reached the point where the slain horse lay, a halt was ordered to enable Comstock and the Indian scouts to thoroughly examine the surrounding ground to discover, if possible, any additional evidence, such as empty cartridge shells, arrows, or articles of Indian equipment, showing that a fight had taken place. All the horse's equipments, saddle, bridle, etc. had been carried away, but whether by friend or foe could not then be determined. While the preponderance of circumstances favored the belief that the horse had been killed by Indians there was still room to hope that he had been killed by Kidder's party and the equipments taken

193

away by them; for it frequently happens on a march that a horse will be suddenly taken ill and be unable for the time being to proceed farther. In such a case, rather than abandon him alive, with a prospect of his recovering and falling into the hands of the Indians to be employed against us, orders are given to kill him, and this might be the true way of accounting for the one referred to.

The scouts being unable to throw any additional light upon the question, we continued our march, closely observing the ground as we passed along. Comstock noticed that instead of the trail showing that Kidder's party was moving in regular order, as when at first discovered, there were but two or three tracks to be seen in the beaten trail, the rest being found on the grass on either side.

We had marched two miles perhaps from the point where the body of the slain horse had been discovered, when we came upon a second, this one, like the first, having been killed by a bullet, and all of his equipments taken away. Comstock's quick eyes were not long in detecting pony tracks in the vicinity, and we had no longer any but the one frightful solution to offer: Kidder and his party had been discovered by the Indians, probably the same powerful and blood-

thirsty band which had been resisted so gallantly by the men under Robbins and Cooke;
and against such overwhelming odds the issue
could not be doubtful.

We were then moving over a high and level plateau unbroken either by ravines or di-
vides, and just such a locality as would be
usually chosen by the Indians for attacking
a party of the strength of Kidder's. The
Indians could here ride unobstructed and
encircle their victims with a continuous line
of armed and painted warriors, while the
beleaguered party, from the even character
of the surface of the plain, would be unable
to find any break or depression from behind
which they might make a successful defense.
It was probably this relative condition of
affairs which had induced Kidder and his
doomed comrades to endeavor to push on in
the hope of finding ground favorable to their
making a stand against their barbarous foes.

The main trail no longer showed the footprints of Kidder's party, but instead Comstock discovered the tracks of shod horses on
the grass, with here and there numerous
tracks of ponies, all by their appearance
proving that both horses and ponies had
been moving at full speed. Kidder's party
must have trusted their lives temporarily to
the speed of their horses—a dangerous ven-

ture when contending with Indians. However, this fearful race for life must have been
most gallantly contested, because we continued our march several miles farther without discovering any evidence of the savages
having gained any advantage.

How painfully, almost despairingly exciting must have been this ride for life! A mere
handful of brave men struggling to escape
the bloody clutches of the hundreds of red-
visaged demons, who, mounted on their
well-trained war ponies, were straining every
nerve and muscle to reek their hands in the
life-blood of their victims. It was not death
alone that threatened this little band. They
were not riding simply to preserve life. They
rode, and doubtless prayed as they rode,
that they might escape the savage tortures,
the worse than death which threatened
them. Would that their prayer had been
granted!

We began leaving the high plateau and to
descend into a valley through which, at the
distance of nearly two miles, meandered a
small prairie stream known as Beaver Creek.
The valley near the banks of this stream was
covered with a dense growth of tall wild
grass intermingled with clumps of osiers. At
the point where the trail crossed the stream
we hoped to obtain more definite informa-

tion regarding Kidder's party and their pursuers, but we were not required to wait so
long. When within a mile of the stream I
observed several large buzzards floating lazily in circles through the air, and but a short
distance to the left of our trail. This, of
itself, might not have attracted my attention
seriously but for the rank stench which per-
vaded the atmosphere, reminding one of the
horrible sensations experienced upon a battle-field when passing among the decaying
bodies of the dead.

As if impelled by one thought Comstock,
the Delawares, and half-a-dozen officers detached themselves from the column and separating into squads of one or two instituted
a search for the cause of our horrible suspicions. After riding in all directions through
the rushes and willows, and when about to
relinquish the search as fruitless, one of the
Delawares uttered a shout which attracted
the attention of the entire command; at the
same time he was seen to leap from his horse
and assume a stooping posture, as if critically
examining some object of interest. Hastening, in common with many others of the
party, to his side, a sight met our gaze which
even at this remote day makes my very
blood curdle. Lying in irregular order, and
within a very limited circle, were the man-

gled bodies of poor Kidder and his party, yet
so brutally hacked and disfigured as to be
beyond recognition save as human beings.

Every individual of the party had been
scalped and his skull broken—the latter done
by some weapon, probably a tomahawk—
except the Sioux chief Red Bead, whose
scalp had simply been removed from his
head and then thrown down by his side.
This, Comstock informed us, was in accordance with a custom which prohibits an Indian from bearing off the scalp of one of his
own tribe. This circumstance, then, told us
who the perpetrators of this deed were. They
could be none other than the Sioux, led in all
probability by Pawnee Killer.

Red Bead, being less disfigured and mutilated than the others, was the only individual capable of being recognized. Even
the clothes of all the party had been carried
away; some of the bodies were lying in beds
of ashes, with partly burned fragments of
wood near them, showing that the savages
had put some of them to death by the terrible tortures of fire. The sinews of the arms
and legs had been cut away, the nose of
every man hacked off, and the features
otherwise defaced so that it would have been
scarcely possible for even a relative to recognize a single one of the unfortunate victims.

THE KIDDER MASSACRE

We could not even distinguish the officer from his men. Each body was pierced by from twenty to fifty arrows, and the arrows were found as the savage demons had left them, bristling in the bodies. While the details of that fearful struggle will probably never be known, telling how long and gallantly this ill-fated little band contended for their lives, yet the surrounding circumstances of ground, empty cartridge shells, and distance from where the attack began, satisfied us that Kidder and his men fought as only brave men fight when the watchword is victory or death.

As the officer, his men, and his no less faithful Indian guide had shared their final dangers together and had met the same dreadful fate at the hands of the same merciless foe, it was but fitting that their remains should be consigned to one common grave. This was accordingly done. A single trench was dug near the spot where they had rendered up their lives upon the altar of duty. Silently, mournfully, their comrades of a brother regiment consigned their mangled remains to mother earth, there to rest undisturbed, as we supposed, until the great day of final review. But this was not to be so; while the closest scrutiny on our part had been insufficient to enable us to detect the slightest evidence which would aid us or others in identifying the body of Lieutenant Kidder or any of his men, it will be seen hereafter how the marks of a mother's thoughtful affection were to be the means of identifying the remains of her murdered son, even though months had elapsed after his untimely death.[25]

On the evening of the day following that upon which we had consigned the remains of Lieutenant Kidder and his party to their humble restingplace, the command reached Fort Wallace on the Smoky Hill route. From the occupants of the fort we learned much that was interesting regarding events which

[25] The story of the identification of Lieutenant Kidder's body is told in one of the *Galaxy* articles which is not reprinted in the present volume. In the late autumn of 1867 Kidder's father came to Custer at Fort Leavenworth seeking to learn where his son had been buried and to obtain a military escort to recover the body for removal to the home of his parents in Dakota. Custer told the father it was impossible to identify the body of his son. In response to his eager inquiries, however, Custer recalled that one of the naked corpses retained the collar band of a black and white shirt. The father stated that upon leaving home for the army Kidder's mother had provided him with several shirts made of this material. Acting upon this clue, the bodies of the massacred party were disinterred and the remains of Lieutenant Kidder were identified and reclaimed by the parent.

had transpired during our isolation from all points of communication. The Indians had attacked the fort twice within the past few days, in both of which engagements men were killed on each side. The fighting on our side was principally under the command of Colonel Barnitz,[26] whose forces were composed of detachments of the Seventh Cavalry. The fighting occurred on the level plain near the fort, where, owing to the favorable character of the ground, the Indians had ample opportunity to display their prowess both as warriors and horsemen.

One incident of the fight was related, which, its correctness being vouched for, is worthy of being here repeated. Both parties were mounted and the fighting consisted principally of charges and countercharges, the combatants of both sides becoming at times mingled with each other. During one of these attacks a bugler boy belonging to the cavalry was shot from his horse; before any of his comrades could reach him a powerfully built warrior, superbly mounted on a

[26] Captain Albert Barnitz enlisted in the First Ohio Cavalry at the beginning of the Civil War and won his promotions through sheer merit and bravery. Wounded in the battle of the Washita—at first believed fatally—on November 27, 1868, he was placed on the retired list. He died in 1912. He was a man of literary tastes and the author of a volume of poems.

war pony was seen to dash at full speed toward the spot where the dying bugler lay. Scarcely checking the speed of his pony, who seemed to divine his rider's wishes, the warrior grasped the pony's mane with one hand and, stooping low as he neared the bugler, seized the latter with the other hand and lifted him from the earth, placing him across his pony in front of him. Still maintaining the full speed of his pony, he was seen to retain the body of the bugler but a moment, then cast it to the earth. The Indians being routed soon after and driven from the field, our troops, many of whom had witnessed the strange and daring action of the warrior, recovered possession of the dead, when the mystery became solved. The bugler had been scalped.

Our arrival at Fort Wallace was most welcome as well as opportune. The Indians had become so active and numerous that all travel over the Smoky Hill route had ceased; stages had been taken off the route, and many of the stage stations had been abandoned by the employees, the latter fearing a repetition of the Lookout Station massacre. No despatches or mail had been received at the fort for a considerable period, so that the occupants might well have been considered as undergoing a state of siege. Added to these embarrassments, which were partly unavoidable, an additional and under the circumstances a more frightful danger stared the troops in the face. We were over two hundred miles from the terminus of the railroad over which our supplies were drawn, and a still greater distance from the main dépôts of supplies. It was found that the reserve of stores at the post was well-nigh exhausted, and the commanding officer reported that he knew of no fresh supplies being on the way. It is difficult to account for such a condition of affairs. Some one must surely have been at fault; but it is not important here to determine who or where the parties were The officer commanding the troops in my absence reported officially to headquarters that the bulk of the provisions issued to his men consisted of rotten bacon and hard bread that was no better. Cholera made its appearance among the men, and deaths occurred daily. The same officer, in officially commenting upon the character of the provisions issued to the troops, added: "The low state of vitality in the men, resulting from the long confinement to this scanty and unwholesome food, will, I think, account for the great mortality among the cholera cases;... and I believe that unless we can obtain a more abundant and better

supply of rations than we have had, it will
be impossible to check this fearful epidemic."

I decided to select upward of a hundred of
the best mounted men in my command and
with this force open a way through to Fort
Harker, a distance of two hundred miles,
where I expected to obtain abundant supplies; from which point the latter could be
conducted, well protected against Indians by
my detachment, back to Fort Wallace. Owing to the severe marching of the past few
weeks, the horses of the command were generally in an unfit condition for further service without rest. So that after selecting upward of a hundred of the best, the remainder
might for the time be regarded as unservice-
able; such they were in fact. There was no
idea or probability that the portion of the
command to remain in camp near Fort Wallace would be called upon to do anything but
rest and recuperate from their late marches.
It was certainly not expected that they
would be molested or called out by Indians;
nor were they.[27] Regarding the duties to be

[27] Here General Custer presents his excuse for leaving
his command, one of the charges upon which he was
convicted in his subsequent court martial. The statement concerning the improbability of Indian attacks
seems to directly contradict the preceding paragraphs of
the chapter, which describe the garrison as in a state of
siege.

performed by the picked detachment as being by far the most important, I chose to accompany it.

The immediate command of the detachment was given to Captain Hamilton, of whom mention has been previously made. He was assisted by two other officers. My intention was to push through from Fort Wallace to Fort Hays, a distance of about one hundred and fifty miles, as rapidly as was practicable; then, being beyond the most dangerous portion of the route, to make the remainder of the march to Fort Harker with half a dozen troopers, while Captain Hamilton with his command should follow leisurely. Under this arrangement I hoped to have a train loaded with supplies at Harker and in readiness to start for Fort Wallace by the time Captain Hamilton should arrive.

Leaving Fort Wallace about sunset on the evening of the 15th of July, we began our ride eastward, following the line of the overland stage route. At that date the Kansas Pacific Railway was only completed as far westward as Fort Harker. Between Forts Wallace and Harker we expected to find the stations of the overland stage company, at intervals of from ten to fifteen miles. In time of peace these stations are generally occupied by half a dozen employees of the

route, embracing the stablemen and relays
of drivers. They were well supplied with
firearms and ammunition, and every facility
for defending themselves against Indians.
The stables were also the quarters for the
men. They were usually built of stone, and
one would naturally think that against Indians no better defensive work would be required. Yet such was not the case. The hay
and other combustible material usually contained in them enabled the savages, by
shooting prepared arrows, to easily set them
on fire, and thus drive the occupants out to
the open plain, where their fate would soon
be settled.

To guard against such an emergency each
station was ordinarily provided with what
on the Plains is termed a dug-out. The name
implies the character and description of the
work. The dugout was commonly located
but a few yards from one of the corners of the
stable, and was prepared by excavating the
earth so as to form an opening not unlike a
cellar, which was usually about four feet in
depth, and sufficiently roomy to accommodate at close quarters half a dozen persons.
This opening was then covered with earth
and loopholed on all sides at a height of a
few inches above the original level of the
ground. The earth was thrown on top until

the dug-out resembled an ordinary mound of earth, some four or five feet in height. To the outside observer, no means apparently were provided for egress or ingress; yet such was not the case. If the entrance had been made above ground, rendering it necessary for the defenders to pass from the stable unprotected to their citadel, the Indians would have posted themselves accordingly and picked them off one by one as they should emerge from the stable. To provide against this danger, an underground passage was constructed in each case, leading from the dug-out to the interior of the stable. With these arrangements for defense a few determined men could withstand the attacks of an entire tribe of savages. The recent depredations of the Indians had so demoralized the men at the various stations that many of the latter were found deserted, their former occupants having joined their forces with those of other stations. The Indians generally burned the deserted stations.

Marching by night was found to be attended with some disadvantages. The men located at the stations which were still occupied, having no notice of our coming, and having seen no human beings for several days except the war parties of savages who had attacked them from time to time, were in a chronic state of alarm, and held themselves in readiness for defense at a moment's notice. The consequence was that as we pursued our way in the stillness of the night, and were not familiar with the location of the various stations, we generally rode into close proximity before discovering them. The station men, however, were generally on the alert, and as they did not wait to challenge us or be challenged, but took it for granted that we were Indians, our first greeting would be a bullet whistling over our heads, sometimes followed by a perfect volley from the dug-out.

In such a case nothing was left for us to do but to withdraw the column to a place of security, and then for one of our number to creep up stealthily in the darkness to a point within hailing distance. Even this was an undertaking attended by no little danger, as by this time the little garrison of the dug-out would be thoroughly awake and every man at his post, his finger on the trigger of his trusty rifle, and straining both eye and ear to discover the approach of the hateful redskins, who alone were believed to be the cause of all this ill-timed disturbance of their slumbers. Huddled together as they necessarily would be in the contracted limits of their subterranean citadel, and all sounds from without being deadened and rendered indistinct by the heavy roof of earth and the few apertures leading to the inside, it is not strange that under the circumstances it would be difficult for the occupants to distinguish between the voice of an Indian and that of a white man. Such was in fact the case, and no sooner would the officer sent forward for that purpose hail the little garrison and endeavor to explain who we were, than, guided by the first sound of his voice, they would respond promptly with their rifles.

In some instances we were in this manner put to considerable delay, and although this was at times most provoking it was not a little amusing to hear the description given by the party sent forward of how closely he hugged the ground when endeavoring to establish friendly relations with the stage people. Finally, when successful and in conversation with the latter, we inquired why they did not recognize us from the fact that we hailed them in unbroken English. They replied that the Indians resorted to so many tricks that they had determined not to be caught even by that one. They were somewhat justified in this idea, as we knew that among the Indians who were then on the war-path there was at least one full blood who had been educated within the limits of civilization, graduated at a popular institution of learning, and only exchanged his civilized mode of dress for the paint, blanket, and feathers of savage life after he had reached the years of manhood. Almost at every station we received intelligence of Indians having been seen in the vicinity within a few days of our arrival.

We felt satisfied they were watching our movements, although we saw no fresh signs of Indians until we arrived near Downer's Station. Here, while stopping to rest our horses for a few minutes, a small party of our men, who had without authority halted some distance behind, came dashing into our midst and reported that twenty-five or thirty Indians had attacked them some five or six miles in rear, and had killed two of their number. As there was a detachment of infantry guarding the station, and time being important, we pushed on toward our destination. The two men reported killed were left to be buried by the troops on duty at the station. Frequent halts and brief rests were made along our line of march; occasionally we would halt long enough to indulge in a few hour's sleep. About three o'clock on the morning of the 18th we reached Fort Hays, having marched about one hundred and fifty miles in fifty-five hours, including all halts.

Some may regard this as a rapid rate of marching; in fact, a few officers of the army who themselves have made many and long marches (principally in ambulances and railroad cars) are of the same opinion. It was far above the usual rate of a leisurely made march, but during the same season and with a larger command I marched sixty miles in fifteen hours. This was officially reported, but occasioned no remark. During the war, and at the time the enemy's cavalry under General J. E. B. Stuart made its famous raid around the Army of the Potomac in Maryland, a portion of our cavalry, accompanied by horse artillery, in attempting to overtake them marched over ninety miles in twenty-four hours. A year subsequent to the events narrated in this chapter I marched a small detachment eighty miles in seventeen hours, every horse accompanying the detachment completing the march in as fresh condition apparently as when the march began.

Leaving Hamilton and his command to rest one day at Hays and then to follow on leisurely to Fort Harker, I continued my ride to the latter post, accompanied by Colonels Cooke and Custer and two troopers. We reached Fort Harker at two o'clock that night, having made the ride of sixty miles without change of animals in less than twelve hours. As this was the first telegraph station, I immediately sent telegrams to headquarters and to Fort Sedgwick announcing the fate of Kidder and his party. General A. J. Smith, who was in command of this military district, had his headquarters at Harker. I at once reported to him in person, and acquainted him with every incident worthy of mention which had occurred in connection with my command since leaving him weeks before. Arrangements were made for the arrival of Hamilton's party and for a train containing supplies to be sent back under their escort. Having made my report to General Smith as my next superior officer, and there being no occasion for my presence until the train and escort should be in readiness to return, I applied for and received authority to visit Fort Riley, about ninety miles east of Harker by rail, where my family was then located.[28]

[28] On July 28 Custer was placed under arrest by his department commander. The first of the seven charges preferred against him was that he disregarded his orders and deserted his command by embarking upon this journey on July 15. The court found him guilty on all counts and sentenced him to suspension from rank and command and to forfeiture of pay for one year. In reviewing the sentence the Board of Review concluded "unavoidably" that Custer's anxiety to see his "family" (which meant Mrs. Custer) at Fort Riley had overcome

"his appreciation of the paramount necessity to obey
orders." In simpler English, he had once again snapped
his fingers at duty when its performance ran counter to
his impulsive desire.

Custer's narrative of his first Indian campaign ends
at this point. His conviction in September, 1867, with
consequent suspension from command and duty for one
year removed him from the seat of warfare until the
following autumn. Meanwhile, General Sheridan had
been placed in command of military operations, and
was making preparations for renewal of an active campaign against the hostile tribes. In response to his request, seconded by General Sherman and others, the
concluding months of Custer's sentence were remitted
and he returned to active duty. Several of his contributions to the *Galaxy* at this point are devoted to the Fetterman massacre of December 21, 1866 and to other
operations concerning which he had no share or personal knowledge, together with an extensive discourse
upon the controversy between the army and the Indian
Department over the conduct of Indian affairs. These
contributions are omitted from the present volume, and
Custer's own story is resumed with his return to the
scene of warfare in September, 1868.

Chapter 8

FUTILE MARCHES AND COUNTERMARCHES

WHEN, in the spring of 1868, the time arrived for the troops to leave their winter quarters and march westward to the Plains, the command with which I had been associated during the preceding year left its station at Fort Leavenworth, Kansas, and marched westward about three hundred miles, there to engage in operations against the Indians. While they, under command of General Sully, were attempting to kill Indians, I was studying the problem of how to kill time in the most agreeable manner. My campaign was a decided success. I established my base of operations in a most beautiful little town on the western shores of Lake Erie, from which I projected various hunting, fishing, and boating expeditions. With abundance of friends and companions, and ample success, time passed pleasantly enough; yet withal there was a constant longing to be with my comrades in arms in the far West, even while aware of the fact that their campaign was not resulting in any material advantage. I had no reason to believe that I would be permitted to rejoin them until the following winter. It was on the evening of the 24th of September, and when about to break bread at the house of a friend in the little town referred to that I received the following telegram:

HEADQUARTERS DEPARTMENT
OF THE MISSOURI,
IN THE FIELD, FORT HAYS, KANSAS,
September 24, 1868.

General G. A. CUSTER, Monroe, Michigan:

Generals Sherman, Sully, and myself, and nearly all the officers of your regiment have asked for you, and I hope the application will be successful. Can you come at once? Eleven companies of your regiment will move about the 1st of October against the hostile Indians, from Medicine Lodge Creek toward the Wichita Mountains.
(Signed)   P. H. SHERIDAN,
Major General Commanding.

The reception of this despatch was a source of unbounded gratification to me, not only because I saw the opportunity of being actively and usefully employed opened before me, but there were personal considerations inseparable from the proposed manner of my return which in themselves were in the highest degree agreeable; so much so that I felt quite forbearing toward each and every one who, whether intentionally or not, had been a party to my retirement, and was almost disposed to favor them with a copy of the preceding despatch, accompanied by an expression of my hearty thanks for the unintentional favor they had thrown in my way.

Knowing that the application of Generals Sherman and Sheridan and the other officers referred to would meet with a favorable reply from the authorities at Washington, I at once telegraphed to General Sheridan that I would start to join him by the next train, not intending to wait the official order which I knew would be issued by the War Department. The following day found me on a railway train hastening to the Plains as fast as the iron horse could carry me. The expected order from Washington overtook me that day in the shape of an official telegram from the Adjutant General of the Army directing me to proceed at once and report for duty to General Sheridan.

At Fort Leavenworth I halted in my journey long enough to cause my horses to be shipped by rail to Fort Hays. Nor must I omit two other faithful companions of my subsequent marches and campaigns, named Blucher and Maida, two splendid specimens of the Scotch staghound, who were destined to share the dangers of an Indian campaign and finally meet death in a tragic manner— the one by the hand of the savages, the other by an ill-directed bullet from a friendly carbine. Arriving at Fort Hays on the morning of the 30th, I found General Sheridan, who had transferred his headquarters temporarily from Fort Leavenworth to that point in order to be nearer the field of operations and better able to give his personal attention to the conduct of the coming campaign. My regiment was at that time on or near the Arkansas River in the vicinity of Fort Dodge, and about three easy marches from Fort Hays.

After remaining at General Sheridan's headquarters one day and receiving his instructions, I set out with a small escort across the country to Fort Dodge to resume command of my regiment. Arriving at Fort Dodge without incident, I found General Sully, who at that time was in command of the district in which my regiment was serving. With the exception of a few detachments, the main body of the regiment was encamped on Bluff Creek, a small tributary of the Arkansas, the camp being some thirty miles southeast from Fort Dodge. Taking with me the detachment at the fort, I proceeded to the main camp, arriving there in the afternoon.

I had scarcely assumed command when a band of Indians dashed close up to our camp and fired upon us. This was getting into active service quite rapidly. I was in the act of taking my seat for dinner, my ride having given me a splendid relish for the repast, when the shouts and firing of the savages informed me that more serious duties were at hand. Every man flew to arms and almost without command rushed to oppose the enemy. Officers and men provided themselves with rifles or carbines, and soon began delivering a deliberate but ineffective fire against the Indians. The latter, as usual, were merely practising their ordinary *ruse de guerre*, which was to display a very small venturesome force in the expectation of tempting pursuit by an equal or slightly superior force, and, after having led the pursuing force well away from the main body, to surround and destroy it by the aid of overwhelming numbers, previously concealed in a ravine or ambush until the proper moment.

On this occasion the stratagem did not succeed. The Indians, being mounted on their fleetest ponies, would charge in single file past our camp, often riding within easy carbine range of our men, displaying great boldness and unsurpassable horsemanship. The soldiers, unaccustomed to firing at such rapidly moving objects, were rarely able to inflict serious damage upon their enemies. Occasionally a pony would be struck and brought to the ground, but the rider always succeeded in being carried away upon the pony of a comrade. It was interesting to witness their marvellous abilities as horsemen; at the same time one could not but admire the courage they displayed. The ground was level, open, and unobstructed; the troops were formed in an irregular line of skirmishers dismounted, the line extending a distance of perhaps two hundred yards. The Indians had a rendezvous behind a hillock on the right, which prevented them from being seen or disturbed by the soldiers. Starting out singly or by twos and threes the warriors would suddenly leave the cover of the hillock and with war whoops and taunts dash over the plain in a line parallel to that occupied by the soldiers, and within easy carbine range of the latter.

The pony seemed possessed of the designs and wishes of his dusky rider, as he seemed to fly unguided by bridle, rein, or spur. The warrior would fire and load and fire again as often as he was able to do, while dashing along through the shower of leaden bullets fired above, beneath, in front, and behind him by the excited troopers, until finally, when the aim of the latter improved and the leaden messengers whistled uncomfortably close, the warrior would be seen to cast himself over on the opposite side of his pony, until his foot on the back and his face under the neck of the pony were all that could be seen, the rest of his person being completely covered by the body of the pony. This maneuver would frequently deceive the recruits among the soldiers; having fired probably about the time the warrior was seen to disappear, the recruit would shout exultingly and call the attention of his comrades to his lucky shot. The old soldiers, however, were not so easily deceived, and often afterwards would remind their less experienced companion of the terrible fatality of his shots.

After finding that their plan to induce a small party to pursue them did not succeed, the Indians withdrew their forces, and, concealment being no longer necessary, we were enabled to see their full numbers as that portion of them which had hitherto remained hidden behind a bluff rode boldly out on the open plain. Being beyond rifle range, they contented themselves with taunts and gestures of defiance, then rode away. From the officers of the camp I learned that the performance of the Indians which had occupied our attention on this afternoon was of almost daily occurrence, and that the savages, from having been allowed to continue in their course unmolested, had almost reduced the camp to a state of siege; so true had this become that at no hour of the day was it safe for individuals to pass beyond the chain of sentinels which enveloped the immediate limits of the camp.

Before it became known that the Indians were so watchful and daring, many narrow escapes were made, and many laughable although serious incidents occurred—laughable, however, only to those who were not the parties most interested. Two of these serio-comic affairs now recur to me. There was a beautiful clear stream of water, named Bluff Creek, running through camp, which supplied bathing facilities to the officers and men, a privilege which but few allowed to pass unimproved. Whether to avoid the publicity attending localities near camp or to seek a point in the bed of the stream where the water was fresh and undisturbed, or from a motive different from either of these, two of our young officers mounted their horses one day without saddles and rode down the valley of the stream perhaps a mile or more in search of a bathing place. Discovering one to their taste, they dismounted, secured their horses, and after disposing of their apparel on the greensward covering the banks were soon floating and floundering in the water like a pair of young porpoises. How long they had been enjoying this healthful recreation, or how much longer they might have remained, is not necessary to the story. One of them happening to glance toward their horses observed the latter in a state of great trepidation. Hastening from the water to the bank, he discovered the cause of the strange conduct on the part of the horses, which was nothing more nor less than a party of about thirty Indian warriors, mounted, and stealthily making their way toward the bathing party, evidently having their eyes on the latter and intent upon their capture.

Here was a condition of affairs that was at least as unexpected as it was unwelcome. Quickly calling out to his companion, who was still in the water unconscious of approaching danger, the one on shore made haste to unfasten their horses and prepare for flight. Fortunately the Indians, who were now within a few hundred yards of the two officers, were coming from the direction opposite camp, leaving the line of retreat of the officers open. No sooner did the warriors find that their approach was discovered than they put their ponies to their best speed, hoping to capture the officers before the latter could have time to mount and get their horses under headway. The two officers in the meanwhile were far from idle; no flesh brushes or bathing towels were required to restore a healthy circulation, nor was time wasted in an idle attempt to make a toilet. If they had sought their bathing ground from motives of retirement or delicacy, no such sentiments were exhibited now, for, catching up their wardrobe from the ground in one hand and seizing the bridle rein with the other, one leap and they were on their horses' backs and riding toward camp for dear life.

They were not exactly in the condition of Flora McFlimsy with nothing to wear, but to all intents and purposes might as well have been so. Then followed a race which, but for the risk incurred by two of the riders, might well be compared to that of John Gilpin. Both of the officers were experienced horsemen; but what experienced horseman would willingly care to be thrust upon the bare back of a flying steed, minus all apparel, neither boots, breeches, nor saddle, not even the spurs and shirt collar which are said to constitute the full uniform of a Georgian colonel, and when so disposed of to have three or four score of hideously painted and feathered savages, well mounted and near at hand, straining every nerve and urging their fleet-footed war ponies to their highest speed in order that the scalps of the experienced horsemen might be added to the other human trophies which grace their lodges? Truly this was one of the occasions when personal appearance is nothing, and "a man's a man for a' that," so at least thought our amateur Mazeppas as they came dashing toward camp, ever and anon casting anxious glances over their shoulders at their pursuers, who, despite every exertion of the former, were surely overhauling their pale-faced brothers.

To the pursued, camp seemed a long way in the distance, while the shouts of the warriors, each time seeming nearer than before, warned them to urge their steeds to their fastest pace. In a few moments the occupants of camp discovered the approach of this strangely appearing party. It was an easy matter to recognize the warriors, but who could name the two who rode at the front? The pursuing warriors, seeing that they were not likely to overtake and capture the two knights of the bath, slackened their pace and sent a volley of arrows after them. A few moments later and the two officers were safe inside the lines, where they lost no time in making their way to their tents to attend to certain matters relating to their toilet which the sudden appearance of their dusky visitors had prevented. It was a long time before they ceased to hear allusions made by their comrades to the cut and style of their riding suit.

The other affair to which I have alluded occurred about the same time, but in a different direction from camp. One of the officers who was commanding a troop concluded one day that it would be safe to grant permission to a part of his command to leave camp for the purpose of hunting buffaloes and obtaining fresh meat for the men. The hunting party, being strong enough to protect itself against almost any ordinary war party of Indians that might present itself, left camp at an early hour in the morning and set out in the direction in which the buffaloes were reported to be. The forenoon passed away, noon came, and still no signs of the return of the hunters. The small hours of the afternoon began to come and go and still no tidings from the hunters, who were expected to return to camp after an absence of two or three hours. The officer to whose troop they belonged, and who was of an exceedingly nervous temperament, began to regret having accorded them permission to leave camp, knowing that Indians had been seen in the vicinity.

The hunting party had gone by a route across the open country which carried them up a long but very gradual ascent of perhaps two miles, beyond which, on the level plain, the buffaloes were supposed to be herding in

large numbers. Anxious to learn something
concerning the whereabouts of his men and
believing he could obtain a view of the country beyond which might prove satisfactory,
the officer, whose suspense was constantly
increasing, determined to mount his horse
and ride to the summit of the ridge beyond
which his men had disappeared in the morning. Taking no escort with him, he leisurely
rode off, guided by the trail made by the
hunters. The distance to the crest proved
much farther than it had seemed to the eye
before starting. A ride of over two miles had
to be made before the highest point was
reached, but once there the officer felt well
repaid for his exertion, for in the dim decep-
tions of a beautiful mirage he saw what to
him was his hunting party leisurely returning
toward camp.

Thinking they were still a long distance
from him and would not reach him for a
considerable time, he did what every prudent
cavalryman would have done under similar
circumstances—dismounted to allow his horse
an opportunity to rest. At the same time he
began studying the extended scenery, which
from his exalted position lay spread in all
directions beneath him. The camp, seen nest-
ling along the banks of the creek at the base
of the ridge, appeared as a pleasant relief to

the monotony of the view, which otherwise was undisturbed. Having scanned the horizon in all directions, he turned to watch the approach of his men; when, behold! instead of his own trusty troopers returning laden with the fruits of the chase the mirage had disappeared and he saw a dozen well-mounted warriors riding directly toward him at full speed. They were still far enough away to enable him to mount his horse and have more than an even chance to outstrip them in the race to camp. But no time was to be thrown away; the beauties of natural scenery had, for the time at least, lost their attraction. Camp never seemed so inviting before. Heading his horse toward camp and gathering the reins in one hand and holding his revolver in the other, the officer set out to make his escape.

Judgment had to be employed in riding this race, for the distance being fully two miles before a place of safety could be reached, his horse, not being high-bred and accustomed to going such a distance at full speed, might, if forced too rapidly at first, fail before reaching camp. Acting upon this idea, a tight rein was held and as much speed kept in reserve as safety would permit. This enabled the Indians to gain on the officer, but at no time did he feel that he could not elude his pursuers. His principal anxiety was confined to the character of the ground, care being taken to avoid the rough and broken places. A single misstep or a stumble on the part of his horse, and his pursuers would be upon him before he could rise. The sensations he experienced during that flying ride could not have been enviable. Soon the men in camp discerned his situation and seizing their carbines hastened out to his assistance. The Indians were soon driven away and the officer again found himself among his friends. The hunters also made their appearance shortly after, well supplied with game. They had not found the buffaloes as near camp as they had expected, and after finding them were carried by a long pursuit in a different direction from that taken by them in the morning. Hence their delay in returning to camp.

These and similar occurrences, added to the attack made by the Indians on the camp the afternoon I joined, proved that unless we were to consider ourselves as actually besieged and were willing to accept the situation some decisive course must be adopted to punish the Indians for their temerity. No offensive measures had been attempted since the infantry and cavalry forces of General Sully had marched up the hill and then, like

the forces of the king of France, had marched
down again.[29] The effect of this movement,
in which the Indians gained a decided advantage, was to encourage them in their attempts to annoy and disturb the troops, not
only by prowling about camp in considerable
numbers and rendering it unsafe, as has been
seen, to venture beyond the chain of sentinels, but by waylaying and intercepting all
parties passing between camp and the base
of supplies at Fort Dodge.

Knowing, from my recent interview with
General Sheridan that activity was to char-
acterize the future operations of the troops,
particularly those of the cavalry, and that
the sooner a little activity was exhibited on
our part the sooner perhaps might we be
freed from the aggressions of the Indians, I

[29] General Alfred Sully, a West Point graduate in the
class of 1841, was a veteran soldier of Mexican, Civil
War, and frontier service. From May 18, 1868 to Feb.
24, 1869 he was commander of the military District of
the Upper Arkansas with headquarters at Fort Harker.
His futile foray from Fort Dodge southward into northwestern Oklahoma in September, 1868 in pursuit of
hostile Indians excited the derision of Custer, and his
subsequent conduct of operations in the winter campaign to establish Camp Supply failed to meet the approval of General Sheridan, who relieved him from the
further command. Sully was one of the officers who
campaigned in an ambulance against warriors mounted
on fleet Indian ponies.

returned from the afternoon skirmish to my
tent and decided to begin offensive movements that same night, as soon as darkness
should conceal the march of the troops. It
was reasonable to infer that the war parties
which had become so troublesome in the
vicinity of camp, and made their appearance
almost daily, had a hiding place or rendezvous on some of the many small streams
which flowed within a distance of twenty
miles of the point occupied by the troops;
and it was barely possible that if a simul-
taneous movement was made by several well-
conducted parties with a view of scouting up
and down the various streams referred to,
the hiding place of the Indians might be discovered and their forays in the future broken
up. It was deemed most prudent, and to
promise greatest chance of success, to make
these movements at night, as during the
hours of daylight the Indians, no doubt, kept
close watch over everything transpiring in
the vicinity of camp, and no scouting party
could have taken its departure in daylight
unobserved by the watchful eyes of the
savages.

Four separate detachments were at once
ordered to be in readiness to move immediately after dark. Each detachment numbered about one hundred cavalry, well mounted

and well armed. Guides who knew the country well were assigned to each, and each party was commanded and accompanied by zealous and efficient officers. The country was divided into four sections and to each detachment was assigned one of the sections, with orders to thoroughly scout the streams running through it. It was hoped that some one of these parties might, if in no other way, stumble upon a camp-fire or other indication of the rendezvous of the Indians; but subsequent experience only confirmed me in the opinion that Indians seldom, if ever, permit hostile parties to stumble upon them unless the stumblers are the weaker party.

Before proceeding further in my narrative I will introduce to the reader a personage who is destined to appear at different intervals and upon interesting occasions as the campaign proceeds. It is usual on the Plains, and particularly during time of active hostilities, for every detachment of troops to be accompanied by one or more professional scouts or guides. These guides are employed by the government at a rate of compensation far in excess of that paid to the soldiers, some of the most experienced receiving pay about equal to that of a subaltern in the line. They constitute a most interesting as well as useful and necessary portion of our frontier population. Who they are, whence they come or whither they go, their names even, except such as they choose to adopt or which may be given them, are all questions which none but themselves can answer. As their usefulness to the service depends not upon the unravelling of either of these mysteries, but little thought is bestowed upon them. Do you know the country thoroughly, and can you speak any of the Indian languages, constitute the only examination which civil or uncivil service reform demands on the Plains.

If the evidence on these two important points is satisfactory the applicant for a vacancy in the corps of scouts may consider his position as secured, and the door to congenial employment, most often leading to a terrible death, opens before him. They are almost invariably men of very superior judgment or common sense, with education generally better than that of the average frontiersman. Their most striking characteristics are love of adventure, a natural and cultivated knowledge of the country without recourse to maps, deep hatred of the Indian and an intimate acquaintance with all the habits and customs of the latter, whether pertaining to peace or war, and last but most necessary to their calling skill in the use of firearms and in the management of a horse. The possessor of these qualifications and more than the ordinary amount of courage may feel equal to discharge the dangerous and trying duties of a scout.

In concentrating the cavalry, which had hitherto been operating in small bodies, it was found that each detachment brought with it the scouts who had been serving with them. When I joined the command I found quite a number of these scouts attached to various portions of the cavalry, but each acting separately. For the purposes of organization it was deemed best to unite them into a separate detachment under command of one of their own number. Being unacquainted personally with the merits or demerits of any of them, the selection of a chief had necessarily to be made somewhat at random. There was one among their number whose appearance would have attracted the notice of any casual observer. He was a man about forty years of age, perhaps older, over six feet in height, and possessing a well-proportioned frame. His head was covered with a luxuriant crop of long, almost black hair, strongly inclined to curl, and so long as to fall carelessly over his shoulders. His face, at least so much of it

CALIFORNIA JOE

as was not concealed by the long, waving brown beard and mustache, was full of intelligence and pleasant to look upon. His eye was undoubtedly handsome, black and lustrous, with an expression of kindness and mildness combined. On his head was generally to be seen, whether asleep or awake, a huge sombrero or black slouch hat. A soldier's overcoat with its large circular cape, a pair of trousers with the legs tucked in the top of his long boots, usually constituted the outside make-up of the man whom I selected as chief scout. He was known by the euphonious title of California Joe; no other name seemed ever to have been given him, and no other name ever seemed necessary.

His military armament consisted of a long breech-loading Springfield musket, from which he was inseparable, and a revolver and hunting-knife, both the latter being carried in his waist-belt. His mount completed his equipment for the field, being instead of a horse a finely-formed mule, in whose speed and endurance he had every confidence. Scouts usually prefer a good mule to a horse, and wisely too, for the reason that in making their perilous journeys, either singly or by twos or threes, celerity is one principal condition to success. The object with the scout is not to outrun or overwhelm the Indians, but to avoid both by secrecy and caution in his movements. On the Plains at most seasons of the year the horse is incapable of performing long or rapid journeys without being supplied with forage on the route. This must be transported, and in the case of scouts would necessarily be transported on the back of the horse, thereby adding materially to the weight which must be carried. The mule will perform a rapid and continuous march without forage, being able to subsist on the grazing to be obtained in nearly all the valleys on the Plains during the greater portion of the year.

California Joe was an inveterate smoker and was rarely seen without his stubby, dingy-looking brierwood pipe in full blast. The endurance of his smoking powers was only surpassed by his loquacity. His pipe frequently became exhausted and required refilling, but California Joe seemed never to lack for material or disposition to carry on a conversation, principally composed of personal adventures among the Indians, episodes in mining life, or experience in overland journeying before the days of steam engines and palace cars rendered a trip across the Plains a comparatively uneventful one. It was evident from the scraps of information volunteered from time to time, that there was but little of the western country from the Pacific to the Missouri River with which California Joe was not intimately acquainted. He had lived in Oregon years before, and had become acquainted from time to time with most of the officers who had served on the Plains or on the Pacific Coast. I once inquired of him if he had ever seen General Sheridan? "What, Gineral Shuridun? Why, bless my soul, I knowed Shuridun way up in Oregon more'n fifteen years ago, an' he wuz only a second lootenant uv infantry. He wuz quartermaster of the fort or something uv that sort, an' I hed the contract uv furnishin' wood to the post, and, would ye b'leve it? I hed a kind of a sneakin' notion then that he'd hurt somebody ef they'd ever turn him loose. Lord, but ain't he old lightnin'?" This was the man whom upon a short acquaintance I decided to appoint as chief of the scouts. This thrust of professional greatness, as the sequel will prove, was more than California Joe aspired to, or, considering some of his undeveloped traits, was equal to; but I am anticipating.

As the four detachments already referred to were to move as soon as it was dark, it was desirable that the scouts should be at once organized and assigned. So, sending

Futile Marches

for California Joe, I informed him of his
promotion and what was expected of him
and his men. After this official portion of
the interview had been completed, it seemed
proper to Joe's mind that a more intimate
acquaintance between us should be cultivated, as we had never met before. His
first interrogatory, addressed to me in
furtherance of this idea, was frankly put
as follows: "See hyar, Gineral, in order that
we hev no misonderstandin', I'd jest like
to ask ye a few questions." Seeing that I
had somewhat of a character to deal with,
I signified my perfect willingness to be inter-
viewed by him. "Are you an ambulance
man ur a hoss man?" Pretending not to discover his meaning, I requested him to explain. "I mean do you· b'leve in catchin'
Injuns in ambulances or on hossback?"
Still assuming ignorance, I replied, "Well,
Joe, I believe in catching Indians wherever
we can find them, whether they are found
in ambulances or on horseback." This did
not satisfy him. "That ain't what I'm
drivin' at. S'pose you're after Injuns and
really want to hev a tussle with 'em, would
ye start after 'em on hossback, or would
ye climb into an ambulance and be haulded
after 'em? That's the pint I'm headin' fur."
I answered that I would prefer the method

239

on horseback provided I really desired to catch the Indians; but if I wished them to catch me, I would adopt the ambulance system of attack.

This reply seemed to give him complete satisfaction. "You've hit the nail squar on the hed. I've bin with 'em on the Plains whar they started out after the Injuns on wheels, jist as ef they war goin' to a town funeral in the States, an' they stood 'bout as many chances uv catchin' Injuns az a six-mule team wud uv catchin' a pack of thievin' Ki-o-tees, jist as much. Why that sort uv work is only fun fur the Injuns; they don't want anything better. Ye ort to've seen how they peppered it to us, an' we a doin' nuthin' a' the time. Sum uv 'em wuz 'fraid the mules war goin' to stampede and run off with the train an' all our forage and grub, but that wuz impossible; fur besides the big loads uv corn an' bacon an' baggage the wagons hed in them, thar war from eight to a dozen infantry men piled into them besides. Ye ort to hev heard the quartermaster in charge uv the train tryin' to drive the infantry men out of the wagons and git them into the fight. I 'spect he wuz an Irishman by his talk, fur he sed to them, 'Git out uv thim wagons, git out uv thim wagons; yez'll hev me tried fur disobadience uv ordhers fur marchin' tin min in a wagon whin I've ordhers but fur ait!'"

How long I might have been detained listening to California Joe's recital of incidents of first campaigns, sandwiched here and there by his peculiar but generally correct ideas of how to conduct an Indian campaign properly, I do not know; time was limited, and I had to remind him of the fact to induce him to shorten the conversation. It was only deferred, however, as on every occasion thereafter California Joe would take his place at the head of the column on the march and his nearest companion was made the receptacle of a fresh instalment of Joe's facts and opinions. His career as chief scout was of the briefest nature.

Everything being in readiness, the four scouting columns, the men having removed their sabers to prevent clanging and detection, quietly moved out of camp as soon as it was sufficiently dark and set out in different directions. California Joe accompanied that detachment whose prospects seemed best of encountering the Indians. The rest of the camp soon afterward returned to their canvas shelter, indulging in all manner of surmises and conjectures as to the likelihood of either or all of the scouting parties meeting with success. As no

tidings would probably be received in camp
until a late hour of the following day, taps,
the usual signal from the bugle for lights
out, found the main camp in almost complete darkness, with only here and there a
stray glimmering of light from the candle of
some officer's tent, who was probably reckoning in his own mind how much he was
losing or perhaps gaining by not accompanying one of the scouting parties. What were
the chances of success to the four detachments which had departed on this all night's
ride? Next to nothing. Still, even if no Indians could be found, the expeditions would
accomplish this much: they would leave
their fresh trails all over the country within
a circuit of twenty miles of our camp, trails
which the practised eyes of the Indians
would be certain to fall upon in daylight,
and inform them for the first time that an
effort was being made to disturb them if
nothing more.

Three of the scouting columns can be
disposed of now by the simple statement
that they discovered no Indians, nor the
remains of any camps or lodging places
indicating the recent presence of a war party
on any of the streams visited by them. The
fourth detachment was that one which California Joe had accompanied as scout. What

a feather it would be in his cap if, after the failure of the scouts accompanying the other columns to discover Indians, the party guided by him should pounce upon the savages and by a handsome fight settle a few of the old scores charged against them!

The night was passing away uninterrupted by any such event, and but a few hours more intervened before daylight would make its appearance. The troops had been marching constantly since leaving camp; some were almost asleep in their saddles when the column was halted and word was passed along from man to man that the advance guard had discovered signs indicating the existence of Indians near at hand. Nothing more was necessary to dispel all sensations of sleep, and to place every member of the command on the alert. It was difficult to ascertain from the advance guard, consisting of a non-commissioned officer and a few privates, precisely what they had seen. It seemed that in the valley beyond into which the command was about to descend, and which could be overlooked from the position the troops then held, something unusual had been seen by the leading troopers just as they had reached the crest. What this mysterious something was or how produced, no one could tell; it appeared simply for a moment and then only as a bright flash of light of varied colors; how far away it was impossible to determine in the heavy darkness of the night.

A hasty consultation of the officers took place at the head of the column, when it was decided that in the darkness which then reigned it would be unwise to move to the attack of an enemy until something more was known of the numbers and position of the foe. As the moon would soon rise and dispel one of the obstacles to conducting a careful attack, it was determined to hold the troops in readiness to act upon a moment's notice, and at the same time send a picked party of men under guidance of California Joe to crawl as close to the supposed position of the Indians as possible and gather all the information available. But where was California Joe all this time? Why was he not at the front where his services would be most likely to be in demand? Search was quietly made for him all along both flanks of the column, but on careful inquiry it seemed that he had not been seen for some hours, and then at a point many miles from that at which the halt had been ordered. This was somewhat remarkable and admitted of no explanation—unless, perhaps, California Joe had fallen asleep during the march and been carried away from the column; but this theory gained no supporters. His absence at this particular time, when his advice and services might prove so invaluable, was regarded as most unfortunate.

However, the party to approach the Indian camp was being selected when a rifle shot broke upon the stillness of the scene, sounding in the direction of the mysterious appearance which had first attracted the attention of the advanced troopers. Another moment, and the most powerful yells and screams rose in the same direction, as if a terrible conflict was taking place. Every carbine was advanced ready for action, each trigger was carefully sought, no one as yet being able to divine the cause of this sudden outcry, when in a moment who should come charging wildly up to the column, now dimly visible by the first rays of the moon, but California Joe, shouting and striking wildly to the right and left as if beset by a whole tribe of warriors.

Here, then, was the solution of the mystery. Not then, but in a few hours, everything was rendered clear. Among the other traits or peculiarities of his character, California Joe numbered an uncontrollable fondness for strong drink; it was his one great weakness—a weakness to which he could only be kept from yielding by keeping all intoxicating drink beyond his reach. It seemed, from an after development of the affair, that the sudden elevation of California Joe, unsought and unexpected as it was, to the position of chief scout was rather too much good fortune to be borne by him in a quiet or undemonstrative manner. Such a profusion of greatness had not been thrust upon him so often as to render him secure from being affected by his preferment. At any rate he deemed the event deserving of celebration—professional duties to the contrary notwithstanding—and before proceeding on the night expedition had filled his canteen with a bountiful supply of the worst brand of whiskey, such as is only attainable on the frontier. He, perhaps, did not intend to indulge to that extent which might disable him from properly performing his duties; but in this, like many other good men whose appetites are stronger than their resolutions, he failed in his reckoning. As the liquor which he imbibed from time to time after leaving camp began to produce the natural or unnatural effect, Joe's independence greatly increased until the only part of the expedition which he recognized as at all important was California Joe. His mule, no longer restrained by his hand, gradually carried him away from the troops, until the latter were left far in the rear.

This was the relative position when the halt was ordered. California Joe, having indulged in drink sufficiently for the time being, concluded that the next best thing would be a smoke; nothing would be better to cheer him on his lonely night ride. Filling his ever present brierwood with tobacco, he next proceeded to strike a light, employing for this purpose a storm or tempest match; it was the bright and flashing colors of this which had so suddenly attracted the attention of the advance guard. No sooner was his pipe lighted than the measure of his happiness was complete, his imagination picturing him to himself, perhaps, as leading in a grand Indian fight. His mule by this time had turned toward the troops, and when California Joe set up his unearthly howls and began his imaginary charge into an Indian village he was carried at full speed straight to the column, where his good fortune alone prevented him from receiving a volley before he was recognized as not an Indian.

His blood was up, and all efforts to quiet or suppress him proved unavailing, until finally the officer in command was forced to bind him hand and foot and in this condition secured him on the back of his faithful mule. In this sorry plight the chief scout continued until the return of the troops to camp, when he was transferred to the tender mercies of the guard as a prisoner for misconduct. Thus ended California Joe's career as chief scout. Another was appointed in his stead, but we must not banish him from our good opinion yet. As a scout, responsible only for himself, he will reappear in these pages with a record which redounds to his credit.

Nothing was accomplished by the four scouting parties except, perhaps, to inspire the troops with the idea that they were no longer to be kept acting merely on the defensive, while the Indians, no doubt, learned the same fact and at the same time. The cavalry had been lying idle, except when attacked by the Indians, for upward of a month. It was reported that the war parties, which had been so troublesome for some time came from the direction of Medicine Lodge Creek, a stream running in the same general direction as Bluff Creek, and about two marches from the latter in a northeasterly direction. It was on this stream—Medicine Lodge Creek—that the great peace council had been held with all the southern tribes with whom we had been and were then at war, the Government being represented at the council by Senators and other members of Congress, officers high in rank in the army, and prominent gentlemen selected from the walks of civil life.[30]

The next move, after the unsuccessful attempt in which California Joe created the leading sensation, was to transfer the troops across from Bluff Creek to Medicine Lodge Creek and to send scouting parties up and down the latter in search of our enemies. This movement was made soon after the return of the four scouting expeditions sent

[30] This council was held in October, 1867 on Medicine Lodge Creek in southern Kansas. A detailed eye-witness report of the proceedings is given by Stanley, *My Life and Adventures*, I, 222–62. The Peace Commission which represented the white government was headed by the Commissioner of Indian Affairs and according to Thoburn (*Standard History of Oklahoma*, I, 397) was the largest and possibly the ablest ever sent out by the Government. About 5000 Kiowas, Comanches, Cheyennes, Arapahoes, and Plains Apaches assembled to confer with the Commissioners and treaties were negotiated establishing a reservation for the Kiowas and Comanches between the Washita and Red rivers westward from the 98th meridian, and another for the Cheyennes and Arapahoes bounded on the north and east by the state of Kansas and the Arkansas River and on the south and west by the Cimarron River. Numerous other provisions concerning schools, rations, etc. were common to both treaties.

out from Bluff Creek. As our first day's march was to be a short one we did not break camp on Bluff Creek until a late hour in the morning. Soon everything was in readiness for the march and like a travelling village of Bedouins the troopers and their train of supplies stretched out into column. First came the cavalry, moving in column of fours; next came the immense wagon train, containing the tents, forage, rations, and extra ammunition of the command, a very necessary but unwieldy portion of a mounted military force. Last of all came the rear guard, usually consisting of about one company.

On this occasion it was the company commanded by the officer whose narrow escape from the Indians while in search of a party of his men who had gone buffalo hunting, has been already described in this chapter. The conduct of the Indians on this occasion proved that they had been keeping an unseen but constant watch on everything transpiring in or about camp. The column had scarcely straightened itself out in commencing the march, and the rear guard had barely crossed the limits of the deserted camp, when out from a ravine near by dashed a war party of fully fifty well-mounted, well-armed warriors. Their first onslaught was directed against the rear guard, and a determined effort was made to drive them from the train and thus place the latter at their mercy, to be plundered of its contents. After disposing of flankers for the purpose of resisting any efforts which might be made to attack the train from either flank, I rode back to where the rear guard were engaged to ascertain if they required reinforcements. At the same time orders were given for the column of troops and train to continue the march, as it was not intended that so small a party as that attacking us should delay our march by any vain effort on our part to ride them down or overhaul them, when we knew they could outstrip us if the contest was to be decided by a race.

Joining the rear guard, I had an opportunity to witness the Indian mode of fighting in all its perfection. Surely no race of men, not even the famous Cossacks, could display more wonderful skill in feats of horsemanship than the Indian warrior on his native plains, mounted on his well-trained war pony, voluntarily running the gantlet of his foes, drawing and receiving the fire of hundreds of rifles and in return sending back a perfect shower of arrows or, more likely still, well-directed shots from some souvenir of a peace commission in the shape of an improved breech-loader.

My Life on the Plains

The Indian warrior is capable of assuming positions on his pony, the latter at full speed, which no one but an Indian could maintain for a single moment without being thrown to the ground. The pony, of course, is perfectly trained, and seems possessed of the spirit of his rider. An Indian's wealth is most generally expressed by the number of his ponies. No warrior or chief is of any importance or distinction who is not the owner of a herd of ponies numbering from twenty to many hundreds. He has for each special purpose a certain number of ponies, those that are kept as pack animals being the most inferior in quality and value; then the ordinary riding ponies used on the march or about camp, or when visiting neighboring villages; next in consideration is the buffalo pony, trained to the hunt and only employed when dashing into the midst of the huge buffalo herds, when the object is either food from the flesh or clothing and shelter for the lodges, to be made from the buffalo hide; last, or rather first, considering its value and importance, is the war pony, the favorite of the herd, fleet of foot, quick in intelligence, and full of courage. It may be safely asserted that the first place in the heart of the warrior is held by his faithful and obedient war pony.

Futile Marches

Indians are extremely fond of bartering and are not behindhand in catching the points of a good bargain. They will sign treaties relinquishing their lands and agree to forsake the burial ground of their forefathers; they will part, for due consideration, with their bow and arrows and their accompanying quiver, handsomely wrought in dressed furs; their lodges even may be purchased at not an unfair valuation, and it is not an unusual thing for a chief or warrior to offer to exchange his wife or daughter for some article which may have taken his fancy. This is no exaggeration; but no Indian of the Plains has ever been known to trade, sell, or barter away his favorite war pony. To the warrior his battle horse is as the apple of his eye. Neither love nor money can induce him to part with it. To see them in battle and to witness how the one almost becomes a part of the other, one might well apply to the warrior the lines—

But this gallant
Had witchcraft in 't; he grew into his seat,
And to such wondrous doing brought his horse,
As he had been encorps'd and demi-natur'd
With the brave beast; so far he passed my thought
That I, in forgery of shapes and tricks,
Come short of what he did.

The officer in command of the rear guard expressed the opinion that he could resist successfully the attacks of the savages until a little later, when it was seen that the latter were receiving accessions to their strength and were becoming correspondingly bolder and more difficult to repulse, when a second troop of cavalry was brought from the column as a support to the rear guard. These last were ordered to fight on foot, their horses, in charge of every fourth trooper, being led near the train. The men being able to fire so much more accurately when on foot, compelled the Indians to observe greater caution in their manner of attack. Once a warrior was seen to dash out from the rest in the peculiar act of "circling," which was simply to dash along in front of the line of troopers, receiving their fire and firing in return. Suddenly his pony while at full speed was seen to fall to the ground, showing that the aim of at least one of the soldiers had been effective. The warrior was thrown over and beyond the pony's head and his capture by the cavalry seemed a sure and easy matter to be accomplished. I saw him fall and called to the officer commanding the troop which had remained mounted to gallop forward and secure the Indian. The troop advanced rapidly, but the comrades of the fallen Indian had also witnessed his mishap and were rushing to his rescue. He was on his feet in a moment, and the next moment another warrior mounted on the fleetest of ponies was at his side, and with one leap the dismounted warrior placed himself astride the pony of his companion; and thus doubly burdened the gallant little steed, with his no less gallant riders, galloped lightly away, with about eighty cavalrymen, mounted on strong domestic horses, in full cry after them.

There is no doubt but that by all the laws of chance the cavalry should have been able to soon overhaul and capture the Indians in so unequal a race; but whether from lack of zeal on the part of the officer commanding the pursuit or from the confusion created by the diversion attempted by the remaining Indians, the pony, doubly weighted as he was, distanced his pursuers and landed his burden in a place of safety. Although chagrined at the failure of the pursuing party to accomplish the capture of the Indians I could not wholly suppress a feeling of satisfaction, if not gladness, that for once the Indian had eluded the white man. I need not add that any temporary tenderness of feeling toward the two Indians was prompted by their individual daring and the heroic display of comradeship in the successful attempt to render assistance to a friend in need.

Without being able to delay our march, yet it required the combined strength and resistance of two full troops of cavalry to defend the train from the vigorous and dashing attacks of the Indians. At last, finding that the command was not to be diverted from its purpose or hindered in completing its regular march, the Indians withdrew, leaving us to proceed unmolested. These contests with the Indians, while apparently yielding the troops no decided advantage, were of the greatest value in view of future and more extensive operations against the savages. Many of the men and horses were far from being familiar with actual warfare, particularly of this irregular character. Some of the troopers were quite inexperienced as horsemen and still more inexpert in the use of their weapons, as their inaccuracy of fire when attempting to bring down an Indian within easy range clearly proved. Their experience, resulting from these daily contests with the red men, was to prove of incalculable benefit and fit them for the duties of the coming campaign.

Our march was completed to Medicine Lodge Creek, where a temporary camp was established while scouting parties were sent both up and down the stream as far as there was the least probability of finding Indians. The party, consisting of three troops, which scouted down the valley of Medicine Lodge Creek, proceeded down to the point where was located and then standing the famous medicine lodge, an immense structure erected by the Indians and used by them as a council house, where once in each year the various tribes of the southern Plains were wont to assemble in mysterious conclave to consult the Great Spirit as to the future and to offer up rude sacrifices and engage in imposing ceremonies, such as were believed to be appeasing and satisfactory to the Indian Deity.

In the conduct of these strange and interesting incantations the presiding or directing personages are known among the Indians as medicine men. They are the high priests of the red man's religion, and in their peculiar sphere are superior in influence and authority to all others in the tribe, not excepting the head chief. No important step is proposed or put in execution, whether relating to war or peace, even the probable success of a contemplated hunt, but is first submitted to the powers of divination confidently believed to be possessed by the medicine man of the tribe. He, after a series

of enchantments, returns the answer supposed to be prompted by the Great Spirit
as to whether the proposed step is well advised and promises success or not. The
decisions given by the medicine men are
supreme and admit of no appeal.

The medicine lodge just referred to had
been used as the place of assembly of the
grand council held between the warlike
tribes and the representatives of the Government, referred to in preceding pages. The
medicine lodge was found in a deserted but
well-preserved condition. Here and there,
hanging overhead, were collected various
kinds of herbs and plants, vegetable offer-
ings no doubt to the Great Spirit; while,
in strange contrast to these peaceful specimens of the fruits of the earth, were trophies
of the war path and the chase, the latter
being represented by the horns and dressed
skins of animals killed in the hunt, some of
the skins being beautifully ornamented in
the most fantastic of styles peculiar to the
Indian idea of art.

Of the trophies relating to war, the most
prominent were human scalps representing
all ages and sexes of the white race. These
scalps, according to the barbarous custom,
were not composed of the entire covering
of the head, but of a small surface surround-

ing the crown and usually from three to four inches in diameter, constituting what is termed the scalp lock. To preserve the scalp from decay a small hoop of about double the diameter of the scalp is prepared from a small withe which grows on the banks of some of the streams in the West. The scalp is placed inside the hoop and properly stretched by a network of thread connecting the edges of the scalp with the circumference of the hoop. After being properly cured, the dried fleshy portion of the scalp is ornamented in bright colors, according to the taste of the captor, sometimes the addition of beads of bright and varied colors being made to heighten the effect. In other instances the hair is dyed, either to a beautiful yellow or golden, or to crimson. Several of these horrible evidences of past depredations upon the defenseless inhabitants of the frontier or overland emigrants were brought back by the troopers on their return from their scout. Old trails of small parties of Indians were discovered, but none indicating the recent presence of war parties in that valley were observable.

The command was then marched back to near its former camp on Bluff Creek, from whence, after a sojourn of three or four days, it marched to a point on the north bank of

the Arkansas River about ten miles below
Fort Dodge, there to engage in earnest preparation and reorganization for the winter
campaign which was soon to be inaugurated,
and in which the Seventh Cavalry was to
bear so prominent a part. We pitched our
tents on the banks of the Arkansas on the
21st of October, 1868, there to remain usefully employed until the 12th of the following month, when we mounted our horses,
bade adieu to the luxuries of civilization,
and turned our faces toward the Wichita
Mountains in the endeavor to drive from
their winter hiding places the savages who
had during the past summer waged such
ruthless and cruel war upon our exposed
settlers on the border. How far and in what
way we were successful in this effort, will
be learned in the following chapter.

Chapter 9

LAUNCHING A WINTER CAMPAIGN

IN concluding to go into camp for a brief period on the banks of the Arkansas two important objects were in view: first, to devote the time to refitting, reorganizing, and renovating generally that portion of the command which was destined to continue active operations during the inclement winter season; second, to defer our movement against the hostile tribes until the last traces of the fall season had disappeared and winter in all its bitter force should be upon us. We had crossed weapons with the Indians time and again during the mild summer months when the rich verdure of the valleys served as bountiful and inexhaustible granaries in supplying forage to their ponies, and the immense herds of buffaloes and other varieties of game roaming undisturbed over the Plains supplied all the food that was necessary to subsist the war parties and at the same time allow their villages to move freely from point to point; and the experience of both officers and men went to prove that in attempting to fight Indians in the summer season we were yielding to them the advantages of climate and supplies; we were meeting them on ground of their own selection, and at a time when every natural circumstance controlling the result of a campaign was wholly in their favor; and as a just consequence the troops, in nearly all these contests with the red men, had come off second best.

During the grass season nearly all Indian villages are migratory, seldom remaining longer than a few weeks at most in any one locality, depending entirely upon the supply of grass; when this becomes exhausted the lodges are taken down and the entire tribe or band moves to some other point, chosen with reference to the supply of grass, water, wood, and game. The distance to the new location is usually but a few miles. During the fall, when the buffaloes are in the best condition to furnish food and the hides are suitable to be dressed as robes, or to furnish covering for the lodges, the grand annual hunts of the tribes take place, by which the supply of meat for the winter is procured. This being done, the chiefs determine upon the points at which the village shall be located; if the tribe is a large one, the village is often subdivided, one portion or band remaining at one point, other portions choosing localities within a circuit of thirty or forty miles.

Launching Winter Campaign

Except during seasons of the most perfect peace, and when it is the firm intention of the chiefs to remain on friendly terms with the whites at least during the winter and early spring months, the localities selected for their winter resorts are remote from the military posts and frontier settlements, and the knowledge which might lead to them carefully withheld from every white man. Even during a moderate winter season it is barely possible for the Indians to obtain sufficient food for their ponies to keep the latter in anything above a starving condition. Many of the ponies actually die from want of forage, while the remaining ones become so weak and attenuated that it requires several weeks of good grazing in the spring to fit them for service—particularly such service as is required from the war ponies.

Guided by these facts, it was evident that if we chose to avail ourselves of the assistance of so exacting and terrible an ally as the frosts of winter—an ally who would be almost as uninviting to friends as to foes—we might deprive our enemy of his points of advantage and force him to engage in a combat in which we should do for him what he had hitherto done for us; compel him to fight upon ground and under circumstances of our own selection. To decide upon making

263

a winter campaign against the Indians was
certainly in accordance with that maxim in
the art of war which directs one to do that
which the enemy neither expects nor desires
to be done. At the same time it would dispel
the old-fogy idea, which was not without
supporters in the army and which was confidently relied on by the Indians themselves,
that the winter season was an insurmount-
able barrier to the prosecution of a successful
campaign. But aside from the delay which
was necessary to be submitted to before the
forces of winter should produce their natural
but desired effect upon our enemies, there
was much to be done on our part before we
could be ready to coöperate in an offensive
movement.

The Seventh Cavalry, which was to operate in one body during the coming campaign,
was a comparatively new regiment, dating
its existence as an organization from July,
1866. The officers and companies had not
served together before with much over half
their full force. A large number of fresh
horses were required and obtained; these had
to be drilled. All the horses in the command
were to be newly shod, and an extra fore and
hind shoe fitted to each horse; these, with
the necessary nails, were to be carried by
each trooper in the saddle pocket. It has

been seen that the men lacked accuracy in the use of their carbines. To correct this, two drills in target practice were ordered each day. The companies were marched separately to the ground where the targets had been erected and under the supervision of the troop officers were practised daily in firing at targets placed one hundred, two hundred, and three hundred yards distant. The men had been previously informed that out of the eight hundred men composing the command a picked corps of sharpshooters would be selected, numbering forty men and made up of the forty best marksmen in the regiment.

As an incentive to induce every enlisted man, whether non-commissioned officer or private, to strive for appointment in the sharpshooters it was given out from headquarters that the men so chosen would be regarded, as they really would deserve to be, as the *élite* of the command; not only regarded as such, but treated with corresponding consideration. For example, they were to be marched as a separate organization, independently of the column, a matter which in itself is not so trifling as it may seem to those who have never participated in a long and wearisome march. Then again no guard or picket duty was to be required of the sharpshooters, which alone was enough to encourage every trooper to excel as a marksman. Besides these considerations, it was known that, should we encounter the enemy, the sharpshooters would be most likely to be assigned a post of honor and would have superior opportunities for acquiring distinction and rendering good service. The most generous as well as earnest rivalry at once sprung up, not only between the various companies, as to which should secure the largest representation among the sharpshooters, but the rivalry extended to individuals of the same company, each of whom seemed desirous of the honor of being considered as one of the best shots.

To be able to determine the matter correctly a record of every shot fired by each man of the command throughout a period of upwards of one month was carefully kept. It was surprising to observe the marked and rapid improvement in the accuracy of aim attained by the men generally during this period. Two drills at target practice each day, and allowing each man an opportunity at every drill to become familiar with the handling of his carbine and in judging of the distances of the different targets, worked a most satisfactory improvement in the av-

266

erage accuracy of fire; so that at the end of
the period named, by taking the record of
each trooper's target practice I was enabled
to select forty marksmen in whose ability
to bring down any warrior, whether mounted
or not, who might challenge us, as we had
often been challenged before, I felt every
confidence.

They were a superb body of men, and
felt the greatest pride in their distinction. A
sufficient number of non-commissioned officers who had proved their skill as marksmen
were included in the organization—among
them, fortunately, a first sergeant whose ex-
pertness in the use of any firearm was well
established throughout the command. I
remember having seen him, while riding at
full speed, bring down four buffaloes by
four consecutive shots from his revolver.
When it is remembered that even experienced hunters are usually compelled to fire
half a dozen shots or more to secure a single
buffalo, this statement will appear the more
remarkable. The forty sharpshooters being
supplied with their complement of sergeants
and corporals and thus constituting an organization by themselves, only lacked one
important element, a suitable commander;
a leader who, aside from being a thorough
soldier, should possess traits of character

which would not only enable him to employ skilfully the superior abilities of those who were to constitute his command, but at the same time feel that *esprit de corps* which is so necessary to both officers and soldiers when success is to be achieved.

Fortunately, in my command were a considerable number of young officers, nearly all of whom were full of soldierly ambition and eager to grasp any opportunity which opened the way to honorable preferment. The difficulty was not in finding an officer properly qualified in every way to command the sharpshooters, but, among so many who I felt confident would render a good account of themselves if assigned to that position, to designate a leader *par excellence.* The choice fell upon Colonel Cooke, a young officer whose acquaintance the reader will remember to have made in connection with the plucky fight he had with the Indians near Fort Wallace the preceding summer. Colonel Cooke, at the breaking out of the rebellion, although then but a lad of sixteen years, entered one of the New York cavalry regiments, commencing at the foot of the ladder. He served in the cavalry arm of the service throughout the war, participating in Sheridan's closing battles near Richmond, his services and gallantry resulting in his promotion to the rank of lieutenant-colonel. While there were many of the young officers who would have been pleased if they instead of another had been chosen, there was no one in the command, perhaps, who did not regard the selection as a most judicious one. Future events only confirmed this judgment.

After everything in the way of reorganization and refitting which might be considered as actually necessary had been ordered another step, bordering on the ornamental perhaps although in itself useful, was taken. This was what is termed in the cavalry "coloring the horses," which does not imply, as might be inferred from the expression, that we actually changed the color of our horses, but merely classified or arranged them throughout the different squadrons and troops according to the color. Hitherto the horses had been distributed to the various companies of the regiment indiscriminately, regardless of color, so that in each company and squadron horses were found of every color. For uniformity of appearance it was decided to devote one afternoon to a general exchange of horses.

The troop commanders were assembled at headquarters and allowed, in the order of their rank, to select the color they preferred. This being done, every public horse in the command was led out and placed in line: the grays collected at one point, the bays, of which there was a great preponderance in numbers, at another, the blacks at another, the sorrels by themselves; then the chestnuts, the blacks, the browns; and last of all came what were jocularly designated the "brindles," being the odds and ends so far as colors were concerned—roans and other mixed colors—the junior troop commander, of course, becoming the reluctant recipient of these last, valuable enough except as to color.

The exchanges having been completed, the men of each troop led away to their respective picket or stable lines their newly-acquired chargers. Arriving upon their company grounds, another assignment in detail was made by the troop commanders. First, the non-commissioned officers were permitted to select their horses in the order of their rank; then the remaining horses were distributed among the troopers generally, giving to the best soldiers the best horses. It was surprising to witness what a great improvement in the handsome appearance of the command was effected by this measure. The change when first proposed had not been greeted with much favor by many of the troopers, who by long service and association in times

of danger had become warmly attached to
their horses; but the same reasons which had
endeared the steed to the soldier in the one
instance soon operate in the same manner to
render the new acquaintances fast friends.

Among the other measures adopted for
carrying the war to our enemy's doors, and
in a manner fight the devil with fire, was the
employment of Indian allies. These were to
be procured from the reservation Indians,
tribes who, from engaging in long and dev-
astating wars with the whites and with other
hostile bands had become so reduced in
power as to be glad to avail themselves of the
protection and means of subsistence offered
by the reservation plan. These tribes were
most generally the objects of hatred in the
eyes of their more powerful and independent
neighbors of the Plains and the latter, when
making their raids and bloody incursions
upon the white settlements of the frontiers,
did not hesitate to visit their wrath equally
upon whites and reservation Indians. To
these smaller tribes it was a welcome opportunity to be permitted to ally themselves to
the forces of the Government and endeavor
to obtain that satisfaction which, acting
alone, they were powerless to secure. The
tribes against which we proposed to operate
during the approaching campaign had been

particularly cruel and relentless in their wanton attacks upon the Osages and Kaws, two tribes living peaceably and contentedly on well-chosen reservations in southwestern Kansas and the northern portion of the Indian Territory.

No assistance in fighting the hostile tribes was desired, but it was believed, and correctly too, that in finding the enemy and in discovering the location of his winter hiding-places, the experience and natural tact and cunning of the Indians would be a powerful auxiliary if we could enlist them in our cause. An officer was sent to the village of the Osages to negotiate with the head chiefs and was successful in his mission, returning with a delegation consisting of the second chief in rank of the Osage tribe, named Little Beaver, Hard Rope, the counsellor or wise man of his people, and eleven warriors, with an interpreter. In addition to the monthly rate of compensation which the Government agreed to give them, they were also to be armed, clothed, and mounted at government expense.

Advices from General Sheridan's headquarters, then at Fort Hays, Kansas, were received early in November, informing us that the time for resuming active operations was near at hand and urging the early completion of all preliminaries looking to that end. Fort Dodge, on the Arkansas River, was the extreme post south in the direction proposed to be taken by us, until the Red River should be crossed and the northwestern posts of Texas could be reached, which were farther south than our movements would probably carry us. To use Fort Dodge as our base of supplies and keep open to that point our long line of communications would have been, considering the character of the country and that of the enemy to be encountered, an impracticable matter with our force. To remedy this a temporary base was decided upon, to be established about one hundred miles south of Fort Dodge at some point yet to be determined, from which we could obtain our supplies during the winter.

With this object in view an immense train consisting of about four hundred army wagons was loaded with forage, rations, and clothing for the supply of the troops composing the expedition. A guard composed of a few companies of infantry was detailed to accompany the trains and to garrison the point which was to be selected as the new base of supplies. Everything being in readiness, the cavalry moved from its camp on the north bank of the Arkansas on the morning of the 12th of November and after fording the river began its march toward the Indian Territory. That night we encamped on Mulberry Creek, where we were joined by the infantry and the supply train. General Sully, commanding the district, here took active command of the combined forces. Much anxiety existed in the minds of some of the officers, remembering no doubt their late experience, lest the Indians should attack us while on the march, when, hampered as we should be in the protection of so large a train of wagons, we might fare badly. The country over which we were to march was favorable to us, as we were able to move our trains in four parallel columns formed close together. This arrangement shortened our flanks and rendered them less exposed to attack.

The following morning after reaching Mulberry Creek the march was resumed soon after daylight, the usual order being: the four hundred wagons of the supply train and those belonging to the troops formed in four equal columns; in advance of the wagons at a proper distance rode the advance guard of cavalry; a corresponding cavalry force formed the rear guard. The remainder of the cavalry was divided into two equal parts, and these parts again divided into three equal detachments; these six detachments were disposed of along the flanks of the column, three on a side, maintaining a distance between themselves and the train of from a quarter to half a mile, while each of them had flanking parties thrown out opposite the train, rendering it impossible for an enemy to appear in any direction without timely notice being received.

The infantry, on beginning the march in the morning, were distributed throughout the train in such manner that should the enemy attack, their services could be rendered most effective. Unaccustomed, however, to field service, particularly marching, the infantry apparently were only able to march for a few hours in the early part of the day, when, becoming weary, they would straggle from their companies and climb into the covered wagons, from which there was no determined effort to rout them. In the afternoon there would be little evidence perceptible to the eye that infantry formed any portion of the expedition save here and there the butt of a musket or point of a bayonet peeping out from under the canvas wagon-covers, or perhaps an officer of infantry "treading alone his native heath," or better still, mounted on an Indian pony, the result of some barter with the Indians when times were a little more peaceable and neither wars nor rumors of wars disturbed the monotony of garrison life.

Nothing occurred giving us any clue to the whereabouts of Indians until we had been marching several days and were moving down the valley of Beaver Creek, when our Indian guides discovered the trail of an Indian war party, numbering, according to their estimate, from one hundred to one hundred and fifty warriors, mounted and moving in a northeasterly direction. The trail was not over twenty-four hours old, and by following it to the point where it crossed Beaver Creek almost the exact numbers and character of the party could be determined from the fresh signs at the crossing. Everything indicated that it was a war party sent from the very tribes we were in search of, and the object, judging from the direction they had been moving and other circumstances, was to make a raid on the settlements in western Kansas.

As soon as we had reached camp for the night, which was but a short distance from the point at which we crossed the Indian trail, I addressed a communication to the senior officer, who was commanding the expedition, and, after stating the facts learned in connection with the trail, requested that I might be permitted to take the cavalry belonging to the expedition, leaving the trains to be guarded by the infantry, whose numbers were ample for this purpose, and with the Indian scouts as trailers set out early the next morning, following the trail of the war party, not in the direction taken by them, as this would be an idle attempt, but in the direction from which they came, expressing the conviction that such a course would in all probability lead us direct to the villages of the marauders, which was the ultimate object of the movement we were thus engaged in. By so doing we might be able to strike a prompt blow against our enemies and visit swift punishment upon the war party, whose hostile purposes were but too evident.

In these views I was sustained by the opinions of our Indian allies, who expressed confidence in their ability to take the trail and follow it back to the villages. The officer to whom my application was submitted, and whose sanction was necessary before I could be authorized to execute my proposed plan, returned an elaborate argument attempting to prove that no successful results could possibly attend the undertaking I had suggested, and ended with the remark that it was absurd to suppose for one moment that a large military force such as ours was, and accompanied by such an immense train

of wagons, could move into the heart of the
Indian country and their presence remain
undiscovered by the watchful savages for
even a single day. This specious reasoning
sounded well—read well—but it gave no
satisfaction to the men and officers of the
cavalry, all of whom thought they saw a fine
opportunity neglected. However, we shall
strike this trail again, but on different ground
and under different circumstances. Great as
was our temporary disappointment at being
restrained, the result satisfied all of us that,
for very different reasons from those adduced
to withhold us from making the proposed
movement, all, as the sequel proved, was for
the best.

On the sixth day after leaving our camp on
the north bank of the Arkansas the expedition arrived at the point which was chosen
as our future base, where the infantry were
to remain and erect quarters for themselves
and storehouses for the military supplies.
The point selected—which was then given
the name it now bears, Camp Supply—was
in the angle formed by Wolf and Beaver
creeks, about one mile above the junction of
these two streams. These streams by their
union form the north fork of the Canadian
River. The exact geographical location of
the point referred to is lat. 36 deg. 30 min.,

long. 99 deg. 30 min., being in the neighborhood of one hundred miles in a southerly direction from Fort Dodge on the Arkansas.

We of the cavalry knew that our detention at this point would be but brief. Within two or three days of our arrival the hearts of the entire command were gladdened by the sudden appearance in our midst of strong reinforcements. These reinforcements consisted of General Sheridan and staff. Hearing of his near approach, I mounted my horse and was soon galloping beyond the limits of camp to meet him. If there were any persons in the command who hitherto had been in doubt as to whether the proposed winter campaign was to be a reality or otherwise, such persons soon had cause to dispel all mistrust on this point. Selecting from the train a sufficient number of the best teams and wagons to transport our supplies of rations and forage, enough to subsist the command upon for a period of thirty days, our arrangements were soon completed by which the cavalry, consisting of eleven companies and numbering between eight and nine hundred men, were ready to resume the march. In addition we were to be accompanied by a detachment of scouts, among the number being California Joe; also our Indian allies from the Osage tribe, headed by

Little Beaver and Hard Rope. As the country in which we were to operate was beyond the limits of the district which constituted the command of General Sully, that officer was relieved from further duty with the troops composing the expedition and in accordance with his instructions withdrew from Camp Supply and returned to his headquarters at Fort Harker, Kansas, accompanied by Colonel Keogh, Seventh Cavalry, then holding the position of staff officer at district headquarters.[31]

After remaining at Camp Supply six days nothing was required but the formal order directing the movement to commence. This came in the shape of a brief letter of instructions from Department headquarters. Of course, as nothing was known positively as to the exact whereabouts of the Indian villages, the instructions had to be general in terms. In substance, I was to march my command in search of the winter hiding-places of the hostile Indians and wherever found to administer such punishment for

[31] Captain Myles W. Keogh, who is characterized by Van De Water as "once a papal zouave, a divil-may-care Irishman with mustache and imperial and an unholy thirst which he could curb only by placing all his cash in the hands of Finnegan, his striker and actual guardian," *Glory Hunter*, 152. Keogh died with Custer at the Little Big Horn in June, 1876.

past depredations as my force was able to. On the evening of November 22d orders were issued to be in readiness to move promptly at daylight the following morning. That night, in the midst of other final preparations for a long separation from all means of communication with absent friends, most of us found time to hastily pen a few parting lines, informing them of our proposed expedition and the uncertainties with which it was surrounded, as none of us knew when or where we should be heard from again once we bade adieu to the bleak hospitalities of Camp Supply. Alas! some of our number were destined never to return.

It began snowing the evening of the 22d and continued all night, so that when the shrill notes of the bugle broke the stillness of the morning air at reveille on the 23d we awoke at four o'clock to find the ground covered with snow to a depth of over one foot, and the storm still raging in full force. Surely this was anything but an inviting prospect as we stepped from our frail canvas shelters and found ourselves standing in the constantly and rapidly increasing depth of snow which appeared in every direction. "How will this do for a winter campaign?" was the half sarcastic query of the Adjutant, as he came trudging back to the tent through a field of snow extending almost to the top of his tall troop boots, after having received the reports of the different companies at reveille. "Just what we want," was the reply. Little grooming did the shivering horses receive from the equally uncomfortable troopers that morning.

Breakfast was served and disposed of more as a matter of form and regulation than to satisfy the appetite; for who, I might inquire, could rally much of an appetite at five o'clock in the morning and when standing around a camp fire almost up to the knees in snow? The signal, "The General," for tents to be taken down and wagons packed for the march, gave every one employment. Upon the principle that a short horse is soon curried, and as we were going to take but little with us in the way of baggage of any description, the duties of packing up were soon performed. It still lacked some minutes of daylight when the various commanders reported their commands in readiness to move, save the final act of saddling the horses, which only awaited the signal sounds of the chief bugler at headquarters. "Boots and saddles" rang forth and each trooper grasped his saddle and the next moment was busily engaged arranging and disposing of the few buckles and straps upon which the safety of his seat and the comfort of his horse depended.

While they were thus employed, my horse being already saddled and held near by, by the orderly, I improved the time to gallop through the darkness across the narrow plain to the tents of General Sheridan and say good-by. I found the headquarters tents wrapped in silence, and at first imagined that no one was yet stirring except the sentinel in front of the General's tent, who kept up his lonely tread, apparently indifferent to the beating storm. But I had no sooner given the bridle-rein to my orderly than the familiar tones of the General called out, letting me know that he was awake and had been an attentive listener to our notes of preparation. His first greeting was to ask what I thought about the snow and the storm, to which I replied that nothing could be more to our purpose. We could move and the Indian villages could not. If the snow only remained on the ground one week, I promised to bring the General satisfactory evidences that my command had met the Indians. With an earnest injunction from my chief to keep him informed, if possible, should anything important occur, and many hearty wishes for a successful issue to the campaign, I bade him adieu.

After I had mounted my horse, and had started to rejoin my command a staff officer of the General, a particular friend, having just been awakened by the conversation, called out, while standing in the door of his tent enveloped in the comfortable folds of a huge buffalo robe, "Good-by, old fellow; take care of yourself!" and in these brief sentences the usual farewell greetings between brother officers separating for service took place. By the time I rejoined my men they had saddled their horses and were in readiness for the march. "To horse" was sounded, and each trooper stood at his horse's head. Then followed the commands "Prepare to mount" and "Mount" when nothing but the signal "Advance" was required to put the column in motion. The band took its place at the head of the column, preceded by the guides and scouts, and when the march began it was to the familiar notes of that famous old marching tune, "The girl I left behind me."

If we had entered into a solemn compact with the clerk of the weather—this being before the reign of "Old Probabilities"—to be treated to winter in its severest aspect, we could have claimed no forfeiture on account of non-fulfilment of contract. We could not refer to the oldest inhabitant, that mythical personage in most neighborhoods, to attest to the fact that this was a storm unparalleled in severity in that section of country. The snow continued to descend in almost blinding clouds. Even the appearance of daylight aided us but little in determining the direction of our march. So dense and heavy were the falling lines of snow that all view of the surface of the surrounding country, upon which the guides depended to enable them to run their course, was cut off. To such an extent was this true that it became unsafe for a person to wander from the column a distance equal to twice the width of Broadway, as in that short space all view of the column was prevented by the storm. None of the command except the Indian guides had ever visited the route we desired to follow, and they were forced to confess that until the storm abated sufficiently to permit them to catch glimpses of the landmarks of the country they could not undertake to guide the troops to the point where we desired to camp that night. Here was a serious obstacle encountered quite early in the campaign.

The point at which we proposed to encamp for the night was on Wolf Creek, only some twelve or fifteen miles from Camp Supply, it not being intended that our first day's progress should be very great. We had started, however, and notwithstanding the discouraging statements of our guides it would never do to succumb to opposition so readily. There was but one course to pursue now that the guides could no longer conduct us with certainty and that was to be guided—like the mariner in mid-ocean—by the never-failing compass. There are few cavalry officers but what carry a compass in some more or less simple form. Mine was soon in my hand, and having determined as accurately as practicable, from my knowledge of the map of the country, the direction in which we ought to move in order to strike Wolf Creek at the desired camping ground, I became for the time guide to the column and after marching until about two P. M. reached the valley of Wolf Creek, where a resting place for the night was soon determined upon.

There was still no sign of abatement on the part of the weather. Timber was found along the banks of the creek in ample quantity to furnish us with fuel, but so imbedded in snow as to render the prospect of a camp fire very remote and uncertain. Our march of fifteen miles through the deep snow and blinding storm had been more fatiguing to our horses than an ordinary march of thirty miles would have been. Our wagons were still far in rear. While they were coming up every man in the command, officers as well as enlisted men, set briskly to work gathering a good supply of wood, as our personal comfort in camp in such weather would be largely dependent on the quality and quantity of our firewood. Fallen and partly seasoned trees were in great demand and when discovered in the huge beds of snow were soon transformed under the vigorous blows of a score of axes into available fuel. It was surprising as well as gratifying to witness the contentment and general good humor everywhere prevailing throughout the command. Even the chill of winter and the bitterest of storms were insufficient to produce a feeling of gloom, or to suppress the occasional ebullition of mirthful feeling which ever and anon would break forth from some Celtic or Teutonic disciple of Mars.

Fires were soon blazing upon the grounds assigned to the different troops and upon the arrival of the wagons, which occurred soon after, the company cooks were quickly engaged in preparing the troopers' dinner, while the servants of the officers were employed in a similar manner for the benefit of the latter. While the cooks were so engaged, officers and men were busily occupied in pitching the tents, an operation which under the circumstances was most difficult to per-

form satisfactorily for the reason that before
erecting the tent it was desirable, almost
necessary, to remove the snow from the surface of the ground intended to form the floor
of the tent; otherwise the snow, as soon as a
fire should be started within the tent, would
melt and reduce the ground to a very muddy
condition. But so rapidly did the large flakes
continue to fall that the most energetic efforts of two persons were insufficient to keep
the ground properly clear; such at least was
the experience of Lieutenant Moylan, the
Adjutant, and myself, in our earnest endeavors to render our temporary abiding place
a fit habitation for the night.

Tents up at last, dinner was not long in
being prepared, and even less time employed
in disposing of it. A good cup of strong coffee
went far toward reconciling us to everything
that had but a few moments before appeared
somewhat uninviting. By this time a cheer-
ful fire was blazing in the center of our tent;
my comfortable bed of buffalo robes was
prepared on a framework of strong boughs,
and with my ever-faithful dogs lying near
me I was soon reclining in a state of comparative comfort, watching the smoke as it
ascended through the narrow apex of the
tent, there to mingle with the descending
flakes of snow. In regard to the storm still

prevailing outside, and which in itself or its effects we were to encounter the following morning and for an indefinite period thereafter, I consoled myself with the reflection that to us it was as an unpleasant remedy for the removal of a still more unpleasant disease. If the storm seemed terrible to us, I believed it would prove to be even more terrible to our enemies, the Indians.

Promptly at the appointed hour, four o'clock the following morning, camp was bustling and active in response to the bugle notes of reveille. The storm had abated, the snow had ceased falling, but that which had fallen during the previous twenty-four hours now covered the ground to a depth of upward of eighteen inches. The sky was clear, however, or, to adopt the expressive language of California Joe, "the travellin' was good overhead." It is always a difficult matter the first few days of a march to inculcate upon the minds of the necessary hangers-on of a camp, such as teamsters, wagon-masters, etc., the absolute necessity of promptness and strict obedience to orders, particularly orders governing the time and manner of marching; and one or two days usually are required to be devoted to disciplining these unruly characters. When the hour arrived which had been previously designated as the one at which the command would begin the second day's march, the military portion were in complete readiness to move out, but it was found that several of the teams were still unharnessed and the tents of the wagon-masters still standing.

This was a matter requiring a prompt cure. The officer of the day was directed to proceed with his guard and after hastening the unfinished preparations for the march to arrest the wagon-masters and most dilatory of the teamsters and compel them to march on foot as a punishment for their tardiness. This was no slight matter, considering the great depth of the snow. So effective was this measure that not many hours had elapsed before the deposed drivers and their equally unfortunate superiors sent through the officer of the guard a humble request that they be permitted to resume their places in the train, promising at the same time never to give renewed cause for complaints of tardiness to be made against them. Their request was granted, and their promise most faithfully observed during the remainder of the campaign.

All of the second day we continued to march up the valley of the stream we had chosen as our first camping ground. The second night we encamped under circumstances very similar to those which attended us the first night, except that the storm no longer disturbed us. The snow did not add to our discomfort particularly, save by increasing the difficulty of obtaining good and sufficient fuel. Our purpose was to strike the Canadian River in the vicinity of Antelope Hills, which are famous and prominent landmarks in that region, and then be governed in our future course by circumstances. Resuming the march at daylight on the morning of the third day, our route still kept us in the valley of Wolf Creek, on whose banks we were to encamp for the third time.

Nothing was particularly worthy of notice during our third day's march except the immense quantities of game to be seen seeking the weak shelter from the storm offered by the little strips of timber extending along the valleys of Wolf Creek and its tributaries. Even the buffaloes, with their huge, shaggy coats—sufficient, one would imagine, to render the wearer indifferent to the blasts of winter—were frequently found huddled together in the timber and so drowsy or benumbed from the effects of the cold as to not discover our approach until we were within easy pistol range, when the Indian guides and our white scouts who rode in advance would single out those appearing in best condition and by deliberate aim bring them down. Details of a few troopers from each company were left at these points to cut up the butchered game and see to its being loaded in the company wagons as the trains came along. In this way a bountiful supply of good fresh meat was laid in, the weather favoring the keeping of the meat for an indefinite period.

Occasionally we would discover a herd of buffaloes on the bluffs overlooking the stream. Then would occur some rare scenes of winter sport: a few of the officers and men would obtain permission to leave the column and join in the chase—an indulgence that could be safely granted, as no fears were entertained that hostile Indians were in our immediate vicinity. The deep snow was a serious obstacle to exhibiting speed, either in the buffalo or his pursuers. It was most laughable to witness the desperate and awkward efforts of buffalo, horse, and rider in the frantic endeavor to make rapid headway through the immense fields of snow. Occasionally an unseen hole or ditch or ravine covered up by the snow would be encountered, when the buffalo or his pursuer, or perhaps all three—horse, rider, and buffalo— would disappear in one grand tumble in the depths of the snowdrifts, and when seen to emerge therefrom it was difficult to determine which of the three was most badly frightened.

Fortunately no accidents occurred to mar the pleasure of the excitement. Seeing a fine herd of young buffaloes a short distance in the advance, I determined to test the courage of my stag-hounds Blucher and Maida. Approaching as near the herd as possible before giving them the alarm, I managed to single out and cut off from the main herd a fine yearling bull. My horse, a trained hunter, was soon alongside, but I was unable to use my pistol to bring the young buffalo down as both the dogs were running close to either side and by resolutely attacking him endeavoring to pull him down. It was a new experience to them; a stag they could easily have mastered, but a lusty young buffalo bull was an antagonist of different caliber. So determined had the dogs become, their determination strengthened no doubt by the occasional vigorous blows received from the ready hoofs of the buffalo, that I could not call them off; neither could I render them assistance from my pistol, for fear of injuring them.

There was nothing left for me to do but to become a silent although far from disinterested participant in the chase. The immense drifts of snow through which we were struggling at our best pace would soon vanquish one or the other of the party; it became a question of endurance simply, and the buffalo was the first to come to grief. Finding escape by running impossible, he boldly came to bay and faced his pursuers; in a moment both dogs had grappled with him as if he had been a deer. Blucher seized him by the throat, Maida endeavored to secure a firm hold on the shoulders. The result was that Blucher found himself well trampled in snow, and but for the latter would have been crushed to death. Fearing for the safety of my dogs I leaped from my horse, who I knew would not leave me, and ran to the assistance of the stag-hounds. Drawing my hunting-knife and watching a favorable opportunity, I succeeded in cutting the hamstrings of the buffalo, which had the effect to tumble him over in the snow, when I was enabled to despatch him with my pistol.

On that afternoon we again encamped in the same valley up which we had been moving during the past three days. The next morning, following the lead of our Indian guides, who had been directed to conduct us to a point on the Canadian River near the Antelope Hills, our course, which so far had been westerly, now bore off almost due south. After ascending gradually for some hours to the crest or divide which sloped on the north down to the valley of the stream we had just left, we reached the highest line and soon began to gradually descend again, indicating that we were approaching a second valley; this the Indians assured us was the valley of the Canadian. Delayed in our progress by the deep snow and the difficulty from the same cause always experienced by our guides in selecting a practicable route, darkness overtook us before the entire command arrived at the point chosen for our camp on the north bank of the Canadian.

As there is little or no timber found along the immediate banks of that river as far up as we then were, we pitched our tent about one mile from the river and near a small fresh-water tributary whose valley was abundantly supplied with wood. If any prowling bands or war parties belonging to either of the tribes with which we were at war were moving across the Canadian in either direction it was more than probable that their crossing would be made at some point above us and not more than ten or fifteen miles distant. The season was rather far advanced to expect any of these parties to be absent from the village, but the trail of the war party discovered by our Indian

guides just before the expedition reached
Camp Supply was not forgotten, and the
heavy storm of the past few days would be
apt to drive them away from the settlements and hasten their return to their village.

We had every reason to believe that the
latter was located somewhere south of the
Canadian. After discussing the matter with
Little Beaver and Hard Rope, and listening
to the suggestions of California Joe and his
confrères, I decided to start a strong force
up the valley of the Canadian at daybreak
the following morning, to examine the banks
and discover, if possible, if Indians had been
in the vicinity since the snow had fallen.
Three full troops of cavalry under Major
Joel H. Elliot, 7th Cavalry, were ordered to
move without wagons or *otro impedimiento*,
each trooper to carry one hundred rounds of
ammunition, one day's rations and forage.
Their instructions were to proceed up the
north bank of the Canadian a distance of
fifteen miles. If any trail of Indians was
discovered pursuit was to be taken up at
once, at the same time sending information
of the fact back to the main command, indicating the number and character of the
Indians as determined by their trail and
particularly the direction in which they were

moving, in order that the main body of the troops might endeavor, if possible, to intercept the Indians, or at least strike the trail by a shorter route than by following the first detachment. A few of our Indian trailers were designated to accompany the party, as well as some of the white scouts. The latter were to be employed in carrying despatches back to the main command should anything be discovered of sufficient importance to be reported.

In the meantime I informed Major Elliot that as soon as it was fairly daylight I would commence crossing the main command over the Canadian—an operation which could not be performed hastily, as the banks were almost overflowing, the current being very rapid and the water filled with floating snow and ice. After making the crossing I would, in the absence of any reports from him, march up the bluffs forming Antelope Hills and strike nearly due south, aiming to encamp that night on some one of the small streams forming the headwaters of the Washita River, where we would again unite the two portions of the command and continue our march to the south.

Major Elliot was a very zealous officer, and daylight found him and his command on the march in the execution of the duty

to which they had been assigned. Those of
us who remained behind were soon busily
occupied in making preparations to effect a
crossing of the Canadian. California Joe
had been engaged since early dawn searching for a ford which would be practicable
for our wagons; the troopers and horses
could cross almost anywhere. A safe fording
place, barely practicable, was soon reported
and the cavalry and wagon train began
moving over. It was a tedious process; sometimes the treacherous quicksand would yield
beneath the heavily laden wagons and double
the usual number of mules would be required
to extricate the load. In less than three hours
the last wagon and the rear guard of the
cavalry had made a successful crossing.

Looming up in our front like towering
battlements were the Antelope Hills. These
prominent landmarks, which can be seen
from a distance of over twenty miles in all
directions, are situated near the south bank
of the Canadian, and at 100 deg. W. longitude. The Antelope Hills form a group of
five separate hillocks, and are sometimes
called Boundary Mountains. They vary in
height above the average level of the Plains
between one hundred and fifty and three
hundred feet. Two of the hills are conical
and the others oblong; they are composed

of porous sandstone, and are crowned with
white and regular terraces about six yards
in depth. From the summit of these terraces one enjoys a most commanding view.
On the left is to be seen the red bed of the
Canadian, whose tortuous windings, coming
from the southwest, direct their course for
a while northwards and finally disappear in
a distant easterly direction. The horizon is
but an immense circle of snowy whiteness,
of which the center is the point of observation. Here and there a few acclivities rise
above the Plains, divided by rows of stunted
trees, indicating a ravine or more frequently
a humble brook such as that on whose banks
we camped the night previous to crossing
the Canadian. It never occurred to any of
us when folding our tents that bleak winter
morning on the bank of the Canadian that
there were those among our number who
had bidden a last and final adieu to the
friendly shelter of their canvas-covered
homes; that for some of us, some who could
but sadly be spared, the last reveille had
sounded, and that when sleep again closed
their eyes it would be that sleep from which
there is no awakening. But I am anticipating.

One by one the huge army wagons with
their immense white covers began the long

ascent which was necessary to be overcome before attaining the level of the Plains. As fast as they reached the high ground the leading wagons were halted and parked to await the arrival of the last to cross the river. In the meantime the cavalry had closed up and dismounted, except the rear guard, which was just then to be seen approaching from the river, indicating that everything was closed up. I was about to direct the chief bugler to sound "To Horse," when far in the distance on the white surface of the snow I descried a horseman approaching us as rapidly as his tired steed could carry him. The direction was that in which Elliot's command was supposed to be, and the horseman approaching could be none other than a messenger from Elliot. What tidings would he bring? was my first thought. Perhaps Elliot could not find a ford by which to cross the Canadian, and simply desired instructions as to what his course should be. Perhaps he has discovered an Indian trail— a fresh one; but it must be fresh if one at all, as the snow is scarcely three days old. If a trail has been discovered, then woe unto the luckless Indians whose footprints are discoverable in the snow; for so long as that remains and the endurance of men and horses holds out, just so long will we follow that trail, until the pursuer and pursued are brought face to face or the one or the other succumbs to the fatigues and exhaustion of the race.

These and a host of kindred thoughts flashed in rapid succession through my mind as soon as I had discovered the distant approach of the scout, for a scout I knew it must be. As yet none of the command had observed his coming, not being on as high ground as where I stood. By means of my field glass I was able to make out the familiar form of Corbin, one of the scouts. After due waiting, when minutes seemed like hours, the scout galloped up to where I was waiting and in a few hurried, almost breathless words informed me that Elliot's command after moving up the north bank of the Canadian about twelve miles had discovered the trail of an Indian war party numbering upwards of one hundred and fifty strong; that the trail was not twenty-four hours old, and the party had crossed the Canadian and taken a course a little east of south. Elliot had crossed his command and at once taken up the pursuit as rapidly as his horses could travel. Here was news and of a desirable character. I asked the scout if he could overtake Elliot if furnished with a fresh horse. He thought he could. A horse was

at once supplied him and he was told to rejoin Elliot as soon as possible, with instructions to continue the pursuit with all possible vigor and I would move with the main
command in such direction as to strike his
trail about dark. If the Indians changed
their general direction, he was to inform me
of the fact; and if I could not overtake him
by eight o'clock that night Elliot was to
halt his command and await my arrival,
when the combined force would move as
circumstances might determine.

My resolution was formed in a moment
and as quickly put in train of execution.
The bugle summoned all the officers to report at once. There was no tardiness on
their part for while they had not heard the
report brought in by the scout they had
witnessed his unexpected arrival and his
equally sudden departure—circumstances
which told them plainer than mere words
that something unusual was in the air.
The moment they were all assembled about
me I acquainted them with the intelligence
received from Elliot, and at the same time
informed them that we would at once set
out to join in the pursuit, a pursuit which
could and would only end when we overtook
our enemies. And in order that we should
not be trammelled in our movements it was
my intention then and there to abandon our

train of wagons, taking with us only such supplies as we could carry on our persons and strapped to our saddles. The train would be left under the protection of about eighty men detailed from the different troops and under command of one officer, to whom orders would be given to follow us with the train as rapidly as the character of our route would permit. Each trooper was to carry with him one hundred rounds of ammunition, a small amount of coffee and hard bread, and on his saddle an equally small allowance of forage for his horse. Tents and extra blankets were to be left with the wagons. We were to move in light marching order as far as this was practicable.

Then taking out my watch, the officers were notified that in twenty minutes from that time "The advance" would be sounded and the march in pursuit begun—the intervening time to be devoted to carrying out the instructions just given. In a moment every man and officer in the command was vigorously at work preparing to set out for a rough ride, the extent or result of which no one could foresee. Wagons were emptied, mess chests called upon to contribute from their stores, ammunition chests opened and their contents distributed to the troopers. The most inferior of the horses were selected to fill up the detail of eighty cavalry which was to remain and escort the train; an extra amount of clothing was donned by some who realized that when the bitter, freezing hours of night came we would not have the comforts of tents and camp-fire to sustain us.

If we had looked with proper dread upon the discomforts of the past three days, the severity of the storm, the deep snow, and our limited facilities for withstanding the inclemencies of midwinter even when provided with shelter, food, and fire, what was the prospect now opened before us when we proposed to relinquish even the few comforts we had at command and start out on a mission not only full of danger, but where food would be very limited, and then only of the plainest kind? Shelterless we should be in the midst of the wide, open Plains, where the winds blow with greater force, and owing to our proximity to the Indians even fires would be too costly an aid to our comfort to be allowed. Yet these thoughts scarcely found a place in the minds of any members of the command. All felt that a great opportunity was before us, and to improve it only required determination and firmness on our part. How thoroughly and manfully every demand of this kind was responded to by my command, I will endeavor to relate in the next chapter.

Chapter 10

THE BATTLE OF THE WASHITA

BEFORE proceeding to narrate the incidents of the pursuit which led us to the battle of the Washita I will refer to the completion of our hasty preparations to detach ourselves from the encumbrance of our immense wagon train. In the last chapter it has been seen that the train was to be left behind under the protection of an officer and eighty cavalrymen, with orders to push after us, following our trail in the snow as rapidly as the teams could move. Where or when it would again join us no one could foretell; in all probability, however, not until the pursuit had terminated and we had met and vanquished our savage foes or had been defeated by them.

Under existing orders the guard for the protection of our train was each day under the command of the officer of the day, the tour of duty of the latter continuing twenty-four hours, beginning in the morning. On that day the duties of officer of the day fell in regular routine upon Captain Louis McLane Hamilton, Seventh Cavalry, a grandson of Alexander Hamilton. Of course this

detail would require him to remain behind
with the train while his squadron, one of
the finest in the command, would move forward to battle under charge of another. To
a soldier of Hamilton's pride and ambition
to be left behind in this inglorious manner
was galling in the extreme. He foresaw the
situation at once, and the moment that intelligence of the proposed movement reached
him he came galloping up from the rear in
search of me. I was busily engaged at the
time superintending the hurried arrangements for commencing the pursuit. Coming
up to me with a countenance depicting the
most earnest anxiety, his first words were
to frame an inquiry as to whether I intended
him to remain behind.

Fully appreciating his anxious desire to
share with his comrades the perils of the
approaching conflict, and yet unable to substitute, without injustice, another officer for
him unless with the consent of the former,
I could not give him the encouragement he
desired. The moment that the plans for
pursuit were being formed I remembered
that the accidents of service were to deprive
the pursuing column of the presence and
aid of one whose assistance in such an emergency could always be confidently relied
upon. Some of his brother officers had be-

thought themselves of the same, and at once came to me with the remark that "we ought to have Hamilton with us." My only reply was that while my desires were all one way my duty prescribed that Hamilton should remain with the guard and train, it being his detail, and it also being necessary that some officer should remain upon this important duty. I answered his repeated request, that while I desired him in command of his squadron, particularly then of all times, I was powerless to have it so without being unjust to some other officer. While forced to admit this to be true, he added, "It seems hard that I must remain."

Finally I said to him that all I could do would be to allow him to get some other officer to willingly take his place with the train, adding that some officer might be found in the command who from indisposition or other causes did not feel able to undertake a rapid and tiresome pursuit, such as we would probably have, and under such circumstances I would gladly order the change. He at once departed in search of some one who would assume his duties with the train and leave him free to resume his post at the head of his splendid squadron— that squadron in whose organization and equipment he had displayed such energy and forethought, and whose superior excellence and efficiency long bore the impress of his hand. I am thus minute in detailing these circumstances affecting the transfer of Captain Hamilton from one duty to another as the sad sequel will show how intimately connected the destiny of one of the parties was with the slight matter of this change.

Hamilton had been absent but a few minutes when he returned overflowing with joy and remarked that an officer had been found who consented to take his place, ending with the question: "Shall I join my squadron?" To this I gladly assented and he galloped to another part of the field, where his men were, to hasten and superintend their preparations for the coming struggle. The officer who had consented to take Hamilton's place with the train had that day been affected with partial snow-blindness and felt himself disqualified and unable to join in the pursuit, and it was exceedingly proper for him, under the circumstances, to agree to the proposed change.

During all this time Elliot with his three companies of calvary was following hard and fast upon the trail left by the Indians in the deep snow. By being informed, as we were, of the direction in which the trail was leading, and that direction being favorable to our position, the main command by moving due south would strike the trail of the Indians, and of Elliot also, at some point not far in rear, perhaps, of Elliot's party. Everything being in readiness to set out, at the expiration of the allotted twenty minutes "The advance" was sounded and the pursuit on our part began. Our route carried us across the broad, open Plains, the snow over a foot in depth, with the surface of course unbroken. This rendered it exceedingly fatiguing to the horses moving in the advance, and changes were frequently rendered necessary. The weather, which during the past few days had been so bitterly cold, moderated on that day sufficiently to melt the upper surface of the snow.

After leaving the wagon train we continued our march rapidly during the remaining hours of the forenoon and until the middle of the afternoon. Still no tidings from Elliot's party nor any sign of a trail. No halt was made during the day either for rest or refreshment. Toward evening we began to feel anxious concerning Elliot's detachment. Could it be that the Indians had discovered that they were pursued, and had broken up into smaller parties or changed the direction of their trail? If so, could Elliot's messengers reach us in time to make the information valuable to us? We had hurried along, our interest increasing with each mile passed over, until the sun was not more than one hour high above the western horizon; and still, strain our eyes as we would and scan the white surface of the Plains in every direction in our front, the snow seemed unbroken and undisturbed as far as the eye could reach.

Our scouts and Indian guides were kept far out in front and on the proper flank to discover, if possible, the trail. At last one of the scouts gave the signal that the trail had been discovered and in a few moments the command had reached it and we were now moving with lighter and less anxious hearts. After studying the trail our Osage warriors informed us that the Indians whose trail we were pursuing were undoubtedly a war party, and had certainly passed where we then were during the forenoon. This was encouraging and a free rein was given to our horses as we hastened along through the snow.

The object now was to overtake as soon as practicable the party of Elliot, which from the heavy trail we could see was in advance of us. The almost level and unbroken character of the country enabled us to see for miles in all directions, and in this way we knew that Elliot must be many miles ahead of our party. At the same time I could see that we were gradually descending into a valley, probably of some stream, and far in advance appeared the dim outline of timber, such as usually fringes the banks of many of the western streams. Selecting a few well-mounted troopers and some of the scouts, I directed them to set out at a moderate gallop to overtake Elliot, with orders to the latter to halt at the first favorable point where wood and water could be obtained and await our arrival, informing him at the same time that after allowing the men an hour to prepare a cup of coffee and to feed and rest their horses it was my intention to continue the pursuit during the night—a measure to which I felt urged by the slight thawing of the snow that day, which might result in our failure if we permitted the Indians to elude us until the snow had disappeared.

Satisfied now that we were on the right course, our anxiety lessened, but our interest increased. Soon after dark we reached the valley whose timbered surface we had caught faint glimpses of hours before. Down this valley and through this sparse timber the trail led us. Hour after hour we struggled on, hoping to overtake the three troops in advance, for hunger, unappeased since before daylight, began to assert its demands in the strongest terms. Our faithful horses were likewise in great need of both food and water as well as rest, as neither had been offered them since four o'clock in the morning. So far had Elliot pushed his pursuit that our scouts were a long time in reaching him and it was nine o'clock at night when the main command arrived at the point where he and his three troops were found halted. A stream of good water with comparatively deep banks ran near by, while the valley at this point was quite heavily timbered.

To enable the men to prepare a cup of coffee, and at the same time give no evidence of our presence to the Indians, who for all we knew might be not far from us, advantage was taken of the deep banks of the creek, and by building small fires down under the edge of the bank they were prevented from being seen except at a small distance. At the same time the horses were relieved of their saddles and unbitted, and a good feed of oats distributed to each. Officers and men were glad to partake of the same quality of simple fare that night, consisting only of a most welcome and refreshing cup of good strong coffee and a handful of army crackers—hard tack. By waiting an hour we not only gained by rest and refreshment, but the light of the moon would then probably be sufficient to guide us on our night ride.

Battle of the Washita

When the hour had nearly expired we began our preparations in the most quiet manner to resume the pursuit. No bugle calls
were permitted as in this peculiar country
sound travels a long distance and we knew not
but that our wily foes were located near by.
Before starting I conferred with our Indian
allies, all of whom were firmly convinced that
our enemy's village was probably not far
away, and most likely was in the valley in
which we then were, as the trail for some
miles had led us down the stream on whose
banks we halted. Little Beaver, who acted
as spokesman for the Osages, seemed confident that we could overtake and surprise
the Indians we had been pursuing and most
probably follow them direct to their village;
but much to my surprise Little Beaver
strongly advised that we delay further pursuit until daylight, remaining concealed in
the timber as we were at the time. When
asked for his reasons for favoring such a
course he could give none of a satisfactory
nature. I then concluded that his disinclination to continue pursuit that night arose from
the natural reluctance, shared by all Indians,
to attack an unseen foe, whether concealed
by darkness or other natural or artificial
means of shelter. Indians rarely attack between the hours of dark and daylight, although their stealthy movements through

the country either in search of an enemy or when attempting to elude them are often executed under cover of night.

As soon as each troop was in readiness to resume the pursuit the troop commander reported the fact at headquarters. Ten o'clock came and found us in our saddles. Silently the command stretched out its long length as the troopers filed off four abreast. First came two of our Osage scouts on foot; these were to follow the trail and lead the command; they were our guides and the panther, creeping upon its prey could not have advanced more cautiously or quietly than did these friendly Indians as they seemed to glide rather than walk over the snow-clad surface. To prevent the possibility of the command coming precipitately upon our enemies the two scouts were directed to keep three or four hundred yards in advance of all others; then came, in single file, the remainder of our Osage guides and the white scouts—among the rest California Joe. With these I rode, that I might be as near the advance guard as possible. The cavalry followed in rear at the distance of a quarter or half a mile; this precaution was necessary from the fact that the snow, which had thawed slightly during the day, was then freezing, forming a crust which, broken by the tread of so many hundreds of feet, produced a noise capable of being heard at a long distance.

Orders were given prohibiting even a word being uttered above a whisper. No one was permitted to strike a match or light a pipe— the latter a great deprivation to the soldier. In this silent manner we rode mile after mile. Occasionally an officer would ride by my side and whisper some inquiry or suggestion, but aside from this our march was unbroken by sound or deed. At last we discovered that our two guides in front had halted and were awaiting my arrival. Word was quietly sent to halt the column until inquiry in front could be made. Upon coming up with the two Osages we were furnished an example of the wonderful and peculiar powers of the Indian. One of them could speak broken English and in answer to my question as to "What is the matter?" he replied: "Me don't know, but me smell fire." By this time several of the officers had quietly ridden up and upon being informed of the Osage's remark each endeavored, by sniffing the air, to verify or disprove the report. All united in saying that our guide was mistaken. Some said he was probably frightened, but we were unable to shake the confidence of the Osage warrior in his first opinion. I then directed him and his companion to advance even more cautiously than before and the column, keeping up the interval, resumed its march.

After proceeding about half a mile, perhaps farther, again our guides halted, and upon coming up with them I was greeted with the remark, uttered in a whisper: "Me told you so;" and sure enough, looking in the direction indicated were to be seen the embers of a wasted fire, scarcely a handful yet enough to prove that our guide was right and to cause us to feel the greater confidence in him. The discovery of these few coals of fire produced almost breathless excitement. The distance from where we stood was from seventy-five to a hundred yards, not in the line of our march, but directly to our left in the edge of the timber. We knew at once that none but Indians, and they hostile, had built that fire. Where were they at that moment? Perhaps sleeping in the vicinity of the fire.

It was almost certain to our minds that the Indians we had been pursuing were the builders of the fire. Were they still there and asleep? We were too near already to attempt to withdraw undiscovered. Our only course was to determine the facts at once, and be prepared for the worst. I called for a few volunteers to quietly approach the fire and discover whether there were Indians in the vicinity; if not, to gather such information as was obtainable as to their numbers and departure. All the Osages and a few of the scouts quickly dismounted and with rifles in readiness and fingers on the triggers silently made their way to the nearest point of the timber, Little Beaver and Hard Rope leading the way. After they had disappeared in the timber they still had to pass over more than half the distance before reaching the fire. These moments seemed like hours and those of us who were left sitting on our horses, in the open moonlight and within easy range from the spot where the fire was located felt anything but comfortable during this suspense. If Indians, as then seemed highly probable, were sleeping around the fire our scouts would arouse them and we would be in fair way to be picked off without being in a position to defend ourselves.

The matter was soon determined. Our scouts soon arrived at the fire and discovered it to be deserted. Again did the skill and knowledge of our Indian allies come in play. Had they not been with us we should undoubtedly have assumed that the Indians who had had occasion to build the fire and those we were pursuing constituted one party. From examining the fire and observing the great number of pony tracks in the snow the

Osages arrived at a different conclusion and were convinced that we were then on the ground used by the Indians for grazing their herds of ponies. The fire had been kindled by the Indian boys, who attend to the herding, to warm themselves by, and in all probability we were then within two or three miles of the village. I will not endeavor to describe the renewed hope and excitement that sprang up. Again we set out, this time more cautiously, if possible, than before, the command and scouts moving at a greater distance in rear.

In order to judge of the situation more correctly I this time accompanied the two Osages. Silently we advanced, I mounted, they on foot, keeping at the head of my horse. Upon nearing the crest of each hill, as is invariably the Indian custom, one of the guides would hasten a few steps in advance and peer cautiously over the hill. Accustomed to this, I was not struck by observing it until once when the same one who discovered the fire advanced cautiously to the crest and looked carefully into the valley beyond. I saw him place his hand above his eyes as if looking intently at some object, then crouch down and come creeping back to where I waited for him. "What is it?" I inquired as soon as he reached my horse's side. "Heaps Injuns down there," pointing in the direction from which he had just come.

Quickly dismounting and giving the reins to the other guide, I accompanied the Osage to the crest, both of us crouching low so as not to be seen in the moonlight against the horizon. Looking in the direction indicated, I could indistinctly recognize the presence of a large body of animals of some kind in the valley below and at a distance which then seemed not more than half a mile. I looked at them long and anxiously, the guide uttering not a word, but was unable to discover anything in their appearance different from what might be presented by a herd of buffaloes under similar circumstances. Turning to the Osage, I inquired in a low tone why he thought there were Indians there. "Me heard dog bark," was the satisfactory reply. Indians are noted for the large number of dogs always found in their villages, but never accompanying their war parties.

I waited quietly to be convinced; I was assured, but wanted to be doubly so. I was rewarded in a moment by hearing the barking of a dog in the heavy timber off to the right of the herd, and soon after I heard the tinkling of a small bell; this convinced me that it was really the Indian herd I then saw, the bell being one worn around the neck of some pony who was probably the leader of the herd. I turned to retrace my steps when another sound was borne to my ear through the cold, clear atmosphere of the valley—it was the distant cry of an infant; and savages though they were and justly outlawed by the number and atrocity of their recent murders and depredations on the helpless settlers of the frontier, I could not but regret that in a war such as we were forced to engage in the mode and circumstances of battle would possibly prevent discrimination.

Leaving the two Osages to keep a careful lookout, I hastened back until I met the main party of the scouts and Osages. They were halted and a message sent back to halt the cavalry, enjoining complete silence and directing every officer to ride to the point we then occupied. The hour was then past midnight. Soon they came and after dismounting and collecting in a little circle I informed them of what I had seen and heard; and in order that they might individually learn as much as possible of the character of the ground and the location of the village I proposed that all should remove their sabers, that their clanking might make no noise, and proceed gently to the crest and there obtain a view of the valley beyond. This was done; not a word was spoken until we crouched together and cast our eyes in the direction of the herd and village. In whispers I briefly pointed out everything that was to be seen, then motioned all to return to where we had left our sabers; then, standing in a group upon the ground or crust of snow, the plan of the attack was explained to all and each assigned his part.

The general plan was to employ the hours between then and daylight to completely surround the village and at daybreak, or as soon as it was barely light enough for the purpose, to attack the Indians from all sides. The command, numbering, as has been stated, about eight hundred mounted men, was divided into four nearly equal detachments. Two of them set out at once, as they had each to make a circuitous march of several miles in order to arrive at the points assigned them from which to make their attack. The third detachment moved to its position about an hour before day, and until that time remained with the main or fourth column. This last, whose movements I accompanied, was to make the attack from the point from which we had first discovered the herd and village. Major Elliot commanded the column embracing G, H, and M troops, Seventh Cavalry, which moved around from our left to a position almost in rear of the village; while

Colonel Thompson commanded the one consisting of B and F troops, which moved in a corresponding manner from our right to a position which was to connect with that of Major Elliot. Colonel Meyers commanded the third column, composed of E and I troops, which was to take position in the valley and timber a little less than a mile to my right.

By this disposition it was hoped to prevent the escape of every inmate of the village. That portion of the command which I proposed to accompany consisted of A, C, D, and K troops, Seventh Cavalry, the Osages and scouts, and Colonel Cooke with his forty sharpshooters. Captain Hamilton commanded one of the squadrons, Colonel West the other. After the first two columns had departed for their posts—it was still four hours before the hour of attack—the men of the other two columns were permitted to dismount, but much intense suffering was unavoidably sustained. The night grew extremely cold towards morning; no fires of course could be permitted, and the men were even ordered to desist from stamping their feet and walking back and forth to keep warm, as the crushing of the snow beneath produced so much noise that it might give the alarm to our wily enemies.

322

THE BATTLE OF THE WASHITA.

During all these long weary hours of this terribly cold and comfortless night each man sat, stood, or lay on the snow by his horse, holding to the rein of the latter. The officers, buttoning their huge overcoats closely about them, collected in knots of four or five, and, seated or reclining upon the snow's hard crust, discussed the probabilities of the coming battle, for battle we knew it would be, and we could not hope to conquer or kill the warriors of an entire village without suffering in return more or less injury. Some, wrapping their capes about their heads, spread themselves at full length upon the snow and were apparently soon wrapped in deep slumber. After being satisfied that all necessary arrangements were made for the attack I imitated the example of some of my comrades and gathering the cavalry cape of my greatcoat about my head lay down and slept soundly for perhaps an hour.

At the end of that time I awoke and on consulting my watch found there remained nearly two hours before we would move to the attack. Walking about among the horses and troopers, I found the latter generally huddled at the feet of the former in squads of three and four, in the endeavor to keep warm. Occasionally I would find a small group engaged in conversation, the muttered

324

tones and voices strangely reminding me of those heard in the death-chamber. The officers had disposed of themselves in similar but various ways; here at one place were several stretched out together upon the snow, the body of one being used by the others as a pillow. Nearly all were silent; conversation had ceased, and those who were prevented by the severe cold from obtaining sleep were no doubt fully occupied in their minds with thoughts upon the morrow and the fate that might be in store for them.

Seeing a small group collected under the low branches of a tree which stood a little distance from the ground occupied by the troops, I made my way there to find the Osage warriors with their chiefs, Little Beaver and Hard Rope. They were wrapped up in their blankets sitting in a circle, and had evidently made no effort to sleep during the night. It was plain to be seen that they regarded the occasion as a momentous one and that the coming battle had been the sole subject of their conference. What the views expressed by them were I did not learn until after the engagement was fought, when they told me what ideas they had entertained regarding the manner in which the white men would probably conduct and terminate the struggle next day. After the success of the

day was decided, the Osages told me that,
with the suspicion so natural and peculiar to
the Indian nature, they had, in discussing
the proposed attack upon the Indian village,
concluded that we would be outnumbered by
the occupants of the village, who of course
would fight with the utmost desperation in
defense of their lives and lodges, and to prevent a complete defeat of our forces or to
secure a drawn battle we might be induced
to engage in a parley with the hostile tribe,
and on coming to an agreement we would
probably, to save ourselves, offer to yield up
our Osage allies as a compromise measure
between our enemies and ourselves.

They also mistrusted the ability of the
whites to make a successful attack upon a
hostile village, located, as this one was known
to be, in heavy timber, and aided by the
natural banks of the stream. Disaster seemed
certain in the minds of the Osages to follow
us, if we attacked a force of unknown strength
and numbers; and the question with them
was to secure such a position in the attack as
to be able promptly to detect any move dis-
advantageous to them. With this purpose
they came to the conclusion that the standard-bearer was a very important personage,
and neither he nor his standard would be
carried into danger or exposed to the bullets

of the enemy. They determined therefore to take their station immediately behind my standard-bearer when the lines became formed for attack, to follow him during the action and thus be able to watch our movements, and if we were successful over our foes to aid us; if the battle should go against us, then they, being in a safe position, could take advantage of circumstances and save themselves as best they might.

Turning from our Osage friends, who were, unknown to us, entertaining such doubtful opinions as to our fidelity to them, I joined another group near by, consisting of most of the white scouts. Here were California Joe and several of his companions. One of the latter deserves a passing notice. He was a low, heavy-set Mexican, with features resembling somewhat those of the Ethiopian—thick lips, depressed nose, and low forehead. He was quite a young man, probably not more than twenty-five years of age, but had passed the greater portion of his life with the Indians, had adopted their habits of life and modes of dress, and had married among them. Familiar with the language of the Cheyennes and other neighboring tribes, he was invaluable both as a scout and interpreter. His real name was Romero, but some of the officers of the command, with whom he was a sort of favorite, had dubbed him Romeo, and by this name he was always known, a sobriquet to which he responded as readily as if he had been christened under it; never protesting, like the original Romeo,

> Tut, I have lost myself; I am not here;
> This is not Romeo, he's some other where.

The scouts like nearly all the other members of the command had been interchanging opinions as to the result of the movements of the following day. Not sharing the mistrust and suspicion of the Osage guides, yet the present experience was in many respects new to them, and to some the issue seemed at least shrouded in uncertainty. Addressing the group, I began the conversation with the question as to what they thought of the prospect of our having a fight. "Fight!" responded California Joe; "I haven't nary doubt concernin' that part uv the business; what I've been tryin' to get through my top-knot all night is whether we'll run aginst more than we bargain fur." "Then you do not think the Indians will run away, Joe?" "Run away! How in creation can Injuns or anybody else run away when we'll have 'em clean surrounded afore daylight?" "Well, suppose then that we succeed in surrounding the village, do you think we can hold our own against the Indians?" "That's the very pint that's been botherin' me ever since we planted ourselves down here, and the only conclusion I kin come at is that it's purty apt to be one thing or t'other; if we jump these Injuns at daylight, we're either goin' to make a spoon or spile a horn, an' that's my candid judgment, sure. One thing's certain, ef them Injuns doesn't har anything uv us till we open on 'em at daylight, they'll be the most powerful 'stonished redskins that's been in these parts lately—they will, sure. An' ef we git the bulge on 'em and keep puttin' it to 'em sort a lively like we'll sweep the platter, thar won't be nary trick left for 'em. As the deal stands now we hold the keerds and are holdin' over 'em; they've got to straddle our blind or throw up their hands. Howsomever, thar's a mighty sight in the draw."

California Joe continued in this strain and by a prolific use of terms connected with other transactions besides fighting Indians did not fail to impress his hearers that his opinion in substance was that our attack in the morning was to result in overwhelming success to us, or that we would be utterly routed and dispersed—that there would be no drawn battle.

The night passed in quiet. I anxiously watched the opening signs of dawn in order to put the column in motion. We were only a few hundred yards from the point from which we were to attack. The moon disappeared about two hours before dawn and left us enshrouded in thick and utter darkness, making the time seem to drag even slower than before.

At last faint signs of approaching day were visible and I proceeded to collect the officers, awakening those who slept. We were standing in a group near the head of the column when suddenly our attention was attracted by a remarkable sight and for a time we felt that the Indians had discovered our presence. Directly beyond the crest of the hill which separated us from the village and in a line with the supposed location of the latter we saw rising slowly but perceptibly, as we thought, up from the village and appearing in bold relief against the dark sky as a background something which we could only compare to a signal rocket, except that its motion was slow and regular. All eyes were turned to it in blank astonishment and but one idea seemed to be entertained, and that was that one or both of the two attacking columns under Elliot or Thompson had encountered a portion of the village and this that we saw was the signal to other portions of the band near at hand. Slowly and majestically it continued to rise above the crest of the hill, first appearing as a small brilliant flaming globe of bright golden hue. As it ascended still higher it seemed to increase in size, to move more slowly, while its colors rapidly changed from one to the other, exhibiting in turn the most beautiful combinations of prismatic tints. There seemed to be not the shadow of doubt that we were discovered.

The strange apparition in the heavens maintained its steady course upward. One anxious spectator, observing it apparently at a standstill, exclaimed: "How long it hangs fire! why don't it explode?" still keeping the idea of a signal rocket in mind. It had risen perhaps to the height of half a degree above the horizon as observed from our position when, lo! the mystery was dispelled. Rising above the mystifying influences of the atmosphere, that which had appeared so suddenly before us and excited our greatest apprehensions developed into the brightest and most beautiful of morning stars. Often since that memorable morning have I heard officers remind each other of the strange appearance which had so excited our anxiety and alarm. In less perilous moments we probably would have regarded it as a beautiful phenomenon of nature, of which so many are to be witnessed through the pure atmosphere of the Plains.

All were ordered to get ready to advance; not a word to officer or men was spoken above undertone. It began growing lighter in the east and we moved forward toward the crest of the hill. Up to this time two of the officers and one of the Osages had remained on the hill overlooking the valley beyond so as to detect any attempt at a movement on the part of the occupants of the village below. These now rejoined the troops. Colonel West's squadron was formed in line on the right, Captain Hamilton's squadron in line on the left, while Colonel Cooke with his forty sharpshooters was formed in advance of the left, dismounted. Although the early morning air was freezingly cold the men were directed to remove their overcoats and haversacks, so as to render them free in their movements.

Before advancing beyond the crest of the hill strict orders were issued prohibiting the firing of a single shot until the signal to attack should be made. The other three detachments had been informed before setting out that the main column would attack promptly at daylight without waiting to ascertain whether they were in position or not. In fact it would be impracticable to communicate with either of the first two until the attack began. The plan was for each party to approach as closely to the village as possible without being discovered and there await the approach of daylight. The regimental band was to move with my detachment and it was understood that the band should strike up the instant the attack opened. Colonel Meyers, commanding the third party, was also directed to move one-half his detachment dismounted.

In this order we began to descend the slope leading down to the village. The distance to the timber in the valley proved greater than it had appeared to the eye in the darkness of the night. We soon reached the outskirts of the herd of ponies. The latter seemed to recognize us as hostile parties and moved quickly away. The light of day was each minute growing stronger and we feared discovery before we could approach near enough to charge the village. The movement of our horses over the crusted snow produced considerable noise and would doubtless have led to our detection but for the fact that the Indians, if they heard it at all, presumed it was occasioned by their herd of ponies. I would have given much at that moment to know the whereabouts of the first two columns sent out. Had they reached their assigned positions, or had unseen and unknown obstacles delayed or misled them? These

333

were questions which could not then be answered. We had now reached the level of the valley and began advancing in line toward the heavy timber in which and close at hand we knew the village was situated.

Immediately in rear of my horse came the band, all mounted and each with his instrument in readiness to begin playing the moment their leader, who rode at their head and who kept his cornet to his lips, should receive the signal. I had previously told him to play Garry Owen as the opening piece. We had approached near enough to the village now to plainly catch a view here and there of the tall white lodges as they stood in irregular order among the trees. From the openings at the top of some of them we could perceive faint columns of smoke ascending, the occupants no doubt having kept up their feeble fires during the entire night. We had approached so near the village that from the dead silence which reigned I feared the lodges were deserted, the Indians having fled before we advanced. I was about to turn in my saddle and direct the signal for attack to be given, still anxious as to where the other detachments were, when a single rifle shot rang sharp and clear on the far side of the village from where we were. Quickly turning to the band leader, I directed him to give us Garry

Battle of the Washita

Owen. At once the rollicking notes of that familiar marching and fighting air sounded forth through the valley and in a moment were reëchoed back from the opposite sides by the loud and continued cheers of the men of the other detachments, who, true to their orders, were there and in readiness to pounce upon the Indians the moment the attack began.

In this manner the battle of the Washita commenced. The bugles sounded the charge and the entire command dashed rapidly into the village. The Indians were caught napping; but realizing at once the dangers of their situation, they quickly overcame their first surprise and in an instant seized their rifles, bows, and arrows, and sprang behind the nearest trees, while some leaped into the stream, nearly waist deep, and using the bank as a rifle-pit began a vigorous and determined defense. Mingled with the exultant cheers of my men could be heard the defiant war-whoop of the warriors, who from the first fought with a desperation and courage which no race of men could surpass. Actual possession of the village and its lodges was ours within a few moments after the charge was made, but this was an empty victory unless we could vanquish the late occupants, who were then pouring in a rapid and well-

335

directed fire from their stations behind trees and banks. At the first onset a considerable number of the Indians rushed from the village in the direction from which Elliot's party had attacked. Some broke through the lines, while others came in contact with the mounted troopers and were killed or captured.

Before engaging in the fight orders had been given to prevent the killing of any but the fighting strength of the village; but in a struggle of this character it is impossible at all times to discriminate, particularly when, in a hand-to-hand conflict such as the one the troops were then engaged in the squaws are as dangerous adversaries as the warriors, while Indian boys between ten and fifteen years of age were found as expert and determined in the use of the pistol and bow and arrow as the older warriors. Of these facts we had numerous illustrations. Major Benteen,[32] in leading the attack of his squadron

[32] Captain Frederick W. Benteen served throughout the Civil War, attaining the rank of lieutenant colonel. He was commissioned captain in the Seventh U.S. Cavalry upon the organization of the regiment in 1866. Temperamental and other differences imbued him with a distinct dislike for Custer, his immediate superior, until the death of the latter in 1876. The imputation that because of this dislike he failed to support Custer loyally in the battle of the Little Big Horn is probably unfounded. In 1882 he became a major in the Ninth

Battle of the Washita

through the timber below the village, encountered an Indian boy scarcely fourteen years of age; he was well mounted and was endeavoring to make his way through the lines. The object these Indians had in attempting this movement we were then ignorant of, but soon learned to our sorrow. This boy rode boldly toward the Major, seeming to invite a contest. His youthful bearing, and not being looked upon as a combatant, induced Major Benteen to endeavor to save him by making peace signs to him and obtaining his surrender, when he could be placed in a position of safety until the battle was terminated; but the young savage desired and would accept no such friendly concessions. He regarded himself as a warrior and the son of a warrior and as such he purposed to do a warrior's part. With revolver in hand he dashed at the Major, who still could not regard him as anything but a harmless lad. Levelling his weapon as he rode, he fired, but either from excitement or the changing positions of both parties his aim was defective and the shot whistled harmlessly by Major Benteen's head. Another followed in quick

U.S. Cavalry, and in 1886 retired from active service. A veteran in the frontier and Indian service, his reputation was clouded by the interminable dispute over the conduct and character of General Custer.

succession, but with no better effect. All this time the dusky little chieftain boldly advanced, to lessen the distance between himself and his adversary. A third bullet was sped on its errand and this time to some purpose, as it passed through the neck of the Major's horse close to the shoulder. Making a final but ineffectual appeal to him to surrender and seeing him still preparing to fire again, the Major was forced in self-defense to level his revolver and despatch him, although as he did so it was with admiration for the plucky spirit exhibited by the lad and regret often expressed that no other course under the circumstances was left him. Attached to the saddle bow of the young Indian hung a beautifully wrought pair of small moccasins elaborately ornamented with beads. One of the Major's troopers afterward secured these and presented them to him. These furnished the link of evidence by which we subsequently ascertained who the young chieftain was, a title which was justly his, both by blood and bearing.

We had gained the center of the village and were in the midst of the lodges, while on all sides could be heard the sharp crack of the Indian rifles and the heavy responses from the carbines of the troopers. After disposing of the smaller and scattering parties of warriors who had attempted a movement down the valley, and in which some were successful, there was but little opportunity left for the successful employment of mounted troops. As the Indians by this time had taken cover behind logs and trees and under the banks of the stream which flowed through the center of the village, from which stronghold it was impracticable to dislodge them by the use of mounted men, a large portion of the command was at once ordered to fight on foot, and the men were instructed to take advantage of the trees and other natural means of cover and fight the Indians in their own style.

Cooke's sharpshooters had adopted this method from the first, and with telling effect. Slowly but steadily the Indians were driven from behind the trees, and those who escaped the carbine bullets posted themselves with their companions who were already firing from the banks. One party of troopers came upon a squaw endeavoring to make her escape, leading by the hand a little white boy, a prisoner in the hands of the Indians, and who doubtless had been captured by some of their war parties during a raid upon the settlements. Who or where his parents were, or whether still alive or murdered by the Indians, will never be known, as the squaw, finding herself and prisoner about to

be surrounded by the troops and her escape
cut off, determined, with savage malignity,
that the triumph of the latter should not
embrace the rescue of the white boy. Casting
her eyes quickly in all directions to convince
herself that escape was impossible, she drew
from beneath her blanket a huge knife and
plunged it into the almost naked body of her
captive. The next moment retributive justice reached her in the shape of a well-directed
bullet from one of the troopers' carbines.
Before the men could reach them life was
extinct in the bodies of both the squaw and
her unknown captive.

The desperation with which the Indians
fought may be inferred from the following:
Seventeen warriors had posted themselves in
a depression in the ground which enabled
them to protect their bodies completely from
the fire of our men, and it was only when the
Indians raised their heads to fire that the
troopers could aim with any prospect of success. All efforts to drive the warriors from
this point proved abortive and resulted in
severe loss to our side. They were only vanquished at last by our men securing positions
under cover and picking them off by sharp-
shooting as they exposed themselves to get a
shot at the troopers. Finally the last one was
despatched in this manner. In a deep ravine

near the suburbs of the village the dead bodies of thirty-eight warriors were reported after the fight terminated.

Many of the squaws and children had very prudently not attempted to leave the village when we attacked it, but remained concealed inside their lodges. All these escaped injury, although when surrounded by the din and wild excitement of the fight and in close proximity to the contending parties their fears overcame some of them and they gave vent to their despair by singing the death song, a combination of weird-like sounds which were suggestive of anything but musical tones. As soon as we had driven the warriors from the village and the fighting was pushed to the country outside I directed Romeo, the interpreter, to go around to all the lodges and assure the squaws and children remaining in them that they would be unharmed and kindly cared for; at the same time he was to assemble them in the large lodges designated for that purpose which were standing near the center of the village. This was quite a delicate mission as it was difficult to convince the squaws and children that they had anything but death to expect at our hands.

It was perhaps ten o'clock in the forenoon and the fight was still raging when to our surprise we saw a small party of Indians collected on a knoll a little over a mile below the village and in the direction taken by those Indians who had effected an escape through our lines at the commencement of the attack. My surprise was not so great at first as I imagined that the Indians we saw were those who had contrived to escape, and having procured their ponies from the herd had mounted them and were then anxious spectators of the fight, which they felt themselves too weak in numbers to participate in.

In the meantime the herds of ponies belonging to the village, on being alarmed by the firing and shouts of the contestants, had, from a sense of imagined security or custom, rushed into the village, where details of troopers were made to receive them. California Joe, who had been moving about in a promiscuous and independent manner, came galloping into the village and reported that a large herd of ponies was to be seen near by, and requested authority and some men to bring them in. The men were otherwise employed just then, but he was authorized to collect and drive in the herd if practicable. He departed on his errand and I had forgotten all about him and the ponies when in the course of half an hour I saw a herd of nearly three hundred ponies coming on the gallop toward the village, driven by a couple of squaws who were mounted, and had been concealed near by, no doubt; while bringing up the rear was California Joe, riding his favorite mule and whirling about his head a long lariat, using it as a whip in urging the herd forward. He had captured the squaws while endeavoring to secure the ponies, and very wisely had employed his captives to assist in driving the herd.

By this time the group of Indians already discovered outside our lines had increased until it numbered upwards of a hundred. Examining them through my field glass, I could plainly perceive that they were all mounted warriors; not only that, but they were armed and caparisoned in full war costume, nearly all wearing the bright-colored war-bonnets and floating their lance pennants. Constant accessions to their numbers were to be seen arriving from beyond the hill on which they stood. All this seemed inexplicable. A few Indians might have escaped through our lines when the attack on the village began, but only a few, and even these must have gone with little or nothing in their possession save their rifles and perhaps a blanket. Who could these new parties be, and from whence came they?

To solve these troublesome questions I sent for Romeo, and taking him with me to one of the lodges occupied by the squaws, I interrogated one of the latter as to who were the Indians to be seen assembling on the hill below the village. She informed me, to a surprise on my part almost equal to that of the Indians at our sudden appearance at daylight, that just below the village we then occupied, and which was a part of the Cheyenne tribe, were located in succession the winter villages of all the hostile tribes of the southern Plains with which we were at war, including the Arapahoes, Kiowas, the remaining band of Cheyennes, the Comanches, and a portion of the Apaches; that the nearest village was about two miles distant, and the others stretched along through the timbered valley to the one farthest off, which was not over ten miles.

What was to be done?—for I needed no one to tell me that we were certain to be attacked and that, too, by greatly superior numbers, just as soon as the Indians below could make their arrangements to do so; and they had probably been busily employed at these arrangements ever since the sound of firing had reached them in the early morning, and been reported from village to village. Fortunately, affairs took a favorable turn in the combat in which we were then engaged, and the firing had almost died away. Only here and there where some warrior still maintained his position was the fight continued. Leaving as few men as possible to look out for these, I hastily collected and reformed my command and posted them in readiness for the attack which we all felt was soon to be made; for already at different points and in more than one direction we could see more than enough warriors to outnumber us and we knew they were only waiting the arrival of the chiefs and warriors from the lower villages before making any move against us.

In the meanwhile our temporary hospital had been established in the center of the village, where the wounded were receiving such surgical care as circumstances would permit. Our losses had been severe; indeed, we were not then aware how great they had been. Hamilton, who rode at my side as we entered the village and whose soldierly tones I heard for the last time as he calmly cautioned his squadron, "Now, men, keep cool, fire low, and not too rapidly," was among the first victims of the opening charge, having been shot from his saddle by a bullet from an Indian rifle. He died instantly. His lifeless remains were tenderly carried by some of his troopers to the vicinity of the hospital. Soon afterwards I saw four troopers coming from the front bearing between them in a blanket a wounded soldier; galloping to them, I discovered Colonel Barnitz, another troop commander, who was almost in a dying condition, having been shot by a rifle bullet directly through the body in the vicinity of the heart. Of Major Elliot, the officer second in rank, nothing had been seen since the attack at daylight, when he rode with his detachment into the village. He, too, had evidently been killed, but as yet we knew not where or how he had fallen. Two other officers had received wounds, while the casualties among the enlisted men were also large. The sergeant-major of the regiment, who was with me when the first shot was heard, had not been seen since that moment.

We were not in as effective condition by far as when the attack was made, yet we were soon to be called upon to contend against a force immensely superior to the one with which we had been engaged during the early hours of the day. The captured herds of ponies were carefully collected inside our lines and so guarded as to prevent their stampede or recapture by the Indians. Our wounded, and the immense amount of captured property in the way of ponies, lodges, etc., as well as our prisoners, were obstacles in the way of our attempting an offensive movement against the lower villages. To have done this would have compelled us to divide our forces, when it was far from certain that we could muster strength enough united to repel the attacks of the combined tribes. On all sides of us the Indians could now be seen in considerable numbers, so that from being the surrounding party, as we had been in the morning, we now found ourselves surrounded and occupying the position of defenders of the village.

Fortunately for us, as the men had been expending a great many rounds, Major Bell, the quartermaster, who with a small escort was endeavoring to reach us with a fresh supply of ammunition, had by constant exertion and hard marching succeeded in doing so and now appeared on the ground with several thousand rounds of carbine ammunition, a reinforcement greatly needed. He had no sooner arrived safely than the Indians attacked from the direction from which he came. How he had managed to elude their watchful eyes I never could comprehend unless their attention had been so completely absorbed in watching our movements inside as to prevent them from keeping an eye out to discover what might be transpiring elsewhere.

Issuing a fresh supply of ammunition to those most in want of it, the fight soon began generally at all points of the circle. For such in reality had our line of battle become, a continuous and unbroken circle of which the village was about the center. Notwithstanding the great superiority in numbers of the Indians, they fought with excessive prudence and a lack of that confident manner which they usually manifest when encountering greatly inferior numbers, a result due, no doubt, to the fate which had overwhelmed our first opponents. Besides, the timber and the configuration of the ground enabled us to keep our men concealed until their services were actually required. It seemed to be the design and wish of our antagonists to draw us away from the village; but in this they were foiled.

Seeing that they did not intend to press the attack just then, about two hundred of my men were ordered to pull down the lodges in the village and collect the captured property in huge piles preparatory to burning. This was done in the most effectual manner. When everything had been collected the torch was applied, and all that was left of the village were a few heaps of blackened ashes. Whether enraged at the sight of this destruction or from other cause, the attack soon be-

came general along our entire line, and pressed
with so much vigor and audacity that every
available trooper was required to aid in
meeting these assaults. The Indians would
push a party of well-mounted warriors close
up to our lines in the endeavor to find a weak
point through which they might venture, but
in every attempt were driven back.

I now concluded, as the village was off our
hands and our wounded had been collected,
that offensive measures might be adopted.
To this end several of the squadrons were
mounted and ordered to advance and attack
the enemy wherever force sufficient was exposed to be a proper object of attack, but at
the same time to be cautious as to ambus-
cades. Colonel Weir, who had succeeded to
the command of Hamilton's squadron, Colonels Benteen and Meyers with their respective
squadrons, all mounted, advanced and engaged the enemy. The Indians resisted every
step taken by the troops, while every charge
made by the latter was met or followed by a
charge from the Indians, who continued to
appear in large numbers at unexpected times
and places. The squadrons acting in support
of each other and the men in each being kept
well in hand, were soon able to force the line
held by the Indians to yield at any point assailed. This being followed up promptly, the

Indians were driven at every point and forced to abandon the field to us. Yet they would go no farther than they were actually driven.

It was now about three o'clock in the afternoon. I knew that the officer left in charge of the train and eighty men would push after us, follow our trail, and endeavor to reach us at the earliest practicable moment. From the tops of some of the highest peaks or round hills in the vicinity of the village I knew the Indians could reconnoiter the country for miles in all directions. I feared if we remained as we were then until the following day the Indians might in this manner discover the approach of our train and detach a sufficient body of warriors to attack and capture it; and its loss to us, aside from that of its guard, would have proved most serious, leaving us in the heart of the enemy's country in midwinter, totally out of supplies for both men and horses.

By actual count we had in our possession eight hundred and seventy-five captured ponies, so wild and unused to white men that it was difficult to herd them. What we were to do with them was puzzling as they could not have been led had we been possessed of the means of doing this; neither could we drive them as the Indians were accustomed to do. And even if we could take them with us, either the one way or the other, it was anything but wise or desirable on our part to do so as such a large herd of ponies, constituting so much wealth in the eyes of the Indians, would have been too tempting a prize to the warriors who had been fighting us all the afternoon, and to effect their recapture they would have followed and waylaid us day and night with every prospect of success until we should have arrived at a place of safety. Besides, we had upwards of sixty prisoners in our hands to say nothing of our wounded, to embarrass our movements. We had achieved a great and important success over the hostile tribes; the problem now was how to retain our advantage and steer safely through the difficulties which seemed to surround our position. The Indians had suffered a telling defeat involving great losses in life and valuable property. Could they succeed, however, in depriving us of the train and supplies and in doing this accomplish the killing or capture of the escort it would go far to offset the damage we had been able to inflict upon them and render our victory an empty one.

As I deliberated on these points in the endeavor to conclude upon that which would be our wisest course, I could look in nearly all directions and see the warriors at a distance collected in groups on the tops of the highest hills, apparently waiting and watching our next move that they might act accordingly. To guide my command safely out of the difficulties which seemed just then to beset them I again had recourse to that maxim in war which teaches a commander to do that which his enemy neither expects nor desires him to do.

Chapter 11

REAPING THE FRUITS OF VICTORY

THE close of the last article left my command on the Washita, still surrounded by a superior but badly defeated force of Indians.[33] We were burdened

[33] Relying upon Custer's careless statements, many writers have greatly exaggerated the number of warriors. Custer himself stated, although with no actual knowledge, that Elliot's party of twenty men had "undoubtedly" been outnumbered 100 to 1, thereby implying the presence of 2000 warriors in this phase of the battle alone. Sheridan, in his *Personal Memoirs* has "thousands" of warriors surrounding Custer, and Nesbitt, a more recent commentator, ascribes "several thousands" to the down river villages (*Chronicles of Oklahoma*, III, 26).

Although precise information is lacking, such statements as these are evidently preposterous. General Hazen, with better sources of information than either Custer or Sheridan possessed, on November 10 estimated the total number of Indians in and near the Washita Valley at 8100 (U.S. Serial, Ex. Doc. 18, p. 17). Of the total, 5000 were assigned to the Comanches alone, yet the warriors encountered in the Washita battle were chiefly Cheyennes and Arapahoes, along with an indeterminate number of Kiowas. The maximum number of warriors in a total population of 8100 must have been considerably less than 2000. But several hundred Indians were at or near Fort Cobb and entirely friendly to the whites (when threatened with attack at Fort Cobb following the battle General Hazen felt confident that 200 warriors would aid the garrison in defending the place), and before the afternoon battle Custer had killed over 100 warriors. Based on General Hazen's information there could hardly have been as many as 1500 surrounding Custer, even though the entire available number had joined in the fight. But individual Indians, in warfare, unlike white soldiers, fought when and how they pleased, and it is extremely unlikely that on this occasion all the available warriors joined in opposing Custer.

Contributory evidence reinforces the foregoing estimates. At the Medicine Lodge Council of October, 1867, Thomas Murphy, Supt. of Indian Affairs, reported that 852 lodges would be in attendance, averaging 6 Indians per lodge, or a total of "over" 5000 souls. Reporter Henry M. Stanley recorded that 756 lodges were in actual attendance. This would imply a total of 750–1000 warriors. On Dec. 7, 1869, Captain Henry E. Alvord at Fort Cobb reported that on Nov. 30 all the hostile elements had assembled at the mouth of the Sweetwater on North Fork of Red River, to the number of 485 lodges, with fighting men averaging "very nearly one to each lodge" (U.S. Serial 1360, Ex. Doc. 18, pp. 35–37). Custer killed 103 warriors in Black Kettle's village of 51 lodges, but this number included members of the war-party which had just returned from a raid toward Kansas. When he marched down river with General Sheridan in early December, it was "computed" that over 600 lodges had stood within five miles of Black Kettle's village, from which, and from others lower down, had come the "immense" number of warriors who engaged in the second battle. Whittaker, *Complete Life*, 454. Since the string of villages extended 10 miles along the Washita, we may reasonably assume the total number of lodges to have been 1200–1300, which at one warrior per lodge gives us the like number of warriors.

with a considerable number of prisoners and quite a number of our own and the enemy's wounded, and had in our possession nearly nine hundred ponies which we had just captured from the enemy. We were far away—just how far we did not know—

In short, it is reasonably evident that the number surrounding Custer in the second battle cannot have exceeded 1500 and quite probably was much smaller than this. That Custer's 700 troopers, in possession of Black Kettle's village (not yet destroyed by Custer) and sheltered by the heavy timber and by the contour of the ground, were in any danger of being overwhelmed is ridiculous to suggest. Moreover, Custer's narrative, reinforced by his list of casualties, discloses that whatever the number of warriors may have been they had little will to fight, and fled en masse at the first sign of Custer's advance.

Save for the loss of Major Elliot's party, Custer's casualties were trifling and practically all of them were incurred in the morning battle for possession of the village. They totalled one officer killed, one severely and two more slightly wounded, and eleven men wounded. The casualties of the four officers were all suffered in the morning battle. Concerning the eleven enlisted men, Custer does not state when their wounds were received, although he twice mentions that his loss in the morning was "severe" and mentions no loss at all in the second battle. On the unlikely assumption that half of the eleven enlisted men were wounded in the second battle it follows that 700 troopers fighting for several hours against an "immensely" superior enemy sustained a total loss of half a dozen wounded. Obviously the fierceness of this second battle has been greatly overstated.

355

from our train of supplies, and the latter with its escort was in danger of capture and destruction by the savages if we did not act to prevent it. We felt convinced that we could not, in the presence of so large a body of hostile Indians, hope to make a long march through their country, the latter favorable to the Indian mode of attack by surprise and ambush, and keep with us the immense herd of captured ponies. Such a course would only encourage attack under circumstances which would almost insure defeat and unnecessary loss to us. We did not need the ponies, while the Indians did. If we retained them they might conclude that one object of our expedition against them was to secure plunder, an object thoroughly consistent with the red man's idea of war. Instead, it was our desire to impress upon his uncultured mind that our every act and purpose had been simply to inflict deserved punishment upon him for the many murders and other depredations committed by him in and around the homes of the defenseless settlers on the frontier.

Impelled by these motives, I decided neither to attempt to take the ponies with us nor to abandon them to the Indians, but to adopt the only measure left—to kill them. To accomplish this seemingly—like most measures of war—cruel but necessary act, four companies of cavalrymen were detailed dismounted, as a firing party. Before they reluctantly engaged in this uninviting work I took Romeo, the interpreter, and proceeded to the few lodges near the center of the village which we had reserved from destruction, and in which were collected the prisoners, consisting of upward of sixty squaws and children. Romeo was directed to assemble the prisoners in one body as I desired to assure them of kind treatment at our hands, a subject about which they were greatly wrought up; also to tell them what we should expect of them and to inform them of our intention to march probably all that night, directing them at the same time to proceed to the herd and select therefrom a suitable number of ponies to carry the prisoners on the march. When Romeo had collected them in a single group, he, acting as interpreter, acquainted them with my purpose in calling them together, at the same time assuring them that they could rely confidently upon the fulfilment of any promises I made them, as I was the big chief. The Indians refer to all officers of a command as chiefs, while the officer in command is designated as the big chief.

After I had concluded what I desired to say to them they signified their approval and satisfaction by gathering around me and going through an extensive series of hand-shaking. One of the middle-aged squaws then informed Romeo that she wished to speak on behalf of herself and companions. Assent having been given to this, she began the delivery of an address which for wisdom of sentiment, and easy, natural, but impassioned delivery, might have been heard with intense interest by an audience of cultivated refinement. From her remarks, interpreted by Romeo, I gathered much—in fact, the first reliable information as to what band we had attacked at daylight, which chiefs commanded, and many interesting scraps of information.

She began by saying that now she and the women and children about her were in the condition of captivity, which for a long time she had prophesied would be theirs sooner or later. She claimed to speak not as a squaw, but as the sister of the head chief of her band, Black Kettle, who had fallen that morning almost the moment the attack was made. He it was who was the first to hear our advance and leaping forth from his lodge with rifle in hand uttered the first war-whoop and fired the first shot as a rally signal to his warriors, and was almost immediately after shot down by the opening volley of the

358

cavalry. Often had she warned her brother of the danger the village, with its women and children, was exposed to, owing to the frequent raiding and war parties which from time to time had been permitted to go forth and depredate upon the settlements of the white men. In the end it was sure to lead to detection and punishment, and now her words had only proved too true. Not a chief or warrior of the village in her belief survived the battle of the forenoon. And what was to become of all these women and children, bereft of everything and of every friend?

True, it was just. The warriors had brought this fate upon themselves and their families by their unprovoked attacks upon the white man. Black Kettle, the head chief and the once trusted friend of the white man, had fallen. Little Rock, the chief second in rank in the village, had also met his death while attempting to defend his home against his enemies; others were named in the order of their rank or prowess as warriors, but all had gone the same way. Who was left to care for the women and children who still lived? Only last night, she continued, did the last war party return from the settlements, and it was to rejoice over their achievements that the entire village were engaged until a late hour dancing and singing. This was why their enemies were able to ride almost into their lodges before they were aroused by the noise of the attack. For several minutes she continued to speak, first upbraiding in the bitterest terms the chiefs and warriors who had been the cause of their capture, then bewailing in the most plaintive manner their sad and helpless condition. Turning to me she added: "You claim to be a chief. This man [pointing to Romeo] says you are the big chief. If this be true and you are what he claims, show that you can act like a great chief and secure for us that treatment which the helpless are entitled to."

After the delivery of this strongly melo-dramatic harangue there was introduced a little by-play, in which I was unconsciously made to assume a more prominent part than either my inclinations or the laws of society might approve. Black Kettle's sister, whose name was Mah-wis-sa, and whose address had just received the hearty approval of her companions by their earnest expression of "Ugh!" the Indian word intended for applause, then stepped into the group of squaws and after looking earnestly at the face of each for a moment approached a young Indian girl—probably seventeen years of age—and taking her by the hand conducted her to where I was standing. Placing the hand of the young girl in mine, she proceeded in the Indian tongue to the delivery of what I in my ignorance of the language presumed was a form of administering a benediction, as her manner and gestures corresponded with this idea.

Never dreaming of her purpose, but remembering how sensitive and suspicious the Indian nature was, and that any seeming act of inattention or disrespect on my part might be misunderstood, I stood a passive participant in the strange ceremony then being enacted. After concluding the main portion of the formalities, she engaged in what seemed an invocation of the Great Spirit, casting her eyes reverently upward, at the same time moving her hands slowly down over the faces of the young squaw and myself. By this time my curiosity got the better of my silence and turning to Romeo, who stood near me and who I knew was familiar with Indian customs, I quietly inquired: "What is this woman doing, Romeo?" With a broad grin on his swarthy face he replied: "Why, she's marryin' you to that young squaw!"

Although never claimed as an exponent of the peace policy about which so much has been said and written, yet I entertained the

361

most peaceable sentiments toward all Indians who were in a condition to do no harm nor violate any law. And while cherishing these friendly feelings and desiring to do all in my power to render our captives comfortable and free from anxiety regarding their future treatment at our hands, I think even the most strenuous and ardent advocate of that peace policy which teaches that the Indian should be left free and unmolested in the gratification of his simple tastes and habits will at least not wholly condemn me when they learn that this last touching and unmistakable proof of confidence and esteem offered by Mah-wis-sa and gracefully if not blushingly acquiesced in by the Indian maiden was firmly but respectfully declined.

The few reasons which forced me to deny myself the advantages of this tempting alliance were certain circumstances over which I then had no control, among which was a previous and already solemnized ceremony of this character, which might have a tendency to render the second somewhat invalid. Then, again, I had not been consulted in regard to my choice in this matter, a trifling considèration, but still having its due influence. I had not had opportunities to become acquainted with the family of the young damsel who thus proposed to link her worldly fate with

mine. Her father's bank account might or
might not be in a favorable condition. No
opportunity had been given me to study the
tastes, disposition, or character of the young
lady, whether she was fond of music, literature, or domestic duties. All these were
questions with which I was not sufficiently
familiar to justify me in taking the important step before me. I did not, however, like
certain candidates for office, thrice decline
by standing up, and with my hand pressed
to my heart say: "Your husband I cannot
be"; but through the intermediation of Romeo, the interpreter, who from the first had
been highly entertained by what he saw was
an excellent joke on the big chief, and wondering in his own mind how I would extricate
myself without giving offense, I explained to
Mah-wis-sa my due appreciation of the kindness intended by herself and her young
friend, but that according to the white man's
laws I was debarred from availing myself of
the offer, at the same time assuring them of
my high consideration, etc.

Glad to get away to duties that called me
elsewhere, I left with Romeo. As soon as we
had turned our backs on the group, I inquired of Romeo what object could have
been in view which induced Black Kettle's
sister to play the part she did. "That's easy

enough to understand; she knows they are
in your power and her object is to make
friends with you as far as possible. But you
don't believe anything she tells you, do you?
Why, that squaw—give her the chance, and
she'd lift your or my scalp for us and never
wink. Lord, I've heerd 'em talk fine too
often to be catched so easy. To hear her
talk and abuse old Black Kettle and the rest
that I hope we've done for, you'd think that
squaw never had had a hand in torturin' to
death many a poor devil who's been picked
up by them. But it's a fact, 'taint no two
ways 'bout it. I've lived with them people
too long not to know 'em—root and branch.
When she was talkin' all that palaver to you
'bout protectin' 'em and all that sort of stuff,
if she could 'a know'd that minute that these
outside Injuns was 'bout to gobble us up
she'd 'a been the very fust one to ram a knife
smack into ye. That's the way they allus
talk when they want anythin'. Do you know
her game in wantin' to marry that young
squaw to you? Well, I'll tell ye; ef you'd 'a
married that squaw, then she'd 'a told ye
that all the rest of 'em were her kinfolks,
and as a nateral sort of a thing you'd 'a been
expected to kind o' provide and take keer of
your wife's relations. That's jist as I tell it
to you—fur don't I know? Didn't I marry a

young Cheyenne squaw and give her old father two of my best ponies for her, and it wasn't a week till every tarnal Injun in the village, old and young, came to my lodge and my squaw tried to make me b'lieve they were all relations of hern and that I ought to give 'em some grub; but I didn't do nothin' of the sort." "Well, how did you get out of it, Romeo?" "Get out of it? Why, I got out by jist takin' my ponies and traps and the first good chance I lit out; that's how I got out. I was satisfied to marry one or two of 'em, but when it come to marryin' an intire tribe, 'scuse me."

At this point Romeo was interrupted by the officer in command of the men detailed to kill the ponies. The firing party was all ready to proceed with its work and was only waiting until the squaws should secure a sufficient number of ponies to transport all the prisoners on the march. The troopers had endeavored to catch the ponies, but they were too wild and unaccustomed to white men to permit them to approach. When the squaws entered the herd they had no difficulty in selecting and bridling the requisite number. These being taken off by themselves, the work of destruction began on the remainder and was continued until nearly eight hundred ponies were thus dis-

posed of. All this time the Indians who had
been fighting us from the outside covered the
hills in the distance, deeply interested spectators of this to them strange proceeding.
The loss of so many animals of value was a
severe blow to the tribe, as nothing so completely impairs the war-making facilities for
the Indians of the Plains as the deprivation
or disabling of their ponies.

In the description of the opening of the
battle in the preceding chapter, I spoke of the
men having removed their overcoats and
haversacks when about to charge the village.
These had been disposed of carefully on the
ground and one man from each company left
to guard them, this number being deemed
sufficient, as they would be within rifle-shot
of the main command; besides, the enemy as
was then supposed would be inside our lines
and sufficiently employed in taking care of
himself to prevent any meddling on his part
with the overcoats and haversacks. This
was partly true, but we had not calculated
upon Indians appearing in force and surrounding us. When this did occur, however,
their first success was in effecting the capture
of the overcoats and rations of the men, the
guard barely escaping to the village. This
was a most serious loss, as the men were destined to suffer great discomfort from the

cold; and their rations being in the haversacks and it being uncertain when we should rejoin our train they were compelled to endure both cold and hunger. It was when the Indians discovered our overcoats and galloped to their capture that one of my staghounds, Blucher, seeing them riding and yelling as if engaged in the chase, dashed from the village and joined the Indians, who no sooner saw him than they shot him through with an arrow. Several months afterward I discovered his remains on the ground near where the overcoats had been deposited on that eventful morning.

Many noteworthy incidents were observed or reported during the fight. Before the battle began our Osage allies, in accordance with the Indian custom, dressed in their war costume, painting their faces in all imaginable colors, except one tall, fine-looking warrior, who retained his ordinary dress. Upon inquiring of the chief, Little Beaver, why this one did not array himself as the others had done he informed me that it was in obedience to a law among all the tribes under which any chief or warrior who has had a near relative killed by an enemy belonging to another tribe is not permitted to don the war costume or put on war paint until he has avenged the murder by taking a scalp from some member of the hostile tribe. A war party of the Cheyennes had visited the Osage village the preceding summer under friendly pretenses. They had been hospitably entertained at the lodge of the warrior referred to by his squaw, he being absent on a hunt. When ready to depart they killed his squaw and destroyed his lodge, and until he could secure a scalp he must go on the war path unadorned by feathers or paint. After the battle had been waged for a couple of hours in the morning I saw this warrior approaching, his horse urged to his highest speed; in his hand I saw waving wildly overhead something I could not distinguish until he halted by my side, when I perceived that it was an entire scalp, fresh and bleeding. His vengeance had been complete and he was again restored to the full privileges of a warrior, a right he was not long in exercising, as the next time I saw him on the field his face was completely hidden under the stripes of yellow, black, and vermilion, the colors being so arranged, apparently, as to give him the most hideous visage imaginable.

Riding in the vicinity of the hospital, I saw a little bugler boy sitting on a bundle of dressed robes near where the surgeon was dressing and caring for the wounded. His face was completely covered with blood, which was trickling down over his cheek from a wound in his forehead. At first glance I thought a pistol bullet had entered his skull, but on stopping to inquire of him the nature of his injury he informed me that an Indian had shot him in the head with a steel-pointed arrow. The arrow had struck him just above the eye and upon encountering the skull had glanced under the covering of the latter coming out near the ear, giving the appearance of having passed through the head. There the arrow remained until the bugler arrived at the hospital, when he received prompt attention. The arrow being barbed could not be withdrawn at once, but by cutting off the steel point the surgeon was able to withdraw the wooden shaft without difficulty. The little fellow bore his suffering manfully. I asked him if he saw the Indian who wounded him. Without replying at once, he shoved his hand deep down into his capacious trousers pocket and fished up nothing more nor less than the scalp of an Indian, adding in a nonchalant manner: "If anybody thinks I didn't see him, I want them to take a look at that." He had killed the Indian with his revolver after receiving the arrow wound in his head.

After driving off the Indians who had attacked us from the outside so as to prevent them from interfering with our operations in the vicinity of the village, parties were sent here and there to look up the dead and wounded of both sides. In spite of the most thorough search, there were still undiscovered Major Elliot and nineteen enlisted men, including the sergeant-major, for whose absence we were unable to satisfactorily account. Officers and men of the various commands were examined, but nothing was elicited from them except that Major Elliot had been seen about daylight charging with his command into the village. I had previously given him up as killed, but was surprised that so many of the men should be missing and none of their comrades be able to account for them. All the ground inside of the advanced lines held by the Indians who attacked us after our capture of the village was closely and carefully examined in the hope of finding the bodies of some if not all the absentees, but with no success. It was then evident that when the other bands attempted to reinforce our opponents of the early morning, they had closed their lines about us in such manner as to cut off Elliot and nineteen of our men.

What had been the fate of this party after leaving the main command? This was a question to be answered only in surmises, and few of these were favorable to the escape of our comrades. At last one of the scouts reported that soon after the attack on the village began he had seen a few warriors escaping, mounted, from the village, through a gap that existed in our line between the commands of Elliot and Thompson, and that Elliot and a small party of troopers were in close pursuit; that a short time after he had heard very sharp firing in the direction taken by the Indians and Elliot's party, but that as the firing had continued for only a few minutes, he had thought nothing more of it until the prolonged absence of our men recalled it to his mind. Parties were sent in the direction indicated by the scout, he accompanying them; but after a search extending nearly two miles all the parties returned, reporting their efforts to discover some trace of Elliot and his men fruitless.

As it was now lacking but an hour of night, we had to make an effort to get rid of the Indians, who still loitered in strong force on the hills within plain view of our position. Our main desire was to draw them off from the direction in which our train might be approaching and thus render it secure from attack until under the protection of the entire command, when we could defy any force our enemies could muster against us.

The last lodge having been destroyed and all the ponies except those required for the pursuit having been killed, the command was drawn in and united near the village. Making dispositions to overcome any resistance which might be offered to our advance by throwing out a strong force of skirmishers, we set out down the valley in the direction where the other villages had been reported and toward the hills on which were collected the greatest number of Indians.

The column moved forward in one body with colors flying and band playing, while our prisoners, all mounted on captured ponies, were under sufficient guard immediately in rear of the advanced troops. For a few moments after our march began the Indians on the hills remained silent spectators, evidently at a loss at first to comprehend our intentions in thus setting out at that hour of the evening and directing our course as if another night march was contemplated; and more than all, in the direction of their villages, where all that they possessed was supposed to be. This aroused them to action, as we could plainly see considerable commotion among them—chiefs riding hither and thither, as if in anxious consultation with each other as to the course to be adopted. Whether the fact that they could not fire upon our

advance without endangering the lives of
their own people who were prisoners in our
hands or some other reason prevailed with
them, they never offered to fire a shot or
retard our movements in any manner, but
instead assembled their outlying detachments as rapidly as possible and began a
precipitate movement down the valley in
advance of us, fully impressed with the idea,
no doubt, that our purpose was to overtake
their flying people and herds and administer
the same treatment to them that the occupants of the upper village had received.

This was exactly the effect I desired, and
our march was conducted with such appearance of determination and rapidity that this
conclusion on their part was a most natural
one. Leaving a few of their warriors to hover
along our flanks and watch our progress, the
main body of the Indians, able to travel
much faster than the troops, soon disappeared from our sight in front. We still
pushed on in the same direction and continued our march in this manner until long
after dark, by which time we reached the
deserted villages, the occupants, at least the
non-combatants and herds, having fled in
the morning when news of our attack on
Black Kettle's village reached them. We
had now reached a point several miles below

373

the site of Black Kettle's village and the darkness was sufficient to cover our movements from the watchful eyes of the Indian scouts, who had dogged our march as long as the light favored them.

Facing the command about, it was at once put in motion to reach our train, not only as a measure of safety and protection to the latter, but as a necessary movement to relieve the wants of the command, particularly that portion whose haversacks and overcoats had fallen into the hands of the Indians early in the morning. By ten o'clock we reached the battle ground, but without halting pushed on, following the trail we had made in striking the village. The march was continued at a brisk gait until about two o'clock in the morning, when I concluded it would be prudent to allow the main command to halt and bivouac until daylight, sending one squadron forward without delay to reinforce the guard with the train. Colonel West's squadron was detailed upon this duty. The main body of the troops was halted and permitted to build huge fires, fuel being obtainable in abundance from the timber which lined the valley of the Washita, our march still leading us up the course of this stream.

At daylight the next morning we were again in our saddles and wending our way hopefully toward the train. The location of the latter we did not know, presuming that it had been pushing after us since we had taken our abrupt departure from it. Great was our joy and satisfaction, about ten o'clock, to discover the train safely in camp. The teams were at once harnessed and hitched to the wagons and without halting even to prepare breakfast the march was resumed, I being anxious to encamp at a certain point that night from where I intended sending scouts through with despatches to General Sheridan.

Early in the afternoon this camp was reached; it was near the point where we had first struck the timbered valley, at the time not knowing that it was the valley of the Washita. Here men and horses were given the first opportunity to procure a satisfactory meal since the few hasty morsels obtained by them during the brief halt made between nine and ten o'clock the night we arrived in the vicinity of the village. After posting our pickets and rendering the camp secure from surprise by the enemy, horses were unsaddled, tents pitched, and every means taken to obtain as comfortable a night as the limited means at our disposal and the severities of the season would permit.

After partaking of a satisfactory dinner I began writing my report to General Sheridan. First I sent for California Joe and informed him that I desired to send a despatch to General Sheridan that night and would have it ready by dark so that the bearer could at once set out as soon as it was sufficiently dark to conceal his movements from the scouts of the enemy, who no doubt were still following and watching us. I told California Joe that I had selected him as the bearer of the despatch and he was at liberty to name the number of men he desired to accompany him, as it was a most perilous mission on which he was going. The exact distance he would have to ride in order to reach General Sheridan's headquarters at Camp Supply could not be determined. The command had occupied four days in accomplishing it, but California Joe, with his thorough knowledge of the country and the experience of our march would be able to follow a much more direct route than a large command moving with a train.

He did not seem in the least disturbed when told of his selection for this errand, so full of danger. When informed that he might name the number of men to accompany him I supposed he would say about twelve or more, under command of a good non-commissioned officer. Very few persons in or out of the military service would have cared to under-

LONE WOLF, HEAD CHIEF OF THE KIOWAS.

take the journey with much less than ten
times that force, but he contented himself by
informing me that before answering that
question he would walk down to where the
scouts were in camp and consult his "pardner." He soon returned saying: "I've just
been talkin' the matter over with my pardner, and him and me both concludes that as
safe and sure a way as any is for him and me
to take a few extra rounds of ammunition
and strike out from here together the very
minnit it's dark. As for any more men, we
don't want 'em, because yer see in a case of
this 'ere kind thar's more to be made by
dodgin' an' runnin' than thar is by fightin',
an' two spright men kin do better at that
than twenty; they can't be seen half as fur.
Besides, two won't leave as much of a trail
for the Injuns to find. If my pardner an' me
kin git away from here as soon as it is plum
dark, we'll be so fur from here by daylight
to-morrer mornin' the Injuns never couldn't
tetch hide nor har of us. Besides, I don't
reckon the pesky varmints 'll be so overly
keen in meddlin' with our business, seein' as
how they've got their han's tolerable full
settin' things to rights at home, owin' to the
little visit we've jist made 'em. I rather
s'pect, all things considerin', them Injuns
would be powerful glad to call it quits for a

spell any way, an' if I ain't off the trail
mightily, some of them 'ere head chiefs as
ain't killed will be headin' for the nighest
Peace Commissioner before they git the war
paint clean off their faces. This thing of
pumpin' 'em when the snow's a foot deep,
and no grass for their ponies, puts a new
wrinkle in these Injuns' scalp, an' they ain't
goin' to git over it in a minnit either. Wal,
I'm goin' back to the boys to see if I can
borrer a little smokin' tobacker. I may want
to take a smoke on the way. Whenever you
git yer dockiments ready jist send your orderly down thar, and me and my pardner
will be ready. I'm mighty glad I'm goin' to-
night, for I know Gineral Sheridan 'll be
monstrous glad to see me back so soon. Did
I tell yer I used to know the Gineral when he
was second or third lootenant and post quartermaster in Oregon? That must 'a been
afore your time."

Leaving California Joe to procure his "tobacker," I assembled all the officers of the
command and informed them that as there
was but an hour or two in which I was to
write my report of the battle of the Washita
I would not have time, as I should have preferred to do, to send to them for regular and
formally written reports of their share in the
engagement; but in order that I might have

the benefit of their combined knowledge of
the battle and its results, each officer in response to my request gave me a brief summary of some of the important points which
his report would have contained if submitted
in writing. With this information in my possession I sat down in my tent and penned, in
as brief manner as possible, a report to General Sheridan detailing our movements from
the time Elliot with his three companies discovered the trail up to the point from which
my despatch was written, giving particularly
the main facts of our discovery, attack, and
complete destruction of the village of Black
Kettle. It was just about dark when I finished this despatch and was about to send for
California Joe, when that loquacious personage appeared at the door of my tent. "I'm
not so anxious to leave yer all here, but the
fact is, the sooner me and pardner are off, I
reckon the better it'll be in the end. I want
to put at least fifty miles 'tween me and this
place by daylight to-morrer mornin', so if
yer'll jest hurry up yer papers, it'll be a lift
for us."

On going outside the tent I saw that the
"pardner" was the scout Jack Corbin, the
same who had first brought the intelligence
of Elliot's discovery of the trail to us at
Antelope Hills. He was almost the antipodes

of California Joe in regard to many points of character, seldom indulging in a remark or suggestion unless prompted by a question. These two scouts recalled to my mind an amicable arrangement said to exist between a harmonious married pair, in which one was willing to do all the talking and the other was perfectly willing he should. The two scouts, who were about to set out to accomplish a long journey through an enemy's country with no guides save the stars, neither ever having passed over the route they proposed to take, and much of the ride to be executed during the darkness of night, apparently felt no greater, if as great, anxiety as to the result of their hazardous mission than one ordinarily feels in contemplating a journey of a few hours by rail or steamboat. California Joe was dressed and equipped as usual. About his waist and underneath his cavalry greatcoat and cape he wore a belt containing a Colt revolver and hunting knife; these, with his inseparable companion, a long Springfield breech-loading rifle, composed his defensive armament. His "pardner," Jack Corbin, was very similarly arrayed except in equipment, his belt containing two revolvers instead of one, while a Sharps carbine supplied the place of a rifle, being more readily carried and handled on horseback. The mounts of the two men were, as different as their characters, California Joe confiding his safety to the transporting powers of his favorite mule, while Corbin was placing his reliance upon a fine gray charger.

Acquainting the men with the probable route we should pursue in our onward march toward Camp Supply, so that, if desirable, they might be able to rejoin us, I delivered my report to General Sheridan into the keeping of California Joe, who, after unbuttoning numerous coats, blouses, and vests, consigned the package to one of the numerous capacious inner pockets with which each garment seemed supplied, with the remark: "I reckon it'll keep dry thar in case of rain or accident." Both men having mounted, I shook hands with them, wishing them Godspeed and a successful journey. As they rode off in the darkness California Joe, irrepressible to the last, called out, "Wal, I hope an' trust yer won't have any scrimmage while I'm gone, because I'd hate mightily now to miss anything of the sort, seein' I've stuck to yer this fur."

After enjoying a most grateful and comparatively satisfactory night's rest, the demands of hunger on the part of man and beast having been bountifully supplied from the stores contained in our train, while a due supply of blankets and robes, with the assistance of huge camp-fires, enabled the men to protect themselves against the intense cold of midwinter, our march was resumed at daylight in the direction of Camp Supply. Our wounded had received every possible care and attention that a skilful and kind-hearted medical officer could suggest. Strange to add, and greatly to our surprise as well as joy, Colonel Barnitz, who had been carried into the village shot through the body and, as all supposed, mortally wounded, with apparently but a few minutes to live, had not only survived the rough jostling of the night march made after leaving the village, but the surgeon, Dr. Lippincott, who was unceasing in his attentions to the wounded, reported indications favorable to a prolongation of life if not a complete recovery. This was cheering news to all the comrades of Colonel Barnitz. I well remember how, when the Colonel was first carried by four of his men, in the folds of an army blanket, into the village, his face wore that pale deathly aspect so common and peculiar to those mortally wounded. He, as well as all who saw him, believed his end near at hand. But like a brave soldier, as he was and had proved himself to be, death had no terrors for him.

When asked by me, as I knelt at the side of
the litter on which he was gasping for breath,
whether he had any messages to send to absent friends he realized the perils of his situation and in half-finished sentences, mingled
with regrets, delivered, as he and all of us
supposed, his farewell messages to be transmitted to dear ones at home. And yet, despite the absence of that care and quiet, not
to mention little delicacies and luxuries, regarded as so essential, and which would have
been obtainable under almost any other circumstances, Colonel Barnitz continued to
improve and before many weeks his attendant medical officer was able to pronounce
him out of danger, although to this day he is,
and for the remainder of life will be, disabled
from further active duty, the ball by which
he was wounded having severed one of his
ribs in such a manner as to render either riding or the wearing of a saber or revolver too
painful to be endured.

By easy marches we gradually neared
Camp Supply, and had begun to descend the
long slope leading down to the valley of
Wolf Creek, the stream on which we had encamped three nights when we first set out
from Camp Supply in search of Indians.
With two or three of the Osage guides and
as many of the officers I was riding some dis-

tance in advance of the column of troops and could indistinctly see the timber fringing the valley in the distance, when the attention of our little party was attracted to three horse-men who were to be seen riding slowly along near the edge of the timber. As yet they evi-dently had not observed us, the troops be-hind us not having appeared in view. We were greatly at a loss to determine who the three horsemen might be; they were yet too distant to be plainly visible to the eye, and the orderly with my field glass was still in rear. While we were halting and watching their movements we saw that they also had discovered us, one of their number riding up to a small elevation near by from which to get a better view of our group. After study-ing us for a few moments he returned at a gallop to his two companions, when all three turned their horses toward the timber and moved rapidly in that direction.

We were still unable to determine whether they were Indians or white men, the distance being so great between us, when my orderly arrived with my field glass, by which I was able to catch a glimpse of them just as they were disappearing in the timber, when whose familiar form should be revealed but that of California Joe, urging his mule to its greatest speed in order to reach the timber before we should discover them. They had evidently taken us for Indians, and well they might, considering that two of our party were Osages and the others were dressed in anything but the regulation uniform. To relieve the anxious minds of California Joe and his companions I put spurs to my horse and was soon bounding down the Plains leading into the valley to join him. I had not proceeded over half way when the scouts rode cautiously out from the timber and California Joe, after shading his eyes with his hand and looking for a few moments, raised his huge sombrero from his matted head and waving it above him as a signal of recognition, pressed his great Mexican spurs deep into the sides of his humble-looking steed, if a mule may receive such an appellation, and the three scouts were soon galloping toward us.

The joy at the meeting was great on both sides, only dampened somewhat on the part of California Joe by the fact that he and his comrades had taken to the timber so promptly when first they discovered us; but he explained it by saying: "I counted on it bein' you all the time when I fust got my eye on yer, until I saw two Injuns in the squad, an' forgettin' all about them Osages we had along, I jumped at the conclusion that if thar war any Injuns around, the comfortablest placed I knowed for us three was to make fur the timber, and there make a stand. We war gettin' ready to give it to yer if it turned out yer war all Injuns. Wal, I'm powerful glad to see yer agin, an' that's sure."

From his further conversation we were informed that Jack Corbin and himself had made their trip to General Sheridan's headquarters without hindrance or obstacle being encountered on their way, and that after delivering the despatches and being well entertained in the meantime, they, with one other scout, had been sent by the General to endeavor to meet us, bringing from him a package of orders and letters.

While the column was overtaking us and while California Joe, now in his element, was entertaining the attentive group of officers, scouts, and Osages who gathered around him to hear him relate in his quaint manner what he saw, heard, and told at General Sheridan's headquarters, I withdrew to one side and opened the large official envelope in which were contained both official and personal despatches. These were eagerly read, and while the satisfaction derived from the perusal of some of the letters of a private and congratulatory nature from personal friends at Camp Supply was beyond expression, the climax of satisfaction was reached when my eye came to an official-looking document bearing the date and heading which indicated department headquarters as its source. We had but little farther to go before going into camp for that night and as the command had now overtaken us we moved down to the timber and there encamped; and in order that the approving words of our chief should be transmitted promptly to every individual of the command, the line was formed and the following order announced to the officers and men:

HEADQUARTERS DEPARTMENT OF THE MIS-
SOURI, IN THE FIELD, DEPOT ON THE NORTH
CANADIAN, AT THE JUNCTION OF BEAVER
CREEK, INDIAN TERRITORY,
November 29, 1868.

GENERAL FIELD ORDERS No. 6.—The Major General commanding announces to this command the defeat, by the Seventh Regiment of cavalry, of a large force of Cheyenne Indians, under the celebrated chief Black Kettle, reinforced by the Arapahoes under Little Raven, and the Kiowas under Satanta, on the morning of the 27th instant, on the Washita River, near the Antelope Hills, Indian Territory, resulting in a loss to the savages of one hundred and three warriors killed, including Black Kettle, the capture of fifty-three squaws and children, eight hundred and seventy-five ponies, eleven hundred and twenty-three buffalo robes and skins, five hundred and thirty-five pounds of powder, one thousand and fifty pounds of lead, four thousand arrows, seven hundred pounds of tobacco, besides

388

rifles, pistols, saddles, bows, lariats, and immense quantities of dried meat and other winter provisions, the complete destruction of their village, and almost total annihilation of this Indian band.

The loss to the Seventh Cavalry was two officers killed, Major Joel H. Elliot and Captain Louis McL. Hamilton, and nineteen enlisted men; three officers wounded, Brevet Lieutenant-Colonel Albert Barnitz (badly), Brevet Lieutenant-Colonel T. W. Custer, and Second Lieutenant T. Z. March (slightly), and eleven enlisted men.

The energy and rapidity shown during one of the heaviest snow-storms that has visited this section of the country, with the temperature below freezing point, and the gallantry and bravery displayed, resulting in such signal success, reflect the highest credit upon both the officers and men of the Seventh Cavalry; and the Major-General commanding, while regretting the loss of such gallant officers as Major Elliot and Captain Hamilton, who fell while gallantly leading their men, desires to express his thanks to the officers and men engaged in the battle of the Washita, and his special congratulations are tendered to their distinguished commander, Brevet Major-General George A. Custer, for the efficient and gallant services rendered, which have characterized the opening of the campaign against hostile Indians south of the Arkansas.

By command of
Major-General P. H. SHERIDAN.
(Signed)   J. SCHUYLER CROSBY, Brevet
Lieutenant-Colonel, A.D.C., A.A.A.
General.

This order, containing as it did the grateful words of approval from our revered commander went far to drown the remembrance of the hunger, cold, and danger encountered by the command in the resolute and united effort made by it to thoroughly discharge its duty. Words like these, emanating from the source they did and upon an occasion such as this was, were immeasurably more welcome, gratifying, and satisfactory to the pride of officers and men than would have been the reception of a budget of brevets worded in the regular stereotyped form and distributed in a promiscuous manner, having but little regard to whether the recipient had bravely imperilled his life on the battle-field in behalf of his country or had taken particular care to preserve that life upon some field far removed from battle.

The last camp before we reached Camp Supply was on Wolf Creek, about ten miles from General Sheridan's headquarters. The weather had now moderated to the mildest winter temperature, the snow having melted and disappeared. From this point I sent a courier to General Sheridan soon after going into camp, informing him of our whereabouts and the distance from his camp, and that we would reach the latter at such an hour in the forenoon, when the officers and men of my

command would be pleased to march in review before him and his staff as we finished
our return march from the opening of the
winter campaign. Officers and men, in view
of this, prepared to put on their best appearance. At the appointed hour on the morning
of December 2 the command moved out of
camp and began its last day's march toward
Camp Supply. Considering the hard and
trying character of the duty they had been
engaged in since leaving Camp Supply, the
appearance of officers, men, and horses was
far better than might naturally have been
expected of them.

When we arrived within a couple of miles
of General Sheridan's headquarters, we were
met by one of his staff officers with a message
from the General that it would give him
great pleasure to review the Seventh Cavalry
as proposed, and that he and his staff would
be mounted, and take up a favorable position for the review near headquarters. In
approaching Camp Supply by the route we
were marching a view of the camp and depot
is first gained from the point where the high
level plain begins to descend gradually to
form the valley in the middle of which Camp
Supply is located; so that by having a man
on the lookout to report when the troops
should first make their appearance on the

heights overlooking Beaver Creek the General was enabled not only to receive timely notice of our approach, but to take position with his staff to witness our march down the long gradual slope leading into the valley. The day was all we could wish, a bright sun overhead, and favorable ground for the maneuvering of troops.

I had taken the precaution to establish the formation of the marching column before we should appear in view from General Sheridan's camp, so that after our march began down the beautifully descending slope to the valley no change was made. In many respects the column we formed was unique in appearance. First rode our Osage guides and trailers, dressed and painted in the extremest fashions of war according to their rude customs and ideas. As we advanced these warriors chanted their war songs, fired their guns in triumph, and at intervals gave utterance to their shrill war-whoops. Next came the scouts riding abreast, with California Joe astride his faithful mule bringing up the rear, but unable, even during this ceremonious and formal occasion, to dispense with his pipe. Immediately in rear of the scouts rode the Indian prisoners under guard, all mounted on Indian ponies, and in their dress, conspicuous by its bright colors, many of them wearing the scarlet blanket so popular with the wild tribes, presenting quite a contrast to the dull and motley colors worn by the scouts. Some little distance in rear came the troops formed in column of platoons, the leading platoon, preceded by the band playing Garry Owen, being composed of the sharpshooters under Colonel Cooke, followed in succession by the squadrons in the regular order of march. In this order and arrangement we marched proudly in front of our chief, who, as the officers rode by giving him the military salute with the saber, returned their formal courtesy by a graceful lifting of his cap and a pleased look of recognition from his eye which spoke his approbation in language far more powerful than studied words could have done.

In speaking of the review afterwards, General Sheridan said the appearance of the troops, with the bright rays of the sun reflected from their burnished arms and equipments as they advanced in beautiful order and precision down the slope, the band playing, and the blue of the soldiers' uniforms slightly relieved by the gaudy colors of the Indians, both captives and Osages, the strangely fantastic part played by the Osage guides, their shouts, chanting their war songs, and firing their guns in air, all com-

393

bined to render the scene one of the most beautiful and highly interesting he remembered ever having witnessed. After marching in review, the troops were conducted across the plain to the border of Beaver Creek, about a quarter of a mile from General Sheridan's camp, where we pitched our tents and prepared to enjoy a brief period of rest.

We had brought with us on our return march from the battle-ground of the Washita the remains of our slain comrade, Captain Louis McLane Hamilton. Arrangements were at once made upon our arrival at Camp Supply to offer the last formal tribute of respect and affection which we as his surviving comrades could pay. As he had died a soldier's death, so like a soldier he should be buried. On the evening of the day after our arrival at Camp Supply the funeral took place. A little knoll not far from camp was chosen as the resting place to which we were to consign the remains of our departed comrade. In the arrangements for the conduct of the funeral ceremonies no preliminary or important detail had been omitted to render the occasion not only one of imposing solemnity, but deeply expressive of the high esteem in which the deceased had been held by every member of the command. In addition to the eleven companies of the Seventh

Reaping Fruits of Victory

Cavalry the regular garrison of Camp Supply, numbering several companies of the Third Regular Infantry, the regiment in which Captain Hamilton had first entered the regular service, was also in attendance. The body of the deceased was carried in an ambulance as a hearse, and covered with a large American flag. The ambulance was preceded by Captain Hamilton's squadron, commanded by Brevet Lieutenant-Colonel T. B. Weir, and was followed by his horse, covered with a mourning sheet and bearing on the saddle—the same in which Captain Hamilton was seated when he received his death wound—the saber and belt and the reversed top-boots of the deceased. The pallbearers were Major-General Sheridan, Brevet Lieutenant-Colonels J. Schuyler Crosby, W. W. Cooke and T. W. Custer, Brevet Major W. W. Beebe, Lieutenant Joseph Hall, and myself.

Our sojourn at Camp Supply was to be brief. We arrived there on the 2d of December, and in less than one week we were to be in the saddle with our numbers more than doubled by reinforcements, and again wending our way southward over the route we had so lately passed over.

Before setting out on the last expedition I had stated to the officers in a casual manner

that all parties engaged in the conduct of
the contemplated campaign against the Indians must reconcile themselves in advance,
no matter how the expedition might result,
to becoming the recipients of censure and
unbounded criticism; that if we failed to engage and whip the Indians, labor as we might
to accomplish this, the people in the West,
particularly along and near the frontier, those
who had been victims of the assaults made
by Indians, would denounce us in unmeas-
ured terms as being inefficient or lukewarm
in the performance of our duty; whereas if we
should find and punish the Indians as they
deserved, a wail would rise up from the hor-
rified humanitarians throughout the country
and we would be accused of attacking and
killing friendly and defenseless Indians.

My predictions proved true; no sooner was
the intelligence of the battle of the Washita
flashed over the country than the anticipated
cry was raised. In many instances it ema-
nated from a class of persons truly good in
themselves and in their intentions, but who
were familiar to only a very limited degree
with the dark side of the Indian question,
and whose ideas were of the sentimental
order. There was another class, however,
equally loud in their utterances of pretended horror, who were actuated by pecuniary

motives alone, and who, from their supposed
or real intimate knowledge of Indian character and of the true merits of the contest
between the Indians and the Government,
were able to give some weight to their expressed opinions and assertions of alleged
facts. Some of these last described actually
went so far as to assert not only that the village we had attacked and destroyed was that
of Indians who had always been friendly and
peaceable toward the whites, but that many
of the warriors and chiefs were partially
civilized and had actually borne arms in the
Union Army during the War of the Rebellion.
The most astonishing fact connected with
these assertions was not that they were
uttered, but that many well-informed people
believed them.

The Government, however, was in earnest
in its determination to administer proper and
deserved punishment to the guilty; and as a
mark of approval of the opening event of the
winter campaign, the following telegram
from the Secretary of War was transmitted
to us at Camp Supply:

LIEUTENANT-GENERAL SHERMAN, St. Louis, Mo.
WAR DEPARTMENT, WASHINGTON CITY,
December 2, 1868.

I congratulate you, Sheridan, and Custer on
the splendid success with which your campaign is

begun. Ask Sheridan to send forward the names of officers and men deserving of special mention. (Signed) J. M. SCHOFIELD, Secretary of War.

It was impracticable to comply with the request contained in the closing portion of the despatch from the Secretary of War for the gratifying reason that every officer and man belonging to the expedition had performed his full part in rendering the movement against the hostile tribes a complete success.

Chapter 12

THE LOT OF TWO WHITE CAPTIVES

THE close of the last chapter left my command in camp near General Sheridan's headquarters, at the point now known as Camp Supply, Indian Territory. We had returned on the second of December from the campaign of the Washita, well satisfied with the result of our labors and exposures; but we were not to sit quietly in our tents or winter quarters and give way to mutual congratulations upon the success which had already rewarded our efforts. The same spirit who in the Shenandoah Valley campaign of 1864 had so successfully inaugurated the "whirling" movement was now present, and it was determined that upon a slightly modified principle, reinforced by the biting frosts of winter, we should continue to press things until our savage enemies should not only be completely humbled, but be forced by the combined perils of war and winter to beg for peace and settle quietly down within the limits of their reservation.

Such was the import of the closing sentences in the Congratulatory Order published by General Sheridan to the Seventh

Cavalry and quoted in the preceding chapter. "The *opening* of the campaign against hostile Indians south of the Arkansas," were the words used. We have seen the opening; if the reader will accompany me I will endeavor to relate that which followed, introducing the principal events which, in connection with the battle of the Washita, resulted in forcing all the hostile Indians south of the Arkansas to a condition of comparative peace, and gave peace and protection to that portion of our frontier which had so long suffered from their murderous and thieving raids.

In less than one week from the date of our arrival at Camp Supply, we were to be again in the saddle and wending our way southward toward the supposed winter haunts of our enemies—this time, however, with more than double our former numbers. So long had the thrifty and enterprising settlers upon the frontier of Kansas, particularly those who had selected homes in the fertile valleys of the Saline, Solomon, and Republican rivers, been subjected to the depredations of the Cheyennes, Arapahoes, Apaches, Kiowas, and Sioux, and so frequent had the murder and capture of settlers by these Indians become, that the citizens and the officials of the State felt forced to take measures in their own defense, and for the purpose of uniting with the forces of the General Government in the attempt to give quiet and protection to life and property to the inhabitants of the border settlements.

The last needed impulse to this movement on the part of the people of Kansas was given when the Indians late in the preceding summer made two raids upon the settlements in the Saline, Solomon, and Republican valleys, and, after murdering many of the men and children, burning houses, and destroying or capturing a vast amount of stock, carried off into captivity two young women or girls, both belonging to highly respected families residing on the exposed border of the State. Although one of the captives was married, her marriage to a farmer having been celebrated less than one month prior to the day of her unfortunate capture by the Indians, yet neither of them could scarcely be said to have passed the line which separates girlhood from womanhood. Mrs. Morgan, the bride, was but nineteen, while her companion in misfortune, Miss White, was still her junior by a year or more. As they played no unimportant part in subsequent operations against the Indians the principal events attending their capture may not be out of place.

Neither knew the other nor had they ever seen each other until they met as captives in an Indian village hundreds of miles from their frontier homes. One can readily imagine with what deep interest and mutual sympathy the acquaintance of these two helpless girls began. Miss White had been captured and carried to the Indian village about one month before the capture of Mrs. Morgan occurred. The brief story of the capture of the former is soon told. One day, her father being at work in the field, she and a younger sister were·engaged in the garden, when she saw four Indians entering the house where her mother and the younger children of the family were. Her first impulse was to fly, but seeing an Indian on the opposite side of the garden she turned and entered the house. One or two of the Indians could speak broken English; all of them assumed a most friendly demeanor and requested something to eat. This request was met by a most prompt and willing response upon the part of Mrs. White and her children. With true western hospitality they prepared for their unbidden guests as bountifully as the condition of the larder would permit. No depredations had been committed in that vicinity for some time, and as it was not an unusual occurrence for small parties of Indians when engaged on hunting excursions to visit the settlements, where they invariably met with kind treatment at the hands of the settlers, it was hoped that after obtaining the desired meal the party would quietly withdraw without committing any depredations.

Such, however, was not the intention of the savages. Already on that day their hands had been dipped in the white man's blood, and the peaceful procurement of something to appease their hunger was merely the dropping of the curtain between two acts of a terrible drama. Having satisfied the demands of their appetites, it was then time for them to throw aside the guise of friendship under which they had entered the house and been treated as favored guests, and to reveal the true object of their visit. Two stalwart warriors grasped Miss White in their arms and rushed toward the door. Neither her shrieks nor the feeble resistance she was able to offer retarded their movements. As she found herself being rapidly carried from the house the last glimpse she obtained of those within revealed her mother engaged in an unequal struggle with a powerful warrior, while another of the savages had felled a younger sister to the floor and was then engaged in destroying such articles of furniture or table-ware as he could lay hands upon. Her two captors hurried her from the house, hastened to the spot where they had left their ponies, and after binding their captive upon the back of one of their ponies and being joined by the others of the party, began their flight from the settlements, well knowing that the alarm would soon be given, and pursuit by the enraged settlers would be the result.

Amid the terrible surroundings of her own situation, the anxieties of the fair captive to know the fate of the dear ones left behind must have been unspeakable. I can scarcely imagine a more deplorable fate than that of which this defenseless girl had become the victim. Torn from her home amid scenes of heartrending atrocities, distracted with anxious thoughts as to the fate which had befallen her mother and sisters, she now found herself a helpless prisoner in the hands of the most cruel, heartless, and barbarous of human enemies. Unable to utter or comprehend a word of the Indian language, and her captors only being able to express the most ordinary words in broken English, her condition was rendered the more forlorn, if possible, by her inability to communicate with those in whose power she found herself.

* * *

The village to which Miss White's captors belonged was located at that time south of

Two White Captives

the Arkansas River, and distant from her
home at least three hundred miles. How
many girls of eighteen years of age possess
the physical ability to survive a journey
such as lay before this lonely captive? Un-
provided with a saddle of any description,
she was mounted upon an Indian pony and
probably required to accomplish nearly, if
not quite, one hundred miles within the first
twenty-four hours, and thus to continue the
tiresome journey with but little rest or nour-
ishment. Added to the discomforts and great
fatigue of the journey was something more
terrible and exhausting than either. The
young captive, although a mere girl, was yet
sufficiently versed in the perils attending
frontier life to fully comprehend that upon
her arrival at the village a fate awaited her
more dreadful than death itself. She realized that if her life had been spared by her
savage captors it was due to no sentiment
of mercy or kindness on their part, but simply that she might be reserved for a doom
far more fearful and more to be dreaded
than death.

The capture of Mrs. Morgan occurred
about one month later and in the same section of country, and the story of her capture
is in its incidents almost a repetition of that
of Miss White. Her young husband was en-

gaged at work in a field not far from the
house when the crack of a rifle from the
woods near by summoned her to the door.
She barely had time to see her husband fall
to the ground, when she discovered several
Indians rushing toward the house. Her first
impulse was to seek safety in flight, but already the Indians had surrounded the house,
and upon her attempting to escape one of the
savages felled her to the ground by a blow
from his war club and she lost all conscious-
ness. When she recovered her senses it was
only to find herself bound upon the back of a
pony which was being led by a mounted warrior, while another warrior rode behind and
urged the pony she was mounted upon to
keep up the trot. There were about fifty
warriors in the party, nearly all belonging to
the Cheyenne tribe, the others belonging to
the Sioux and Arapahoes. As in the case of
the capture of Miss White, a rapid flight
immediately followed the capture.[34]

[34] Nineteenth century Victorian prudery prevented
the author from stating in plain English the fact that
the Plains Indians habitually repeatedly raped their female captives and this was the fate in store for Miss
White and her companion in misfortune, Mrs. Morgan.
Somewhat extensive biographies of both women are
appended to D. L. Spotts, *Campaigning with Custer*,
207–15. Miss Sarah White was the eldest of seven children whose parents settled on a claim in Cloud County,

Two White Captives

It was the story oft repeated of outrages like these, but particularly of these two, that finally forced the people of Kansas to take up arms in their own defense. Authority was obtained from the General Government to raise a regiment of cavalry, whose services were to be accepted for a period of six months. So earnest and enthusiastic had the people of the frontier become in their determination to reclaim the two captives, as well as ad-

Kansas following the close of the Civil War. Until her return from captivity she believed that all her family had been slain. She subsequently taught school, married H. C. Brooks, a neighboring claim owner, and reared a family of seven children. She was still living, aged nearly eighty, in 1928, when Spotts' narrative was published.

Sadder was the life of Mrs. Anna Morgan. She was born December 10, 1844 near Trenton, New Jersey. Her father and one brother were killed in the Civil War. David, the remaining brother, was also a soldier. Following the war he entered a claim in Ottawa County, Kansas, where Anna presently joined him, her mother having died in an insane asylum in Pennsylvania a short time before. On September 13, 1868 she married a neighbor, James S. Morgan, and within a month was carried into captivity by a Cheyenne raiding party. Both girls were eventually taken to the Texas Panhandle, where they were rescued by General Custer in March, 1869. Mrs. Morgan resumed life with her husband, but never fully recovered from the hardships endured during her captivity. Eventually she was consigned to the Home for the Feeble Minded at Topeka, where she died June 11, 1902.

minister justly-merited punishment, that people of all classes and callings were eager to abandon their professions and take up arms against the traditional enemy of the frontier. The Governor of the State, Hon. S. J. Crawford, resigned the duties of the Executive of the State into the hands of the Lieutenant-Governor, and placed himself at the head of the regiment which was then being organized and equipped for service during the winter campaign.[35]

After the return of the Seventh Cavalry from the Washita campaign we were simply waiting the arrival at Camp Supply of the Kansas volunteers before again setting out to continue the campaign whose opening had begun so auspiciously. Severe storms de-

[35] Samuel J. Crawford, a lawyer and native of Indiana, settled in Kansas in 1859. During the Civil War he won favorable notice as an officer and leader of Kansas Volunteer troops and in 1864 while still in military service and less than thirty years of age was elected Governor of the State. In response to the Indian raids upon the frontier settlers of Kansas, Crawford organized a cavalry regiment and on Nov. 4, 1868 resigned the governorship to lead it in person. The resultant campaign, in association with the Seventh U.S. Cavalry under Custer, achieved the objective of humbling the Indians and rescuing some of the captives they had taken, and Crawford's career both in the army and in politics came to an end, although he lived for almost half a century, until October 21, 1913.

layed the arrival of the Kansas troops beyond the expected time. They reached Camp
Supply, however, in time for the 7th of December to be fixed upon as the date of our
departure. My command, as thus increased,
consisted of eleven companies of the Seventh
United States Cavalry; ten companies of the
Nineteenth Kansas Volunteer Cavalry, Colonel S. J. Crawford commanding; a detachment of scouts under Lieutenant Silas Pepoon, Tenth Cavalry; and between twenty
and thirty whites, Osage and Kaw Indians,
as guides and trailers. As our ultimate
destination was Fort Cobb, Indian Territory, where we would obtain a renewal of our
supplies after the termination of our proposed march, and as General Sheridan desired to transfer his headquarters "in the
field" to that point, he decided to accompany my command, but generously declined
to exercise any command of the expedition,
merely desiring to avail himself of this opportunity of an escort without rendering a
detachment for that purpose necessary; and,
as he remarked when announcing his intention to accompany us, he simply wished to
be regarded as a passenger.[36]

[36] In 1858 Major Earl Van Dorn established a post
which was named Camp Radziminski in Otter Creek
Canon in southern Kiowa County, Oklahoma. In

My Life on the Plains

The day prior to our departure I was standing in front of my tent when a young man probably twenty-one or two years of age accosted me and began a conversation by inquiring when I expected the expedition would move. Any person who has had much to do with expeditions in the Indian country knows how many and how frequent are the applications made to the commanding officer to obtain employment as scouts or guides. Probably one in fifty of the applicants is deserving of attention, and if employed would prove worthy of his hire. Taking but a glance at the young man who addressed me, and believing him to be one of the numerous applicants for employment, my attention being at the time absorbed with other matters I was in no mood to carry on a conversation which I believed would terminate in an

December, 1859 it was abandoned in favor of a new post on the west side of the Washita at its junction with Pond Creek in Caddo County, Oklahoma, which was named Fort Cobb. During the Civil War, Confederates occupied the post for a time. Following the war it was abandoned until General W. B. Hazen reoccupied it in early November, 1868 to serve as headquarters for the Indian Agency in charge of the southern plains tribes, General Sheridan disliked the location and ordered the establishment of new Fort Sill in January, 1869, to which place garrison and Indians were removed from Fort Cobb several weeks later.

offer of services not desired. I was disposed to be somewhat abrupt in my answers, but there was something in the young man's earnest manner, the eagerness with which he seemed to await my answers, that attracted and interested me. After a few questions on his part as to what portion of the country I expected to march through, what tribes I might encounter, and others of a similar nature, he suddenly said: "General, I want to go along with you."

This only confirmed my first impression, although from his conversation I soon discovered that he was not one of the professional applicants for employment as a scout or guide, but more likely had been seized with a spirit of wild romance and imagined the proper field for its display would be discovered by accompanying an expedition against the Indians. Many instances of this kind had previously fallen under my observation and I classed this as one of them; so I simply informed him that I had already employed as many scouts and guides as were required and that no position of that character, or any other in fact, was open to him. Not in the least discouraged by this decided refusal, he replied: "But you do not understand me; I do not desire employment in your command, nor any position requiring pay. I only ask permission to accompany your expedition. I have neither arms nor horse; if you will furnish me these and permit me to go with you I will serve you in any capacity I can, and will expect no pay."

My curiosity was now excited; I therefore pressed him to explain his motive in desiring to accompany the expedition.

"Well, I'll tell you; it's a sad story. About four months ago the Indians attacked my home and carried off my only sister, a girl nineteen years of age. Since that day I have heard not a word as to what has become of her. I know not whether she is among the living or dead; but when I think of what must be her fate if among the living, I am almost tempted to wish she was quietly resting among the dead. I do not even know what tribe was engaged in her capture, but hearing of your expedition I thought it might afford me the means of getting some clue to my sister's fate. You may have a council with some of the chiefs, or some of the prisoners you captured at the battle of the Washita may tell me something of her; or if I can only learn where she is, perhaps you can exchange some of your prisoners for her; at any rate, the only chance I have to learn anything concerning her is by being permitted to accompany your expedition."

Two White Captives

Of course he was permitted to accompany the expedition; not only that, but he was provided with a horse and arms and appointed to a remunerative position. I asked him why he had not informed me at first as to his object in desiring to go with us. He replied that he feared that if it was known that he was in search of a lost sister and we should afterward have interviews with the Indians, as we certainly would at Fort Cobb, he might not be as successful in obtaining information as if the object of his mission was unknown.

The name of this young man was Brewster, and the lost sister in whose search he was so earnestly engaged was Mrs. Morgan, whose capture has already been described. From him I learned that Mrs. Morgan's husband, although shot down at the first fire of the Indians, was in a fair way to recover, although crippled probably for life. But for his wounds, he too would have joined the brother in a search for the sister and for his bride, whose honeymoon had met with such a tragic interruption. Young Brewster remained with my command during the entire winter, accompanying it and every detachment made from it in the eager hope to learn something of the fate of his sister. In his continued efforts to discover some clue lead-

413

ing to her he displayed more genuine courage, perseverance, and physical endurance,
and a greater degree of true brotherly love
and devotion, than I have ever seen combined in one person. We will hear from him
as the story progresses.

It was decided to send the captives taken
at the Washita to Fort Hays, Kansas, where
they could not only be safely guarded, but be
made far more comfortable than at Camp
Supply. Before the expedition moved I suggested to General Sheridan that I should
take with the expedition three of the squaws
who were prisoners in our hands, with a view
to rendering their services available in establishing communication with the hostile villages, if at any time this should become a
desirable object. General Sheridan approved
of the suggestion and I selected three of the
captives who were to accompany us. The
first was Mah-wis-sa, the sister of Black
Kettle, whose acquaintance the reader may
have formed in the preceding chapter; the
second was a Sioux squaw, probably fifty
years of age, whom Mah-wis-sa expressed a
desire to have accompany her, and who at
times was disposed to be extremely communicative in regard to the winter resorts of
the various tribes and other matters connected with the purposes of the expedition.

414

Two White Captives

The third was the daughter of Little Rock, the chief second in rank to Black Kettle, who had been killed at the battle of the Washita.

Little Rock's daughter was an exceedingly comely squaw, possessing a bright, cheery face, a countenance beaming with intelligence, and a disposition more inclined to be merry than one usually finds among the Indians. She was probably rather under than over twenty years of age. Added to bright, laughing eyes, a set of pearly teeth, and a rich complexion, her well-shaped head was crowned with a luxuriant growth of the most beautiful silken tresses, rivalling in color the blackness of the raven and extending, when allowed to fall loosely over her shoulders, to below her waist. Her name was Mo-nah-se-tah, which, anglicized, means "The young grass that shoots in the spring." Mo-nah-se-tah, although yet a maiden in years and appearance, had been given in marriage, or, more properly speaking, she had been traded in marriage, as an Indian maiden who should be so unfortunate as to be given away would not be looked upon as a very desirable match. In addition to her handsome appearance both in form and feature and to any other personal attraction which might be considered peculiarly her own, Mo-nah-se-tah, being the daughter of a chief high in rank,

was justly considered as belonging to the
cream of the aristocracy, if not to royalty
itself; consequently the suitors who hoped to
gain her hand must be prepared, according
to the Indian custom, to pay handsomely
for an alliance so noble. Little Rock, while
represented as having been a kind and af-
fectionate father, yet did not propose that
the hand of his favorite daughter should
be disposed of without the return of a due
equivalent.

Among the young warriors of the tribe
there were many who would have been proud
to call Mo-nah-se-tah to preside over the
domestic destinies of their lodge, but the
price to be paid for so distinguished an alliance was beyond the means of most of them.
Among the number of young braves who aspired to the honor of her hand was one who,
so far as worldly wealth was concerned, was
eligible. Unfortunately, however, he had
placed too much reliance upon this fact, and
had not thought that while obtaining the
consent of paterfamilias it would be well also
to win the heart of the maiden; or perhaps he
had, in seeking her hand, also attempted to
gain her heart, but not meeting with the desired encouragement from the maiden of his
choice was willing to trust to time to accomplish the latter, provided only he could se-

cure the first. According to Indian custom
the consent of the bride to a proposed marriage, while it may be ever so desirable, is not
deemed essential. All that is considered absolutely essential is that the bridegroom shall
be acceptable to the father of the bride, and
shall transfer to the possession of the latter
ponies or other articles of barter in sufficient
number and value to be considered a fair
equivalent for the hand of the daughter.
When it is stated that from two to four
ponies are considered as the price of the
average squaw, and that the price of the
hand of Mo-nah-se-tah as finally arranged
was eleven ponies, some idea can be formed
of the high opinion entertained of her.

It proved, however, so far as the young
warrior was concerned an unsatisfactory in-
vestment. The ponies were transferred to
Little Rock and all the formalities were duly
executed which by Indian law and custom
were necessary to constitute Mo-nah-se-tah
the wife of the young brave. She was forced
to take up her abode in his lodge, but refused
to acknowledge him as her husband, or to
render him that obedience and menial service which the Indian husband exacts from
his wife. Time failed to soften her heart, or
to cause her to look kindly upon her self-con-
stituted but unrecognized lord and master.

Here was a clear case of incompatibility of disposition; and within the jurisdiction of some of our State laws a divorce would have been granted almost unquestioned. The patience of the young husband having become exhausted, and he having unsuccessfully resorted to every measure of kindness deemed likely to win the love and obedience of his wife, he determined to have recourse to harsher measures—if necessary, to employ force. Again he mistook the character of her upon whose apparently obdurate heart neither threats nor promises had produced the faintest effect. Mo-nah-se-tah had probably been anticipating such a decision and had prepared herself accordingly. Like most Indian women, she was as skilful in the handling and use of weapons as most warriors are; and when her husband, or rather the husband who had been assigned to her, attempted to establish by force an authority which she had persistently refused to recognize she reminded him that she was the daughter of a great chief and rather than submit to the indignities which he was thus attempting to heap upon her she would resist even to the taking of life; and suiting the action to the word, she levelled a small pistol which she had carried concealed beneath her blanket and fired, wounding him in the knee and disabling him for life.

Two White Captives

Little Rock, learning of what had occurred and finding upon investigation that his daughter had not been to blame, concluded to cancel the marriage—to grant a divorce— which was accomplished simply by returning to the unfortunate husband the eleven ponies which had been paid for the hand of Mo-nah-se-tah. What an improvement upon the method prescribed in the civilized world! No lawyer's fees, no publicity nor scandal; all tedious delays are avoided, and the result is as nearly satisfactory to all parties as is possible.

Having sent a messenger to ask the three Indian women referred to to come to my tent, I acquainted them with my intention of taking them with the expedition when we moved in search of the hostile villages. To my surprise they evinced great delight at the idea, and explained it by saying that if they accompanied us they might be able to see or communicate with some of their people, while by remaining with the other prisoners and becoming farther separated from their own country and hunting-grounds they could entertain little or no hope of learning anything concerning the fate of other portions of their tribe. They gladly acceded to the proposition to accompany the troops. I then inquired of them in which mode they preferred to travel, mounted upon ponies as was their custom, or in an ambulance. Much to my surprise, remembering how loath the Indian is to adopt any contrivance of the white man, they chose the ambulance, and wisely, too, as the season was that of mid-winter and the interior of a closely covered ambulance was a much less exposed position than that to be found on the back of a pony.

Chapter 13

FORAGE for the horses and mules and rations for the men, sufficient of both to last thirty days, having been loaded on the wagons, the entire command, composed as previously stated and accompanied by General Sheridan and staff, left Camp Supply early on the morning of December 7, and turning our horses' heads southward we marched in the direction of the battle-ground of the Washita. Our march to the Washita was quiet and uneventful if we except the loquacity of California Joe, who, now that we were once more in the saddle with the prospect of stirring times before us, seemed completely in his element and gave vent to his satisfaction by indulging in a connected series of remarks and queries, always supplying the answer to the latter himself if none of his listeners evinced a disposition to do so for him. His principal delight seemed to be in speculating audibly as to what would be the impression produced on the minds of the Indians when they discovered us returning with increased numbers both of men and wagons.

421

"I'd jist like to see the streaked count'-
nances of Satanta, Medicine Arrow, Lone
Wolf, and a few others of 'em when they
ketch the fust glimpse of the outfit. They'll
think we're comin' to spend an evenin' with
'em sure, and hev brought our knittin' with
us. One look'll satisfy 'em thar'll be sum of
the durndest kickin' out over these plains
that ever war heern tell uv. One good thing,
it's goin' to cum as nigh killin' uv 'em to start
'em out this time uv year as ef we hed an out
an' out scrummage with 'em. The way I
looks at it they hev jist this preference: them
as don't like bein' shot to deth kin take ther
chances at freezin'." In this interminable
manner California Joe would pursue his
semi-soliloquies, only too delighted if some
one exhibited interest sufficient to propound
an occasional question.

As our proposed route bore to the southeast after reaching the battlefield, our course
was so chosen as to carry us to the Washita
River a few miles below, at which point we
encamped early in the day. General Sheridan desired to ride over the battle-ground
and we hoped by a careful examination of
the surrounding country to discover the remains of Major Elliot and his little party, of
whose fate there could no longer be the faintest doubt. With one hundred men of the

Winter Campaign

Seventh Cavalry under command of Captain Yates we proceeded to the scene of the battle and from there dispersed in small parties in all directions, with orders to make a thorough search for our lost comrades. We found the evidences of the late engagement much as we had left them. Here were the bodies, now frozen, of the seven hundred ponies which we had slain after the battle; here and there, scattered in and about the site of the former village of Black Kettle, lay the bodies of many of the Indians who fell during the struggle. Many of the bodies, however, particularly those of Black Kettle and Little Rock, had been removed by their friends. Why any had been allowed to remain uncared for could only be explained upon the supposition that the hasty flight of the other villages prevented the Indians from carrying away any except the bodies of the most prominent chiefs or warriors, although most of those remaining on the battle-ground were found wrapped in blankets and bound with lariats preparatory to removal and burial. Even some of the Indian dogs were found loitering in the vicinity of the places where the lodges of their former masters stood; but, like the Indians themselves, they were suspicious of the white man and could hardly be induced to establish friendly relations. Some

423

of the soldiers, however, managed to secure possession of a few young puppies; these were carefully brought up and to this day they or some of their descendants are in the possession of members of the command.

After riding over the ground in the immediate vicinity of the village I joined one of the parties engaged in the search for the bodies of Major Elliot and his men. In describing the search and its result I cannot do better than transcribe from my official report, made soon after to General Sheridan:

"After marching a distance of two miles in the direction in which Major Elliot and his little party were last seen, we suddenly came upon the stark, stiff, naked, and horribly mutilated bodies of our dead comrades. No words were needed to tell how desperate had been the struggle before they were finally overpowered. At a short distance from where the bodies lay could be seen the carcasses of some of the horses of the party, which had probably been killed early in the fight. Seeing the hopelessness of breaking through the line which surrounded them, and which undoubtedly numbered more than one hundred to one, Elliot dismounted his men, tied their horses together, and prepared to sell their lives as dearly as possible. It may not be improper to add that in describing, as far as

424

possible, the details of Elliot's fight I rely not only upon a critical and personal examination of the ground and attendant circumstances, but am sustained by the statements of Indian chiefs and warriors who witnessed and participated in the fight, and who have since been forced to enter our lines and surrender themselves up under circumstances which will be made to appear in other portions of this report.

"The bodies of Elliot and his little band, with but a single exception, were found lying within a circle not exceeding twenty yards in diameter. We found them exactly as they fell, except that their barbarous foes had stripped and mutilated the bodies in the most savage manner.

"All the bodies were carried to camp. The latter was reached after dark. It being the intention to resume the march before daylight the following day, a grave was hastily prepared on a little knoll near our camp and, with the exception of that of Major Elliot, whose remains were carried with us for interment at Fort Arbuckle,[37] the bodies of the

[37] In May, 1850 Captain Randolph B. Marcy conducted a company of the Fifth U.S. Infantry which established Fort Arbuckle on the south side of the Canadian River in eastern McLain County, Oklahoma. The following year the post was relocated on Wild

entire party, under the dim light of a few
torches held by sorrowing comrades, were
consigned to one common resting place. No
funeral note sounded to measure their passage to the grave. No volley was fired to tell
us a comrade was receiving the last sad rites
of burial, that the fresh earth had closed over
some of our truest and most daring soldiers.[38]

* * *

"The forest along the banks of the Washita
from the battle-ground a distance of twelve
miles was found to have been one continuous

Horse Creek in the southern part of present-day Gar-
vin County, a few miles from the Washita River. It
was occupied (during much of the Civil War by Confederate troops) until it was rendered useless by the
establishment of present-day Fort Sill under orders of
General Sheridan in 1869.

[38] At this point the author supplies a surgical report
upon the mutilations inflicted upon the bodies of fifteen of the dead soldiers. The description of Major
Elliot's body will suffice as a sample of them all: "two
bullet holes in head, one in left cheek, right hand cut
off, left foot almost cut off, . . . deep gash in right groin,
deep gashes in calves of both legs, little finger of left
hand cut off, and throat cut." The words omitted presumably recite indecencies deemed unfit to print. Three
of the corpses—two of them beheaded—were unidenti-
fied. General Sheridan, in a report of December 19, 1868
stated that the bodies of Elliot and 16 of his men were
found. The fate of the three missing troopers thus
remains a matter for speculation.

Indian village. Black Kettle's band of
Cheyennes was above; then came other hostile tribes camped in the following order:
Arapahoes under Little Raven; Kiowas under Satanta and Lone Wolf; the remaining
bands of Cheyennes, Comanches, and Apaches. Nothing could exceed the disorder and
haste with which these tribes had fled from
their camping grounds. They had abandoned thousands of lodge poles, some of
which were still standing as when last used.
Immense numbers of camp kettles, cooking
utensils, coffee-mills, axes, and several hundred buffalo robes were found in the abandoned camps adjacent to Black Kettle's village, but which had not been visited before
by our troops. By actual examination it was
computed that over six hundred lodges had
been standing along the Washita during the
battle, and within five miles of the battle-
ground, and it was from these villages, and
others still lower down the stream that the
immense number of warriors came who, after
our rout and destruction of Black Kettle and
his band, surrounded my command and
fought until defeated by the Seventh Cavalry about 3 P. M. on the 27th ult. . . . In the
deserted camp lately occupied by Satanta
with the Kiowas my men discovered the
bodies of a young white woman and child,

427

the former apparently about twenty-three years of age, the latter probably eighteen months old. They were evidently mother and child and had not long been in captivity, as the woman still retained several articles of her wardrobe about her person, among others a pair of cloth gaiters but little worn, everything indicating that she had been but recently captured and upon our attacking and routing Black Kettle's camp her captors, fearing she might be recaptured by us and her testimony used against them, had deliberately murdered her and her child in cold blood. The woman had received a shot in the forehead, her entire scalp had been removed, and her skull horribly crushed. The child also bore numerous marks of violence."[39]

At daylight on the following morning the entire command started on the trail of the Indian villages, nearly all of which had moved down the Washita toward Fort Cobb, where they had good reason to believe they

[39] The slain captives were Mrs. Clara Blinn and her two-year-old son, Willie, who had been taken in the capture of a wagon train near Fort Lyon, Colorado, on October 9, 1868. Efforts to recover them had been made, and a pathetic letter was written by Mrs. Blinn on November 7, appealing for their continuance. For it and further details of her fate see Rister, *Border Command* 116-18.

would receive protection. The Arapahoes and remaining band of Cheyennes left the Washita Valley and moved across in the direction of Red River. After following the trail of the Kiowas and other hostile Indians for seven days over an almost impassable country, where it was necessary to keep two or three hundred men almost constantly at work with picks, axes, and spades before being able to advance with our immense train, my Osage scouts came galloping back on the morning of the 17th of December and reported a party of Indians in our front bearing a flag of truce.

It is to this day such a common occurrence for Indian agents to assert in positive terms that the particular Indians of their agency have not been absent from their reservation nor engaged in making war upon the white men, when the contrary is well known to be true, that I deem it proper to introduce one of the many instances of this kind which have fallen under my observation, as an illustration not only of how the public in distant sections of the country may be misled and deceived as to the acts and intentions of the Indians, but also of the extent to which the Indian agents themselves will proceed in attempting to shield and defend the Indians of their particular agency.

My Life on the Plains

Sometimes, of course, the agent is the victim of deception and no doubt conscientiously proclaims that which he firmly believes; but I am forced by long experience to the opinion that instances of this kind are rare, being the exception rather than the rule. In the example to which I refer, the high character and distinction as well as the deservedly national reputation achieved by the official then in charge of the Indians against whom we were operating will at once absolve me from the imputation of intentionally reflecting upon the integrity of his action in the matter. The only point to occasion surprise is how an officer possessing the knowledge of the Indian character, derived from an extensive experience on the frontier, which General Hazen could justly lay claim to should be so far misled as to give the certificate of good conduct which follows. General Hazen had not only had superior opportunities for studying the Indian character, but had participated in Indian wars, and at the very time he penned the following note he was partially disabled from the effects of an Indian wound. The Government had selected him from the large number of intelligent officers of high rank whose services were available for the position, and had assigned him with plenary powers to the superintendency of the Southern Indian District, a position in which almost the entire control of all the southern tribes was vested in the occupant. If gentlemen of the experience and military education of General Hazen, occupying the intimate and official relation to the Indians which he did, could be so readily and completely deceived as to their real character it is not strange that the mass of the people living far from the scene of operations and only possessing such information as reaches them in scraps through the public press, and generally colored by interested parties, should at times entertain extremely erroneous impressions regarding the much-vexed Indian question. Now to the case in point:[40]

With the Osage scouts who came back from the advance with the intelligence that a party of Indians were in front, also came a scout who stated that he was from Fort Cobb and delivered to me a despatch which read as follows:

[40] When this installment of Custer's narrative was published in the *Galaxy*, General Hazen submitted to the Editor his own version of the action complained of, and a condensed summary of it was published in the July, 1874 issue. Hazen's entire rebuttal was privately published at St. Paul in 1875, entitled *Some Corrections to my Life on the Plains.*" It was subsequently reprinted in *Chronicles of Oklahoma*, Vol. III, 295-318.

My Life on the Plains

Headquarters Southern Indian District,
Fort Cobb, 9 p. m. December 16, 1868.

To the Officer, commanding troops in the Field.

Indians have just brought in word that our troops to-day reached the Washita some twenty miles above here. I send this to say that all the camps this side of the point reported to have been reached are friendly, and have not been on the war path this season. If this reaches you it would be well to communicate at once with Satanta or Black Eagle, chiefs of the Kiowas, near where you now are, who will readily inform you of the position of the Cheyennes and Arapahoes, also of my camp.

Respectfully,
(Signed) W. B. Hazen, Brevet Major-General.

This scout at the same time informed me that a large party of Kiowa warriors under Lone Wolf, Satanta, and other leading chiefs were within less than a mile of my advance, and notwithstanding the above certificate regarding their friendly character they had seized a scout who accompanied the bearer of the despatch, disarmed him, and held him a prisoner of war. Taking a small party with me I proceeded beyond our lines to meet the flag of truce. I was met by several of the leading chiefs of the Kiowas, including those above named. Large parties of their warriors could be seen posted in the neighboring

432

Winter Campaign

ravines and upon the surrounding hilltops.
All were painted and plumed for war and
nearly all were armed with one rifle, two revolvers, bow and arrow, some of their bows
being strung, and their whole appearance
and conduct plainly indicating that they had
come for war. Their declarations to some of
my guides and friendly Indians proved the
same thing, and they were only deterred
from hostile acts by discovering our strength
to be far greater than they had imagined,
and our scouts on the alert. Aside, however,
from the question as to what their present or
future intentions were at that time, how deserving were those Indians of the certificate
of good behavior which they had been shrewd
enough to obtain? The certificate was dated
December 16, and stated that the camps had
not been on the war path "this season."

What were the facts? On the 27th of November, only twenty-one days prior to the
date of the certificate, the same Indians
whose peaceable character was vouched for
so strongly had engaged in battle with my
command by attacking it during the fight
with Black Kettle. It was in their camp that
the bodies of the murdered mother and child
were found, and we had followed day by day
the trail of the Kiowas and other tribes leading us directly from the dead and mangled

433

bodies of our comrades, slain by them a few
days previous, until we were about to overtake and punish the guilty parties, when the
above communication was received, some
forty or fifty miles from Fort Cobb in the
direction of the Washita battle-ground.

This of itself was conclusive evidence of
the character of the tribes we were dealing
with; but aside from these incontrovertible
facts, had additional evidence been needed
of the openly hostile conduct of the Kiowas
and Comanches and of their active participation in the battle of the Washita, it is only
necessary to refer to the collected testimony
of Black Eagle and other leading chiefs.
This testimony was written and was then in
the hands of the agents of the Indian Bureau.
It was given voluntarily by the Indian chiefs
referred to and was taken down at the time
by the Indian agents, not for the army or
with a view of furnishing it to officers of the
army, but simply for the benefit and information of the Indian Bureau. This testimony, making due allowance for the concealment of much that would be prejudicial
to the interests of the Indians, plainly states
that the Kiowas and Comanches took part
in the battle of the Washita: that the former
constituted a portion of the war party whose
trail I followed, and which led my command

into Black Kettle's village: and that some of the Kiowas remained in Black Kettle's village until the morning of the battle.

This evidence is all contained in a report made to the Superintendent of Indian Affairs by one Philip McCuskey, United States interpreter for the Kiowa and Comanche tribes. This report was dated Fort Cobb, December 3, while the communication from General Hazen, certifying to the friendly disposition and conduct of these tribes was dated at the same place thirteen days later. Mah-wis-sa also confirmed these statements and pointed out to me, when near the battle-ground, the location of Satanta's village. It was from her, too, that I learned that it was in Satanta's village that the bodies of the white woman and child were found. As I pen these lines the daily press contains frequent allusions to the negotiations which are being conducted between the Governor of Texas and the General Government looking to the release of Satanta from the Texas penitentiary, to which institution Satanta, after a trial before the civil authorities for numerous murders committed on the Texas frontier, was sent three or four years ago to serve out a life sentence.

After meeting the chiefs who with their bands had approached our advance under flag of truce, and compelling the release of the scout whom they had seized and held prisoner, we continued our march toward Fort Cobb, the chiefs agreeing to ride with us and accompany my command to that place. Every assurance was given me that the villages to which these various chiefs belonged would at once move to Fort Cobb and there encamp, thus separating themselves from the hostile tribes, or those who preferred to decline this proposition of peace and to continue to wage war; and as an evidence of the sincerity of their purpose some eighteen or twenty of the most prominent chiefs, generally Kiowas, voluntarily proposed to accompany us during the march of that day and the next, by which time it was expected that the command would reach Fort Cobb. The chiefs only requested that they might send one of their number mounted on a fleet pony to the villages, in order to hasten their movement to Fort Cobb. How eager for peace were these poor, confiding sons of the forest is the mental ejaculation of some of my readers, particularly if they are inclined to be converts to the humanitarian doctrines supposed to be applicable in the government of Indians. If I am addressing any of this class, for whose kindness of heart I have the utmost regard, I regret to be compelled to disturb the illusion.

Peace was not included among the purposes which governed the chiefs who so freely and unhesitatingly proffered their company during our march to Fort Cobb. Nor had they the faintest intention of either accompanying us or directing their villages to proceed to the fort. The messenger whom they seemed so anxious to despatch to the village was not sent to hasten the movement of their villages toward Fort Cobb, as claimed by them, but to hasten their movement in a precisely opposite direction, viz., towards the head waters of Red River near the northwestern limits of Texas. This sudden effusion of friendly sentiments rather excited my suspicions, but I was unable at first to divine the real intents and purposes of the chiefs. Nothing was to be done but to act so as to avoid exciting their suspicions, and trust to time to unravel the scheme.

When we arrived at our camping ground on the evening of that day the chiefs requested permission to despatch another messenger to their people to inform them where we were encamped. To this proposition no objection was made. That evening I caused an abundant supply of provisions, consisting principally of beef, bread, coffee, and sugar,

to be distributed among them. In posting
my pickets that night for the protection of
the camp I arranged to have the reserve stationed within a short distance of the spot on
which the chiefs were to encamp during the
night, which point was but a few paces from
my headquarters. Before retiring, I took
Romeo, the interpreter, and strolled down to
pay a visit to the chiefs. The latter, after the
substantial meal in which they had just indulged, were seated, Indian fashion, around
a small fire, enjoying such comfort as was to
be derived from the occasional whiffs of
smoke which each in proper turn inhaled
from the long-stemmed pipe of red clay that
was kept passing from right to left around
the circle. Their greeting of me was cordial
in the extreme, but, as in the play—of
Richelieu, I believe—they "bowed too low."

Through Romeo I chatted on indifferent
subjects with the various chiefs, and from
nearly all of them received assurances of
their firmly fixed resolution to abandon forever the dangers and risks of the war path,
to live no longer at variance with their white
brothers, to eschew henceforth all such unfriendly customs as scalp-taking, murdering
defenseless women and children, and stealing
stock from the settlers of the frontier. All
this was to be changed in the future. It

seemed strange, listening to these apparently
artless sons of nature, that men entertaining
the ardent desire for repose which they professed had not turned their backs on the war
path long ago and settled down to the quiet
enjoyment of the blessings of peace. But
better that this conclusion should be arrived
at late than not at all. The curtain had fallen
from their eyes and they were enabled to see
everything in its proper light. To adopt their
own language, "their hearts had become
good," "their tongues had become straight,"
they had cast aside the bad ways in which
they had so long struggled unsuccessfully
and had now resolved to follow the white
man's road, to adopt his mode of dress, till
the soil, and establish schools for the education of their children, until in time the white
man and the red man would not only be
brothers in name, but would be found travelling the same road with interests in common.

Had I been a latter-day Peace Commissioner, I should have felt in duty bound to
send a despatch to the chief of the proper
bureau at Washington, in terms somewhat
as follows:

* * *

Not being an orthodox Peace Commissioner in good standing in that fraternity, I
did not send a despatch of this character.

439

What I did, however, answered every purpose. I went to the station of the guard near by and directed the non-commissioned officer in charge to have his men keep a watchful eye upon those same untutored sons of the forest, as I felt confident their plans boded us no good. Romeo was also told to inform the chiefs that after the camp had quieted down for the night it would not be prudent for them to wander far from their camp fire, as the sentries might mistake them for enemies and fire upon them. This I knew would make them hug their fire closely until morning.

Before daylight we were again in the saddle and commencing the last march necessary to take us to Fort Cobb. Again did it become important, in the opinion of the chiefs, to despatch another of their number to hurry up the people of their villages, in order, as they said, that the villages might arrive at Fort Cobb at the same time we did. As the march progressed these applications became more frequent, until most of the chiefs had been sent away as messengers. I noticed, however, that in selecting those to be sent the chiefs lowest in rank and importance were first chosen, so that those who remained were the highest. When their numbers had dwindled down to less than half the original party I saw that instead of acting in good faith this party of chiefs was solely en-

gaged in the effort to withdraw our attention
from the villages, and, by an apparent offer
on their part to accompany us to Fort Cobb,
where we were encouraged to believe the villages would meet us, prevent us from watching and following the trail made by the
lodges which had already diverged from the
direct route to Fort Cobb, the one the villages would have pursued had that fort been
their destination.

It became palpably evident that the Indians were resorting, as usual, to stratagem
to accomplish their purpose, which of course
involved our deception. Fortunately their
purpose was divined in time to thwart it. As
no haste was necessary, I permitted the remaining chiefs to continue the march with
us without giving them any grounds to suppose that we strongly doubted their oft-
repeated assertions that their hearts were
good and their tongues were straight. Finally as our march for that day neared its
termination and we were soon to reach our
destination, the party of chiefs, which at first
embraced upwards of twenty, had become
reduced until none remained except the two
head chiefs, Lone Wolf and Satanta, and
these no doubt were laughing in their
sleeves, if an Indian may be supposed to
possess that article of apparel, at the happy
and highly successful manner in which they

had hoodwinked their white brethren. But had they known all that had been transpiring they would not have felt so self-satisfied. As usual, quite a number of officers and orderlies rode at the head of the column, including a few of General Sheridan's staff.

As soon as the scheme of the Indians was discovered, I determined to seize the most prominent chiefs as hostages for the fulfilment of their promises regarding the coming on of the villages; but as for this purpose two hostages were as valuable as twenty, I allowed all but this number to take their departure apparently unnoticed. Finally when none but Lone Wolf and Satanta remained, and they no doubt were prepared with a plausible excuse to bid us in the most improved Kiowa *au revoir*, the officers just referred to, at a given signal, drew their revolvers and Lone Wolf and Satanta were informed through Romeo that they were prisoners.[41]

[41] Lone Wolf was one of the nine signers of the treaty of Medicine Lodge in 1867, by which the Kiowa first agreed to be placed on a reservation. In 1873 his son was killed by Texans and he became the leader of the hostile Kiowas in the outbreak of 1874. Following their surrender, Lone Wolf was condemned by the military commission which sat at Fort Sill in 1875 and imprisoned in Fort Marion at St. Augustine. He died in 1879, shortly after his release from this imprisonment. For Satanta see *Post*, 533.

Chapter 14

RED AND WHITE DIPLOMACY

NOT even the proverbial stoicism of the red man was sufficient to conceal the chagrin and disappointment recognizable in every lineament of the countenances of both Satanta and Lone Wolf when they discovered that all their efforts at deception had not only failed, but left them prisoners in our hands. Had we been in doubt as to whether their intention had really been to leave us in the lurch or not, all doubt would have been dispelled by a slight circumstance which soon after transpired. As I before stated we had almost reached Fort Cobb, which was our destination for the time being. The chiefs who had already made their escape now became anxious in regard to the non-arrival in their midst of Satanta and Lone Wolf. The delay of the last two could not be satisfactorily accounted for. Something must have gone amiss.

Again was stratagem resorted to. We were marching along without interruption or incident to disturb our progress, such of us as were at the head of the column keeping watchful eyes upon our two swarthy prisoners who rode sullenly at our sides, and whose past career justified us in attributing to them the nerve and daring necessary to induce an effort to secure their liberty should there be the slightest probability of success. Suddenly a mounted Indian appeared far away to our right and approached us at a gallop until almost within rifle range, when halting his well-trained pony upon a little hillock which answered his purpose, he gracefully detached the scarlet blanket he wore and began waving it in a peculiar but regular manner. Both chiefs looked anxiously in the direction of the warrior, then merely glanced toward me as if to see if I had also observed this last arrival; but too proud to speak or prefer a request, they rode silently on, apparently indifferent to what might follow. Turning to Romeo, who rode in rear, I directed him to inquire of the chiefs the meaning of the signals which the warrior was evidently endeavoring to convey to them. Satanta acted as spokesman and replied that the warrior in sight was his son, and that the latter was signalling to him that he had something important to communicate and desired Satanta to ride out and join him.

To have seen the innocent and artless expression of countenance with which Satanta made this announcement one would not have imagined that the son had been sent as a decoy to cover the escape of the father, and that the latter had been aware of this fact from the first. However, I pretended to humor Satanta. Of course there was no objection to his galloping out to where his son awaited him, because, as he said, that son was, and for good reason perhaps, unwilling to gallop in to where his father was. But if Satanta was so eager to see and communicate with his son, there should be no objection to the presence of a small escort—not that there existed doubts in my mind as to Satanta's intention to return to us, because no such doubt existed. I was positively convinced that once safely beyond our reach the place at the head of the column which had known him for a few brief hours would know him no more forever. I told Romeo to say to Satanta that he might ride across the plain to where his son was, and not only that, but several of us would do ourselves the honor to volunteer as his escort.

The most careless observer would have detected the air of vexation with which Satanta turned his pony's head, and taking me at my word started to meet his son. A brisk gallop soon brought us to the little hillock upon which Satanta's son awaited us. He was

there, a tall, trimly built, warrior-like young
fellow of perhaps twenty, and bore himself
while in our presence as if he would have us
to understand he was not only the son of a
mighty chief but some day would wear that
title himself. What was intended to be
gained by the interview did not become evident, as the presence of Romeo prevented
any conversation between father and son
looking to the formation of plans for escape.
Questions were asked and answered as to
where the village was, and in regard to its
future movements, but nothing satisfactory
either to Satanta or his captors was learned
from the young warrior. Finally, I suggested
to Satanta that as we only intended to proceed a few miles farther, being then in the
near vicinity of Fort Cobb and would there
encamp for an indefinite period, his son had
better accompany us to camp, where Lone
Wolf and Satanta would be informed what
was to be required of them and their people,
and then, after conferring with each other,
the two chiefs could send Satanta's son to
the village with any message which they
might desire to transmit to their people. At
the same time I promised the young warrior
good treatment, with permission to go and
come as he chose, and in no manner to be
regarded or treated as a prisoner.

Red and White Diplomacy

This proposition seemed to strike the Indians favorably, and much to my surprise, knowing the natural suspicion of the Indian, the young warrior readily consented to the plan and at once placed himself in our power. Turning our horses' heads, we soon resumed our places at the head of the column, the three Indians riding in silence, brooding, no doubt, over plans looking to their freedom.[42]

* * *

Upon our arrival at Fort Cobb, the day of the seizure of the two chiefs, Lone Wolf and Satanta, we selected a camp with a view of remaining at that point during the negotiations which were to be conducted with the various tribes who were still on the war path. So far as some of the tribes were concerned, they were occupying that equivocal position which enabled them to class themselves as friendly and at the same time engage in hostilities. This may sound ambiguous, but is easily explained. The chiefs and old men with the women and children of the tribe were permitted to assemble regularly at the agency near Fort Cobb, and as regularly were bountifully supplied with food and

[42] A digression at this point in the original narrative recounts the details of a series of shooting matches in which Custer and the son of Satanta engaged.

clothing sufficient for all their wants; at the same time the young men, warriors, and war chiefs of the tribe were almost continually engaged in making war upon the frontier of northern Texas and southeastern Kansas. Indeed, we established the fact while at or near Fort Cobb that while my command was engaged in fighting the warriors and chiefs of certain tribes at the battle of the Washita the families of these same warriors and chiefs were being clothed and fed by the agent of the Government then stationed at Fort Cobb.

Surprising as this may seem, it is not an unusual occurrence. The same system has prevailed during the past year. While my command was resisting the attacks of a large body of warriors on the Yellowstone River last summer the families of many of these warriors, the latter representing seven tribes or bands, were subsisting upon provisions and clothed in garments issued to them at the regular Indian agencies by the Government. But of this more anon.

The three tribes which became at that time the special objects of our attention, and with whom we were particularly anxious to establish such relations as would prevent in the future a repetition of the murders and outrages of which they had so long been guilty, were the Kiowas, Cheyennes, and Arapahoes; the object being to complete our work by placing these three tribes upon reservations where they might be cared for and at the same time be kept under proper surveillance. The Washita campaign had duly impressed them with the power and purpose of the Government to inflict punishment upon all who chose to make war; and each tribe, dreading a repetition of the blow upon themselves, had removed their villages to remote points where they deemed themselves secure from further chastisement. Having Lone Wolf and Satanta, the two leading chiefs of the Kiowas, in our hands, we thought that through them the Kiowas could be forced to a compliance with the just and reasonable demands of the Government, and with the terms of their treaty providing for the reservation system.

All demands upon the Kiowas were communicated by me to Lone Wolf and Satanta under the instructions of General Sheridan, who, although on the ground, declined to treat directly with the faithless chiefs. The Kiowas were informed that unless the entire tribe repaired to the vicinity of the agency, then located not far from Fort Cobb, the war which had been inaugurated with such vigor and effect at the Washita would be renewed and continued until the terms of their

treaty had been complied with. This proposition was imparted to Lone Wolf and Satanta and by them transmitted to their tribe
through the son of the latter, who acted as a
sort of diplomatic courier between the Kiowa
village and our camp.

The Kiowas, while sending messages apparently in accord with the proposition, and
seeming to manifest a willingness to come in
and locate themselves upon their reservation,
continued, after the manner of Indian diplomacy, to defer from time to time the promised movement. There was every reason to
believe that finding the military disposed to
temporarily suspend active operations and
resort to negotiation, the Kiowas had located
their village within a short distance of our
camp, as Satanta's son in going and coming
with messages from one to the other easily
made the round journey in a single day; so
that had they been so disposed the Kiowas
could have transferred their village to our
immediate vicinity, as desired by the military authorities, in one day. The truth was,
however, that while manifesting an apparent
desire to conform to this requirement, as a
precedent to final peace, they had not intended at any time to keep faith with the
Government, but, by a pretended acquies-
cence in the proposed arrangement secure

the release of the two head chiefs, Lone Wolf
and Satanta, and then hasten with the entire
village to join forces with the other two
tribes, the Cheyennes and Arapahoes, who
were then represented as being located
somewhere near the source of Red River, and
on the border of the Llano Estacado, or
Staked Plain, a region of country supposed
to be impenetrable by civilized man. Every
promise of the Kiowas to come in was always
made conditional upon the prior release of
Lone Wolf and Satanta.

Their efforts to procrastinate or evade a
fulfilment of their part of the agreement finally exhausted the forbearance which thus
far had prompted none but the mildest
measures on the part of the military authorities, in the efforts of the latter to bring
about a peaceful solution of existing difficulties. It had become evident that, instead of
intending to establish relations of permanent
peace and friendship with the whites, the
majority of the tribe were only waiting the
release of Lone Wolf and Satanta to resume
hostilities, or at least to more firmly ally
themselves with the extremely hostile tribes
then occupying the head waters of Red River.
Spring was approaching, when the grass
would enable the Indians to recuperate their
ponies, which, after the famished condition

to which winter usually reduced them, would soon be fleet and strong, ready to do duty on the war path. It was therefore indispensable that there should be no further delay in the negotiations, which had been needlessly prolonged through several weeks.

General Sheridan promptly decided upon the terms of his ultimatum. Like most of the utterances of that officer, they were brief and to the point. I remember the day and the circumstances under which they were given. The General and myself were standing upon opposite sides of a rude enclosure which surrounded the space immediately about his tent, composed of a single line of rough poles erected by the unskilled labor of some of the soldiers. The day was one of those bright, warm, sunshiny days so frequent in the Indian Territory, even in winter. I had left my tent, which was but a few paces from that of General Sheridan, to step over and report, as I did almost daily, the latest message from the Kiowas as to their intention to make peace. On this occasion as on all former ones there was a palpable purpose to postpone further action until Lone Wolf and Satanta should be released by us.

After hearing the oft-repeated excuses of the Kiowas, General Sheridan communicated his resolve to me in substance as follows:

Red and White Diplomacy

"Well, Custer, these Kiowas are endeavoring to play us false. Their object is to occupy us with promises until the grass enables them to go where they please and make war if they choose. We have given them every opportunity to come in and enjoy the protection of the Government if they so desired. They are among the worst Indians we have to deal with, and have been guilty of untold murders and outrages, at the same time they were being fed and clothed by the Government. These two chiefs, Lone Wolf and Satanta, have forfeited their lives over and over again. They could now induce their people to come in and become friendly if they chose to exert their influence in that direction. This matter has gone on long enough and must be stopped, as we have to look after the other tribes before spring overtakes us. You can inform Lone Wolf and Satanta that we shall wait until sundown to-morrow for their tribe to come in; if by that time the village is not here, Lone Wolf and Satanta will be hung and the troops sent in pursuit of the village."

This might be regarded as bringing matters to a crisis. I proceeded directly to the lodge in which Lone Wolf and Satanta were prisoners, accompanied by Romeo as interpreter. I found the two chiefs reclining lazily

453

upon their comfortable if not luxurious
couches of robes. Satanta's son was also
present. After a few preliminary remarks, I
introduced the subject which was the occasion of my visit by informing the chiefs that
I had just returned from General Sheridan's
tent, where the question of the failure of the
Kiowas to comply with their oft-repeated
promises had been discussed, and that I had
been directed to acquaint them with the
determination which had been formed in regard to them and their people. At this announcement I could see that both chiefs became instantly and unmistakably interested
in what was being said.

I had so often heard of the proverbial
stoicism of the Indian character that it occurred to me that this was a favorable moment for judging how far this trait affects
their conduct. For it will be readily acknowledged that the communication which I
was about to make to them was one likely, at
all events, to overturn any self-imposed sto-
lidity which was not deeply impregnated in
their nature. After going over the subject of
the continued absence of the Kiowas from
their reservation, their oft-made promises,
made only to be violated, I told them that
they were regarded, as they had a right to be,
as the two leading and most influential chiefs

of the tribe; that although they were prisoners, yet so powerful were they among the people of their own tribe that their influence, even while prisoners, was greater than that of all the other chiefs combined; hence all negotiations with the Kiowas had been conducted through them, and although they had it in their power, by a single command, to cause a satisfactory settlement of existing difficulties to be made, yet so far they had failed utterly to exert an influence for peace between their people and the Government. The announcement then to be made to them must be regarded as final, and it remained with them alone to decide by their action what the result should be.

In as few words as possible I then communicated to them the fate which undoubtedly awaited them in the event of the non-appearance of their tribe. Until sunset of the following day seemed a very brief period, yet I failed to detect the slightest change in the countenance of either when told that that would be the extent of their lives if their tribe failed to come in. Not a muscle of their warrior-like faces moved. Their eyes neither brightened nor quailed; nothing in their actions or appearance gave token that anything unusual had been communicated to them. Satanta's son alone of the three seemed to realize that matters were becoming serious, as could readily be told by watching his anxious glances, first at his father, then at Lone Wolf; but neither spoke.

Realizing the importance of time, and anxious to bring about a peaceful as well as satisfactory termination of our difficulties with the Kiowas, and at the same time to afford every facility to the two captive chiefs to save their oft-forfeited lives—for all familiar with their bloody and cruel career would grant that they merited death—I urged upon them the necessity of prompt action in communicating with their tribe and pointed to Satanta's son, who could be employed for this purpose. Quickly springing to his feet and not waiting to hear the opinions of the two chiefs the young warrior rushed from the lodge and was soon busily engaged in tightening the girths of his Indian saddle preparatory to a rapid gallop on his fleet pony.

In the mean time Lone Wolf and Satanta began exchanging utterances, at first slow and measured, in tones scarcely audible. Gradually they seemed to realize how desperate was the situation they were in, and how much depended upon themselves. Then, laying aside the formality which had up to that moment characterized their deportment, they no longer appeared as the dignified, reserved, almost sullen chiefs, but acted and spoke as would be expected of men situated as they were. In less time than I have taken to describe the action Satanta's handsome son appeared at the entrance of the lodge, mounted and in readiness for his ride.

Although he seemed by his manner to incline toward his father as the one who should give him his instructions, yet it was soon apparent that a more correct understanding existed between the two captives. Lone Wolf was the head chief of their tribe, Satanta the second in rank. The occasion was too important to leave anything to chance. A message from Satanta might receive prompt attention; a command from the head chief could not be disregarded; hence it was that Satanta stood aside and Lone Wolf stepped forward and addressed a few hasty but apparently emphatic sentences to the young courier, who was all eagerness to depart on his mission. As Lone Wolf concluded his instructions and the young warrior was gathering up his reins and lariat and turning his pony from the lodge in the direction of the village, Satanta simply added, in an energetic tone, "Hoodle-teh, hoodle-teh" (make haste, make haste); an injunction scarcely needed, as the young Indian and his pony were the the next moment flying across the level plain.

I then reëntered the lodge with Lone Wolf and Satanta, accompanied by Romeo. Through the latter Lone Wolf informed me that he had sent orders to the Kiowa village, which was not a day's travel from us, to pack up and come in as soon as the courier should reach them. At the same time he informed them of what depended upon their coming. He had also sent for Black Eagle, the third chief in rank, to come in advance of the village, bringing with him a dozen or more of the prominent chiefs. I inquired if he felt confident that his people would arrive by the appointed time? He almost smiled at the question, and assured me that an Indian would risk everything to save a comrade, leaving me to infer that to save their two highest chiefs nothing would be permitted to stand in the way. Seeing, perhaps, a look of doubt on my face, he pointed to that locality in the heavens which the sun would occupy at two o'clock and said: "Before that time Black Eagle and the other chiefs accompanying him will be here; and by that time," indicating in a similar manner sunset, "the village will arrive."

No general commanding an army, who had transmitted his orders to his corps commanders directing a movement at daylight the following morning could have exhibited more confidence in the belief that his orders would be executed than did this captive chief in the belief that, although a prisoner in the hands of his traditional enemies, his lodge closely guarded on all sides by watchful sentinels, his commands to his people would meet with a prompt and willing compliance. After a little further conversation with the two chiefs I was preparing to leave the lodge when Lone Wolf, true to the Indian custom, under which an opportunity to beg for something to eat is never permitted to pass unimproved, called me back and said that the next day his principal chiefs would visit him, and although he was a prisoner, yet he would be glad to be able to entertain them in a manner befitting his rank and importance in the tribe, and therefore I was appealed to to furnish the provisions necessary to provide a feast for a dozen or more hungry chiefs and their retainers; in reply to which modest request I made the heart of Lone Wolf glad, and called forth in his most emphatic as well as delighted manner the universal word of approval, "How," by informing him that the feast should certainly be prepared if he only would supply the guests.

The next day was one of no little interest, and to none more than to the two chiefs, who expected to see the first step taken by their people which would terminate in their release from a captivity which had certainly become exceedingly irksome, not to mention the new danger which stared them in the face. Lone Wolf, however, maintained his confidence and repeatedly assured me during the forenoon that Black Eagle and the other chiefs whom he had sent for by name would arrive not later than two o'clock that day. His confidence proved not to be misplaced. The sun had hardly marked the hour of one in the heavens when a small cavalcade was seen approaching in the distance from the direction of the Kiowa village. The quick eye of Satanta was the first to discover it. A smile of haughty triumph lighted up the countenance of Lone Wolf when his attention was called to the approaching party, his look indicating that he felt it could not be otherwise: had he not ordered it?

On they came, first about a dozen chiefs riding at a deliberate and dignified pace, they and their ponies richly caparisoned in the most fantastic manner. The chiefs wore blankets of bright colors, scarlet predominating, with here and there a bright green. Each face was painted in brilliant colors, yellow, blue, green, red, black, and combinations of all of them, no two faces being ornamented alike, and each new face seeming more horrible than its predecessor. The ponies had not been neglected, so far as their outward make-up was concerned, eagle feathers and pieces of gaudy cloth being interwoven in their manes and tails.

Following the chiefs rode a second line, only less ornamented than the chiefs themselves. These were warriors and confidential friends and advisers of the chiefs in whose train they rode. In rear of all rode a few meek-looking squaws, whose part in this imposing pageant became evident when the chiefs and warriors dismounted, giving the reins of their ponies to the squaws, who at once busied themselves in picketing the ponies of their lords, and, in every sense of the word, masters, wherever the grazing seemed freshest and most abundant. This being done, their part was performed and they waited near the ponies the return of the chiefs and warriors.

The latter, after forming in one group, and in similar order to that in which they rode, advanced toward the lodge outside of which, but within the chain of sentinels, stood Lone Wolf and Satanta. The meeting between the captive chiefs and their more fortunate com-

461

rades occasioned an exhibition of more feeling and sensibility than is generally accredited to the Indian. A bevy of school girls could not have embraced each other, after a twenty-four hours' separation, with greater enthusiasm and demonstrations of apparent joy than did these chieftains, whose sole delight is supposed to be connected with scenes of bloodshed and cruelty. I trust no gentle-minded reader imbued with great kindness of heart will let this little scene determine his estimate of the Indian character; for be it understood, not one of the chiefs who formed the group of which I am writing but had participated in acts of the most barbarous and wanton cruelty. It was a portion of these chiefs who had led and encouraged the band that had subjected the Box family to such a horrible fate, of which Major-General Hancock made full report at the time.

Immediately after greetings had been exchanged between the captives and their friends I was requested, by a message from Lone Wolf, to repair to his lodge in order to hear what his friends had to say. As I entered the lodge the entire party of chiefs advanced to meet me, and began a series of handshaking and universal "Hows," which in outward earnestness made up for any lack of real sincerity, and to an inexperienced observer or a tender-hearted peace commissioner might well have appeared as an exhibition of indubitable friendship if not affection. After all were seated and the ever-present long red clay pipe had passed and repassed around the circle, each chief indulging in a few silent whiffs, Black Eagle arose, and after shaking hands with me proceeded, after the manner of an oration, to inform me, what I had had reason to expect and what the reader no doubt has also anticipated, that the entire Kiowa village was at that moment on the march and would arrive in the vicinity of our camp before dark. No reference was made to the fact that this general movement on their part was one of compulsion, but on the contrary to have heard Black Eagle, who was an impressive orator, one might well have believed that, no longer able to endure the separation from their brothers, the white men, who, as Black Eagle said, like themselves were all descended from one father, the Kiowas had voluntarily resolved to pack up their lodges, and when they next should put them down it would be alongside the tents of their white friends.

In nothing that was said did it appear that the impending execution of Lone Wolf and Satanta had aught to do with hastening the arrival of their people. At the termination of the conference, however, Black Eagle intimated that as the tribe was about to locate near us, it would be highly agreeable to them if their two head chiefs could be granted their liberty and permitted to resume their places among their own people.

That evening the Kiowa village, true to the prediction of Lone Wolf, arrived, and was located a short distance from our camp. The next morning the family or families of Satanta appeared in front of headquarters and made known their desire to see Satanta, to which, of course, no objection was made, and the guards were instructed to permit them to pass the lines. Satanta's home circle was organized somewhat on the quadrilateral plan; that is, he had four wives. They came together, and so far as outward appearances enabled one to judge they constituted a happy family. They were all young and buxom, and each was sufficiently like the others in appearance to have enabled the lot to pass as sisters; and, by the way, it is quite customary among the Indians for one man to marry an entire family of daughters as rapidly as they reach the proper age. To those who dread a multiplicity of mothers-in-law this custom possesses advantages.

To add in a material as well as maternal way to the striking similarity in appearance presented by Satanta's dusky spouses, each bore on her back, encased in the capacious folds of a scarlet blanket, a pledge of affection in the shape of a papoose, the difference in the extreme ages of the four miniature warriors, or warriors' sisters, being too slight to be perceptible. In single file the four partners of Satanta's joys approached his lodge, and in the same order gained admittance. Satanta was seated on a buffalo robe when they entered. He did not rise—perhaps that would have been deemed unwarriorlike—but each of his wives advanced to him, when, instead of going through the ordinary form of embracing with its usual accompaniments, on such occasions considered proper, the papoose was unslung—I know of no better term to describe the dexterous manner in which the mother transferred her offspring from its cozy resting-place on her back to her arms—and handed to the outstretched arms of the father, who kissed it repeatedly, with every exhibition of paternal affection, scarcely deigning to bestow a single glance on the mother, who stood by meekly, contenting herself with stroking Satanta's face and shoulders gently, at the same time muttering almost inaudible expressions of Indian endearment.

This touching little scene lasted for a few moments, when Satanta, after bestowing a kiss upon the soft, cherry lips of his child, transferred it back to its mother, who passed on and quietly took a seat by Satanta's side. The second wife then approached, when precisely the same exhibition was gone through with, not being varied from the first in the slightest particular. This being ended, the third took the place of the second, the latter passing along with her babe and seating herself next to the first, and so on, until the fourth wife had presented her babe, received it back, and quietly seated herself by the side of the third; not a word being spoken to or by Satanta from the beginning to the end of this strange meeting.

The Kiowas were now all located on their reservation, except a single band of the tribe led by a very wicked and troublesome chief named Woman Heart, although his conduct and character were anything but in keeping with the gentleness of his name. He had taken his band and moved in the direction of the Staked Plains, far to the west of the Kiowa reservation.

However, the Indian question, so far as the Kiowas were concerned, was regarded as settled, at least for the time being, and it became our next study how to effect a similar settlement with the Cheyennes and Arapahoes, who had fled after the battle of the

Washita and were then supposed to be somewhere between the Wichita Mountains and
the western border of Texas, north of the
head-waters of Red River. It was finally
decided to send one of the friendly chiefs of
the Apaches, whose village was then near the
present site of Fort Sill,[43] and one of the three
captive squaws whom we had brought with
us.

All the chiefs of that region who were interested in promoting peace between the

[43] Fort Sill, 36 miles south of Fort Cobb, at the eastern base of the Wichita Mountains, in central Comanche County, Oklahoma, was established on January 7, 1869 in pursuance of an order of General Sheridan, who named it in honor of a former classmate who
had been killed in the battle of Stone River. It was an
important center of operations during the remaining
Indian warfare in the Southwest. Subsequently it became an artillery school, and during World War I the
site of Camp Doniphan. Here in the winter of 1874-
75, in response to the insistence of General Sheridan, a
military commission tried and condemned 75 Indians
for their participation in the recent warfare in Texas
and elsewhere, and all were sent to St. Augustine,
Florida for imprisonment. This action seems to have
marked the origin of the policy subsequently applied
to the Apaches in the 1880's, for which see Britton
Davis, *The Truth About Geronimo*, the Lakeside Classics
volume for 1951. Fort Sill, also, was the scene of the
imprisonment of the Apaches from 1897 to 1912, when
the survivors were given the choice of remaining per-
manently in Oklahoma or being transferred to the
Mescalero Apache Reservation in New Mexico.

whites and Indians were assembled at my
headquarters, when I informed them of the
proposed peace embassy and asked that some
chief of prominence should volunteer as bearer of a friendly message to the Cheyennes
and Arapahoes. A well-known chief of the
Apaches named Iron Shirt promptly offered
himself as a messenger in the cause of peace.
In reply to my inquiry he said he could be
ready to depart upon his commendable errand on the following day, and estimated the
distance such that it would be necessary to
take provision sufficient to last him and his
companion three weeks.

Having arranged all the details of the journey the assemblage of chiefs dispersed, the
next step being to decide which of the three
squaws should accompany Iron Shirt to her
tribe. I concluded to state the case to them
and make the selection a matter for them to
decide. Summoning Mah-wis-sa, Mo-nah-
see-tah, and the Sioux squaw, their companion, to my tent, I, through Romeo, acquainted
them with the desire of the Government to
establish peace with their people and with
the Arapahoes, and in order to accomplish
this we intended despatching a friendly message to the absent tribes, which must be
carried by some of their own people. After
conferring with each other a few minutes

Red and White Diplomacy

they concluded that Mah-wis-sa, the sister of Black Kettle, should return to her people. Every arrangement was provided looking to the comfort of the two Indians who were to undertake this long journey. A bountiful supply of provisions was carefully provided in convenient packages, an extra amount of clothing and blankets being given to Mah-wis-sa in order that she should not return to her people empty-handed. To transport their provisions and blankets a mule was given them to be used as a pack-animal.

It was quite an event, sufficient to disturb the monotony of camp, when the hour arrived for the departure of the two peace commissioners. I had told Iron Shirt what he was to say to the chiefs of the tribes who still remained hostile, which was in effect that we were anxious for peace, and to that end invited them to come at once and place themselves and their people on the reservations, where we would meet and regard them as friends and all present hostilities, as well as reckoning for past differences, should cease; but if this friendly proffer was not accepted favorably and at once we would be forced to regard it as indicating their desire to prolong the war, in which event the troops would be sent against them as soon as practicable. I relied not a little on the good influence of

469

Mah-wis-sa, who, as I have before stated, was a woman of superior intelligence, and was strongly impressed with a desire to aid in establishing a peace between her people and the white men. Quite a group, composed of officers, soldiers, teamsters, guards, and scouts, assembled to witness the departure of Iron Shirt and Mah-wis-sa, and to wish them God-speed in their mission.

After Iron Shirt and Mah-wis-sa had seated themselves upon their ponies and were about to set out, Mah-wis-sa, suddenly placing her hand on the neat belt which secured her blanket about her indicated that she was un-provided with that most essential companion of frontier life, a *mutch-ka* as she expressed it, meaning a hunting-knife. Only those who have lived on the Plains can appreciate the unpurchasable convenience of a hunting-knife. Whether it is to carve a buffalo or a mountain trout, mend horse equipments, or close up a rent in the tent, there is a constant demand for the services of a good hunting-knife. Mah-wis-sa smiled at the forgetful-ness which had made her fail to discern this omission sooner, but I relieved her anxiety by taking from my belt the hunting-knife which hung at my side and giving it to her, adding as I did so that I expected her to return it to me before the change in the moon, that being fixed as the extreme limit of their absence. When all was ready for the start Iron Shirt rode first, followed by the pack-mule, which he led, while Mah-wis-sa, acting as a driver to the latter and well mounted, brought up the rear.

As they rode away amid the shower of good wishes which was bestowed upon them and their mission, many were the queries as to the probable extent of their journey, their return, and whether they would be successful. For upon the success or failure of these two Indians depended in a great measure the question whether or not we were to be forced to continue the war; and among the hundreds who watched the departing bearers of the olive branch there was not one but hoped earnestly that the mission would prove successful, and we be spared the barbarities which a further prosecution of the war would necessarily entail. Yet there are those who would have the public believe that the army is at all times clamorous for an Indian war. I have yet to meet the officer or man belonging to the army, who, when the question of war or peace with the Indians was being agitated, did not cast the weight of his influence, the prayers of his heart, in behalf of peace. When I next called Mah-wis-sa's attention to the *mutch-ka* (knife) it was far from the locality we then occupied, and under very different circumstances.

After the departure of Iron Shirt and Mah-wis-sa we were forced to settle down to the dullest routine of camp life, as nothing could be done until their return. It was full three weeks before the interest in camp received a fresh impetus by the tidings which flew from tent to tent that Iron Shirt had returned. He did return, but Mah-wis-sa did not return with him. His story was brief. He and Mah-wis-sa, after leaving us and travelling for several days westward, had arrived at the Cheyenne and Arapahoe villages. They delivered their messages to the chiefs of the two tribes, who were assembled in council to hear them, and after due deliberation thereon Iron Shirt was informed that the distance was too great, the ponies in too poor condition, to permit the villages to return. In other words, these two tribes had virtually decided that rather than return to their reservation they preferred the chances of war. When asked to account for Mah-wis-sa's failure to accompany him back, Iron Shirt stated that she had desired to fulfill her promise and return with him, but the chiefs of her tribe would not permit her to do so.

The only encouragement derived from Iron Shirt was in his statement that Little

Robe, a prominent chief of the Cheyennes, and Yellow Bear, the second chief of the Arapahoes, were both extremely anxious to effect a permanent peace between their people and the Government, and both had promised Iron Shirt that they would leave their villages soon after his departure and visit us with a view to prevent a continuation of the war. Iron Shirt was rewarded for his journey by bountiful presents of provisions for himself and his people. True to their promises made to Iron Shirt, it was but a short time before Little Robe and Yellow Bear arrived at our camp and were well received.

They reported that their villages had had under consideration the question of accepting our invitation to come in and live at peace in the future, and that many of their people were strongly in favor of adopting this course, but for the present it was uncertain whether or not the two tribes would come in. The two tribes would probably act in concert and if they intended coming would make their determination known by despatching couriers to us in a few days. In spite of the sincerity of the motives of Little Robe and Yellow Bear, whom I have always regarded as two of the most upright and peaceably inclined Indians I have ever known,

473

and who have since that time paid a visit to the President at Washington, it was evident that the Cheyennes and Arapahoes, while endeavoring to occupy us with promises and pretenses, were only interested in delaying our movements until the return of spring, when the young grass would enable them to recruit the strength of their winter-famished ponies and move when and where they pleased.

After waiting many long weary days for the arrival of the promised couriers from the two tribes, until even Little Robe and Yellow Bear were forced to acknowledge that there was no longer any reason to expect their coming, it occurred to me that there was but one expedient yet untried which furnished even a doubtful chance of averting war. This could only be resorted to with the approval of General Sheridan, whose tent had been pitched in our midst during the entire winter, and who evidently proposed to remain on the ground until the Indian question in that locality should be disposed of. My plan was as follows:

We had some fifteen hundred troops, a force ample to cope with all the Indians which could then, or since, be combined at any one point on the Plains. But in the state of feeling existing among those Indians at

YELLOW BEAR, SECOND CHIEF
OF THE ARAPAHOES.

that time, consequent upon the punishment which they had received at and since the Washita campaign, it would have been an extremely difficult if not impracticable matter to attempt to move so large a body of troops near their villages and retain the latter in their places, so fearful were they of receiving punishment for their past offenses. It would also have been impracticable to move upon them stealthily, as they were then, for causes already given, more than ever on the alert, and were no doubt kept thoroughly informed in regard to our every movement.

It was thus considered out of the question to employ my entire command of fifteen hundred men in what I proposed should be purely a peaceful effort to bring about a termination of the war, as so large a force would surely intimidate the Indians, and cause them to avoid our presence. I believed that if I could see the leading chiefs of the two hostile tribes and convince them of the friendly desire of the Government, they might be induced to relinquish the war and return to their reservation. I have endeavored to show that I could not go among them with my entire command, neither was I sufficiently orthodox as a peace commissioner to believe what so many of that order preach, but fail to practise, that I could take an olive branch in

476

one hand, the plan of a school-house in the
other, and, unaccompanied by force, visit the
Indian villages in safety. My life would certainly have been the price of such temerity.
Too imposing a force would repel the Indians; too small a force would tempt them to
murder us, even though our mission was a
friendly one.

After weighing the matter carefully in my
own mind I decided that with General Sheridan's approval I would select from my command forty men, two officers, and a medical
officer, and, accompanied by the two chiefs,
Little Robe and Yellow Bear, who regarded
my proposition with favor, I would set out
in search of the hostile camp, there being but
little doubt that with the assistance of the
chiefs I would have little difficulty in discovering the whereabouts of the villages;
while the smallness of my party would prevent unnecessary alarm or suspicion as to our
intentions. From my tent to General Sheridan's was but a few steps, and I soon submitted my proposition to the General, who
from the first was inclined to lend his approval to my project. After discussing it
fully, he gave his assent by saying that the
character of the proposed expedition was
such that he would not order me to proceed
upon it, but if I volunteered to go he would

give me the full sanction of his authority and every possible assistance to render the mission a successful one; in conclusion urging me to exercise the greatest caution against the stratagems or treachery of the Indians, who no doubt would be but too glad to massacre my party in revenge for their recent well-merited chastisement. Returning to my tent, I at once set about making preparations for my journey, the extent or result of which now became interesting subjects for deliberation. The first thing necessary was to make up the party which was to accompany me.

As the number of men was to be limited to forty, too much care could not be exercised in their selection. I chose the great majority of them from the sharpshooters, men who, in addition to being cool and brave, were experienced and skilful marksmen. My standard-bearer, a well-tried sergeant, was selected as the senior non-commissioned officer of the party. The officers who were to accompany me were my brother, Colonel Custer, Captain Robbins, and Dr. Renick, Acting Assistant Surgeon U. S. Army. As guide I had Neva, a Blackfoot Indian, who had accompanied General Fremont in his explorations, and who could speak a little English. Little Robe and Yellow Bear were also to be relied upon as guides, while Romeo accompanied us as interpreter. Young Brewster, determined to miss no opportunity of discovering his lost sister, had requested and been granted permission to become one of the party.

This completed the *personnel* of the expedition. All were well armed and well mounted. We were to take no wagons or tents; our extra supplies were to be transported on pack-mules. We were to start on the evening of the second day, the intervening time being necessary to complete our preparations. It was decided that our first march should be a short one, sufficient merely to enable us to reach a village of friendly Apaches located a few miles from our camp, where we would spend the first night and be joined by Little Robe and Yellow Bear, who at that time were guests of the Apaches. I need not say that in the opinion of many of our comrades our mission was regarded as closely bordering on the imprudent, to qualify it by no stronger term.

So confident did one of the most prudent officers of my command feel in regard to our annihilation by the Indians that in bidding me good-by he contrived to slip into my hand a small pocket Derringer pistol, loaded, with the simple remark, "You had better take it, General; it may prove useful to you." As I was amply provided with arms, both revolvers and rifle, and as a pocket Derringer may not impress the reader as being a very formidable weapon to use in Indian warfare, the purpose of my friend in giving me the small pocket weapon may not seem clear. It was given me under the firm conviction that the Indians would overwhelm and massacre my entire party; and to prevent my being captured, disarmed, and reserved for torture, that little pistol was given me in order that at the last moment I might become my own executioner, an office I was not seeking, nor did I share in my friend's opinion.

Everything being ready for our departure, we swung into our saddles, waved our adieus to the comrades who were to remain in camp, and the next moment we turned our horses' heads westward and were moving in the direction of the Apache village.

Chapter 15

A PEACE MISSION AND ITS RESULTS

THE Apache village had been represented as located only five or six miles from our camp, but we found the distance nearly twice as great; and although we rode rapidly, our horses being fresh, yet it was quite dark before we reached the first lodge, the location of the rest of the village being tolerably well defined by the apparently countless dogs whose barking at our approach called forth most of the inhabitants of the village.

As our coming had been previously announced by Little Robe and Yellow Bear, our arrival occasioned no surprise. Inquiring of the first we saw where the stream of water was, as an Indian village is invariably placed in close proximity to water, we were soon on our camp ground, which was almost within the limits of the village. Our horses were soon unsaddled and picketed out to graze, fires were started by the men preparatory to the enjoyment of a cup of coffee, and every preliminary made for a good night's rest and early start in the morning. But here the officers of the party encountered their first drawback. From some unexplained cause the pack-mule which carried our blankets had with his attendant failed thus far to put in an appearance.

His head leader had probably fallen behind and in the darkness lost the party. The bugler was sent to a neighboring eminence to sound signals with his bugle in the hope that the absent man with his mule might make his way to us, but all to no purpose. We were soon forced to relinquish all hope of seeing either man, mule, or blankets until daylight, and consequently the prospect of enjoying a comfortable rest was exceedingly limited. Saddle blankets were in great demand, but I was even more fortunate. A large number of the Apaches had come from their lodges out of mere curiosity to see us, hoping no doubt, too, that they might secure something to eat. Among them was one with whom I was acquainted, and to whom I made known the temporary loss of my blankets. By promising him a pint of sugar and an equal amount of coffee on my return to my camp he agreed to loan me a buffalo robe until morning. With this wrapped around me and the aid of a bright blazing camp fire I passed a most comfortable night among my less fortunate companions as we all lay stretched out on the ground, using our saddles for pillows.

A Peace Mission

Early next morning (our pack animals having come up in the night) we were in our saddles, and on our way, ready and eager for whatever might be in store for us. The route taken by the guides led us along the northern border of the Wichita Mountains, our general direction being nearly due west. As soon as it had become known in the main camp that the expedition of which I now write was contemplated, young Brewster, who had never relinquished his efforts or inquiries to determine the fate of his lost sister, came to me with an earnest request to be taken as one of the party, a request which I was only too glad to comply with. No person who has not lived on the frontier and in an Indian country can correctly realize or thoroughly appreciate the extent to which a frontiersman becomes familiar with, and apparently indifferent to, the accustomed dangers which surround him on every side. It is but another verification of the truth of the old saying, familiarity breeds contempt.

After getting well on our way I began, through Romeo, conversing with the two chiefs, Little Robe and Yellow Bear, who rode at my side, upon the topic which was uppermost in the minds of the entire party: when and where should we probably find their people? Before our departure they had given me to understand that the villages might be found on some one of the small streams flowing in a southerly direction past the western span of the Wichita mountains, a distance from our main camp not exceeding sixty or seventy miles; but I could easily perceive that neither of the chiefs spoke with a great degree of confidence. They explained this by stating that the villages would not remain long in one place and it was difficult to say positively in what locality or upon what stream we should find them; but that when we reached the last peak of the Wichita Mountains, which commanded an unlimited view of the plains beyond, they would send up signal smoke and perhaps be able to obtain a reply from the village.

In the evening we reached a beautiful stream of water with abundance of wood in the vicinity; here we halted for the night. Our horses were fastened to the trees, while the officers and men spread their blankets on the ground and in groups of twos and threes prepared for the enjoyment of a good night's rest. One sentry remained awake during the night, and in order that the loss of sleep should be as little as might be consistent with our safety the relief, instead of being composed of three men, each of whom would have to remain on duty two hours for every four hours of rest, was increased in number so that each member thereof was required to remain on post but a single hour during the night. While I felt confidence in the good intentions of the two chiefs I did not neglect to advise the guards to keep a watchful eye upon them, as we could not afford to run any avoidable risks.

Long after we had sought the solace of our blankets and I had dropped into a comfortable doze I was awakened by an Indian song. There was, of course, no occasion for alarm from this incident, yet it was sufficient to induce me to get up and make my way to the small fire, around which I knew the three Indians and Romeo to be lying, and from the vicinity of which the singing evidently came. As I approached the fire I found Neva, the Blackfoot, replenishing the small flame with a few dried twigs, while Romeo and Yellow Bear were sitting near by enjoying some well-broiled beef ribs. Little Robe was reclining in a half-sitting position against a tree and, apparently oblivious of the presence of his companions, was singing or chanting an Indian melody, the general tenor of which seemed to indicate a lightness of spirits. Young Brewster—unable, perhaps, to sleep, owing to thoughts of his lost sister— had joined the group, and appeared an interested observer of what was going on. I inquired of Romeo why Little Robe had selected such an unreasonable hour to indulge in his wild melodies. Romeo repeated the inquiry to Little Robe, who replied that he had been away from his lodge for a long time and the thought of soon returning and of being with his people once more had filled his heart with a gladness which could only find utterance in song.

Taking a seat on the ground by the side of young Brewster, I joined the group. As neither Little Robe nor Yellow Bear could understand a word of English and Neva was busily engaged with his culinary operations, young Brewster, with unconcealed delight, informed me that from conversations with Little Robe, who appeared in a more communicative mood than usual, he felt cheered by the belief that at last he was in a fair way to discover the whereabouts of his captive sister. He then briefly detailed how Little Robe, little dreaming that his listener was so deeply interested in his words, had admitted that the Cheyennes had two white girls as prisoners, the date of the capture of one of them, and the personal description given by Little Robe closely answering to that of Brewster's sister. In the hope of gleaning other valuable information from time to time, I advised the young man not to acquaint the Indians with the fact that he had lost a sister by capture; else, becoming suspicious, the supply of information might be cut off.

The tidings in regard to the captured girls were most encouraging and spurred us to leave no effort untried to release them from the horrors of their situation. Before daylight the following morning we had breakfasted, and as soon as it was sufficiently light to enable us to renew our march we set out, still keeping almost due west. In the afternoon of that day we reached the last prominent peak of the Wichita Mountains, from which point Little Robe and Yellow Bear had said they would send up a signal smoke. I had often during an Indian campaign seen these signal smokes on my front, on my right and left—everywhere, in fact—but could never catch a glimpse of the Indians who were engaged in making them, nor did I comprehend at the time the precise import of the signals. I was glad, therefore, to have an opportunity to stand behind the scenes, as it were, and not only witness the *modus operandi*, but understand the purpose of the actors.

Arriving at the base of the mountain or peak, the height of which did not exceed one thousand feet, we dismounted, and leaving our horses on the plain below, owing to the rough and rocky character of the ascent, a small portion of our party, including, of course, the two chiefs, climbed to the summit. After sweeping the broad horizon which spread out before us and failing to discover any evidence of the presence of an Indian village anywhere within the scope of our vision, the two chiefs set about to make preparations necessary to enable them to "call to the village," as they expressed it.

I have alluded in a former chapter to the perfect system of signals in use among the Indians of the Plains. That which I am about to describe briefly was but one of many employed by them. First gathering an armful of dried grass and weeds, this was carried and placed upon the highest point of the peak, where, everything being in readiness, the match was applied close to the ground; but the blaze was no sooner well lighted and about to envelop the entire amount of grass collected than Little Robe began smothering it with the unlighted portion. This accomplished, a slender column of gray smoke began to ascend in a perpendicular column. This, however, was not enough, as such a signal, or the appearance of such, might be created by white men or

488

might rise from a simple camp fire. Little Robe now took his scarlet blanket from his shoulders and with a graceful wave threw it so as to cover the smouldering grass, when, assisted by Yellow Bear, he held the corners and sides so closely to the ground as to almost completely confine and cut off the column of smoke. Waiting but for a few moments, and until he saw the smoke beginning to escape from beneath, he suddenly threw the blanket aside and a beautiful balloon shaped column puffed upward, like the white cloud of smoke which attends the discharge of a field piece.

Again casting the blanket on the pile of grass the column was interrupted as before, and again in due time released, so that a succession of elongated, egg-shaped puffs of smoke kept ascending toward the sky in the most regular manner. This beadlike column of smoke, considering the height from which it began to ascend, was visible from points on the level plain fifty miles distant.

The sight of these two Indian chiefs so intently engaged in this simple but effective mode of telegraphing was to me full of interest, and this incident was vividly recalled when I came across Stanley's painting of "The Signal," in which two chiefs or warriors are standing upon a large rock with lighted torch in hand, while far in the distance is to be seen the answering column as it ascends above the tops of the trees from the valley where no doubt the village is pleasantly located.[44] In our case, however, the picture was not so complete in its results. For strain our eager eyes as we might in every direction no responsive signal could be discovered, and finally the chiefs were reluctantly forced to acknowledge that the villages were not where they expected to find them and that to reach them would probably involve a longer journey than we had anticipated. Descending from the mountain, we continued our journey, still directing our course nearly due west as the two chiefs felt confident the villages were in that direction. That day and the next passed without further incident.

After arriving at camp on the second evening a conversation with the two Indian chiefs

[44] "The Signal" was one of the paintings of John Nix Stanley (1814–72) who from about the year 1838 devoted almost a lifetime of travel and labor to painting scenes and portraits associated with the American Indians. His great collection of 150 portraits of 43 Indian tribes obtained at the cost of two years' travel throughout the western country was deposited with the Smithsonian Institution in 1852 where in 1865 all but 5 of the paintings were burned "an irreparable loss to students of history and ethnology."

made it seem probable that our journey would have to be prolonged several days beyond the time which was deemed necessary when we left the main camp. And as our supply of provisions was limited to our supposed wants during the shorter journey, it was necessary to adopt measures for obtaining fresh supplies. This was the more imperative as the country through which we were then. passing was almost devoid of game. Our party was so small in number that our safety would be greatly imperilled by any serious reduction, yet it was a measure of necessity that a message should be sent back to General Sheridan, informing him of our changed plans and providing for a renewal of our stores.

I acquainted the men of my command with my desire and it was not long before a soldierly young trooper announced that he would volunteer to carry a despatch safely through. The gallant offer was accepted and I was soon seated on the ground, pencil in hand, writing to General Sheridan a hurried account of our progress thus far and our plans for the future, with a request to forward to us a supply of provisions; adding that the party escorting them could follow on our trail, and I would arrange to find them when required. I also requested that

Colonel Cooke, who commanded the sharp-shooters, should be detailed to command the escort, and that California Joe might also be sent with the party.

It was decided that the despatch bearer should remain in camp with us until dark and then set out on his return to the main camp. Being well mounted, well armed, and a cool, daring young fellow, I felt but little anxiety as to his success. Leaving him to make his solitary journey guided by the light of the stars, and concealing himself during the day, we will continue our search after what then seemed to us the two lost tribes.

Daylight as usual found us in our saddles, the country continuing interesting but less rolling and (we judge by appearances) less productive. We saw but little game along our line of march and the importance of time rendered delays of all kinds undesirable. The countenances of Little Robe and Yellow Bear wore an anxious look, and I could see that they began to doubt their ability to determine positively the locality of the villages. Neva, the Blackfoot, was full of stories connected with his experiences under General Fremont, and appeared more hopeful than the two chiefs. He claimed to be a son-in-law of Kit Carson, his wife, a half-breed, being deceased. Carson, it appeared, had always regarded Neva with favor, and often made him and his family handsome presents. I afterwards saw a son of Neva, an extremely handsome boy of fourteen, whose comely face and features clearly betrayed the mixture of blood indicated by Neva.

Yellow Bear finally encouraged us by stating that by noon the following day we would arrive at a stream, on whose banks he expected to find the Arapaho village and perhaps that of the Cheyennes. This gave us renewed hope, and furnished us a topic of conversation after we had reached our camp that night. Nothing occurred worthy of note until about noon next day when Yellow Bear informed me that we were within a few miles of the stream to which he had referred the day before, and added that if the village was there his people would have a lookout posted on a little knoll which we would find about a mile from the village in our direction; and as the appearance of our entire force might give alarm, Yellow Bear suggested that he, with Little Robe, Romeo, Neva, myself, and two or three others, should ride some distance in advance.

Remembering the proneness of the Indians to stratagem, I was yet impressed not only

493

with the apparent sincerity of Yellow Bear thus far, but by the soundness of the reasons he gave for our moving in advance. I assented to his proposition, but my confidence was not sufficiently great to prevent me from quietly slipping a fresh cartridge in my rifle as it lay in front of me across my saddle-bow, nor from unbuttoning the strap which held my revolver in place by my side. Fortunately, however, nothing occurred to make it necessary to displace either rifle or revolver. After riding in advance for a couple of miles Yellow Bear pointed out in the distance the little mound at which he predicted we would see something posted in the way of information concerning his tribe. If the latter was not in the vicinity a letter would no doubt be found at the mound, which now became an object of interest to all of us, each striving to be the first to discover the confirmation of Yellow Bear's prediction.

In this way we continued to approach the mound until not more than a mile of level plain separated us from it and still nothing could be seen to encourage us, when, owing to my reason being quickened by the excitement of the occasion, thus giving me an advantage over the chiefs, or from other causes, I caught sight of what would ordinarily have been taken for two half-round stones or

small boulders, just visible above the upper
circle of the mound, as projected against the
sky beyond. A second glance convinced me
that instead of the stones which they so
closely resembled they were neither more
nor less than the upper parts of the heads
of two Indians, who were no doubt studying our movements with a view of determining whether we were a friendly or war
party.

Reassuring myself by the aid of my field
glass, I announced my discovery to the chiefs
and the rest of the party. Yellow Bear immediately cantered his pony a few yards to
the front, when, freeing his scarlet blanket
from his shoulders, he waved it twice or
thrice in a mysterious manner and waited
anxiously the response. In a moment the
two Indians, the tops of whose heads had
alone been visible, rode boldly to the crest of
the mound and answered the signal of Yellow Bear, who uttered a quick, oft-repeated
whoop, and at my suggestion galloped in advance to inform his people who we were and
our object in visiting them. By the time we
reached the mound all necessary explana-
tions had been made, and the two Indians
advanced at Yellow Bear's bidding and
shook hands with me, afterward going
through the same ceremony with the other

officers. Yellow Bear then despatched one of the Indians to the village, less than two miles distant, to give news of our approach.

It seemed that they had scarcely had time to reach the village before young and old began flocking out to meet us, some on ponies, others on mules, and occasionally two full-grown Indians would be seen mounted on one diminutive pony. If any of our party had feared that our errand was attended with risk, their minds probably underwent a change when they looked around and upon all sides saw armed warriors whose numbers exceeded ours more than ten to one, and whose entire bearing and demeanor toward us gave promise of any but hostile feelings.

Not deeming it best to allow them to encircle us too closely, I requested Yellow Bear, in whose peaceable desires I had confidence, to direct his people to remain at some distance from us, so as not to impede our progress; at the same time to inform them that it was our purpose to pitch our camp immediately alongside of theirs, when full opportunity would be given for interchange of visits. This proposition seemed to meet with favor and our route was left unobstructed. A short ride brought us to the village, the lodges composing which were dotted in a

A Peace Mission

picturesque manner along the left branch of
Mulberry Creek, one of the tributaries of
Red River.

I decided to cross the creek and bivouac
on the right bank, opposite the lower end of
the village and within easy pistol range of the
nearest lodge. This location may strike the
reader with some surprise, and may suggest
the inquiry why we did not locate ourselves
at some point farther removed from the
village. It must be remembered that in
undertaking to penetrate the Indian country
with so small a force I acted throughout
upon the belief that if proper precautions
were adopted the Indians would not molest
us. Indians contemplating a battle, either
offensive or defensive, are always anxious to
have their women and children removed
from all danger thereof. By our watchfulness we intended to let the Indians see that
there would be no opportunity for them to
take us by surprise, but that if fighting was
intended it should not be all on one side. For
this reason I decided to locate our camp as
close as convenient to the village, knowing
that the close proximity of their women and
children and their necessary exposure in
case of conflict would operate as a powerful
argument in favor of peace when the question of peace or war came to be discussed.

But right here I will do the Arapahoes justice by asserting that after the first council, which took place in my camp the same evening, and after they had had an opportunity to learn the exact character and object of our mission as told to them by me and confirmed by the earnest addresses of Yellow Bear and Little Robe they evinced toward us nothing but friendly feeling, and exhibited a ready willingness to conform to the only demand we made of them, which was that they should proceed at once with their entire village to our main camp within their reservation, and then report to General Sheridan.

Little Raven,[45] the head chief, spoke for his people and expressed their gratification at the reports brought to them by Yellow Bear and Little Robe. They accepted with gladness the offer of peace, and promised to set

[45] Little Raven had joined in the warfare upon the Kansas settlers in the sixties, but after signing the treaty of Medicine Lodge in 1867, accepting placement on a reservation he remained constantly friendly to the whites, exerting his influence over the Arapahoes in favor of peace. Largely due to him, they refused to join in the uprising of 1874 when their allies, the Cheyennes and Kiowas, resumed the warpath. Little Raven died at Cantonment, Oklahoma, in 1889, after twenty years of leadership of the progressive element of his tribe.

498

LITTLE RAVEN, HEAD CHIEF
OF THE ARAPAHOES.

out in three days to proceed to our main camp near the site of Fort Sill. As it was quite late before the council concluded the discussion of questions pertaining to the Arapahoes, no reference was made to the Cheyennes; besides, I knew that Little Robe would be able to gather all possible information concerning them.

Little Raven invited me to visit him the following day in his village, an invitation I promised to accept. Before the chiefs separated I requested Little Raven to give notice through them to all his people that after it became dark it would no longer be safe for any of them to approach our camp, as, according to our invariable custom, guards would be posted about camp during the entire night; and as we could not distinguish friends from foes in the darkness, the sentries would be ordered to fire on every object seen approaching our camp. To this Little Raven and his chiefs promised assent. I then further informed him that during our stay near them we should always be glad, during the hours of daylight, to receive visits from him or from any of his people, but to prevent confusion or misunderstanding, not more than twenty Indians would be permitted to visit our camp at one time. This also was agreed to and the chiefs, after shaking hands and uttering the customary "How," departed to their village. Yellow Bear remained only long enough to say that, his family being in the village, he preferred, of course, to be with them, but assured us that his people were sincere in their protestations of peace and that we might sleep as soundly as if we were back among our comrades in the main camp, with no fears of unfriendly interruption.

After tethering our horses and pack mules securely in our midst and posting the guards for the night each one of our little party, first satisfying himself that his firearms were in good order and loaded, spread his blanket on the ground and with his saddle for a pillow, the sky unobscured by tent or roof above him, was soon reposing comfortably on the broad bosom of mother earth, where, banishing from the mind as quickly as possible all visions of Indians, peace commissioners, etc., sleep soon came to the relief of each, and we all, except the guards, rested as peacefully and comfortably as if at home under our mother's roof; and yet we all, in seeking our lowly couches that night, felt that the chances were about even whether or not we should be awakened by the war whoop of our dusky neighbors. Nothing occurred, however, to disturb our dreams or break our slumber, save, perhaps, in my own case.

My Life on the Plains

From a greater sense of responsibility, perhaps, than rested on my comrades, but not greater danger, I awoke at different hours during the night and to assure myself that all was well rose up to a sitting posture on the ground and, aided by the clear sky and bright starlight, looked about me, only to see, however, the dim outlines of my sleeping comrades as they lay in all manner of attitudes around me, wrapped in their blankets of gray, while our faithful horses, picketed in the midst of their sleeping riders, were variously disposed, some lying down, resting from the fatigues of the march, others nibbling the few tufts of grass which the shortness of their tether enabled them to reach. That which gave me strongest assurance of safety, however, as I glanced across the little stream and beheld the conical forms of the white lodges of the Indians was the silent picture of the sentry as he paced his lonely post within a few feet of where I lay. And when to my inquiry, in subdued tones, if all had been quiet during the night, came the prompt, soldierly response, "All quiet, sir," I felt renewed confidence, and again sought the solace of my equestrian pillow.

Breakfasting before the stars bade us good night, or rather good morning, daylight

found us ready for the duties of the day. As
soon as the Indians were prepared for my
visit Yellow Bear came to inform me of the
fact, and to escort me to Little Raven's
lodge. Romeo and Neva accompanied me,
the former as interpreter. I directed Captain Robbins, the officer next in rank, to
cause all men to remain closely in camp during my absence and to be careful not to permit more than the authorized number of
Indians to enter; also to watch well the Indian village, not that I believed there would
be an attempt at stratagem, but deemed it
well to be on guard. To convince the Indians
of my own sincerity I left my rifle and revolver with my men, a measure of not such
great significance as it might at first seem, as
the question of arms or no arms would have
exercised but little influence in determining
my fate had the Indians, as I never for a
moment believed, intended treachery.

Arrived at Little Raven's lodge, I found
him surrounded by all his principal chiefs, a
place being reserved by his side for me. After
the usual smoke and the preliminary moments of silence, which strongly reminded
me of the deep silence which is the prelude to
religious services in some of our churches,
Little Raven began a speech which was
mainly a review of what had been agreed

upon the evening before, and closed with the
statement that his people were highly pleased
to see white men among them as friends, and
that the idea of complying with my demand
in regard to proceeding to our main camp
had been discussed with great favor by all of
his people, who were delighted with this
opportunity of terminating the war. All
questions affecting the Arapahoes being satisfactorily disposed of, I now introduced the
subject of the whereabouts of the Cheyenne
village, stating that my purpose was to extend to them the same terms as had been
accepted by the Arapahoes.

To this I could obtain no decisive or satisfactory reply. The Cheyennes were represented to be moving constantly, hence the
difficulty in informing me accurately as to
their location; but all agreed that the Cheyennes were a long distance west of where we
then were. Finally, I obtained a promise
from Little Raven that he would select two
of his active young warriors who would accompany me in my search for the Cheyenne
village, and whose knowledge of the country
and acquaintance with the Cheyennes would
be of incalculable service to me. As the limited amount of provisions on hand would not
justify us in continuing our search for the
Cheyennes, I decided to await the arrival of

A Peace Mission

Colonel Cooke, who, I felt confident, would reach us in a few days.

In the meanwhile the day fixed for the departure of the Arapahoes came and the village was all commotion and activity, lodges being taken down and packed on ponies and mules; the activity, I might mention, being confined, however, to the squaws, the noble lords of the forest sitting unconcernedly by, quietly smoking their long red clay pipes. I was sorry to lose the services of Yellow Bear, but it was necessary for him to accompany his people, particularly as he represented the peace element. I gave him a letter to General Sheridan, in which I informed the latter of our meeting with the Arapahoes, the council and the final agreement. In view of the farther extension of our journey I requested a second detachment to be sent on our trail, with supplies, to meet us on our return. Everything being in readiness, the chiefs, commencing with Little Raven, gathered around me and bade me good-by, Yellow Bear being the last to take his leave. This being ended, the entire village was put in motion and soon stretched itself into a long, irregular column.

The chiefs formed the advance; next came the squaws and children and the old men, followed by the pack animals bearing the lodges and household goods; after these came the herd, consisting of hundreds of loose ponies and mules, driven by squaws; while on the outskirts of the entire cavalcade rode the young men and boys, performing the part of assistants to the herders, but more important as flankers or videttes in case of danger or attack. Nor must I omit another important element in estimating the population of an Indian village, the dogs. These were without number and of all colors and sizes. It was difficult to determine which outnumbered the other, the dogs, or their owners. Some of the former were mere puppies, unable to travel; these were carefully stowed away in a comfortable sort of basket, made of willows and securely attached to the back of one of the pack animals, the mother of the interesting family trotting along contentedly by the side of the latter.

After the excitement attending the departure of the Indians had passed and the last glimpse of the departing village had been had, our little party seemed lonely enough as we stood huddled together on the bank of Mulberry Creek. There was nothing to be done until the arrival of our expected supplies. Little Robe, impatient at the proposed delay, concluded to start at once in quest of his people, and if possible persuade them to meet us instead of awaiting our arrival. He evidently was anxious to have peace concluded with the Cheyennes, and thus enable his people to be placed on the same secure footing with the Arapahoes. Instead of opposing, I encouraged him in the execution of his plan, although loath to part with him. The two young Arapahoes were to remain with me, however, and by concert of plan between them and Little Robe we would be able to follow the trail.

It was agreed that if Little Robe should come up with his people and be able to induce them to return he was to send up smoke signals each morning and evening, in order that we might receive notice of their approach and be able to regulate our march accordingly. Giving him a sufficient supply of coffee, sugar, and hard bread, we saw Little Robe set out on his solitary journey in the character of a veritable peace commissioner.

I might fill several pages in describing the various expedients to which our little party resorted in order to dispose of our time while waiting the arrival of our supplies. How Romeo, by the promise of a small reward in case he was successful, was induced to attempt to ride a beautiful Indian pony which we had caught on the plains, and which was still as wild and unbroken as if he had never felt the hand of man. The ground selected was a broad border of deep sand, extending up and down the valley. Two long lariats were securely fastened to the halter. At the end of one was my brother. I officiated at the end of the other, with the pony standing midway between us, some twenty feet from either, and up to his fetlocks in sand, an anxious spectator of what was going on. Everything being in readiness, Romeo, with never a fear or doubt as to the result, stepped quietly up to the side of the pony, who, turning his head somewhat inquiringly, uttered a few snorts indicative of anything but gentleness. Romeo, who was as active as a cat, succeeded in placing his hands on the pony's back, and with an injunction to us to keep firm hold on the lariats he sprang lightly upon the back of the pony and seized the mane.

I have seen trained mules, the delight of boys who attend the circus, and sometimes of persons of more advanced age, and have witnessed the laughable efforts of the youngsters who vainly endeavor to ride the contumacious quadruped once around the ring; but I remember nothing of this description to equal or resemble the frantic plunges of the Indian pony in his untrained efforts to free his back from its burden, nor the equally frantic and earnest efforts of the rider to maintain his position. Fortunately for the holders of the lariats they exceeded the length of the pony's legs, or his heels, which were being elevated in all directions and almost at the same time, would have compelled us to relinquish our hold and leave Romeo to his fate. As both pony and rider seemed to redouble their efforts for the mastery the scene became more ludicrous, while the hearty and prolonged shouts of laughter from the bystanders on all sides seemed only to add intensity to the contest.

This may strike the reader as a not very dignified proceeding, particularly upon the part of one of the lariat holders; but we were not studying how to appear dignified, but how to amuse ourselves. So exhausted did I become with unrestrained laughter as I beheld Romeo in his lofty gyrations about a center which belonged to the movable order, that a much further prolongation of the sport would have forced me to relinquish my hold on the lariat. But I was spared this result. The pony, as if studying the problem, had indulged in almost every conceivable form of leaping, and now, rising almost perpendicularly on his hind legs, stood erect, pawing the air with his fore legs and com-

pelling Romeo, in order to prevent himself
from sliding off, to clasp him about the neck
with both arms. The pony seemed almost as
if waiting this situation, as with the utmost
quickness, and before Romeo could resume
his seat, he descended from his elevated attitude and the next moment his head was almost touching the ground, and his heels occupied the space just vacated by his head in
mid air. This sudden change was too much
for Romeo, and as if projected from an an-
cient catapult he departed from his place on
the back of the pony and landed on the deep,
soft sand, many feet in advance of his late
opponent. Three times was this repeated
with almost the same result until finally Romeo, as he brushed the sand from his matted
locks, expressed it as his opinion that no one
but an Indian could ride that pony. As Romeo was half Indian, the distinction seemed
finely drawn.

Innumerable were the tricks played on
each other by one and all; everything seemed
legitimate sport which tended to kill time.
Three days after the departure of the Arapahoe village the lookout reported that parties were in sight some three or four miles in
the direction taken by the village. This created no little excitement in camp. Field-
glasses were brought into immediate requisi-

tion, and after a careful examination of the parties, who could be plainly seen approaching us in the distance, we all came to the conclusion that what we saw must be the escort with our supplies. A few horses were soon saddled and two of the officers, with some of the men, galloped out to meet the advancing party. It proved to be Colonel Cooke, with California Joe and a dozen men, bringing with them several pack animals loaded with fresh supplies.

I need not say how we welcomed their arrival. It was too late in the day to make it desirable for us to set out on the trail of Little Robe, as it was necessary to unpack and issue rations and repack the remainder; so that it was concluded to remain until next morning, an additional reason in favor of this resolution being that the horses of Colonel Cooke's party would have the benefit of rest. The account given by Colonel Cooke and California Joe concerning their march was exceedingly interesting. It will be remembered that it was the expectation that we would find the Arapahoe village nearer our main camp than we afterward did, and in my letter to General Sheridan I had intimated that Colonel Cooke would probably overtake us at a point not far from the termination of the Wichita Mountains.

Colonel Cooke arrived at the designated point, but we, of course, had gone, and not finding any letter or signal at our deserted camp he became, not unnaturally, anxious as to where we had gone. This will not be wondered at when it is remembered that he had but thirteen men with him and was then in a hostile country and far from all support. However, he had nothing to do but to continue on our trail. That night will no doubt live long in the memory of Colonel Cooke.

After reaching camp with his little party in a small piece of timber, he, as he afterward related to me, began taking a mental survey of his situation. For fear of misleading the reader, I will here remark, as I have indicated in previous chapters, that fear, or a lack of the highest order of personal courage, was not numbered among the traits of character possessed by this officer. After seeing that the animals were properly secured for the night, and his men made comfortable, he sat down by the camp fire awaiting the preparation of his evening meal. In the meantime California Joe found him, and entered into a discussion as to the probabilities of overtaking us soon, and in a kind of Jack Bunsby style suggested, if not, why not?[46]

[46] Jack Bunsby was an outlandish character in *Dombey and Sons* by Charles Dickens, who was enor-

A Peace Mission

The more Colonel Cooke looked at the matter, the more trying seemed his position. Had he known, as we then knew, that the Arapahoes had been found and a peaceful agreement entered into, it would have solved all his difficulty. Of this he of course was ignorant, and thoughts ran through his mind that perhaps my little party had been led on only to be massacred, and his would follow blindly to the same fate. This recalled all former Indian atrocities with which he was familiar, while prominent above them all rose before him the fate of young Kidder and party, whose fate is recorded in a former chapter.

In thinking of this, Colonel Cooke was struck by a coincidence. Kidder's party consisted of almost the identical number which composed his own. Kidder had a guide, and Cooke had California Joe; all of which, without attaching any importance to his words, the latter took pains to remind Colonel Cooke of. By the time supper was prepared Colonel Cooke felt the responsibilities of his position

mously popular in America at the time Custer's narrative was written. Bunsby had a very large head "with one staring eye" and one revolving one, "shaggy hair like oakum" and "a perfect desert of a chin." Moreover he was a philosopher and quite an oracle, able and willing to expound his views on any subject.

too strongly to have any appetite for food, so
that when supper was commenced he simply
declined it and invited California Joe to help
himself, an invitation the latter was not slow
in accepting. Posting his guards for the
night, Colonel Cooke felt that to sleep was
impossible. He took his seat by the camp
fire and with his arms by his side impatiently
waited the coming of dawn.

California Joe, who regarded the present
as of far more importance than the future,
and whose slumber would have been little
disturbed even had he known that hostile
Indians were soon to be encountered, disposed of Colonel Cooke's supper, and then,
wrapping himself up in his blanket, stretched
himself under a tree near the fire and was
soon sleeping soundly. His brief account of
the enjoyment he derived from Colonel
Cooke's supper was characteristic: "Thar I
sot an' sot a eatin' uv that young man's
wittles, while he in his cavalry boots, with
his pistol in his belt, stood a lookin' inter the
fire."

Early next morning, as soon as the light
was sufficient to enable them to follow our
trail, Colonel Cooke and his party were on
their way. About noon, as they were passing
over a low ridge, yet sufficiently high to enable them to see for miles beyond, the eyes

of one of the party caught a view of a long line of dark-looking objects miles in advance, yet directly in their path. Each moment the objects became more distinct, until finally Colonel Cooke, who was studying them intently through his glass, pronounced the simple word, "Indians." "Ef that is so, Colonel, thar's a many one uv 'em," was the sober response of California Joe, who rode at his side.

By this time the Indians could be plainly seen, although numbers of them continued to gallop up from the rear. It was evident from their movements that they had discovered Colonel Cooke's party almost as soon as he had seen them, and that the entire body of Indians was directing its march toward the little eminence from which the white men were now watching their movements. "What do yer think about it now, Colonel?" said California Joe, at last breaking the silence. "Well, Joe, we must do the best we can; there is no use in running." "You're right," replied Joe; "an Injun 'll beat a white man runnin' every time, so I 'spect our best holt is fitin', but, Lor' a' mercy! look at 'em; thar ain't enuff uv us to go half round!"

Getting his little party collected in good order, and speaking words of encouragement to all, Colonel Cooke quietly awaited further developments. His thoughts in the meanwhile must have been such as he probably never wishes to indulge in again. All sorts of terrible visions and ideas flashed through his mind; the most prominent as well as plausible being that the Indians had made away with my party and from Little Robe and Yellow Bear had learned of the expected supplies, with their small escort, and were now in search of the latter. Whatever varied thoughts of this character chased each other through his brain, he at once came to the firm resolve that whatever fate was in store for him he would meet it like a soldier, and if the worst came he would fight to the last.

By this time it was seen that a single Indian was galloping in advance of the rest, as if hastening to reach the white men. "That's a queer dodge," remarked California Joe; but the mystery was soon cleared away as the Indian began to draw near to the party without slackening his pace. Colonel Cooke and California Joe instinctively advanced to meet him, when to their great joy and surprise it proved to be none other than the faithful Yellow Bear, who, realizing the situation, had ridden in advance of his people in order to assure the whites of their friendly character. His coming no doubt caused the hearts of Colonel Cooke and his party to beat lighter. Or, as California Joe expressed it: "When I seed it wuz Yaller Bar I knowed we wuz all right." From Yellow Bear Colonel Cooke learned where he might expect to find us, and thus another cause of anxiety was lifted from his mind.

The morning after my party had been reinforced by the arrival just described, we set out under guidance of Neva and the two young Arapahoe warriors and followed the direction in which Little Robe had gone. It being one of the winter months, the Indian ponies were still in unfit condition to make long or rapid marches; for this reason the two Arapahoes had left their ponies with the village and were accompanying or rather preceding us on foot; an undertaking which they seemed to have no difficulty in accomplishing. The grazing became more indifferent each day as we journeyed toward the west, until finally we ceased to rely upon it, but as a substitute fed our horses upon the bark of the young cottonwood trees which are generally found fringing the borders of the streams. In spite, however, of our utmost care our horses and pack animals, having exhausted their supply of forage, began to fail in strength and condition under their cottonwood bark diet.

After reaching and crossing Red River at
a point west of that at which the survey of
Marcy and McClellan crossed it,[47] and failing to discover any indication of the recent
occupation of the ground by Indians, I had
fears that if I prolonged my journey much
farther our animals would not be able to
reach the main camp, so famished had they
become in the last few days. I therefore,
after consultation with Neva and the two
Arapahoes, decided to recross to the north
bank of Red River and follow up its course
until we should reach a small tributary coming in from the northwest, and which Neva
informed me would furnish a good camp
ground. In the meanwhile Neva, who was
well mounted on a hardy, active mule, was to
take with him the two young Arapahoes and

[47] In the spring of 1852 Captain Randolph B. Marcy
and Lieutenant George B. McClellan were ordered to
explore the sources of Red River. Both officers became
generals in the Civil War, in which McClellan attained
permanent fame. In 1852, however, Marcy outranked
him. Marcy's narrative of the expedition is "even yet
a splendid description of the natural features of the
country through which it passed." It was published
as Sen. Ex Doc. 64, 32nd Cong., 2nd sess. For a brief
appreciative account of the expedition see Joseph Thoburn, *Standard History of Oklahoma*, I, 216–18. The
entire report, edited by Grant Foreman, was reprinted
by the University of Oklahoma Press at Norman in
1937, titled *An Adventure on Red River*.

push on in advance in search of the Cheyenne
village, the understanding being that I should
follow in his direction until the stream referred to was reached, where I would await
his return for three days. Should he fail to
rejoin us in that time, we would commence
our return march to the main camp.

When it was known that this plan had
been definitely settled upon, young Brewster,
who never for a moment had become discouraged as to his final success in discovering
his lost sister, came to me and in the most
earnest manner asked permission to accompany Neva in his search for the Cheyenne
village. I did everything I could to dissuade
him from so dangerous a project. No arguments were of any avail. He felt satisfied
that his sister was a prisoner in the Cheyenne
village, and this was his last and only opportunity to gain a knowledge of the fact; and
even with the chances of death or torture
staring him in the face he preferred to risk
all and learn the truth rather than live longer
in a state of horrible uncertainty. Against
my judgment in the matter, I was forced by
his importunate manner to grant him permission to accompany Neva.

Taking a suitable amount of supplies with
them, the three Indians and young Brewster
set out, Neva being the only one of the party

mounted. After they had left us we moved in the same direction, with the intention of halting on the stream indicated by Neva, there to await their return. While the reader is also waiting their return, I will refer to an incident which should have appeared in an earlier part of this chapter. It was neither more nor less than what might, among fashionable notices in the Indian press, provided they had one, have been termed an elopement in high life.

One evening after we had gone into camp many long weary miles from our point of starting, and when we supposed we had left all the Kiowas safely in camp awaiting the release of their two chiefs, Lone Wolf and Satanta, we were all surprised to see a young and handsome Kiowa warrior gallop into our midst accompanied by a young squaw, who certainly could not have reached the age which distinguishes the woman from the girl. In a few moments our little party gathered about these two wayfarers, eager to learn the cause of their sudden and unexpected visit. The girl was possessed of almost marvelous beauty, a beauty so remarkable that my companions of that march refer to her to this day as the most beautiful squaw they have ever seen. Her graceful and well-rounded form, her clearly-cut features, her dark ex-

pressive eyes, fringed with long silken lashes,
cheeks rich with the color of youth, teeth of
pearly whiteness occasionally peeping from
between her full, rosy lips, added withal to
a most bewitching manner, required not the
romance of her story to make her an object
of deep interest in the eyes of the gallants of
our party. But to their story:

She was the daughter of Black Eagle, at
that time the acting head chief of the Kiowas.
The young warrior who rode at her side was
somewhat of a young Lochinvar in disposition. It was the old, old story, only to be
repeated again by these representatives of
the red man—mutual and determined love
on the part of the youngsters, opposition
equally determined upon the part of Black
Eagle; not that the young warrior was ob-
jectionable, but unfortunately, as is but too
often the case, he was poor, and could not
offer in exchange for the hand of a chief's
daughter the proper number of ponies. Black
Eagle was inexorable—the lovers, constancy
itself. There was but one thing for them to
do, and they did it.

Aware of our proposed expedition in search
of the Cheyennes and Arapahoes, they timed
their affairs accordingly. Giving us time to
get two days the start, they slipped away
from their village at dusk the evening of the

second day after our departure, and hastening unperceived to a thicket near by, where the lover had taken the precaution to conceal two of the fleetest ponies of the village already saddled, they were soon in their saddles and galloping for love and life away from the Kiowa village. I say galloping for life, for by the Indian law if the father or relatives of the girl could overtake the lovers within twenty-four hours the life of the young woman would pay the forfeit.

They followed our trail in order to avail themselves of our protection by travelling with us as far as our course might lead them in the direction of the Staked Plains, on the borders of which a straggling band of Kiowas under the chief Woman Heart was supposed to be, and which the lovers intended to join, at least until the rage of *paterfamilias* should subside and they be invited to return. This in brief was their story. I need not add that they found a hearty welcome in our midst and were assured that they need no longer fear pursuit.

That evening after the camp fires were lighted the officers of our party, with Romeo as interpreter, gathered about the camp fire of the bridal couple and passed a pleasant hour in conversation. Their happiness and exultation at their success in escaping from their village were too powerful to be restrained, and in many delicate little ways the bride—for by Indian law twenty-four hours' absence from the village with her lover made her a bride—plainly betrayed her exceeding fondness for him who had risked all to claim her as his own.

After my return to the main camp I met Black Eagle and informed him that his daughter and her husband had been companions of our march. "Yes. Why did you not kill him?" was his reply, which upon inquiry he explained by saying that if some person had kindly put an end to the life of his son-in-law it would have benefited him to the value of several ponies; his difficulty seeming to be in overcoming the loss of the ponies which should have been paid for his daughter's hand. I afterwards learned, however, that the haughty chief became reconciled to the wilful lovers and invited them to return to his lodge, an invitation they were not tardy in accepting.

We pitched our camp at the point agreed upon between Neva and myself, and prepared to await the return of his party. Neva had been informed that our delay could not extend beyond three days, as our store of provisions and forage was almost exhausted, and this fact alone would force us to retrace our steps. I had hoped that during the time we were to spend in camp hunting parties might be able to bring in a sufficient amount of game to satisfy our wants; but although parties were despatched in all directions not an animal or bird could be found. So barren was the country as to offer no inducements that would attract game of any species.

Our last ounce of meat had been eaten and the men, after one day's deprivation of this essential part of their rations, were almost ravenous. Our horses had several days since eaten their last ration of grain and the grass was so sparse and indifferent as to furnish insufficient diet to sustain life. Resort was had to cottonwood bark, to obtain which we cut down large numbers of the trees and fed our horses upon the young bark of the branches. Knowing that in answer to my second request supplies of provisions both for men and horses must be on their way and probably near to us, I determined to begin our return march one day sooner than I had expected when Neva and his companions left us, as they would be able on finding our camp to follow our trail and overtake us.

We moved only a few miles, but even this short distance was sufficient to demonstrate how weak and famished our horses had become, one of them dying from starvation be-

fore we reached camp the first day of our
return march. This circumstance, however,
was turned to our advantage. Much has been
said and written in praise of the savoriness of
horseflesh as a diet. Our necessities compelled us to put this question to practical
test, and the animal had scarcely fallen, unable to rise again, when it was decided to
prepare his carcass for food. That evening
the men treated themselves to a bountiful
repast made up of roasts, steaks, and broils,
all from the flesh of the poor animal, whose
death was attributable to starvation alone.
Judging, however, from the jolly laughter
which rang through camp at supper time, the
introduction of this new article of diet met
with a cordial reception.

Soon after finishing our supper we discovered in the distance and following in our trail
a horseman. We at once concluded that this
must be Neva, a fact rendered conclusive by
the aid of a field-glass. Various were the surmises indulged in by the different members
of our party as to the success of Neva's mission. What had become of his companions,
particularly young Brewster? These and
many other inquiries suggested themselves
as we watched his approach. We could almost read the answer on Neva's face when
he reached us as to the success of his search

for the Cheyennes. Disappointment, hunger, and fatigue were plainly marked in his features as he dismounted and shook hands with us.

Knowing that one of the characteristics of the Indian is to talk but little until the wants of the inner man have been fully attended to, I at once ordered him a steak. One of the party, however, fearing that if he knew the exact character of the diet offered him he might from some superstitious cause decline it, suggested that Neva be asked if he would like a nice buffalo steak, a deception which seemed somewhat justifiable under the circumstances. To this Neva returned a hearty affirmative, when one of the men placed before him a raw steak whose dimensions would have amply gratified the appetites of an ordinary family of half a dozen. Having held the steak over the blazing fire until sufficiently done to suit his taste, Neva seated himself on the ground near by and began helping himself liberally to the dripping morsel. After he had indulged for some time in this pleasing entertainment, and having made no remark, one of the officers inquired of him if he was hungry.

"Yes," was his reply, but added in his very indifferent English, "Poor buffano, poor buffano." None of us ever informed him of the little deception which had been practised upon him.

His account of his journey was brief. He had travelled nearly due west, accompanied by Brewster and the two young Arapahoes, and had discovered a trail of the Cheyenne village some two weeks old leading still farther to the west, and under circumstances which induced him to believe the village had moved far away. Under these circumstances there was no course left to him but to return. The Arapahoes decided to follow on and join the Cheyenne village. Neva and young Brewster began their return together, but the latter, being unable to travel as fast as Neva, fell behind. Neva, anxious to keep his promise and rejoin us at the time and place indicated, pushed forward as rapidly as possible. Young Brewster, however, manfully struggled along, and reached our camp a few hours after Neva's arrival.

The next morning we set out on our homeward or return march. During the night one of our horses strayed away from camp and as one of the men thought he could find it before we made our start in the morning, he left camp with that purpose. Failing to rejoin us at the proper time, I sent parties in search of him, but they returned unsuccessful. We were compelled by our necessities to

move without further delay. Weeks and
months elapsed, and no tidings of the lost
trooper reached us, when one day while encamped near Fort Hays, Kansas, hundreds
of miles from the locality of which I am now
writing, who should step up to my tent but
the man who was lost from us in northwestern Texas. He had become bewildered after
losing sight of our camp, took the wrong
direction, and was never able thereafter during his wanderings to determine his course.
Fortunately he took a southerly route, and
after nearly two months of solitary roaming
over the plains of northern Texas he arrived
at a military post south of Red River in
Texas, and by way of Galveston, the Gulf of
Mexico, the Mississippi and Missouri rivers,
rejoined his regiment in Kansas. As we
gained the crest of the hill from which we obtained a view of the white tents which formed
our camp, there was no one of our little party
who did not enjoy a deep feeling of gratitude
and thankfulness that our long and trying
journey was about to end under happier
auspices than many might have supposed
when we began it.

Chapter 16

OUR arrival in camp created a sensation among our comrades, who had seen us depart upon what they might well have considered an errand of questionable prudence. Leaving my companions of the march to answer the many queries of those who had not accompanied us, I galloped across the narrow plain which separated General Sheridan's tents from my camp and was soon greeted by the General and staff in terms of hearty welcome. Repairing to the General's tent, I soon recounted the principal incidents of my expedition, with most of which the reader has been already made acquainted. I found that the Arapahoes had kept their promise made to me while I was in their village, and that the village was then located near our main camp.

It might be proper here to remark that although a period of several years has elapsed since the Arapahoes were induced to accept the offer of peace made to them, and promised to relinquish in the future their predatory mode of life, yet to this day, so far as I know, they as a tribe have remained at peace with the white men. This remark may not, and probably does not, apply to particular individuals of the tribe, but it is due to the tribe to state that their conduct, since the events related in the preceding chapter has been greatly to their credit, as well as to the peace and comfort of the settlers of the frontier; results wholly due to the Washita campaign and the subsequent events with which the reader of these articles is familiar. The conduct of the Cheyennes, however, in declining our proffers of peace, left the Indian question in that section of country still unsettled; but this only rendered new plans necessary, plans which were quickly determined upon.

Other events of great public importance rendered General Sheridan's presence necessary elsewhere at an early day. It was therefore decided that he, accompanied by his escort of scouts under Lieutenant Pepoon, should proceed northward to Camp Supply, while I, with the Seventh Regulars and the Nineteenth Kansas Cavalry and my Osage scouts, a force numbering about fifteen hundred men, should move westward in quest of the recalcitrant Cheyennes and administer to them such treatment as their past conduct might merit and existing circumstances demanded. Satanta and Lone Wolf were still prisoners in our hands, a portion of their tribe having failed thus far to comply with the terms of the agreement by which they were to settle down peaceably on their reservation. As the greater portion of the tribe, however, was then encamped near us, and as both Satanta and Lone Wolf were loud in their protestations of peace, it was decided to release them. Accordingly, after conference with General Sheridan, I went to the lodge in which I kept the two chiefs closely guarded as prisoners and informed them of the decision which had been arrived at in their behalf, the only response being a most hearty and emphatic "How" from the two robust chieftains.

General Sheridan had up to this time declined all their requests for an interview, but now deemed it best to see them and speak a few words of warning and caution as to their future conduct. No peace commissioners were ever entertained by promises of good behavior, peaceable intentions, and regrets for past offenses which smacked of greater earnestness and sincerity than those volunteered by Lone Wolf and Satanta when informed that they were free to rejoin their people. According to their voluntary representations their love for their white brothers

531

was unbounded; their desire for peace, their hatred of war, ungovernable; and nothing would satisfy them in future but to be permitted to lead their people "the white man's road," by cultivating the soil, building schoolhouses and churches, and forever eschewing a predatory or warlike life.

Alas, the instability of human resolutions, particularly of the human in an Indian! and the resolutions are expressed—not formed—simply to obtain a certain advantage, or, as is most usually the case, to tickle the fanciful imagination of some thoroughly well-meaning but utterly impractical peace commissioner, whose favorable influence is believed by the Indian to be all-potent in securing fresh invoices of new blankets, breech-loading arms, and provisions. Neither blankets, breech-loading arms, nor an unnecessary amount of provisions were distributed by the military among the adherents of Satanta and Lone Wolf.

Scarcely one year had elapsed, however, before Satanta defiantly informed the General of the Army, then on a visit to Fort Sill, that he had just returned from an expedition to Texas during which he and his party had murdered and robbed several white men. It was this confession which led to Satanta's trial, conviction, and sentence to death by

jFurtfjer Cfjepenne Pursuit

the civil authorities of Texas. Through the intercession of the General Government, the Executive of Texas was induced to commute the punishment of Satanta from hanging to imprisonment for life, a step which all familiar with Indians and Indian management knew would result sooner or later in his release, and that of his confederate, Big Tree.

Importuned constantly by the tenderhearted representations of the peace commissioners, who could not be induced to look upon Satanta and Big Tree as murderers, the Governor of Texas very unwisely yielded to their persistent appeals and upon the strength of promises solemnly made by the peace commissioners, according to which not only Satanta and Big Tree were to abstain from acts of bloodshed and murder in the future, but their entire tribe was also to remain at peace and within their reservation limits, the two chiefs who had unfortunately escaped the halter were again turned loose to engage in acts of hostility against the whites; an opportunity they and their treacherous people have not been slow to improve from that day to this.[48]

[48] Satanta was renowned as an orator and during his later years ranked next to Lone Wolf as chief of the Kiowas. In 1871 he raided the Texas frontier and sub-

⚙y Life on the Plains

The winter of 1868–'69 was rapidly terminating, acting as a forcible reminder to us
that if we hoped to operate in the field with
any advantage over the Cheyennes the movement must be made before the spring grass
should make its appearance for the benefit of
the Indian ponies. Accordingly, as soon as
our arrangements were perfected our camp
at the present site of Fort Sill, Indian Territory, was broken up and General Sheridan,
accompanied by his staff and escort, set out
for Camp Supply in the north, while my command faced westward and began its search
for the Cheyennes, passing along the southern base of the Wichita Mountains on the
afternoon of inauguration day old Camp

sequently boasted before General Sherman of his responsibility for the killings that were committed. For
his crimes he was sentenced to death but the sentence
was commuted to life imprisonment in the Texas state
penitentiary, from which he was released two years
later by Governor Davis, conditioned upon the continued good behavior of the Kiowas. General Sherman
sharply protested the release and expressed the hope
that when the Kiowas resumed their killings the Governor's scalp might be the first one taken. Davis, in
defense, protested his lack of authority, and pressure
upon him by the Federal Government. The Kiowas
again went on the warpath in 1874, and when they
were subdued Satanta was returned to his Texas prison.
Here he committed suicide on March 11, 1878 by
throwing himself from an upper story of the prison.

Further Cheyenne Pursuit

Radziminski, a station which had been occupied by our troops prior to the war between the Northern and Southern States, and whose name, no doubt, will recall pleasant reminiscences to many who afterwards wore the blue or the gray.

On the morning of the first day after leaving the Wichita Mountains behind us no little excitement was created throughout the command by the discovery of a column of smoke directly on our course, and apparently about fifteen or twenty miles in front of us. That Indians had originated the fire was beyond a doubt, as we all knew that beyond us in the direction of the smoke the country was inhabited by no human beings save hostile Indians. I at once decided to push on with the command to the point from which the smoke was ascending and discover, if possible, some trace of the Indians. Be it understood that neither I nor any members of my command supposed for one moment that when we arrived at the desired point we would find the Indians there awaiting our arrival, but we did hope to discover their trail. Of the many experienced frontiermen embraced in the command, including, of course, California Joe, there were none who judged the distance which separated us from the smoke as greater than could be easily passed over by us before three or four o'clock that afternoon.

It was evidently not a signal smoke, ascending from a single point and regulated by human control, but appeared from our standpoint more like a fire communicated to the prairie grass from an abandoned or neglected camp fire. Pushing on as rapidly as our horses could travel, we were again reminded from time to time of the deceptive character of the Plains as regards distances. When three o'clock arrived, and we had been marching steadily for nine hours, the dense and changing columns of deep gray smoke which had been our guiding point all day seemed as far distant as when our march began in the morning. Except to water our animals and once to enable the men to prepare a cup of coffee no halts were made from six o'clock in the morning until we finally reached the desired locality—not at three or four o'clock in the afternoon, but at two o'clock that night.

Our surmises proved correct. The fire had evidently been communicated to the dry winter grass from some Indian camp fire. The Indians, of course, had gone; but where? As this was a question that could not be solved until daylight and as all of us were glad enough of an opportunity to get a few hours' repose, the troops bivouacked in promiscuous order as they arrived. Only those who have enjoyed similar experiences know how brief the preparation required for sleep. As for myself, as soon as the necessary directions had been given relating to the command I unsaddled my horse, arranged my saddle for my pillow, tethered my horse within easy reach, and in less time than has been required to write these few lines I was enjoying one of those slumbers which only come as the reward of a day of earnest activity in the saddle.

As soon as it was light enough for our purpose we were in the saddle and searching in all directions for the trail left by the Indians who had fired the prairie. Our Osage scouts were not long in making the desired discovery. The trail led westward, following the general course of a small valley in which it was first discovered. The party was evidently a small one numbering not more than fifteen persons, but the direction in which they were moving led me to hope that by following them carefully and with due caution to prevent discovery of our pursuit we might be led to the main village. All that day our Osage scouts clung to the trail with the pertinacity of sleuth hounds. The course led us up and across several different streams

537

of beautiful, clear water; but to our great disappointment and to that of our horses as well we discovered, upon attempting to quench our thirst at different times, that every stream was impregnated to the fullest degree with salt.

Later in the day this became a serious matter, and had we not been on an Indian trail I should have entertained earnest apprehensions as to whether or not we were destined to find pure water by continuing farther in the direction we were then moving; but I felt confident that the Indians we were pursuing were familiar with the country and would no doubt lead us, unintentionally of course, to streams of fresh water.

One of the streams we crossed was so strongly impregnated with salt that the edges near the banks were covered with a border of pure white salt, resembling the borders of ice often seen along rivulets in winter. This border was from one to three feet in width and sufficiently thick to support the weight of a horse. Fortunately the Indian trail, as I had anticipated, led us to a refreshing spring of pure, cold water near by. Here we halted to prepare a cup of coffee before continuing the pursuit.

While halted at this point I observed a trooper approaching with an armful of huge cakes of pure white salt gathered from the salt stream just described, and which flowed at the foot of the hill from which also bubbled forth the spring of fresh water to which we were indebted for the means of preparing our first meal on that day. Salt was not an abundant article with us at that time and the trooper referred to, aware of this fact, had, in behalf of himself and comrades, collected from the literal "salt of the earth" a quantity ample for all present need. After conveying his valuable load to the vicinity of the cook fire he broke the cakes of salt into small particles with an axe, and then passing the fragments through a coffee-mill he was in possession of table salt whose quality would have satisfied a more exacting epicure than a hungry cavalryman.

Finishing our meal, which not only was our breakfast for that day, but a late dinner as well, we resumed the pursuit, observing before doing so that the Indians had also made a brief halt at the same point and had built a fire and prepared their meal, as we had done after them. Crossing a high ridge, or divide, the trail led us down into a beautiful open valley. After following up the course of the latter several miles the freshness of the trail indicated that the Indians had passed over it that same day. As it was not our purpose to overtake them, but to follow as closely as prudence would allow, I determined to go into camp until the following morning. Soon after resuming the pursuit next day rain began to fall, at first slowly, but later in the day in copious showers. I knew the Indians would not travel in the rain if they could avoid it, unless they knew they were pursued, and of this fact I had reason to believe they were still ignorant as evidences found all along the trail indicated that they were moving very leisurely.

To avoid placing ourselves in too close proximity to them, I ordered a halt about noon and began preparation for camping for the night. Our wagons were still in rear. In the meantime the horses were all unsaddled and picketed out in the usual manner to graze. As was my usual custom upon halting for the night, I had directed the Osage scouts, instead of halting and unsaddling to advance in the direction we were to follow next day and examine the country for a distance of a few miles. We had barely completed the unsaddling of our horses and disposed of them over the grazing ground when I discovered the Osage scouts returning over the ridge in front of us as fast as their ponies could carry them. Their story was soon told. Disliking to travel in the rain, the Indians whom we were pursuing had gone into camp also, and the Osage scouts had discovered them not more than a mile from us, the ridge referred to preventing the Indians from seeing us or being seen by us.

Quickly the words "Saddle up" flew from mouth to mouth, and in a marvellously brief time officers and men were in the saddle and under the guidance of the Osage scouts were moving stealthily to surprise the Indian camp. Passing around a little spur of the dividing ridge, there before us, at a distance of but a few hundred yards, stood the half-erected lodges of the Indians, while scattered here and there in the immediate vicinity were to be seen the Indian ponies and pack animals, grazing in apparent unconsciousness of the close proximity of an enemy. At a given signal the cavalry put spurs to their steeds, drew their revolvers, and in a few moments were in possession of the Indian camp, ponies and all—no, not all, for not a single Indian could be discovered.

The troops were deployed at a gallop in all directions, but failed to find the trace of an Indian. Our capture was apparently an empty one. How the occupants of the Indian camp had first discovered our presence and afterwards contrived to elude us was a mystery which even puzzled our Osage scouts. This mystery was afterwards explained, and in order to avoid detaining the reader I will anticipate sufficiently to state that in the course of subsequent events we came face to face, under a flag of truce, with the late occupants of the Indian camp, and learned from them that in this instance history had reproduced itself. Rome was saved by the cackling of geese: the Indians owed their safety to the barking of dogs, not the barking of dogs belonging to their own camp, but to ours.

It seemed that during the haste and excitement attendant upon the discovery of the close proximity of the Indian camp to ours, two of our dogs, whether or not sharing in the bellicose humor of their masters, engaged in a quarrel, the noise of which reached the quick ears of the Indians nearly one mile distant. Comprehending the situation at once, the Indians, realizing the danger of delay, abandoned their camp and ponies and fled on foot, the better to effect concealment and elude pursuit.

On the following day we resumed the march. There being no longer any trail for us to follow we continued in the same direction, believing that the small party we had been pursuing had been directing their course toward the location of the main village, which was somewhere to the westward of us. Day after day we travelled in this direction, hoping to discover some sign or trail which might give us a clue to the whereabouts of the Cheyenne village. We had left the Indian Territory far behind us and had advanced into Texas well toward the 102d meridian of longitude. Nearly all hope of discovering the Indians had vanished from the minds of the officers and men when late in the afternoon the trail of a single lodge was discovered, leading in a southwesterly direction. The trail was nearly if not quite one month old; hence it did not give great encouragement. To the surprise of most of the command I changed the direction of our march at once and put the Osages on the trail, having decided to follow it.

This may seem to the reader an ill-advised move, but the idea under which the decision was made was that the owner of the lodge, the trail of which we had discovered, had probably been absent from the main village in search of game, as is customary for small parties of Indians at that season of the year. In the spring, however, the entire tribe assembles at one point and determines its plans and movements for the summer, whether relating to war or hunting. There was a chance —a slight one, it is true—that the trail of the

543

single lodge just discovered might lead us to the rendezvous of the tribe. I deemed it worthy of our attention, and a pursuit of a few days at furthest would determine the matter.

Following our faithful Osages, who experienced no difficulty in keeping the trail, we marched until near sundown, when we arrived at the banks of a small stream upon which, and near a cool, bubbling spring, we discovered the evidences of an Indian camp, which must have not only included the lodge whose trail we had been following, but about a dozen others. Here was a speedier confirmation of my hopes than I had anticipated. Here I determined to encamp until morning, and while the cavalry were unsaddling and pitching their tents I asked Mo-nah-see-tah to examine the Indian camp minutely and to tell me how long a time had elapsed since its occupation by the Indians, how many constituted the party, and the character and probable indications of the latter.

No detective could have set about the proposed examination with greater thoroughness than did this Indian girl. The ashes of the camp fires were raked carefully away and examined with all the scrutiny of a chemical analysis. Bits of cloth or fragments of the skins of animals found within the limits of the camp were lifted from their resting-places as tenderly as if they were articles of greatest value. Here and there were to be seen the bones of deer or antelope which had been obtained by the Indians as food. These Monah-see-tah examined carefully; then, shattering them between two stones, the condition of the marrow seemed a point of particular importance to her as tending to determine the length of time the bones had been lying in the camp. After many minutes spent in this examination, during which I accompanied her, a silent but far from disinterested spectator, she, apparently like a judge who had been carefully reviewing all the evidence, gave me her conclusions, communicating with me through the medium of the sign language with a grace characteristic of the Indian race, and which added to the interest of her statements.

Briefly summed up, her conclusions were as follows: twelve lodges had encamped at that point, probably constituting the band of some petty chief, the different members of which, like the one whose trail we had that day discovered, had been separated for purposes of hunting, but had been called together at that point preparatory to joining the main village. The lodges had left this camp not to exceed two weeks previous to that date, and in all probability had moved to the rendezvous appointed for the main tribe, which would without doubt be found by other small bands from time to time until the village would all be assembled at one point. Moving in this manner and at this early season of the year, when grass was scarce and no enemy known to be in the country, the Indians would make very short moves each day, passing merely from one stream to another, not accomplishing in one day a greater distance, probably, than the cavalry would in two or three hours.

This intelligence, of course, was most gratifying, and for encouragement was soon communicated to the individual members of the command. The trail was found to lead almost in a northerly direction, slightly inclining to the east. Perhaps no one of the command experienced such a feeling of hope and anxious suspense as the new discoveries gave rise to in the breast of young Brewster, who now more than ever believed, and with reason too, that he was soon to unravel or forever seal the fate of his lost sister, whose discovery and release had been the governing impulses of his life for months past.

With renewed interest the cavalry resumed the pursuit at daylight the following morning. We had marched but a few miles before we reached a second camping ground, which had been occupied not only by those whose trail we were then following, but the number of fires showed that the strength of the Indians had been increased by about twenty-five lodges, thus verifying the correctness of the surmises advanced by Mo-nah-see-tah.

Continuing our progress, we had the satisfaction of seeing still further accessions to the trail until it was evident that at least one hundred lodges had united and passed in one body on the trail. As we marched in one day over the distance passed over in three by the Indians, and as the latter were moving unsuspicious of the presence of an enemy in that section of the country, the trail was becoming freshened as we advanced. That night we encamped with every precaution calculated to conceal our presence from the Indians. No fires were permitted until after dark, and then but small ones, for fear the quick and watchful eye of the Indian might detect the ascending columns of smoke. As soon as the men had prepared their suppers the fires were put out. In the morning breakfast was prepared before daylight, and the fires at once smothered by heaping damp earth over them.

Resuming the pursuit as soon as it was sufficiently light to follow the trail, we soon arrived at the camp vacated by the Indians the previous day, the extent of which showed that from three to four hundred lodges of Indians had occupied the ground. In many places the decayed embers of the lodge fires were still glowing; while the immense quantity of young cottonwood timber found cut and lying throughout the camp stripped of its young bark showed that the Indian ponies were being mainly subsisted on cottonwood bark, the spring grass not being sufficiently advanced to answer the purpose. Nothing indicated that the Indians had departed in a precipitate manner or that they had discovered our approach. It was reasonable, therefore, to suppose that we would come in contact with them that day, if not actually reach the village.

All our plans were made accordingly. The Osages, as usual, were kept in the advance, that their quick eyes might the sooner discover the Indians should they appear in our front. In order to avail myself of the earliest information, I, with Colonel Cooke, accompanied the Osages. Two of the latter kept in advance of all, and as they neared a ridge or commanding piece of ground they would cautiously approach the crest on foot and peer beyond, to ascertain whether an enemy was in sight before exposing our party to discovery. This proceeding, a customary one with Indians, did not excite unusual attention upon the part of Colonel Cooke and myself until once we saw Hard Rope, the head warrior, who was in advance, slowly ascend a slight eminence in our front, and after casting one glimpse beyond descend the hill and return to us as rapidly as his pony could carry him. We almost anticipated his report, so confident was everybody in the command that we were going to overtake the village.

In a few words Hard Rope informed us that less than a mile beyond the hill from which he had obtained a view there was in plain sight a large herd of Indian ponies grazing, being herded and driven by a few Indian boys. As yet they had not seen us, but were liable to discover the column of troops farther to the rear. To judge of the situation I dismounted, and, conducted by Hard Rope, advanced to the crest of the hill in front and looked beyond; there I saw in plain view the herd of ponies, numbering perhaps two hundred and being driven in the opposite direction toward what seemed the valley of a stream, as I could see the tops of the forest trees which usually border the water courses.

The ponies and their protectors soon disappeared from view, but whether they had discovered us yet or not I was unable to determine. Sending a messenger back as rapidly as his horse could carry him, I directed the troops to push to the front, and to come prepared for action. I knew the village must be near at hand, probably in the vicinity of the trees seen in the distance. As the country was perfectly open, free from either ravines or timber capable of affording concealment to Indians, I took my orderly with me and galloped in advance in the direction taken by the Indians, leaving Colonel Cooke to hasten and direct the troops as the latter should arrive.

After advancing about half way to the bluff overlooking the valley I saw about half a dozen Indian heads peering over the crest, evidently watching my movements; this number was soon increased to upwards of fifty. I was extremely anxious to satisfy myself as to the tribe whose village was evidently near at hand. There was but little doubt that it was the Cheyennes, for whom we had been searching. If this should prove true the two white girls, whose discovery and release from captivity had been one of the objects of the expedition, must be held prisoners in the village which we were approaching; and to effect their release unharmed then became my study, for I remembered the fate

of the white woman and child held captive
by a band of this same tribe at the battle of
the Washita.

I knew that the first shot fired on either
side would be the signal for the murder of the
two white girls. While knowing the Cheyennes to be deserving of castigation, and feeling assured that they were almost in our
power, I did not dare to imperil the lives of
the two white captives by making an attack
on the village, although never before or since
have we seen so favorable an opportunity for
administering well-merited punishment to
one of the strongest and most troublesome of
the hostile tribes. Desiring to establish a
truce with the Indians before the troops
should arrive, I began making signals inviting a conference. This was done by simply
riding in a circle and occasionally advancing
toward the Indians on the bluff in a zigzag
manner. Immediately there appeared on the
bluffs about twenty mounted Indians; from
this group three advanced toward me at a
gallop, soon followed by the others of the
party. I cast my eyes behind me to see if the
troops were near, but the head of the column
was still a mile or more in rear. My orderly
was near me and I could see Colonel Cooke
rapidly approaching about midway between
the column and my position.

Directing the orderly to remain stationary, I advanced toward the Indians a few paces, and as soon as they were sufficiently near made signs to them to halt, and then for but one of their number to advance midway and meet me. This was assented to, and I advanced with my revolver in my left hand, while my right hand was held aloft as a token that I was inclined to be friendly. The Indian met me as agreed upon and in response to my offer exchanged friendly greetings and shook hands. From him I learned that the village of the entire Cheyenne tribe was located on the stream in front of us, and that Medicine Arrow, the head chief of the Cheyennes, was in the group of Indians then in view from where we stood. Little Robe, with his band numbering about forty lodges, was a short distance farther down the stream. I asked the Indian to send for Medicine Arrow, as I desired to talk with the head chief. Calling to one of his companions who had halted within hailing distance, the latter was directed to convey to Medicine Arrow my message, to do which he set off at a gallop.

At this juncture I perceived that the Indians to the number of twenty or more had approached quite near, while some of the party seemed disposed to advance to where I was. To this I had decided objections, and so indicated to the Indian who was with me. He complied with my wishes and directed his companions to remain where they were. As a precaution of safety, I took good care to keep the person of the Indian between me and his friends. Medicine Arrow soon came galloping up accompanied by a chief.

While engaged in shaking hands with him and his companions and exchanging the usual salutation, "How," with the new arrivals, I observed that the Indians who had been occupying a retired position had joined the group, and I found myself in the midst of about twenty chiefs and warriors. Medicine Arrow exhibited the most earnest desire to learn from me the number of troops following me. Whether this question was prompted by any contemplated act of treachery in case my followers were few in number, or not, I do not know. But if treachery was thought of, the idea was abandoned when I informed him that my followers numbered fifteen hundred men, the advance guard being then in sight. Medicine Arrow then informed me that his village was near by, and that the women and children would be greatly excited and alarmed by the approach of so large a body of troops. To give assurance to them he urged me to accompany him to his village in advance of the troops, and by my presence

553

satisfy his people that no attack upon them would be made. This I consented to do.

By this time Colonel Cooke had again joined me, also Dr. Lippincott. Leaving the doctor with directions for the troops, and taking Colonel Cooke with me, I started with Medicine Arrow and a considerable party of his warriors to the village, Medicine Arrow urging us to put our horses to the gallop. The reader may regard this movement on my part as having been anything but prudent, and I will admit that viewed in the ordinary light it might seem to partake somewhat of a foolhardy errand. But I can assure them that no one could be more thoroughly convinced of the treachery and bloodthirsty disposition of the Indian than I am, nor would I ever trust life in their hands except it was to their interest to preserve that life; for no class of beings act so much from self-interest as the Indian, and on this occasion I knew, before accepting the proposal of the chief to enter his village, that he and every member of his band felt it to be to their interest not only to protect me from harm, but to treat me with every consideration, as the near approach of the troops and the formidable number of the latter would deter the Indians from any act of hostility, knowing as they did that in case of an outbreak of any kind it would be impossible for a great portion of the village, particularly the women and children, to escape. I considered all this before proceeding to the village.

As we were turning our horses' heads in the direction of the village I caught sight of a familiar face in the group of Indians about me; it was that of Mah-wis-sa, the squaw whom I had sent as peace commissioner from our camp near Fort Sill, and who had failed to return. She recognized me at once and laughed when I uttered the word *Mutah-ka* referring to the hunting-knife I had loaned her as she was about to depart on her errand of peace. A brisk gallop soon brought us to the village, which was located beneath the trees on the bank of a beautiful stream of clear running water. The name of the latter I found to be the Sweetwater; it is one of the tributaries of Red River, and is indicated on the map as crossing the 100th meridian not far south of the Canadian River.

Medicine Arrow hurried me to his lodge, which was located almost in the center of the village, the latter being the most extensive I had ever seen. As soon as I had entered the lodge I was invited to a seat on one of the many buffalo robes spread on the ground about the inner circumference of the lodge. By Medicine Arrow's direction the village crier in a loud tone of voice began calling the chiefs together in council. No delay occurred in their assembling. One by one they approached and entered the lodge until fifteen of the leading chiefs had taken their seats in the circle within the lodge in the order of their rank. I was assigned the post of honor, being seated on the right of Medicine Arrow, while on my immediate right sat the medicine man of the tribe, an official scarcely second in influence to the head chief.

The squaw of Medicine Arrow built a huge fire in the center of the lodge. As soon as all the chiefs had assembled, the ceremonies, which were different from any I ever witnessed before or since, began. The chiefs sat in silence while the medicine man drew forth from a capacious buckskin tobacco pouch, profusely ornamented with beads and porcupine quills, a large red clay pipe, with a stem about the size of an ordinary walking-stick. From another buckskin pouch which hung at his girdle he drew forth a handful of kinnikinick,[49] and placed it on a

[49] Kinnikinick, the Indian substitute for tobacco, was commonly the inner bark of the red willow. In different tribes, and dependent upon the exigencies of

cloth spread on the ground before him; to this he added, in various amounts, dried leaves and herbs, with which he seemed well supplied. After thoroughly mixing these ingredients, he proceeded with solemn ceremony to fill the pipe with the mixture, muttering at times certain incantations, by which no doubt it was intended to neutralize any power or proclivity for harm I may have been supposed to possess.

To all of this I was a silent but far from disinterested spectator. My interest perceptibly increased when the medicine man, who was sitting close to me, extended his left hand and grasped my right, pressing it strongly against his body over the region of his heart, at the same time and with complete devoutness of manner engaging in what seemed to me a petition or prayer to

the moment, however, the bark of any one of a variety of trees, or dry leaves of plants, might be used. Frequently, too, as in the present instance, the substance thus employed was mixed with actual tobacco, if any of the latter was available. Mrs Custer stated: "It is a mixture of willow bark, sumac leaves, sage leaf and tobacco, and this is thoroughly mingled with marrow from buffalo bones." *Following the Guidon*, 101. George B. Grinnell, author of *The Fighting Cheyennes*, who obtained the Indian version of this council, states that, unknown to Custer, Medicine Arrow was placing a curse upon him.

557

the Great Spirit; the other chiefs from time
to time ejaculating, in the most earnest manner, their responses, the latter being made
simultaneously. To the Indians it was a
most solemn occasion, and scarcely less impressive to me, who could only judge of what
was transpiring by catching an occasional
word and by closely following their signs.

After the conclusion of the address or
prayer by the medicine man the latter released my hand, which up to this time had
been tightly grasped in his, and taking the
long clay pipe in both hands, it likewise was
apparently placed under an imaginary po-
tent spell by a ceremony almost as long as
that which I have just described. This being
ended, the medicine man, first pointing slowly with the stem of the pipe to each of the
four points of the compass, turned to me
and without even so much as saying,
"Smoke, sir?" placed the mouthpiece of the
long stem in my mouth, still holding the
bowl of the pipe in his hand.

Again taking my right hand in his left,
the favor or protecting influence of the Great
Spirit was again invoked in the most earnest
and solemn manner, the other chiefs joining
at regular intervals with their responses.
Finally, releasing my hand, the medicine
man lighted a match, and applying it to

the pipe made signs to me to smoke. A desire to conform as far as practicable to the wishes of the Indians and a curiosity to study a new and interesting phase of the Indian character prompted me to obey the direction of the medicine man, and I accordingly began puffing away with as great a degree of nonchalance as a man unaccustomed to smoking could well assume. Now being, as I have just stated, one of that class which does not number smoking among its accomplishments, I took the first few whiffs with a degree of confidence which I felt justified in assuming, as I imagined the smoking portion of the ceremony was to be the same as usually observed among Indians so devoted to the practice, in which each individual takes the pipe, enjoys half a dozen whiffs, and passes it to his next neighbor on his left. That much I felt equal to; but when, after blowing away the first half dozen puffs of smoke from my face, the medicine man still retained his hold of the pipe, with an evident desire that I should continue the enjoyment of this Indian luxury, I proceeded more deliberately, although no such rule of restraint seemed to govern the volubility of the medicine man, whose invocation and chants continued with unabated vigor and rapidity.

When the first minute had added to itself four more, and still I was expected to
make a miniature volcano of myself, minus
the ashes, I began to grow solicitous as to
what might be the effect if I was subjected
to this course of treatment. I pictured to
myself the commander of an important expedition seated in solemn council with a
score and a half of dusky chieftains, the
pipe of peace being passed, and before it had
left the hands of the aforesaid commander,
he becoming deathly sick, owing to lack of
familiarity with the noxious weed or its sub-
stitutes. I imagined the sudden termination
of the council, the absurdity of the figure
cut, and the contempt of the chiefs for one
who must, under the circumstances, appear
so deficient in manly accomplishments.
These and a hundred similar ideas flashed
through my mind as I kept pulling vigorously at the pipe, and wondering when this
thing would terminate.

Fortunately for my peace of body as well
as of mind, after a period which seemed to
me equal to a quarter of an hour at least, I
felt relieved by the medicine man taking the
pipe from my mouth, and after refilling it
handing it to the head chief, sitting on my
left, who, drawing three or four long, silent
whiffs, passed it to his next neighbor on his

left; and in similar manner it made the circle of the chiefs until it finally returned to the medicine man, who, after taking a few final whiffs, laid it aside, much to my relief, as I feared the consequences of a repetition of my former effort.

Romeo, the interpreter, having been mounted upon an indifferent animal, had fallen to the rear of the column during the march that day and I was deprived of his services during my interview with the chief. Colonel Cooke, during this time, was in an adjoining lodge, each moment naturally becoming more solicitous lest upon the arrival of the troops there should be a collision between the Indians and the excited volunteers. To the inquiries of the chiefs I explained the object of our march without alluding to the two captive girls, the time not having arrived for discussing that subject. Having resolved to obtain the release of the captives, all other purposes were necessarily laid aside; and as I knew that the captives could not be released should hostilities once occur between the troops and Indians, I became for the time being an ardent advocate of peace measures, and informed the chiefs that such was my purpose at the time. I also requested them to inform me where I would find the most suitable camping ground in the vicinity of the village, to which request Medicine Arrow replied that he would accompany me in person and point out the desired ground.

When this offer was made I accepted it as a kindness, but when the chief conducted me to a camp ground separated from the village and from all view of the latter I had reason to modify my opinion of his pretended kindness, particularly when coupled with his subsequent conduct. My command soon came up and was conducted to the camp ground indicated by Medicine Arrow, the distance between the camp and the village not exceeding three-fourths of a mile. I was still uncertain as to whether there were any grounds to doubt that the two white girls were captives in Medicine Arrow's village. I anxiously awaited the arrival of Mo-nah-see-tah, who could and would solve this question. She came with the main body of the troops and I at once informed her whose village it was alongside of which we were located.

To my inquiry as to whether the two white girls were prisoners in Medicine Arrow's village she promptly replied in the affirmative, and at the same time exhibited a desire to aid as far as possible in effecting their release. It was still early in the afternoon and I did not deem it necessary, or even advisable, to proceed with undue haste in the negotiations by which I expected to bring about the release of the two captives. Although our camp, as already explained, was cut off from a view of the village, yet I had provided against either surprise or strategem by posting some of my men on prominent points near by from which they obtained a full view of both our camp and the village and thus rendered it impossible for any important movement to take place in the latter without being seen. I felt confident that as soon as it was dark the entire village would probably steal away and leave us in the lurch; but I proposed to make my demand for the surrender of the captives long before darkness should aid the Indians in eluding us.

From fifty to one hundred chiefs, warriors, and young men were assembled at my headquarters, or about the camp fire built in front of headquarters. Apparently they were there from motives of mere curiosity, but later developments proved they had another object in view. Finally Medicine Arrow came to my camp, accompanied by some of his head men, and after shaking hands with apparent cordiality stated that some of his young men, desirous of manifesting their friendship for us, would visit our camp in a few minutes and entertain us by a serenade. This idea was a novel one to me, and I awaited the arrival of the serenaders with no little curiosity.

Before their arrival, however, my lookouts reported unusual commotion and activity in the Indian village. The herd of the latter had been called in, and officers sent by me to investigate this matter confirmed the report and added that everything indicated a contemplated flight on the part of the Indians. I began then to comprehend the object of the proposed serenade; it was to occupy our attention while the village could pack up and take flight. Pretending ignorance of what was transpiring in the village, I continued to converse, through Romeo, with the chiefs, until the arrival of the Indian musicians. ·These, numbering about a dozen young men, were mounted on ponies which, like themselves, were ornamented in the highest degree, according to Indian fashion. The musicians were feathered and painted in the most horrible as well as fantastic manner. Their instruments consisted of reeds, the sounds from which more nearly resembled those of the fife than any other, although there was a total lack of harmony between the various

Further Cheyenne Pursuit

pieces. As soon as the musicians arrived they began riding in a gallop in a small circle, of which circle our little group, composed of a few officers and the chiefs, composed the center. The display of horsemanship was superb, and made amends for the discordant sounds given forth as music.

During all this time reports continued to come in leaving no room to doubt that the entire village was preparing to decamp. To have opposed this movement by a display of force on the part of the troops would have only precipitated a terrible conflict, for which I was not yet prepared, keeping in mind the rescue of the white girls. I did not propose, however, to relinquish the advantage we then had by our close proximity to the village and permit the latter to place several miles between us.

Knowing that the musicians would soon depart and with them perhaps the chiefs and warriors then grouped about my camp fire, I determined to seize the principal chiefs then present, permit the village to depart if necessary, and hold the captured chiefs as hostages for the surrender of the white girls and the future good behavior of the tribe. This was a move requiring not only promptness but most delicate and careful handling in order to avoid bloodshed. Quiet-

565

ly passing the word to a few of the officers who sat near me around the camp fire, I directed them to leave the group one by one and in such manner as not to attract the attention of the Indians proceed to their companies and select quickly some of their most reliable men, instructing the latter to assemble around and near my camp fire, well armed, as if merely attracted there by the Indian serenade. The men thus selected were to come singly, appear as unconcerned as possible, and be in readiness to act promptly, but to do nothing without orders from me.

In this manner about one hundred of my men were in an inconceivably short space of time mingled with the Indians, who, to the number of forty or more, sat or stood about my camp fire, laughing in their sleeves (had they not been minus these appendages), no doubt, at the clever dodge by which they were entertaining the white men while their village was hastening preparations for a speedy flight. When the musicians had apparently exhausted their program, they took their departure, informing us that later in the evening they would return and repeat the performance; they might have added, "with an entire change of program."

Further Cheyenne Pursuit

After their departure the conversation continued with the chiefs until, by glancing about me, I saw that a sufficient number of my men had mingled with the Indians to answer my purpose. Of the forty or more Indians in the group there were but few chiefs, the majority being young men or boys. My attention was devoted to the chiefs, and acting upon the principle that for the purposes desired half a dozen would be as valuable as half a hundred, I determined to seize the principal chiefs then present and permit the others to depart. To do this without taking or losing life now became the problem.

Indicating in a quiet manner to some of my men who were nearest to me to be ready to prevent the escape of three or four of the Indians whom I pointed out, I then directed Romeo to command silence on the part of the Indians and to inform them that I was about to communicate something of great importance to them. This was sufficient to attract their undivided attention. I then rose from my seat near the fire and unbuckling my revolver from my waist asked the Indians to observe that I threw my weapons upon the ground as an evidence that in what I was about to do I did not desire or propose to shed blood unless forced to do so. I then asked the chiefs to look about them and count the armed men whom I had posted among and around them, completely cutting off every avenue of escape. They had attempted, under pretense of a friendly visit to my camp, to deceive me, in order that their village might elude us, but their designs had been frustrated and they were now in our power. I asked them to quietly submit to what was now inevitable, and promised them that if they and their people responded in the proper manner to the reasonable demands which I intended to make all would be well and they would be restored to their people.

The reader must not imagine that this was listened to in tame silence by the thoroughly excited Indians, old and young. Upon the first intimation from me regarding the armed men and before I could explain their purpose every Indian who was dismounted sprang instantly to his feet, while those who were mounted gathered the reins of their ponies; all drew their revolvers or strung their bows, and for a few moments it seemed as if nothing could avert a collision, which could only terminate in the annihilation of the Indians and an equal or perhaps greater loss on our part. A single shot fired, an indiscreet word uttered, would have been the signal to commence. My men behaved admirably, taking their positions in such manner that each Indian was confronted by at least two men. All this time the Indians were gesticulating and talking in the most excited manner; the boys and young men counselling resistance, the older men and chiefs urging prudence until an understanding could be had.

The powers of Romeo as interpreter were employed without stint in repeating to the chiefs my urgent appeals to restrain their young men and avoid bloodshed. Even at this date I recall no more exciting experience with Indians than the occasion of which I now write. Near me stood a tall, gray-haired chief, who, while entreating his people to be discreet, kept his cocked revolver in his hand ready for use, should the emergency demand it. He was one of the few whom I had determined to hold. Near him stood another, a most powerful and forbidding-looking warrior, who was without firearms, but who was armed with a bow already strung and a quiver full of iron-pointed arrows. His coolness during this scene of danger and excitement was often the subject of remark afterward between the officers whose attention had been drawn to him. He stood apparently unaffected by

the excitement about him, but not unmindful of the surrounding danger. Holding his
bow in one hand, with the other he continued to draw from his quiver arrow after
arrow. Each one he would examine as cool-
ly as if he expected to engage in target
practice. First he would cast his eye along
the shaft of the arrow, to see if it was perfectly straight and true. Then he would
with thumb and finger gently feel the point
and edge of the barbed head, returning to
the quiver each one whose condition did not
satisfy him.

In this manner he continued until he had
selected perhaps half a dozen arrows with
which he seemed satisfied, and which he retained in his hand, while his quick eye did
not permit a single incident about him to
escape unnoticed. The noise of voices and
the excitement increased until a movement
began on the part of the Indians who were
mounted, principally the young men and
boys. If the latter could be allowed to escape and the chiefs be retained, the desired
object would be gained. Suddenly a rush
was made. But for the fact that my men
were ordered not to fire, the attempt of the
Indians would not have been successful. I,
as well as the other officers near me, called
upon the men not to fire. The result was

that all but four broke through the lines
and made their escape. The four detained,
however, were those desired, being chiefs
and warriors of prominence.

Forming my men about them in such impassable ranks that a glance was sufficient
to show how futile all further efforts to escape would prove, I then explained to the
four captive Indians that I knew the design
under which they had visited our camp;
that I also knew that in their village were
held as captives two white girls whose release the troops were there to enforce, and
to effect their release, as well as to compel
the Cheyennes to abandon the war path
and return to their reservation, I had seized
the four Indians as hostages. To prove my
sincerity and earnest desire to arrange these
matters amicably and without resort to
force the Indians were told they might select
one of their number whom I would release
and send as a messenger of peace to the
village, the latter having left in indiscrimi-
nate flight as soon as the seizure of the
chiefs was made.

It became a matter of great difficulty
without the employment of force to induce
the four Indians to give up their arms. I
explained to them that they were prisoners,
and it was one of our customs to disarm all

men held as prisoners. Should they be released, however, I assured them their arms would be restored to them. No argument could prevail upon them to relinquish their arms until I stated to them that a persistence in their refusal would compel me to summon a sufficient number of men to take the arms by force; and it was even necessary to parade the men in front of them before the arms were finally given up. After a lengthy conference with each other they announced that they had agreed upon one of their number who, in accordance with my promise, should be released and sent to the tribe as bearer of my demands and of any messages they might desire to send to their people.

I accordingly caused bountiful presents of coffee and sugar to be given the one so chosen, returned to him his pony and arms, and intrusted him with verbal messages to his tribe, the substance of which was as follows: First, I demanded the unconditional surrender of the two white girls held captive in the village; hitherto surrenders of white captives by Indians had only been made on payment of heavy ransom. Second, I required the Cheyenne village, as an evidence of peaceable intentions and good faith on their part, to proceed at once to their reservation and to locate near Camp Supply, reporting to the military commander at that station. Third, I sent a friendly message to Little Robe, inviting him to visit me with a view to the speedy settlement of the questions at issue, promising him unmolested transit coming and returning for him and as many of his people as chose to visit me. In case of failure to comply with the first two of my demands hostilities would be continued, and my command would at once commence the pursuit of the village, which, considering its size and the poor condition of the ponies at that early season of the year, would be unable to escape from the cavalry.

The Indian who was to go as bearer of these demands was also invited to return, assured that whether the response of his people should prove favorable or not he should be granted a safe-conduct between the camp and the village. Inwardly congratulating himself, no doubt, upon the good fortune which gave him his liberty, the messenger of peace or war, as his tribe might elect, took his departure for his village. With him went the earnest wishes for success of every inmate of the camp; but if this was the feeling of the command generally, who can realize the intense interest and

573

anxiety with which young Brewster now awaited the result of this effort to secure the freedom of his sister? And if the two forlorn, helpless girls knew of the presence of troops of their own race, what must have been the bitter despondency, the painful relinquishment of all hope as they saw the village and its occupants commencing a hasty flight and no apparent effort upon the part of the troops to effect their release?

What comfort it would have been to these ill-fated maidens could they have known, before being hurried from the village, of the steps already taken to restore them to home and friends, or better still if one of them could have known that almost within the sound of her voice a brother was patiently but determinedly biding the time that should restore his sister to his arms.

Chapter 17

RELYING upon the influence which I believed Little Robe would exert upon his people, and knowing the pressure we were able to bring to bear through the three chiefs we held as hostages, I felt confident that sooner or later the Cheyennes would be forced to release the two white girls from their captivity. Placing a strong guard over the three chiefs, and warning them not to attempt to escape if they valued their lives, I returned to my tent after having ordered every comfort possible to be provided for our prisoners consistent with their position.

It was perhaps an hour or more after dark when an Indian voice was heard calling from one of the hillocks overlooking the camp. I proceeded to the guard fire near which the three chiefs were still seated engaged in conversation and through Romeo inquired who the parties were whose voices we heard, and their object. They informed me that the voices were those of some of their young men who were anxious to ascertain if their friends, the captives, were still alive. Anxious that they should not only see that their friends were alive, but well treated, I desired to induce them to come within our lines and visit the captive chiefs. This was communicated to them through the chiefs, who called to them in tones capable of being heard far beyond the point at which the young Indians were posted. But this did not satisfy their suspicious natures; they imagined some trap, and declined to accept the invitation. Romeo, the only one who could converse freely in the Indian tongue, might have been able to persuade them to come in, but it was not safe for him to venture beyond the line of our pickets and trust himself in the power of the young Indians.

In this emergency I thought of Mo-nah-see-tah, in whom I had every confidence, and who I believed might be successful in inducing her friends to come in. Sending for her, I soon acquainted her with my plan to which she gave her ready assent, only expressing an apprehension that in passing our own chain of sentries in the darkness they might mistake her for an enemy and fire upon her. This difficulty I removed by offering to escort her safely through the line of pickets and there await her return. Starting at once in the darkness, she clinging to my hand with the natural timidity of a girl, we proceeded to the picket station nearest to the point from which the sound of voices had come and after explaining to the sentry our purpose, passed beyond as far as it was prudent to do, and then, bidding Mo-nah-see-tah to proceed on her mission, I halted to await her return. A few moments later I heard her voice in the darkness calling to her friends beyond; back came the quick response, and soon after I could distinguish the tones of the assembled group as Mo-nah-see-tah endeavored to convince them of their security in trusting to the promises made them.

Her arguments finally prevailed over their suspicions, and in the dim light of the stars I could see her returning, accompanied by four or five others. Not caring to tempt them by meeting them alone so far from support, I slowly retired until I was near the picket post. Here the Indians found me and after the form of an introduction by Mo-nah-see-tah and a general hand-shaking the entire party proceeded without hesitation to the guard fire, where they joined their less fortunate chiefs.

It may strike the reader with some surprise that Mo-nah-see-tah, herself a captive in our hands, should have voluntarily returned to us that night after once being

577

safely beyond our lines. But she only confirmed the confidence that was placed in her. During her imprisonment, if her stay in our camp without a guard may be termed imprisonment, she had become a great favorite with the entire command; not only this, but she believed she would in due time be given up to her own people, and that until then she would receive kind treatment at our hands and be exposed to less personal danger and suffering during hostilities than if with her village.

The visit of the young men to our camp that night could not but have a beneficial influence upon the tribe, as they were enabled to see that the three chiefs were being treated with the utmost consideration and were being held, as informed at first, simply as hostages to enforce compliance with demands which even an Indian's ideas of right and wrong must pronounce just. After a lengthy conversation between the captives and their friends the latter took their departure, charged with messages to the village, both from the captive chiefs and me, similar to those transmitted through the chief who had been released for that purpose.

The following day was passed without incident in awaiting the arrival of tidings from the village. Early in the afternoon the pickets reported a small body of Indians in sight. Upon a nearer approach the party appeared to consist of about fifty mounted Indians. They rode steadily in the direction of the camp with no apparent wish to conceal their movements, thus indicating that they were on an errand of peace. When within half a mile or less of camp the entire party dismounted, and after picketing their ponies out to graze, advanced on foot directly toward camp. So strange a proceeding, and at a time when the excitement regarding our relations with the Indians ran high, was sufficient to assemble nearly all the occupants of camp to watch the approach of this delegation of Indians. The latter were apparelled in their best and most highly colored clothes. As they came near it was perceived that several paces in advance of the main group strode two chiefs, evidently leaders of the party; both advanced with uncovered heads. Suddenly I thought I detected a familiar face and form in the taller of the two chiefs in front, and on more careful scrutiny I recognized my former friend and guest, Little Robe, who had thus quickly responded to my invitation to cast aside all doubts and come and visit me with a view to bringing about more friendly relations between his people and the whites.

579

As soon as I recognized him I advanced
to meet him. He grasped my hand and embraced me with what seemed to me real
cordiality. Waiting until the other members
of his party came up, I shook hands with
each individual and then invited them to
my tent. As the tent would not accommodate the entire party Little Robe designated
about a dozen of the most important, who
entered, while the others remained outside.
I soon found that in Little Robe I had a
hearty coadjutor in the work before me.
He admitted that the white girls were held
as captives in the Cheyenne village, which
was the first positive evidence received of
this fact. He also stated, what I had no
reason to doubt, that he had at various times
attempted to purchase them with a view, if
successful, of returning them to the nearest
military post; but his efforts in this direction
had always failed. He admitted the justice
of my demands upon his people and assured
me that to bring about a satisfactory condition of affairs he would use every exertion
and employ all the influence at his command. It was to assure me of this desire
on his part that he had hastened to visit me.

Knowing that the surest and speediest
way to establish a state of good feeling in
an Indian is to provide liberally for the

wants of his stomach, I ordered a beef to be killed and distributed among the followers of Little Robe; with this also were distributed the usual supplies of coffee, sugar, flour, etc., so that the recipients were not only prepared to regard us as at least very kindly disposed, but I knew the effect on the village, when the result of the visit and the treatment extended to our guests was described, would materially aid us in our negotiations with the tribe. Little Robe, while earnest in his desire to see the white girls returned to us, frankly admitted that his influence was not supreme and there were those who would object to their release, at least without compensation; and it might be that a satisfactory settlement of the question might be delayed for many days.

After partaking of a bountiful repast Little Robe and his party set out for the village, promising to send me word the following day as to his success. Another day was passed in waiting, when the chief who had accompanied Little Robe the previous day again visited us, but brought no decisive or satisfactory reply. The substance of the reply was that the Cheyennes desired us to release the three chiefs then held by us as hostages, after which they would be prepared to consider the question of the release of the two white girls. To this I sent back a reply that we would remain in the camp we then occupied until the following day, when, if a favorable answer should not have been received, we would follow on their trail and encamp nearer to the village, the great distance then separating us, about twelve miles, being a hindrance in the way of transmitting messages promptly from one to the other.

I knew that the village was in no condition for a rapid or extended flight, and could be overhauled by the cavalry whenever desired; at the same time, to allow as much freedom in their deliberations as possible, I had not been unwilling that a few miles should separate us. No reply was received; consequently we packed up and marched down the Sweetwater, on the trail of the village, about ten miles and went into camp. Here I received another visit from the chief who had previously acted as diplomatic courier between the camp and village, but the response of the Cheyennes was still unsatisfactory and exhibited a disinclination on their part to make any decided promises respecting the release of the captive white girls. They insisted as preliminary to such decision that the three chiefs held by us should be restored to liberty, after which we might discuss the question relating to the release of the girls.

Successful Ending of Campaign

I will not weary the reader by describing the various subterfuges resorted to by the Indians by which they strove to avoid or delay the surrender of the white girls without first, as had been customary, receiving a ransom. Finally, after I had almost exhausted the patience of the troops, particularly of the Kansas regiment, which had been raised and organized mainly to effect the recapture of the white girls or else avenge the outrage of which they had been the victims, I determined to force matters to an issue without further quibbling on the part of the Indians.

I sent for a delegation of chiefs from the Cheyenne village to receive my ultimatum. They came, and upon their arrival I assembled them in my tent, the three captured chiefs being also permitted to be present, as the conference, as will be seen, was to be of deep interest to them. After recounting to the chiefs the incidents of our pursuit of the village, their surprise at being overtaken, the strategems by which they hoped to elude us, the steps we had already taken to obtain the release of the white girls, and the delays interposed by the Indiáns, I stated that I had but one other message to send to the village; and upon the chiefs of the latter would rest the responsibility of peace or war.

Further delay would not be submitted to on our part. We knew they had two of our race captives in the village, and we were there to demand and enforce the demand for their release, cost what it might. I then informed them that if by sunset the following day the two white girls were not restored to our hands unharmed the lives of the three chiefs would be forfeited and the troops would resume active hostilities.

At the same time I called attention to the fact that in the famished condition of their ponies they could not expect to escape the pursuit of the cavalry. Every argument which might have weight in influencing a favorable decision was stated to them. The conference then broke up and the three chiefs were remanded to the custody of the guard. The delegation from the village, after a brief interview with their captive comrades, took a hasty departure and set out upon their return to the village, deeply impressed, apparently, with the importance of promptness in communicating to the chiefs at the village the decision which had been arrived at regarding the captives. The terms given to the Indians soon became known to every individual in the command, and naturally excited the deepest interest. All hoped for a favorable issue, but no one regarded the events then transpiring with the intense interest and anxiety felt by young Brewster, who now saw that his long-cherished hope to recover his sister was either about to be realized, or forever sealed in disappointment.

The captive chiefs did not pretend to conceal their solicitude as to the part they were involuntarily made to play in the events then transpiring. I did not expect prompt action on the part of the chiefs in the village. I knew they would practise every delay conceivable before complying with our demands; but when the question was forced upon them as to whether they preferred to deliver up the white girls to us or to force, by their refusal, the execution of the three chiefs, their decision would be in favor of their people.

Three o'clock arrived, and no tidings from the village. By this time the officers and men of the command had assembled near headquarters and upon the small eminences near by, eagerly watching the horizon in the direction of the village to catch the first glimpse of the messengers who must soon arrive to avert the execution of the three chiefs. Even the three chiefs became despondent as the sun slowly but surely approached the horizon, and no tidings from the village reached them. Finally, Romeo came to me and stated that the three chiefs desired to see me. I repaired to their place of confinement at once and was asked by the younger of the three if it was my firm purpose to make good my words in the event of the failure of their people to release the white girls. I replied in the affirmative. The chief then attempted a little Indian diplomacy by assuring me that in the village and among his own people he was a man of great consequence and could exert a wide influence; for this reason he requested me to release him and he would hasten to the village, obtain the release of the two girls, and return in time to save his two companions.

When this proposition was first made I attributed it to fear that the chiefs in the village might decline to restore the two girls to liberty and the lives of the three chiefs would be sacrificed thereby; but subsequent events proved that while this consideration may have had its influence, the principal motive which prompted the proposition was a desire to escape from our hands before the white girls should be restored to us, as the chief referred to had been a party to their capture and to the subsequent ill treatment they had received. I replied to his proposal that if he was of such importance in his tribe as he claimed to be he was the most proper

586

person for me to retain possession of, as his people would be more likely to accede to my demands to save his life than that of a person of less consequence.

The sun was perhaps an hour high when the dim outlines of about twenty mounted figures were discerned against the horizon, on a high hill two or three miles to the west of us. Instantly all eyes were directed to the party, but the distance was too great to enable any of us to clearly define either the number or character of the group. The eyes of the three chiefs perceptibly brightened with hope. Securing my field glass, I carefully scanned the party on the hill. Every one about me waited in anxious suspense the result of my examination. Gradually, under the magnifying powers of the glass I was able to make out the figures in sight. I could only determine at first that the group was, as might be imagined, composed of Indians, and began counting them audibly, when I discovered two figures mounted upon the same pony.

As soon as this was announced several of my companions at once exclaimed: "Can they be the girls?" I could detect nothing, however, in their appearance warranting such a conclusion, their dress apparently being the same as that of the other individuals of the group. While endeavoring to make out something more definite in regard to the party I saw the two figures descend from the pony and, leaving the rest of the group, advance toward us on foot. All this I reported to the anxious bystanders, who became now more than ever convinced that the two figures approaching must be the two girls. I began describing the appearance of the two as well as I could with the aid of the glass: "One seems to have a short, heavy figure; the other is considerably taller and more slender." Young Brewster, who stood at my side, immediately responded, "The last one must be my sister; she is quite tall. Let me go and meet them; this anxiety is more than I can endure." But this I declined, fearing that should one of the two now approaching us prove to be his sister, seeing her in the forlorn condition in which she must be might provoke young Brewster beyond control, and induce him to attempt to obtain revenge in a manner not governed by either prudence or propriety. So I reluctantly declined to permit him to advance beyond our lines. But by this time the two figures had approached near enough to enable me clearly to determine that they were really of white complexion and undoubtedly the two girls whose release we were so impatiently waiting for.

Successful Ending of Campaign

As the Kansas volunteers had left their homes and various occupations in civil life to accomplish, among other results, the release of the two girls who had been abducted from the frontier of their State, I deemed it appropriate that that regiment should be the first to welcome the two released captives to friends and freedom. Accordingly, the three senior officers of the regiment were designated to proceed beyond our lines and conduct the two girls to camp, a duty whose performance carried its pleasure with it. The three officers advanced to meet the two figures (I use the term figures, as the dress was of that nondescript pattern which renders this term most appropriate). They had passed one-fourth of the distance, perhaps, when young Brewster, whom I had detained at my side with difficulty, bounded away and the next moment was running at full speed to greet his long-lost sister. Dashing past the three officers, he clasped in his arms the taller of the two girls. This told us all we had hoped for. We awaited their approach, and as they drew near to the little brook which flowed just beyond the point occupied by the group of officers around me, I stepped forward, and extending my hands to the two girls bade them a hearty welcome to liberty. In a moment officers and men were struggling about them upon all sides, eager to take them by the hand and testify the great joy felt at their deliverance from a life of captivity.

Men whom I have seen face death without quailing found their eyes filled with tears, unable to restrain the deep emotion produced by this joyful event. The appearance of the two girls was sufficient to excite our deepest sympathy. Miss White, the younger of the two, though not beautiful, possessed a most interesting face. Her companion would have been pronounced beautiful by the most critical judge, being of such a type as one might imagine Maud Müller to be.

Their joy at their deliverance, however, could not hide the evidences of privation and suffering to which they had been subjected by their cruel captors. They were clothed in dresses made from flour sacks, the brand of the mills being plainly seen on each dress; showing that the Indians who had held them in captivity had obtained their provisions from the Government at some agency. The entire dress of the two girls was as nearly like the Indian mode as possible; both wore leggings and moccasins; both wore their hair in two long braids, and as if to propitiate us, the Indians, before releasing them, had added to the wardrobe of the two girls various rude ornaments, such as are worn by squaws. About their wrists they wore coils of brass wire; on their fingers had been placed numerous rings, and about their necks strings of variously colored beads. Almost the first remark I heard young Brewster make after the arrival of the two girls was: "Sister, do take those hateful things off."

Fortunately they were not the only white women in camp. I had a white woman as cook, and to enable the two girls to improve their wardrobe a little before relating to us the history of their capture and captivity they were conducted to the tent of the white woman referred to, from whose limited wardrobe they were able to obtain enough to replace the dresses made of flour sacks, and in a few minutes reappeared presenting a much more civilized appearance than when they first entered camp.

In a previous chapter I have given the main incidents of their capture. The story of their captivity was that of hundreds of other women and girls whose husbands, fathers, or brothers take their lives in their hands and seek homes on the frontier. There was much in their story not appropriate for these pages. They described how great their joy was at encountering each other for the first time as prisoners in the hands of the

591

Indians. They had been traded repeatedly
from the hands of one chief to those of
another, the last transfer having been effected only two weeks prior to their release.
Soon after their first meeting it was their
good fortune, comparatively, to become the
property of one chief. This threw them into
each other's society and tended to lighten
the horrors of their captivity. While thrown
together in this manner they planned an
escape. Their plan, it seems, was more the
result of desperation than of careful deliberation, as they had no idea as to what state
or territory the village was then in, nor in
what direction to travel should they escape
from the village. Indeed, one of their first
questions on entering our lines was to ask in
what part of the country we were.

Determining at all hazards, however, to
flee from their captors at the first opportunity and trust to chance to lead them to
the settlements or to some military post, they
escaped from the village one night and travelled for several hours in a northerly direction. During this attempt to regain their
liberty they reached a wagon road over
which wagons and horses had passed recently and were congratulating themselves upon
the success of their effort, when a bullet
whistled past them and in close proximity

to them. Casting an anxious look, they saw to their horror and disappointment, their late captor or owner riding at full speed in pursuit. Escape was impossible. Nothing remained but to await the arrival of the chief, who came up excited with savage rage at the idea of their attempt to escape him.

Marching back on foot to the village, they became the recipients of renewed insults and taunts. Nor did it end here. The squaws of the village, always jealous of white women when captives, took this opportunity to treat them with the greatest severity for their attempt to regain their liberty. The old chief, also, decided upon a change of program. He had invested several ponies when he became the possessor of the two girls and he did not propose to risk the loss of this property. So he determined to separate the two girls by selling one of them, and the two friends in misfortune were torn from each other. Miss White, in consideration of three ponies given in exchange, passed into the hands of another chief, whose lodge was generally located some miles from that of her late master.

The story of the two girls, containing accounts of wrongs and ill treatment sufficient to have ended the existence of less determined persons, is too long to be given here.

Besides indignities and insults far more terrible than death itself, the physical suffering
to which the two girls were subjected was too
great almost to be believed. They were required to transport huge burdens on their
backs, large enough to have made a load for
a beast of burden. They were limited to
barely enough food to sustain life; sometimes
a small morsel of mule meat not more than
an inch square was their allowance of food
for twenty-four hours. The squaws beat
them unmercifully with clubs whenever the
men were not present. Upon one occasion
one of the girls was felled to the ground by a
blow from a club in the hands of one of the
squaws. Their joy, therefore, at regaining
their freedom after a captivity of nearly a
year can be better imagined than described;
while that of the brother who had struggled
so long and determinedly to regain his sister
could not be expressed in words.

After the momentary excitement consequent upon the safe arrival of the girls in
camp had subsided, officers, particularly of
the Kansas volunteers, came to me with the
remark that when we first overtook the
Cheyenne village and I failed to order an
attack when all the chances were in our favor,
they mentally condemned my decision as a
mistake; but with the results accomplished

afterwards they found ample reason to amend their first judgment and frankly and cordially admit that the release of the two captives was far more gratifying than any victory over the Indians could have been if purchased by the sacrifice of their lives.

With this happy temination of this much of our negotiations with the Indians, I determined to march in the morning for Camp Supply, Indian Territory, satisfied that with the three chiefs in our possession and the squaws and children captured at the Washita still held as prisoners at Fort Hays, Kansas, we could compel the Cheyennes to abandon the war path and return to their reservation. The three chiefs begged to be released, upon the ground that their people had delivered up the two girls; but this I told them was but one of the two conditions imposed; the other required the tribe to return to their reservation and until this was done they need not hope for freedom; but in the meanwhile I assured them of kind treatment at our hands.

Before dark a delegation of chiefs from the village visited camp to likewise urge the release of the three chiefs. My reply to them was the same as that I had given to the captives. I assured them, however, that upon complying with their treaty obligations, and returning to their reservation the three chiefs

595

would be restored to their people and we
would return to them also the women and
children captured at the Washita. Seeing
that no modification of these terms could be
obtained, they finally promised to accede to
them, saying that their ponies, as I knew to
be the fact, were in no condition to travel,
but as soon as practicable they would surely
proceed with their entire village to Camp
Supply and abandon the war path forever; a
promise which, as a tribe, they have adhered
to from that day to this with strict faith, so
far as my knowledge extends.[50]

[50]Custer's last campaign on the Southern Plains,
whose recital concludes at this point, was a remarkable
performance which deserves far greater renown than
has ever been accorded it. In its conduct he displayed
a complete mastery of Indian psychology and of the art
of frontier warfare. If even a tithe of the attention that
has been accorded his final defeat at the Little Big Horn
were devoted to this campaign his reputation would
profit enormously.

The regrettable fact remains that despite the data
supplied in his own report and elsewhere it is impossible
to identify his route, save in broad outline. Perhaps
the general reader will be satisfied with the statement
that he proceeded westwardly and northwardly from
Fort Sill into the Texas Panhandle and after an extensive circuitous march over the area lying eastward of
Amarillo eventually rejoined the remainder of his command (which he had detached at the crossing of North
Fork of Red River early in the campaign) at the
Washita battleground near Cheyenne, Oklahoma, on

Successful Ending of Campaign

I had not heard from General Sheridan since we separated at Fort Sill; he to set out for Camp Supply and I with my command to begin my present movement. But when near Camp Supply a courier met me with despatches from General Sheridan, who had been meanwhile summoned to Washington, informing me in regard to the arrangements made for my command upon its arrival at Camp Supply. The Kansas volunteers were

March 23. In exactly three weeks he had executed a march of hundreds of miles through an arid wilderness, had found and, without fighting a battle, had completely subdued the hostile Cheyennes, and had rescued from impending death the two captive girls.

The difficulty encountered in identifying Custer's route is due in part to the fact that it led across the open Plains, bereft of recognizable landmarks, but even more to the contemporary imperfect geographical knowledge of the area and the easy habit of calling the rivers encountered "sweet," "sandy," "salt," etc. Even the location of Medicine Arrow's village, high point of the entire campaign, is problematical. Professor Carl C. Rister, outstanding scholar in southwestern history, doubts that any living person can trace the route followed by the cavalry, and ventures the guess that Custer's "Sweetwater" where the Cheyenne village was found may have been a southerly tributary of North Fork of Red River in southwestern Gray County. My own tentative plotting (See map, page 2) of Custer's route, although based upon as careful study of the sources as I have been able to make, undertakes to do no more than to visualize for the reader the general area in which the campaign was waged.

597

to march to Fort Hays and there be mustered out of the service. The Seventh Cavalry was also to proceed to the same point and there await further orders, as the General in his note stated that he had concluded to draw in the Seventh and end the campaign.

In reply to my letter, written subsequently from Camp Supply, giving him a detailed account of our operations, including the release of the two white girls, I received a letter of warm encouragement from the General, written from Chicago, where he had just established his present headquarters. In that letter he wrote: "I am very much rejoiced at the success of your expedition, and feel proud of our winter's operations and of the officers and men who have borne its privations and hardships so manfully. . . . Give my kind regards to the officers, and say how happy I should be to see them should any of them come this way on leave." These words of hearty sympathy and approval from one who had not only shared but appreciated at their true worth our "privations and hardships," were far more cheering and valued than the empty honor contained in half a dozen brevets bestowed grudgingly and recalled in a moment of pique.

Making a brief halt at Camp Supply to rest our animals and replenish our stores, my command continued its march to Fort Hays, crossing the Arkansas River at Fort Dodge, Kansas. Upon our arrival at Fort Hays we were met by the husband of young Brewster's sister, who had learned of her restoration to liberty from the published despatches which had preceded us to Fort Hays. He was still lame from the effects of the bullet wound received at the time the Indians carried off his bride, whom he had given up as dead or lost to him forever. The joy of their meeting went far to smooth over their late sorrow. They could not find language to express their gratitude to the troops for their efforts in restoring them to each other. As the Indians had robbed them of everything at the time of the attack, a collection was taken up among the troops for their benefit, which resulted in the accumulation of several hundred dollars, to be divided between the two captives. The time came for our guests to leave us and rejoin their people, or such of them as had survived the attack of the Indians. Goodbys were spoken and the two girls, so lately victims of the most heartless and cruel captivity, departed with husband, brother, and friends for their frontier homes, bearing with them the warm sympathies and cordial good wishes of every soldier in the command.

599

Mo-nah-see-tah was anxious to visit her friends who were now captives at Fort Hays, and who were kept in a large stockade at the post, our camp being placed some two or three miles below the post. Accordingly she repaired to the stockade and spent several hours relating, no doubt, the story of our march since they had separated from each other. She preferred to live in the cavalry camp, where she was allowed to roam without the restraint of a guard; but it was deemed advisable soon after to place her with the other women and children inside the stockade.

The three captive chiefs were also transferred to the same place for safe keeping. Here a most unfortunate misunderstanding arose. The chiefs had been confined inside the same enclosure with the women and children, but in separate tents. The commanding officer of the post decided to remove them to rooms in the guardhouse, adjoining the stockade. This was decided upon as a measure of security. There was no interpreter kept at the post; consequently there was no way of communicating with the Indians except by rude signs, and even this method was but indifferently understood by the infantry soldiers constituting the garrison of the post. From accounts given me by the Indians afterwards, it seems the men of the guard, in the execution of the order to transfer the three chiefs, entered the stockade muskets in hand, and upon the failure of the chiefs to comprehend what was required of them the soldiers attempted to push the chiefs from the stockade by force, pointing with their bayonets to the outside. The chiefs, failing to understand a word spoken to them, and with the natural suspicion of their race, imagined that they were being led or driven forth to execution and determined to die there and then. An attack was at once made upon the guard with knives which they carried beneath their blankets. The sergeant of the guard received a stab in the back which almost proved mortal. This was the signal for a determined fight between the three chiefs and the guard, the latter having the decided advantage in numbers and weapons. The result could not be long doubtful. One of the chiefs, Big Head, the young man who had proposed to proceed to the village and obtain the release of the two white girls, fell dead at the first fire of the guard. The oldest of the three, Dull Knife, received a bayonet wound through the body which proved fatal in a few days. The third, Fat Bear, was felled by a blow from the butt of a musket, but did not receive serious injury.

Knowing that I could converse with the Indians, and from my acquaintance with them might be able to quiet the excitement among the remaining prisoners, the commanding officer of the post sent to me for assistance. Upon repairing to the stockade I found the women and children in a state of great excitement and huddled together inside their tents. Entering the stockade, I soon learned their version of the affair, which did not vary materially from that just given. Mo-nah-see-tah pointed to a bullet-hole in her blanket, the effect of a stray shot fired during the mélée. The affair was a source of deep regret to all.

The Cheyennes, in accordance with their promise made to me, returned to their reservation; and having thus far complied with the terms of the agreement then made, it devolved upon the military authorities to return to them their people whom we had up to that time and since the battle of the Washita retained as prisoners of war. An order was accordingly issued releasing the only surviving chief, Fat Bear, and the women and children then held at Fort Hays. Wagons and subsistence were furnished them from Fort Hays to Camp Supply and a squadron of the Seventh Cavalry escorted them to the latter point, where they were

received by their own people. Mo-nah-see-
tah, although gladdened by the prospect of
being restored to her people, exhibited
marked feelings of regret when the time for
her departure arrived. She had grown quite
accustomed to the easy, idle life she had led
among the troops as compared with that
mere existence of toil and drudgery to which
all tribes of Indians consign their squaws.

Romeo, who had accompanied us throughout the events described in these pages as
interpreter, took unto himself a wife from
the Cheyenne village and thereafter became
a sort of trader between the whites and Indians. I believe he is still acting in that
capacity. Lone Wolf is still the leading chief
of the Kiowas; but if public and private
advices are to be relied upon he has acted
with extremely bad faith toward the Government, and even as these lines are being
penned is reported as absent from his reservation, leading a war party of his people in
committing depredations upon the people of
the Texas frontier. Satanta, since his release
from the Texas state prison, has led a comparatively quiet and uneventful life. How
much of this is due to his incarceration in
prison for a short term of years can only be
inferred. Little Raven continues to exercise
the powers of head chief of the Arapahoes,

although he is too old and infirm to exercise active command. My former friend and companion, Yellow Bear, is the second chief in rank to Little Raven, and probably will succeed to the dignities of the latter ere many years have rolled around. Little Robe, of the Cheyennes, whose acts and words were always on the side of peace, died some three years ago.

A few words in regard to one other character with whom the reader of these sketches has been made acquainted and I shall have disposed of the principal personages, not included in the military, whom the reader has encountered from time to time. California Joe accompanied my command to Fort Hays, Kansas, on the Kansas Pacific Railroad, when the troops were partially disbanded and sent to different stations. California Joe had never seen a railroad nor a locomotive, and here determined to improve his first opportunity in these respects and to take a trip in the cars to Leavenworth, distant about four hundred miles. A few days afterward an officer of my command, happening to be called to Leavenworth, thought he recognized a familiar form and face in front of the leading hotel of the city. A closer scrutiny showed that the party recognized was none other than California Joe. But how changed!

Successful Ending of Campaign

Under the manipulations of the barber, and through the aid of the proprietor of a gentleman's furnishing store, the long, curly locks and beard of California Joe, both of which had avoided contact with comb, brush, or razor for many years, had undergone a complete metamorphosis. His hair and beard were neatly trimmed and combed, while his figure, a very commanding one, had discarded the rough suit of the frontiersman and was now adorned by the latest efforts of fashion. If the reader imagines, however, that these changes were in keeping with the taste of California Joe, the impression is wholly incorrect. He had effected them simply for a sensation. The following day he took the cars for the West, satisfied with the faint glimpse of civilization he had had.

As I soon after left that portion of the Plains in which these scenes are laid I saw no more of California Joe; but I often wondered what had become of my loquacious friend, whose droll sayings and quaint remarks had often served to relieve the tedium of the march or to enliven the group about the camp-fire. I had begun, after a few years had passed without trace or tidings from Joe, to fear that he had perhaps gone to that happy hunting ground to which he no doubt had sent more than one dusky enemy, when

605

a few weeks ago I was most agreeably surprised to receive indubitable evidence that California Joe was still in the land of the living, but exactly where I could not determine, as his letter was simply dated "Sierre Nevade Mountains, California." Now as this range of mountains extends through the entire length and embraces a considerable portion of the State of California, Joe's address could not be definitely determined. But as his letter is so characteristic of the man, I here introduce it as the valedictory of California Joe:

SIERRE NEVADE MOUNTAINS,
CALEFORNIA, March 16, 1874.

Dear General after my respets to you and Lady i thought that i tell you that i am still on top of land yit i hev been in the rockey mountain the most of the time sence last I seen you but i got on the railroad and started west and the first thing I knew I landed in san Francisco so I could not go any further except goin by water and salt water at that so i turned back and headed for the mountains once more resolved never to go railroading no more i drifted up with the tide to sacramento city and i landed my boat so i took up through town they say thar is 20 thousand people living thar but it looks to me like to be 100 thousand counting chinaman and all i cant describe my wolfish feeling but i think that i look just like i did when we was chasing Buffalo on the cimarone so I struck up through town and i come to a large fine building crowded with people so i bulged in to see what was going on and when i got in to the counsil house i took a look around at the crowd and i seen the most of them had bald heads so i thought to myself i struck it now that they are indian peace commissioners so i look to see if i would know any of them but not one so after while the smartess lookin one got up and said gentlemen i introduce a bill to have speckle mountain trout and fish eggs imported to california to be put in the american Bear and yuba rivers—those rivers is so muddy that a tadpole could not live in them caused by mining—did any body ever hear of speckle trout living in muddy water and the next thing was the game law and that was very near as bad as the Fish for they aint no game in the country as big as mawking bird i heard some fellow behind me ask how long is the legislaturs been in session then i dropt on myself it wuzent Indian commissioners after all so i slid out took across to chinatown and they smelt like a kiowa camp in August with plen-ty buffalo meat around—it was gettin late so no place to go not got a red cent so i happen to think of an old friend back of town that i knowed 25 years ago so i lit out and sure enough he was thar just as i left him 25 years ago baching [leading the life of bachelor—G. A. C.] so i got a few seads i going to plant in a few days give my respects to the 7th calvery and except the same yoursly

CALIFORNIA JOE.

The events described in this chapter terminated my service in the field on what is known as the southern and middle Plains, embracing all that portion of the plains south of the Platte River. From and after the Washita campaign the frontiers of Kansas have enjoyed comparative peace and immunity from Indian depredations. No general Indian war has prevailed in that part of the country, nor is it probable that anything more serious in this way than occasional acts of horse-stealing will occur hereafter. Many of my friends have expressed surprise that I have not included in *My Life on the Plains* some of the hunting scenes and adventures which have formed a part of my experience; but I feared the introduction of this new feature, although probably the pleasantest and in many respects most interesting of my recollections of border life, might prolong the series of articles far beyond the length originally assigned to them. I hope, however, at an early day to relate some of my experiences with the large game so abundant on the Plains, and in this way fill up a blank in these articles which my friends who are lovers of sport have not failed to observe.

As I pen these lines I am in the midst of scenes of bustle and busy preparation attendant upon the organization and equipment of a large party for an important exploring expedition, on which I shall start before these pages reach the publishers' hands.[51] During my absence I expect to visit a region of country as yet unseen by human eyes, except those of the Indian—a country described by the latter as abounding in game of all varieties, rich in scientific interest, and of surpassing beauty in natural scenery. Bidding adieu to civilization for the next few months, I also now take leave of my readers, who, I trust, in accompanying me through my retrospect, have been enabled to gain a true insight into a cavalryman's *Life on the Plains.*

[51] This was the expedition conducted by Custer throughout the months of July and August, 1874 from Fort Abraham Lincoln, near Bismarck, North Dakota, to the Black Hills region; it resulted in the discovery of gold and induced an inrush of gold seekers which proved an important factor in the renewal of warfare with the Sioux, which had been temporarily ended by the Fort Laramie Treaty of 1868.

Index

Index

Index

Benteen, Capt. Frederick, criticizes Custer, XLIII; career, 336–37; in Washita battle, 336–38, 349.

Big Head, Cheyenne chief, killed, 601.

Big Tree, Kiowa chief, 533.

Black Eagle, Kiowa Chief, 432, 434, 458, 460; orator, 463; daughter elopes, 520–23.

Black Kettle, Cheyenne chief, village destroyed, 321–52, 427; killed, 358; conduct of sister, 358–65; body missing, 423. See also Mah-wis-sa.

Blinn, Mrs. Clara, captivity story, 427–28.

Blucher, Custer's dog, 217, 293–94, 367.

Bluff Creek, military activities on, 217–19, 259.

Box family, captivity story, 102–106, 462.

Brewster, search for sister, 410–14, 483–87, 519–27, 588–91.

Brooks, H. C., husband of Sarah White, 407.

Buffaloes, habitat, 12–15; hunted, 80–85, 111, 226–29, 291–94.

Buffalo bulls, rivalry for leadership, 14.

Buffalo flies, as pests, 15–16.

Buffalo grass, 11–12.

Buffalo trails, described, 13.

Buffalo wallows, 13–15.

Bull Bear, role in Hancock campaign, 44–50.

Burials, Indian, described, 119–21.

CALIFORNIA Joe, scouting services, 234–49, 279, 289, 298, 314, 327–29, 342, 421–22, 512–17, 535; dispatch bearer, 376–82, 385–87; in regimental review, 392; visits Leavenworth, 604–605; writes letter, 606–607.

Calhoun, John C., recommends Indian reserve, 4.

Camp Doniphan, 467.

Camp Radziminski, history, 409–410; site passed, 534–35.

Camp Supply, established, 278–79; final campaign ends, 597. See also Washita River and Washita battle.

Index

Canadian River, boundary of buffalo range, 12; military activities on, 294–96.

Captives, Indian, 40–42; taken in Washita battle, 341, 357–65, 372–73, 392–93, 414, 602–603; taken at Medicine Arrow's village, 567–603.

Captives, white, Box family, 102–106; Fletcher child, 106–108; slain, 339–40, Mrs. Clara Blinn, 427–28; Sarah White and Mrs. Anna Morgan, 401–407, 562–94, 599.

Carr, Major E. A. defeats Tall Bull, 40.

Carrington, Col. Henry B., Indian Department opposes, XXXVII; at Fort McPherson, 112; at Julesburg, 130.

Carrington, Mrs. Margaret I., *Absaraka, Home of the Crow* cited, XXXVI–XXXVII, 112, 127, 130.

Carson, Kit, son-in-law, 492–93.

Cheyenne Indians, role in Hancock campaign, 33–111; in councils, 38–40, 249; Washita campaign, 280–352; retire to Red River, 451; peace mission to, 466–72; final conquest, 530–96; camp surprised, 540–41; chiefs seized, 565–72; surrender terms, 572–73; fate of captive chiefs, 600–602.

Chivington Massacre, 40–42; Indians fear, 50.

Cholera, at Fort Wallace, 204–205.

Cimarron River, boundary of Indian reservation, 249.

Circling, maneuver explained, 165–66.

Civil War, career of General Custer, XXVII–XXXIII; writes memoirs, XLV–XLVI.

Coates, Dr., in Hancock campaign, 56–64; escapes Indians, 146–49; night ride with Custer, 173–77.

Coloring the horses, described, 269–71.

Comanche Indians, in council, 249; villages, 249, 427; role in Washita battle, 434.

Comstock, Will, scouting service, 112–13, 122–23, 154–70, 188–98.

Cooke, Col., Wm. W., career, 133; role in Indian campaigns, 133–70; 179–80, 212, 548–51, 554, 561; com-

Index

mands sharpshooters, 268–69; in Washita battle, 322, 332, 339; commands relief detachment, 492, 505, 510–17.

Cooper, Col. Wickliffe, 114.

Corbin, Jack, scouting service, 300–302, 380–82, 385–87.

Cottonwood trees, horses eat bark, 10–11, 517, 548.

Councils, 38–40, 99–102, 124–25, 139–43, 249.

Council House, on Medicine Lodge Creek described, 257–59.

Crawford, Gov. Samuel J., career, 408; leads Kansas regiment, 408–409.

Cresaptown, Custers settle at, XIX–XX.

Custer, Gen. George A., characterized, XVII–XLIX; ancestry, XVIII–XXII; West Point career, XXIII–XXVII; Civil War career, XXVII–XXXIII; "luck", XXIX–XXXII; friendship of Sheridan, XXXII–XXXIII, XLI, 214, 216; career on Plains, XXXIII–XLV, 31–608; uxoriousness, XXXVIII–XXXIX; callousness, XXXIX–XLI; conduct in Washita campaign, XLI–XLIII; writings, XLIV–XLIX; campaigns of 1867, 31–214; campaigns of 1868–69, 215–608; occupies Cheyenne-Sioux village, 51–65; pursues Cheyennes, 65–78; hunting exploits, XXXVIII, 79–85; 122–23, 293–94; council with Pawnee Killer, 139–43; court martial, 35, 185, 205, 213–14; story of Fletcher child, 106–108; marches, 114–27, 172–77, 206–13, 249–56, 273–78; quells deserters, 182–88; recalled to duty, 215–18; Indians attack, 134–38, 218–30; hunting dogs, 79–83, 217, 293–94, 367; directs search for hostiles, 231–60; prepares for winter campaign, 260–72; conducts Washita campaign, 279–394; marriage proposal, 358–65; second Washita campaign, 400, 408–67; criticism of Indian Department, 429–35; forces surrender of Kiowas, 435–66; conducts peace mission, 474–528; obtains surrender of Arapahoes, 495–506; final campaign, 529–608; interview with Medicine

616

Index

Arrow, 552–62; seizure of chiefs, 563–73; recovers
captive women, 572–91; route of final campaign,
596–97; Black Hills expedition, 608–609.

Custer, Mrs. Elizabeth, narrative cited, XXXVIII–
XXXIX, 68, 557; at Fort Hays, 96, 115; fears for
safety, 152, 156.

Custer, Thomas, XXI–XXII; role in Indian campaigns, 132–70, 212, 478.

Cut Nose, Cheyenne chief, captor of Fletcher family,
106–108.

Davis, Governor Edmund J., pardons Satanta, 533–34.

Delaware Indians, history, 67; scouting service, 67–78,
112, 192–97.

Desertions, from army, 109–10, 182–88.

Dogs, of Gen. Custer, 79–83, 217, 293–94, 367; of
Indians, 506; Indians eat, 60–61; die on march, 173;
alarm Indian camp, 542.

Dog Soldiers, in council, 38–40, 42.

Downer's Station, history, 86; soldiers killed, 211.

Dugouts, at stage stations, described, 207–10.

Dull Knife, Cheyenne chief, killed, 601.

Elizabethtown, Custer stationed at, XLV.

Elliot, Major Joel H., abandoned, XLI–XLIII; career,
131–32; commands detachment, 131–51, 174; ap-
prehends deserters, 185–86; in Washita campaign,
296–302, 308–12, 321–22, 330, 346; search for, 370–
71, 422, 424–26.

Fat Bear, Cheyenne chief, released, 601–602.

Fires, Indians set, 43, 315–17, 535–36.

Fletcher family, atrocities committed upon, 106–108.

Forsyth, Col. George A., in Beecher Island battle, 74.

Fort Arbuckle, history, 425–26.

Fort Cobb, history, 409–10; march of army to, 421–47;
Indians assemble at, 428, 436–37.

Fort Cottonwood. See Fort McPherson.

Fort Dodge, history, 100; military activities at, 218–49,
260, 273.

617

Index

Fort Ellsworth. See Fort Harker.

Fort Harker, history, 36; military activities at, 35, 206, 280.

Fort Hays, Custer stationed at, XLIV; elevation 7; history, 95-96; military activities at, 109, 112, 114-27, 206-12, 218, 272, 598-99, 604; Indian captives at, 414; prison riot, 600-609.

Fort Larned, military activities at, 35-37, 42; council held, 100.

Fort Leavenworth, Custer stationed at, XLIV-XLV; history, 36; military headquarters, 35, 111, 217-18.

Fort Lyon, Chivington massacre near, 42; wagon train captured, 428.

Fort McPherson, history, 112; military activities at, 114-27.

Fort Marion. See St. Augustine.

Fort Phil Kearny, XXXVI-XXXVII, 112.

Fort Riley, military activities at, 35; history, 36.

Fort Sedgwick, history 129-30; military operations at, 130-51, 172-78.

Fort Sill, history, 410, 467.

Fort Wallace, history, 130; military activities at, 114, 130-72, 178-201; Indians attack, 202-203; cholera epidemic, 204-205.

Fremont, John C., stories about, 478, 492.

Frontiersmen, aversion to Indian wars, 25, 29-30.

GALAXY, publishes Custer writings, XLV-XLIX.

Game, wild, of Great Plains area, 12; migrations, 18-19; abundance, 79; hunted, 121-23; supports war parties, 261. See also Buffaloes and Beavers.

Garry Owen, Seventh Cavalry song, 334-35, 393.

Gold, discovery of, 609.

Graft, in army contracts, 110.

Grass, of Great Plains area, 11-12.

Gray Beard, Cheyenne chief, role in Hancock campaign, 48, 50.

Index

Great American Desert, described, 3–5. See also Great Plains.

Great Plains, described, 3–20; characterized, 21–24; peace restored, 608.

Grover, Abner S., scouting incident, 113.

Guerrier, Ed, interpreter, 50–51, 56–64.

HAMILTON, Capt. Louis McLane, career, 144; skirmish with Indians, 144–50; commands expedition, 206–12; in Washita campaign, 305–308, 332; killed, 345; burial, 394–95.

Hancock, Gen. W. S., wages Indian campaign, 34–111; career, 31–32; holds councils, 37–40, 100, 109; orders Cheyenne-Sioux village destroyed, 97; criticized, 31, 97–99.

Hard Rope, Osage chief, scouting service, 272, 280, 296, 548–49.

Hazen, Gen. W. B., dispute with Custer, XLV; reports number of Indians, 353–54; conduct of Indian Agency, 410, 429–35.

Hickok, James B. (Wild Bill), career, 67–71.

Horses, eat cottonwood bark, 10–11, 517, 548; Indians steal, 121; importance to Indians, 252–53; captured in Washita battle, 342–43, 350–51, 356–57, 365–66; bucking exhibition, 507–10; starvation of, 524–25; eaten, 525–26.

INDIANS, governmental relations with, XXXIII–XXXVII; attack wagon trains, XLIII–XLIV, 154–71, 250–56, 428; Custer's camp, 134–38, 218–30; Great Plains reserved for, 4–5; characterized, 21–24; responsibility for wars, 25–34; Hancock campaign against, 34–111; battle array described, 44–47; treatment of captives, 102–108, 339–40, 401–407, 427–28, 562–94; village described, 49–50; burial customs, 119–21; councils with whites, 37–40, 99–102, 124–25, 249; importance of horses, 250–52; medicine men, 257–58, 556–61; migratory habits, 262; employed as scouts, 67–78, 112, 192–97, 271–72, 276–

Index

80, 285–86, 294–98, 310, 313–20, 325–27, 332, 367–68, 384–86, 392–93, 409, 431, 530, 537, 540–41, 543–44, 548–49; mutilate foes, 27–28, 197–200, 425–26; romances, 415–19, 520–23; kinnikinick, 555–56.

Indian Department, dispute with Army, XXXVI–XXXVII, 31, 45, 214, 429–35, 448; venality of agents, 34, 97–99.

Iron Shirt, Apache chief, peace mission, 468–72.

JULESBURG, history, 129–30.

KANSAS, Indian raids upon settlers, 34, 400–401; regiment raised to fight Indians, 407–408. See also Nineteenth Kansas Cavalry, White captives, and the several military campaigns.

Kansas River, elevation, 7.

Kaw Indians, 272; scouting service, 409.

Keogh, Capt. Myles W., career, 280.

Kicking Bird, Kiowa chief, attends council, 100.

Kidder, Lieut., expedition of, 178–81, 188–201; massacre reported, 213; fate recalled, 513.

Kinnikinick, described, 556–57.

Kiowa Indians, council with Gen. Hancock, 99–102; attend. Medicine Lodge Creek Council, 249; villages, 344, 427; complicity in Washita hostilities, 427–35; army conquers, 435–66.

Kirkpatrick, Lydia, half-sister of General Custer, XXI–XXIII.

Kirkpatrick, Maria, wife of Emanuel H. Custer, XXI.

Knives, utility on Plains, 470; story of Custer's knife, 470–71, 555.

LEFT Hand, Sioux chief, 48.

Lippincott, Dr., 383, 554.

Little Bear, Sioux chief, 48.

Little Beaver, Osage chief, scouting service, 272, 280, 296, 367.

Little Big Horn battle, men distrust General Custer, XLIV.

Little Bull, Sioux chief, 48.

Index

Little Raven, Arapahoe chief, 100, 427, peace mission
to, 477–506; career, 498.

Little Robe, Cheyenne chief, peace efforts, 473–74,
477–507, 511, 517, 552, 573, 579–81; song, 485–86;
death, 604.

Little Rock, Cheyenne chief, killed, 359, 415, 423. See
also Mo-nah-se-tah.

Lone Wolf, Kiowa chief, attends council, 100; village,
427; army compels surrender, 435–66; career, 442;
raids Texas frontier, 603.

Lookout Station, Indians destroy, 94–95.

McClellan, Gen. George B., surveys Red River, 518.

McCuskey, Philip, reports Indian hostilities, 435.

Mah-wis-sa, sister of Black Kettle, role in Washita battle, 358–65; accompanies army, 414, 419–20; testimony concerning Washita battle, 435; on peace
mission, 468–72, 555.

Maida, Custer's dog, 217, 293–94.

Marcy, Capt. Randolph B., founds Fort Arbuckle,
425–26; surveys Red River, 518.

Medicine Lodge Creek, military activities on, 248–59.

Medicine Lodge Creek Council, 249.

Medicine Lodge Creek Council House, 257–59.

Medicine Lodge Treaty, signers, 442, 498.

Medicine men, authority of, 257–58; proceedings
described, 556–61.

Medicine Wolf, Cheyenne chief, role in Hancock campaign, 48, 50.

Meyers, Lieut. Col. Edward, role in Indian campaigns,
152–70, 322, 333, 349; career, 153.

Mirages, on Great Plains, 16–18, 88–93.

Missouri River, boundary of Great American Desert, 3;
of hostile tribes, 5.

Mo-nah-se-tah, daughter of Little Rock, romance, 415–
19; accompanies army, 415, 419–20, 468, 562;
analyzes abandoned camp, 543–47; peace mission,
576–78; imprisonment, 600, 602; released, 603.

621

Index

Monroe, Mich., home of Gen. Custer, XX–XXV, 215–16.

Morgan, Mrs. Anna, captivity narrative, 401–407, 591–94; rescued, 550–90; reunion with husband, 599; career, 407.

Morning Star, phenomenon of, 330–31.

Morrow, Jack, rancher, 126–27.

Moylan, Lieut. Myles, career, 173–74; in Washita campaign, 281–82, 288.

Mulberry Creek, army encamps, 274, 497–517; Arapahoe village on, 497.

Mules, superiority to horses, 236–37. See also California Joe.

Murphy, Thomas, reports number of Indians, 354.

My Life on the Plains, Custer writes, XLV–XLIX.

NEVA, Blackfoot guide, guides expedition, 478, 485–86; relations with Gen. Fremont, 478, 492; with Kit Carson, 492–93; scouting service, 519–27.

New Rumley, Custers settle at, XX.

Nineteenth Kansas Cavalry, organized, 407–408; in campaigns, 409, 530–98; officers receive captive women, 589; congratulate Custer, 594–95; mustered out of service, 597–98.

OSAGE Indians, scouting service. See entries under Indians, employed as scouts.

PAWNEE Fork, route via, 42.

Pawnee Killer, Sioux chief, in Hancock campaign, 43, 48; councils with, 124–25, 139–43; search for, 126–27; massacres Kidder party, 198.

Peace Commission, negotiates Medicine Lodge Creek treaties, 249; criticized, 549.

Pennsylvania Dutch, XVIII–XX.

Pepoon, Lieut. Silas, in winter campaign, 409; leads scouts, 530.

Pike, Zebulon M., myth of Great American Desert, 4–5.

Poplar trees, on Great Plains, 10.

Platte River, boundary of hostile tribes, 5; of buffalo

Index

range, 12; military activities on, 99, 114, 123–28, 172–79.

RED Bead, Sioux chief, guides Kidder expedition, 178–200.

Red River, boundary of Indian reservation, 249; refuge of hostile tribes, 429, 437, 451; survey of, 518; Custer expedition ascends, 518–27.

Reed, David, marries Lydia Kirkpatrick, XXII, XXIV.

Renick, Dr., accompanies peace mission, 478.

Republican River, military activities on, 114, 121, 129–30, 172–73, 178–201; settlements raided, 400–401.

Rister, Prof. Carl C., statements cited, XLVII, 40, 428, 597.

Riverside Station, objective of campaign, 172, 179.

Robbins, Lieut. Samuel M., escorts wagon train, 133–71, 179–80; career, 133; accompanies peace mission, 478.

Rocky Mountains, boundary of Great American Desert, 3.

Roman Nose, role in Hancock campaign, 48, 50; career, 73–74.

Romeo (Romero), characterized, 327–28; interpreter, 341, 344, 357–65, 438–46, 453, 468, 478–79, 483, 485, 493, 522, 561, 567–69, 575–76, 586; rides Indian pony, 507–10; marriage, 603.

ST. AUGUSTINE, imprisonment of Indians, 442, 467.

Saline River, military activities on, 118; settlements raided, 400–401.

Salt water streams, army encounters, 538–39.

Sand Creek Massacre, 40–42.

Satanta, Kiowa chief, attends council, 100–102; murders captives, 427, 435; army compels surrender, 435–66; wives, 464–66; son, 444–47, 450, 455–57; released, 531; orator, 533; later career, 532–34, 603.

Scalps, described, 258–59; Kidder party scalped, 198; bugler, 202–203.

Schofield, Gen. J. M., congratulates victors, 397–98.

623

Index

Scouts, services described, 232–34. See also Delaware Indians, Osage Indians, Romeo, Will Comstock, Jack Corbin, and California Joe.

Seventh U.S. Cavalry, Custer leads, XXXIII, XXXVII, 216–18; preparations to mount, 51–53, 117–18; preparations for campaign, 261–73; sharpshooters organized, 268–69; coloring the horses, 269–71; Gen. Sheridan reviews, 392–94; campaigns in 1867, 31–214; in 1868–69, 215–598.

Sharpshooters, unit organized, 265–69; in Washita battle, 322, 332, 339; accompany peace mission, 478.

Sheridan Gen. Philip, friendship for Custer, XXXII–XXXIII, XLI, 214, 216; *Memoirs* cited, XLI, 113, 353; protests Indian policy, XXXVI; directs military operations, 216, 230, 272, 279, 283, 399–400, 409, 597–98; report of Washita battle sent to, 375–87; congratulates Seventh Regiment, 388–89; reviews Regiment, 390–94; visits Washita battleground, 422–28; ultimatum to Kiowa chiefs, 452–53; founds Fort Sill, 467; approves peace mission, 474–78; leaves Southwest, 530–32.

Sherman, Gen. Wm. T., directs military operations, 124–25, 130, 172, 178; asks recall of Custer, 214, 216; protests release of Indian convicts, 534.

Signals, Indians use, 77, 495; methods, 138, 487–90.

Sioux Indians, role in Hancock campaign, 33–111; raid settlements, 34; massacre Kidder party, 198; renew hostilities, 609.

Smith, Gen. Andrew J., career, 47–48; commands district, 213.

Smoky Hill River, military activities on, 86–99, 114, 179–201; route of stage line, 86–95. See also Stage stations.

Snowstorms, 37, 281–92. See also Winter.

Stage Company, horses stolen, 121.

Stage stations, Indians attack, 33, 177–78, 207–10; on Smoky Hill route, 86–95; described, 206–11.

Index

Index

More Intriguing History Books
Available From Carol Publishing Group

Ask for the books listed below at your bookstore. Or to order direct from the publisher call 1-800-447-BOOK (MasterCard or Visa) or send a check or money order for the books purchased (plus $3.00 shipping and handling for the first book ordered and 50¢ for each additional book) to Carol Publishing Group, 120 Enterprise Avenue, Dept. 1439, Secaucus, NJ 07094.

The Black 100: A Ranking of the Most Influential African-Americans, Past and Present by Columbus Salley, hardcover $21.95 (#51299)

Chaining the Hudson: The Fight for the River in the American Revolution by Lincoln Diamant, hardcover $21.95 (#40502)

Christopher Columbus, In His Own Words: Four Voyages to the New World, paperback $9.95 (#51337)

A Documentary History of the Negro People in the United States, Edited by Herbert Aptheker
African-Americans tell the story of their experiences in this country in their own words
Volume 1: From Colonial Times Through the Civil War, paperback $14.95 (#50168)

Volume 2: From the Reconstruction Years to the Founding of the NAACP in 1910, paperback $14.95 (#50167)

Volume 3: From the Emergence of the NAACP to the Beginning of the New Deal, paperback $14.95 (#51006)

Volume 4: From the Beginning of the New Deal to the End of the Second World War, paperback $14.95 (#51007)

Volume 5: From the End of the Second World War to the Korean War, paperback $16.95 (#51421)

Volume 6: From the Korean War to the Emergence of Martin Luther King, Jr., paperback $16.95 (#51431)

Prices subject to change;
books subject to availability

League of the Iroquois: A Classic Study of An American Indian Tribe, With the Original Illustrations by Lewis Henry Morgan, paperback $10.95 (#50917)

The Life and Major Writings of Thomas Paine, paperback $15.95 (#50414)

My Captivity Among the Sioux Indians by Fanny Kelly, paperback $10.95 (#51434)

My Life on the Plains, by General George Armstrong Custer, paperback $12.95 (#51439)

On Fifth Avenue: Then & Now by Ronda Wist, hardcover $25.00 (#72155)

The 100: A Ranking of the Most Influential Persons in History by Michael Hart, paperback $18.95 (#51350)

The Picture Book of Greenwich Village, written & compiled by R. Bruce Gaylord, paperback $16.95 (#51236)

Stamping Our History: The Story of the United States Portrayed On Its Postage Stamps by Charles Davidson & Lincoln Diamant, hardcover $49.95 (#40532)

To Be Free: Studies in American Negro History, edited by Herbert Aptheker, paperback $9.95 (#51257)

Up From Slavery: The Autobiography of Booker T. Washington, paperback $9.95 (#60184)

The Wit and Wisdom of Abraham Lincoln, paperback $7.95 (#51456)

The Wisdom of FDR, paperback $7.95 (#51462)